FAMILY THERAPY SOURCEBOOK

THE GUILFORD FAMILY THERAPY SERIES
ALAN S. GURMAN, EDITOR

Family Therapy Sourcebook
Fred P. Piercy, Douglas H. Sprenkle, and Associates

Family Paradigms: The Practice of Theory in Family Therapy
Larry L. Constantine

Systems Consultation: A New Perspective for Family Therapy
Lyman C. Wynne, Susan H. McDaniel, and Timothy T. Weber, *Editors*

Clinical Handbook of Marital Therapy
Neil S. Jacobson and Alan S. Gurman, *Editors*

Marriage and Mental Illness: A Sex-Roles Perspective
R. Julian Hafner

Living through Divorce: A Developmental Approach to Divorce Therapy
Joy K. Rice and David G. Rice

Generation to Generation: Family Process in Church and Synagogue
Edwin H. Friedman

Failures in Family Therapy
Sandra B. Coleman, *Editor*

Casebook of Marital Therapy
Alan S. Gurman, *Editor*

Families and Other Systems: The Macrosystemic Context of Family Therapy
John Schwartzman, *Editor*

The Military Family: Dynamics and Treatment
Florence W. Kaslow and Richard I. Ridenour, *Editors*

Marriage and Divorce: A Contemporary Perspective
Carol C. Nadelson and Derek C. Polonsky, *Editors*

Family Care of Schizophrenia: A Problem-Solving Approach to the Treatment of Mental Illness
Ian R. H. Falloon, Jeffrey L. Boyd, and Christine W. McGill

The Process of Change
Peggy Papp

Family Therapy: Principles of Strategic Practice
Allon Bross, *Editor*

Aesthetics of Change
Bradford P. Keeney

Family Therapy in Schizophrenia
William R. McFarlane, *Editor*

Mastering Resistance: A Practical Guide to Family Therapy
Carol M. Anderson and Susan Stewart

Family Therapy and Family Medicine: Toward the Primary Care of Families
William J. Doherty and Macaran A. Baird

Ethnicity and Family Therapy
Monica McGoldrick, John K. Pearce, and Joseph Giordano, *Editors*

Patterns of Brief Family Therapy: An Ecosystemic Approach
Steve de Shazer

The Family Therapy of Drug Abuse and Addiction
M. Duncan Stanton, Thomas C. Todd, and Associates

From Psyche to System: The Evolving Therapy of Carl Whitaker
John R. Neill and David P. Kniskern, *Editors*

Normal Family Processes
Froma Walsh, *Editor*

Helping Couples Change: A Social Learning Approach to Marital Therapy
Richard B. Stuart

FAMILY THERAPY SOURCEBOOK

FRED P. PIERCY, Ph.D.
DOUGLAS H. SPRENKLE, Ph.D.
AND ASSOCIATES

THE GUILFORD PRESS
New York   London

Printed in the United States of America
Last digit is print number 9 8 7 6 5 4

Library of Congress Cataloging in Publication Data

Piercy, Fred P.
    Family therapy sourcebook.

    (The Guilford family therapy series)
    Includes bibliographies and index.
    1. Family psychotherapy.   I. Sprenkle, Douglas H.
II. Title.   III. Series.   [DNLM: 1. Family therapy.
WM 430.5.F2 P618f]
RC488.5.P54   1986   616.89′156   86-19588
ISBN 0-89862-071-6
ISBN 0-89862-913-6 (pbk.)

CONTRIBUTORS

PRINCIPAL AUTHORS

Fred P. Piercy, Ph.D.   Associate Professor of Family Therapy and Director of Training and Research, Family Therapy Program, Department of Child Development and Family Studies, Purdue University, West Lafayette, IN 47906.

Douglas H. Sprenkle, Ph.D.   Associate Professor and Director, Family Therapy Program, Department of Child Development and Family Studies, Purdue University, West Lafayette, IN 47906.

ASSOCIATES

Judith Myers Avis, Ph.D.   Associate Professor, Department of Family Studies, University of Guelph, Guelph, Ontario N16 2WI, Canada.

Dennis A. Bagarozzi, Ph.D.   Private Practice, Alliance for Counseling and Therapeutic Services (ACTS), 174 West Wienca Road, Atlanta, GA 30342.

Bradford P. Keeney, Ph.D.   Director, Family Therapy Doctoral Program, Department of Human Development and Family Studies, Texas Tech University, Lubbock, TX 79409.

David R. Mace, Ph.D.   Founder, Association for Couples for Marriage Enrichment (ACME), Highland Farms, Black Mountain, NC 28711.

Frank N. Thomas, M.Div. Ph.D. Candidate,   Family Therapy Doctoral Program, Department of Human Development and Family Studies, Texas Tech University, Lubbock, TX 79409.

WITH SPECIAL THANKS TO:

Joseph L. Wetchler, M.S.
Marcia Brown-Standridge, Ph.D.
Mary Jo Zygmond, Ph.D.
Linda Stone Fish, Ph.D.
Roslyn G. Cantrell

ACKNOWLEDGMENTS

No man is an island entire of itself; every man is a piece of the continent, a part of the main . . .

—John Donne

Consistent with Donne's famous lines, we wish to emphasize the collaborative nature of this sourcebook. In writing it, we were reminded not only of our indebtedness to the pioneers of family therapy, but also to many people closer to home. While the writing was often a solitary, time-consuming endeavor, the many forms of aid and support we received were invaluable. The result must be considered a team effort.

We are particularly indebted to our colleagues and friends, Judith Myers Avis, Dennis Bagarozzi, Bradford Keeney, Frank Thomas, and David Mace for their own contributions to this volume. Their areas of expertise in feminist issues, premarital counseling, ecosystemic epistemology, and enrichment, respectively, have enhanced considerably the breadth and depth of this sourcebook. Similarly, our students, Joseph L. Wetchler and Marcia Brown-Standridge, were instrumental in exploring the dark and musty corners of the Purdue library system and writing the initial versions of many of the annotated citations in the sourcebook. Many other people have shared in breathing life into this project, and are cited at the conclusions of various chapters. We especially wish to acknowledge the excellent secretarial support of Roberta Thayer, Jean Greives, Carole Alexander, and Becky Harshman. Finally, we were energized and touched by the support we received from those near and dear to us. Consequently, we offer our sincere thanks to our parents and to our immediate family members, Susan, David, Stephen, Mark, and Rob, for all the usual reasons and for many, many more.

Fred P. Piercy, Ph.D.
Douglas H. Sprenkle, Ph.D.

FOREWORD

As should be the case, it is unusual for the editor of a book series to write a Foreword to a book in his or her series. But, then, this is an unusual book, so it deserves a different kind of introduction.

Unlike some books about family therapy, this one will not grab you emotionally, and keep your eyes riveted to its pages as you plumb the passions and complexities of detailed case studies of family treatment. Unlike some other books, this one also will not put you to sleep with its neutral, distant, noncommittal discussions of one theory after another. Unlike most family therapy books, this is one you will want to keep within reach. Think of it as a reliable, consistent friend, almost always there to help you, but never pushing itself on you. This is a book all your students or fellow students will want to borrow, and one that most of your colleagues *should* borrow. But it is one you should not lend, because you will probably never get it back.

No book can actually teach someone how to do family therapy, including this one. But this one is probably the most *useful* (literally: full of uses) one you can find. It is, at once, a superior glossary of core family therapy terms and concepts; a carefully selected annotated bibliography; a consumer's guide to many of the best video teaching tapes; and a compact introductory mini-text on the major methods of family therapy. And its dozens of thought-provoking experiential learning exercises will be welcomed by all teachers of family therapy: The less ambitious will simply use them to great advantage, and the more energetic will be stimulated by them to create many new, active, teaching/learning adventures. Moreover, the section written by the authors for most of the chapters on "Research Issues" can be used both for in-depth discussion of research matters and as a reliable summary of a great number of the most pressing theoretical and clinical issues and questions in the field still requiring systematic empirical scrutiny (for graduate students, an undeniable bonanza of meaningful thesis or dissertation topics!).

As the authors make clear, this is not a textbook; it is a sourcebook. It is a guide to where the field of family therapy has been, where it is, and where it is going. The pedagogically outstanding structure of the chapters in this book allows for maximal utility as a secondary text for any course on family therapy. "Secondary" here does not mean "optional"—this book should be a mandatory companion volume used along with any combination of required primary source books.

The authors, eminent teachers in their own right, are to be commended for creating such a uniquely valuable addition to the literature of family therapy. Interestingly, almost two dozen of Piercy and Sprenkle's students had a hand, in one way or another, in getting this book together—prima facie evidence of what can happen when students are excited about learning and teachers are excited about teaching.

Alan S. Gurman, Ph.D.

PREFACE

This book is the result of an increasing wave of interest in family therapy, a discipline virtually unknown 30 years ago. The American Association for Marriage and Family Therapy (AAMFT) has increased in membership by 500% in 10 years. Traditional disciplines, such as psychiatry, psychology, social work, counselor education, and pastoral counseling, are all developing coursework and training experiences in family therapy. The field is literally exploding with books, journals, and newsletters.

While some authors have written books surveying the field, the present volume provides something different: a road map to both classic and state-of-the-art information on foundational issues related to the theory, research, and practice of family therapy. This book, then, is a "sourcebook" rather than a "textbook," because it is a guide to the studying and teaching of the original source materials. Rather than simply summarizing primary sources for the reader, the sourcebook points the student or teacher of family therapy to these original materials. This sourcebook is intended to provide the reader with easy access to annotated listings of key books and articles, as well as with concepts, skills, and research issues associated with the various theoretical approaches to family therapy; creative assignments and experiential activities are also provided for teaching these approaches. In addition, chapters are dedicated to such important family therapy topics as supervision, outcome research, the feminist critique of family therapy, and ethical, legal, and professional issues. We hope that this sourcebook will prove to be a useful reference for all those interested in broadening their knowledge of the expanding field of family therapy. For the newcomer to family therapy, the volume can serve as an overview of key concepts and issues in the field. For the experienced family therapist, the book should be a helpful resource in keeping up with the more recent literature, particularly in those areas in which he/she does not specialize.

Of course, no one volume could capture either the full essence or the breadth of this exciting field. Such a task would be doomed to fail. For this reason, this volume should be considered neither definitive nor exhaustive. And, depending upon the reader's biases, sins of omission and commission will be evident in every chapter. Rather than try to map every road, hill, and valley, we have attempted to include major thoroughfares and to sketch a landscape in broad strokes that, albeit incomplete, reflects the beauty and texture of the scenery.

We have undertaken the writing of this book in a critical manner, attempting to hold our own biases in check. While these biases may occasionally peek through, we hope that our commentary and the relative number of key citations in each chapter reflect more the state of the field than the state of the authors. And some decisions were not always easy. For example, our choice not to cover psychodynamic family therapy beyond our discussion of object relations could be argued. Even within the obviously broad and far-reaching scope of this book, certain limits had to be set.

We hope that students and teachers alike will use the information discussed and sources cited in this book to expand their own knowledge and appreciation of the field of family therapy. As this sourcebook amply reflects, there is much to be known and appreciated.

F. P. P.
D. H. S.

CONTENTS

1

TRANSGENERATIONAL FAMILY THERAPIES

Transgenerational approaches to family therapy have grown out of the work of such pioneers as Murray Bowen, Ivan Boszormenyi-Nagy, James Framo, Norman Paul, and, more recently, Donald Williamson. One theoretical influence cutting across most transgenerational therapies is that of the object relations concepts of W. R. D. Fairbairn and Henry Dicks. Each of these key therapists/theorists, and the basic theoretical tenets of object relations theory, are introduced briefly below.

MURRAY BOWEN

Murray Bowen (1960) conducted important clinical studies during 1954–1959 at the National Institute of Mental Health (NIMH), in which entire families lived on a psychiatric ward with their schizophrenic family members. Bowen noticed a striking lack of ego boundaries between the schizophrenic patient and at least one other family member (usually the mother). Often one person would speak for the other, and anxiety was transmitted easily from one family member to the other.

Bowen's observations in these early clinical studies led to theoretical concepts that explain schizophrenia and other disorders in terms of family dynamics. The health of each family member, Bowen contends, is a function of his/her degree of differentiation. The higher the level of one's differentiation of self, the more distinguishable are his/her emotional and intellectual systems. That is, a differentiated person can participate emotionally without fear of becoming fused in the family's "undifferentiated family ego mass" (see "Key Concepts"). A critical goal of therapy, then, is to help family members differentiate from the family's emotional "togetherness." When one person is able to differentiate, a ripple effect is likely to occur throughout the family.

A knowledge of triangles is particularly useful in the conduct of therapy, since, according to Bowen, the triangle is the basic building block of

1

an emotional system. When anxiety increases between two family members, a vulnerable third person is predictably and automatically involved in the emotional issue. This "triangling" of the third person ultimately reduces the anxiety level. The therapist coaches family members in "detriangling"— that is, reading the automatic emotional triangling among family members and controlling one's own automatic emotional participation. Although no one (including the therapist) really stays outside of an emotional system, a knowledge of triangles makes it possible to "get out" (i.e., stay rational) while not losing emotional contact. An important goal of therapy is to increase the degree to which one is able to distinguish between the feeling process and the intellectual process.

Continued undifferentiation in the family may result in marital conflict, dysfunction in one spouse, or impairment of one or more children. Bowen (1978) contends that this impairment from undifferentiation may be transmitted across multiple generations, with generations of the most undifferentiated offspring marrying partners with similar levels of undifferentiation. The eventual result is, according to Bowen, a schizophrenic offspring.

In March 1967, at a national conference, Bowen described how he had employed his theoretical concepts with his own family of origin (Anonymous, 1972). His provocative presentation helped focus national attention on his theory and emphasized the importance of family-of-origin therapy as a viable therapeutic tool. Subsequently, he began using family-of-origin strategies in teaching young family therapy residents. Several of these therapists began using detriangling procedures with their own parental families. Bowen noticed that it was these therapists who seemed to be more effective with patient families. Consequently, family-of-origin work with trainees themselves has become one of the most important aspects of Bowen's postgraduate family therapy training program.

Similarly, Bowen has found that helping adult family members differentiate from their own families of origin often has surprisingly positive effects on the patients' relationships with their spouses and children. His findings have led to the use of family-of-origin procedures as the treatment of choice for most family problems. Bowen (1978) states:

> [F]amilies in which the focus is on the differentiation of self in the families of origin automatically make as much or more progress in working out the relationship system with spouses and children as families seen in formal family therapy in which there is a principal focus on the interdependence in the marriage. My experience is going in the direction of saying that the most productive route to change, for families who are motivated, is to work at defining self in the family of origin, and to specifically avoid focus on the emotional issues in the nuclear family. (p. 545, italics in original)

Bowen coaches his patients to differentiate from their families of origin by such methods as developing person-to-person relationships with significant family members, becoming better observers, controlling emotional reactiveness, and learning how to detriangle from emotional family situations (Bowen, 1974).

IVAN BOSZORMENYI-NAGY

Ivan Boszormenyi-Nagy and his colleagues have emphasized the importance of transgenerational entitlements and indebtedness in the formation of symptoms within the family (e.g., Boszormenyi-Nagy, 1965, 1972; Boszormenyi-Nagy & Spark, 1973; Boszormenyi-Nagy & Ulrich, 1981). According to Boszormenyi-Nagy, invisible, often unconscious loyalties or bonds across generations greatly influence present behavior. For example, a scapegoated child's misbehavior may be his/her means of loyally acting out his/her parents' need for a focus of anger (a cycle that may have connections to behavioral sequences begun generations before). Such loyalties arise from the basic human concern for fairness and result in unconscious "ledgers" of what has been given and what is owed. One accumulates merit by the extent to which he/she "balances the ledger."

Boszormenyi-Nagy's concept of unconscious legacy obligations provides an interesting rationale for a variety of maldaptive behaviors. For example, an abused child may grow up to balance his/her ledger in the only way he/she may know how: by becoming an abusive parent.

Ledgers carry a statement of entitlement and indebtedness for each individual in the family. However, the parent–child relationship is asymmetrical, in that the child's entitlement naturally exceeds his/her indebtedness. Consequently, it is eventually possible to "buy into" the expectation that the debt to the parents is important enough to become a lifelong, consuming enterprise.

Boszormenyi-Nagy and Ulrich (1981) discuss contextual therapy as a means of dealing directly with the web of invisible loyalties influencing family members' behavior. In contextual therapy, the therapist explores legacies, invisible loyalties, and ledger balances, and thus guides family members toward those tasks necessary to restore some balance in the ledger. The therapist's aim is to "loosen the chains of invisible loyalty and legacy, so each person can give up symptomatic behaviors and explore new options" (Boszormenyi-Nagy & Ulrich, 1981, p. 174). Through contextual therapy the family's resources for trustworthiness are unlocked, and these allow them to preserve loyalty in more adaptive ways and to exonerate previous generations. Exoneration involves helping family members realize that, however much their parents have failed, neither was a monster. Each was unconsciously driven by his/her own loyalty commitments, however irrational or destructive.

JAMES FRAMO

For James Framo, the relationship between intrapsychic and transactional influences is primary. Framo (1980) states:

> [I]t is just as important to know what goes on inside people as to know what goes on between them. . . . I think it is the *relationship* between the intrapsychic and interpersonal that will provide the greatest understanding and therapeutic leverage, that is, how internalized conflicts from past family relationships are being lived through the spouse and the children in the present. (p. 58)

Framo's (1982) theory of symptoms is based largely on the object relations concepts of Fairbairn (1952) and Dicks (1967), described later in this chapter. Framo emphasizes transgenerational projective identification, in which children subtly collude in identifying and acting out the projected "introjects" (i.e., bad objects) of their parents.

Framo's therapeutic approach is eclectic, in that he employes varied intervention formats such as couples groups and family-of-origin therapy sessions. Framo (1981) believes that couples group therapy (with groups of three couples) is the treatment of choice in premarital, living-together, marital, and separation or divorce relationship problems.

In virtually all of his couples therapy, Framo initially suggests that most of his other clients have found it helpful to bring in their families of origin at some point during the course of treatment, typically toward the end. While Framo (1982) does not have as ritualized a set of pre-family-of-origin-session activities as Williamson (1982a) (see below), his goals are similar—that is, to "put the burden of responsibility on the individuals to think about and take up with their family the issues about the family relationships that have concerned them throughout the years" (Framo, 1982, p. 174).

Framo's (1982) family-of-origin sessions provide important diagnostic information regarding how past family problems are being lived in the present. More important, however, are the corrective experiences of (1) discovering previously unknown information about the family; (2) clarifying old misunderstandings rooted in childhood misperceptions; (3) demystifying magical meanings that family members have for one another; (4) getting to know one's parents as real people; and (5) opening up the possibility of establishing adult-to-adult relationships with one's aging parents. Moreover, Framo (1976) contends that dealing with the real, external figures (i.e., the adult clients' parents) within the therapy session loosens the grip of the internalized representatives of these figures, with the result that both the adult clients and their parents are freer to be themselves in the future. Having "returned" to their families of origin, the adult clients are subsequently more able to respond to their spouses and children as real people and not as the targets of disowned parts of themselves.

NORMAN PAUL

Norman Paul believes that the feelings family members most tenaciously withhold are those associated with grief. His major contribution involves treatment procedures derived from his contention that a direct relationship exists between family members' maladaptive responses to the death of a loved one and the subsequent rigidity of family patterns. Paul believes that the family tends to return to a "pathological stable equilibrium" when grief is not appropriately expressed. A family scapegoat generally maintains this steady state, serving the symbiotic function of averting the family's attention away from their recognition of grief (Paul, 1974; Paul & Grosser, 1965).

The goal of therapy is "operational mourning," where the family's pathologically fixed patterns are dislodged, and the grief feelings that have been distorted to maintain the rigid family equilibrium are exposed, released, neutralized, and resolved within therapy (Paul & Grosser, 1965).

In operational mourning, Paul deliberately introduces a belated grief experience through "cross-confrontation" (Paul, 1977). For example, he may directly ask about past losses or may play audio- or videotapes of family members' discussions of such losses.

Paul also has used positive labels such as "sympathy" and "loyalty" rather than "grief" or "depression" to positively connote what appear to be depressive patterns and incompetent behaviors of family members, so that all family members, scapegoat included, can unite as partners in the same project—mourning a mutual loss rather than being locked into a rigid system of family equilibrium. In all of his work, Paul enables clients to consider unpleasant feelings as normal consequences of living, thus making them easier to be shared.

DONALD WILLIAMSON

Donald Williamson (1981) hypothesizes that a family life cycle stage occurs at about the fourth decade of life, the goal of which is to terminate the hierarchical power structures governing the relationships between the adult and his/her older parents. This process involves the redistribution of power between the two generations. Williamson contends that the termination of hierarchical boundaries between the adult clients and his/her "former parents" facilitates the client's own "personal authority," and encourages a more intimate peer relationship across generations.

Williamson's theoretical suppositions are generally consistent with those of Bowen, Framo, and Boszormenyi-Nagy and Spark. However, Williamson (1982a), perhaps more than any other intergenerational family therapist, has clearly described the procedures he uses to affect change in the power structure across generations. Williamson suggests the assignment of a series of tasks (e.g., the writing of an autobiography, the making of audiotaped letters to each parent, the audiotaping of telephone conversations with each parent) as a prelude to a 3-day, in-office consultation with the adult client and his/her parents. In this consultation, the therapist allows the client freedom and authority to renegotiate the politics of his/her relationship with the parents. The adult client, first talking with each parent separately and then together, deals with a variety of issues and at some point simply and poignantly declares, "I am no longer your little girl (or little boy)" (Williamson, 1982a, p. 34). After an appropriate period of debriefing, a supportive peer relationship develops in which grief, anxiety, happiness, guilt, and other strong emotions are shared freely among all members of the family.

While Williamson's goal of intergenerational "peerhood" may seem solemn and forbidding, he addresses therapy with a playfulness and humor that both support the family members and remind them of the absurdity of the human condition (Williamson, 1982b). Williamson's (1982b) humor also helps diffuse the intensity of emotional issues and often takes the form of relabeling and paradoxical statements, which are more typically associated with structural and strategic therapies.

OBJECT RELATIONS THEORY AND MARITAL RELATIONSHIPS

Fairbairn (1952) contended that a fundamental motive of human life is the development of satisfying object relationships. By this, he meant the resolution of conflict developed by internalizing a parent image that is both loved (e.g., a mother's breast that is accessible to a hungry infant) and hated (e.g., a mother's breast that is inaccessible) in order to master and control the ambivalent image intrapsychically. The results of such internalized images' being split into good and bad objects are "introjects," or psychological representations of these objects that unconsciously influence one's relationships. According to Framo (1970; cited from Framo, 1982),

> life situations in outer reality are not only unconsciously interpreted in the light of the inner-object world, resulting in distorted expectations of

other people, *but active unconscious attempts are made to force and change close relationships into fitting the internal role models.* (p. 26, italics in original)

Henry Dicks (1963, 1967) was one of the first to apply Fairbairn's (1954) object relations concepts to marriage. Dicks (1963) stated that distressed marriages are characterized by "mutual attribution and projection . . . , with each spouse perceived to a degree as an internal object" (p. 126). Dicks's conceptualizations are useful in understanding why many neurotic "cat-and-dog" marriages stay together but seem impervious to change. Each spouse's ego identity (which includes both good and bad objects) is, in effect, preserved by having one or more bad objects split off onto his/her partner. In other words, each spouse disowns his/her own bad-object introjects, and thus needs the other to accept the projection of these introjects. Each begins to subtly conform to the inner role model of the other in a collusive manner. Dicks (1963) believed that this collusive process continues because both spouses hope for integration of lost introjects by finding them in the other.

Resulting unconscious marital bargains (cf. Sager, 1976) may take many forms (e.g., "You be my courage, and I will be your support," "You be tender, and I will be strong"). The distressed marriage, then, represents a total personality that, according to Dicks, is problematic. Therapists employing object relations theory (e.g., Framo) attempt in various ways to help couples own their introjects and begin seeing their spouses for the people they really are, and not projected parts of themselves. (While Bowen himself explicitly denies the use of psychoanalytic concepts, his approach may also be viewed in terms of object relations theory.)

OBJECT RELATIONS THEORY AND INTERGENERATIONAL RELATIONSHIPS

Object relations theory can also be applied to relationships across generations. For example, children unconsciously may be perceived by a parent as projections of the parent's own split-off traits. Children, in turn, may subtly conform to these projections and act out the parent's introjects. For example, one child may be unconsciously chosen as the "promiscuous one" to act out the impulsive sexual behavior that his/her parent has internalized as a bad object and then projected onto the child. Another child may be the "feelings" of a highly rational parent. The role of each family member, according to Brodey (1959), "allows the internal conflict of each member to be acted out within the family, rather than within the self . . ." (p. 392).

The family-of-origin therapies of Bowen (1974), Framo (1976), and Williamson (1981, 1982a, 1982b) either explicitly or implicitly acknowledge the potential risks of parental projections and attempt to weaken their hold by helping adult clients renegotiate their relationships with their aging parents. Framo (1976) contends that "dealing with the real, external figures loosens the grip of the internalized representatives of these figures and exposes them to current realities" (p. 194).

KEY CONCEPTS

Differentiation of self. The extent to which one's emotional and intellectual systems are distinguishable. According to Bowen's (1978) theory, the more autonomous one's intellect is from automatic emotional forces, the more differentiated one is.

Differentiation of Self Scale. A theoretical scale postulated by Bowen (1978) for evaluating the lowest possible level of "undifferentiation," which is 0 on the scale, to the highest level of "differentiation," which is 100 on the scale. One's degree of undifferentiation (no self) is directly correlated with one's degree of emotional fusion into a common self with others (undifferentiated ego mass). The scale, then, is a means of conceptualizing one's basic level of self.

Emotional cutoff. The process of separation, isolation, withdrawal, running away, or denying the importance of one's parental family. Dealing with unresolved attachment in this manner may be problematic. According to Bowen (1978), "the more intense the cutoff with the past, the more likely the individual is to have an exaggerated version of his parental family problem in his own marriage" (p. 382).

Emotional divorce. A process of distancing between spouses. According to Bowen (1978), when spouses' individual selves begin to fuse together into an individual oneness, the result is typically a loss of individual identity, emotional turmoil, and conflict. As a response to this fusion, each spouse retreats in order to gain enough aloofness and distance to maintain his/her autonomy.

Family projection process. According to Bowen (1978), a process in which parents may project part of their immaturity onto one or more of their children. The child who is the object of the projection develops the lowest level of differentiation of self and is more likely to be symptomatic in the future.

Genogram. A written symbolic diagram of the family system, not unlike a "family tree." Many transgenerational therapists use the genogram both diagnostically and therapeutically (e.g., Guerin & Pendagast, 1976).

Introject. A psychological representation of one's interpretation of the external world. Object relations theory maintains that one's introjects often are split intrapsychically into good and bad "objects" that either may be eventually integrated into one's personality or denied and projected onto others.

Ledger. According to Boszormenyi-Nagy and Ulrich (1981), an accumulation of the accounts of what has been given and what is owed. Merit may be accumulated through contribution to the welfare of another, while debts and entitlements relate to the relative balance of the ledger. For example, a kind alcoholic father may accrue entitlements from his daughter that she then unconsciously "pays back" by becoming a nun.

Legacy. According to Boszormenyi-Nagy (1976), a specific configuration of expectations that originate, not from the merit of the parents, but simply from the universal implication of being born of parents. In other words, there is a chain of destiny anchored in every parent–child relationship. Certain debts and entitlements are dictated by one's legacy, and payment of debts typically occurs in the way one has been taught to pay. For example, an abused child may become a child-abusing parent.

Loyalty. A central concept of Boszormenyi-Nagy and Spark (1973) in understanding family behavior. Internalized expectations, injunctions, and obligations in relation to one's family of origin have powerful interpersonal influences. What to an outsider may seem like irrational or pathological behavior may, in fact, conform to a basic family loyalty. For example, a scapegoated, irresponsible child may be unconsciously acting out this loyalty message: "I will be the bad one to help you look good, since you have done so much for me."

Multigenerational transmission process. A pattern that develops over several generations in which children grow up and marry partners with similar levels of differentiation to themselves. Bowen (1978) believes that schizophrenia is the result of several generations of individuals with low levels of differentiating ("weak links") marrying other low-level individuals, and producing one or more children with low levels of differentiation. Bowen believes it may take several generations for such a process to develop a schizophrenic offspring.

Nuclear family emotional system. Bowen (1978) uses the term "emotional system" to describe the triangular emotional patterns typical of all close relationships. In the nuclear family emotional system, parental undifferentiation may produce (1) marital conflict, (2) dysfunction in a spouse, and/or (3) projection to one or more children.

Personal authority. Described by Williamson (1982b) as a synthesizing construct arising from the Hegelian dialectic of autonomy and intimacy. When an individual has personal authority, he/she is in charge of his/her own thoughts and opinions, acts freely and responsibly, and maintains appropriate social connection with others.

Sibling position. Birth order; emphasized by both Toman (1961) and Bowen (1978) as an important factor in the development of personality characteristics. Bowen also suggests that sibling position is useful in understanding how a particular child is chosen as the object of the family projection process.

Societal regression. A concept applying Bowen's theory to society in general. That is, during periods of societal anxiety, society responds emotionally with problematic "Band-Aid" legislation that simply increases problems. What is needed is better differentiation between emotion and intellect, allowing more constructive societal decisions to be made.

Triangle. A three-person system; according to Bowen (1978), the smallest stable relationship system. Bowen contends that a two-person system is an unstable system that forms a triangle under stress. More than three people in a system form themselves into a series of interlocking triangles.

Undifferentiated family ego mass. A term of Bowen's (1978) used to describe the emotional "struck-togetherness" or fusion in the nuclear family.

CLINICAL SKILLS

Transgenerational family therapy skills are not as easily isolated, identified, or operationalized as are those in present-centered, problem-focused therapies such as behavioral and strategic family therapy. Perhaps this is because such goals as differentiation, insight, and renegotiation of interpersonal power are emphasized more in transgenerational family therapies than are explicit problem-centered techniques. This is not to say that transgenerational family therapies are void of systematic procedures to meet these goals (cf. Framo, 1976; Williamson, 1982a, 1982b), but simply that these procedures can more typically be considered clinical processes than skills. Below are several representative clinical processes/skills.

Coaching. A term used by Bowen (1978) to describe his role in supervising patients and trainees in the process of differentiation of self. Bowen believes that his relationship is similar to that of a coach's relationship to an athlete, in that his initial goal is to get the patient (and trainee) started. However, the actual work is done by the patient, and the learning comes as the patient works toward his/her goal outside the therapy session.

Cross-Confrontation and Self-Confrontation. Norman Paul uses emotionally charged "stressor stimuli" in the form of audio- and videotapes (often of former clients), letters, pieces of literature, and poems with his clients in order to normalize unpleasant feeling states. His client's reactions to these stressor stimuli are also audio- or videotaped and are later played back to them as a type of self-confrontation (Paul, 1976).

Detriangling. The process whereby an individual keeps himself/herself (or someone else) outside the emotional field of two others. For example, since spouses will automatically attempt to involve a third person when anxiety increases, if the therapist can stay rational and not respond as others do to their emotional attempts at triangulation, then the spouses can begin to deal more directly with each other and patterns can change.

Exoneration. In contextual family therapy (Boszormenyi-Nagy & Ulrich, 1981), a process by which the therapist attempts to help the client see the positive intent and intergenerational loyalty issues behind the behavior of members of previous generations. Regardless of how destructive their behavior may have been to the client, if their behavior can be seen in a human context, exoneration occurs, loosening the hold of the past behavior on the client.

Operational Mourning. Norman Paul (1974) states that, "there is a direct relationship between the maladaptive response to the death of a loved one and the fixity of symbolic relationships within the family." Operational mourning, according to Paul, involves dislodging those fixed and distorted feelings through introducing a belated grief experience. In therapy, these feelings, which are often associated with grief, can be neutralized and resolved through empathic intervention and procedures such as cross confrontation.

Person-to-person relationship. A relationship in which two family members relate personally to each other about each other; that is, they do not talk about others (triangling) and do not talk about impersonal issues. Person-to-person relationships among family members may be facilitated, for example, by having an adult patient write separate letters to "Mother" and "Father," and by having him/her spend portions of visits home in personal discussions with each alone.

TEACHING TOOLS AND TECHNIQUES

Training Videotapes

A list and description of videotapes which discuss and/or demonstrate transgenerational family therapies may be secured from:

- AAMFT Master Series, AAMFT, 1717 K Street, N.W., Suite 407, Washington, DC 20006
- Boston Family Institute, 251 Harvard Street, Brookline, MA 02146
- Georgetown Family Center, 4380 MacArthur Blvd., N.W., Washington, DC 20007.

Family Autobiography

A student may be asked to write a 15- to 20-page family autobiography in which he/she discusses the dynamics of his/her own family of origin, utilizing the terminology and theoretical rationale of such writers as Bowen (1978), Framo (1982), Williamson (1981), and Boszormenyi-Nagy and Spark

(1973). While such a retrospective analysis is obviously biased, it does provide students the opportunity to apply ideas from family-of-origin readings to personally meaningful family relationships.

Object Relations: In-Class Simulation

After reading appropriate object relations literature (e.g., Dicks, 1963; Fairbairn, 1954; Stewart, Peters, Marsh, & Peters, 1975; Framo, 1982), students or trainees may be asked to get into triads and discuss one of the situations below. After each situation is discussed for 5–10 minutes, the essence of the small-group discussions should be shared in the large group.

1. Two of you are parents and one of you is a child. Both parents are projecting negative introjects onto the child. Decide what these introjects might be and what symptom the child might develop to accommodate to these introjects.
2. The child has the following symptom. What parental projections of introjects might account for this symptom? (Give a different symptom to each triad.)
   a. Sexual acting out.
   b. Running away.
   c. Drug abusing.
   d. Overachieving.
   e. Getting poor grades.

Nicknames from Past

As an introductory exercise, students/trainees can each be asked to think of two labels (nicknames, adjectives, or phrases) that were often applied to them as children—one that felt positive and one that felt negative. Then have them mill around the room and introduce themselves to each person in the room by these traits. For example, one student might say, "Hi, I'm Joe. I'm irresponsible and can really catch a football." After the milling, ask each person to find a partner and discuss the derivation of the descriptions or labels he/she used—where they came from and what they mean. Each dyad should also discuss whether the labels are true today. If not, what happened to them? (This exercise is adapted from Duhl, 1983.)

Family-of-Origin Audiotape

One of the sequential steps that Williamson (1982a) suggests adult clients engage in to begin negotiating "peership" with their parents is an audiotape exercise. Williamson's clients are asked to make an audiotape to each of their parents in which they tell each parent reactions to growing up in their family, as well as any "unfinished business" related to their past and/or present relationships with their parents. Students may be asked to do the same thing in order to make Williamson's process more immediate and meaningful. Students are then asked to write reaction papers describing how they felt while making the audiotapes to their parents and what they may have learned. In order to make this assignment less anxiety-provoking, students are *not* required to turn in the audiotapes or give them to their parents.

Simulation Activities

Simulation activities may include written papers that allow students to apply the concepts they are learning from their readings. For example, below is a simulation assignment intended to strengthen the students' understanding of object relations concepts:

> Choose a character from literature, stage, screen, radio, or TV who has some problematic characteristic or personality trait. Using object relations theory, discuss the possible etiology and present purpose of this characteristic. Also, discuss how a psychotherapy based on object relations theory might be employed to deal with your character's problematic trait.

Birth Order Exercise

The students/trainees may be asked to divide into the following four groups based upon their sibling positions in their own families of origin: (1) oldest child, (2) youngest child, (3) middle child, and (4) only child. The members of these groups then discuss their early growing-up years and what roles and ways of "fitting in" they developed within their families. Each person should note any trends within his/her group. These trends are later presented by a group spokesperson to the rest of the class. After each group spokesperson's report, the instructor summarizes what Toman (1961) has written about the particular sibling position of that group.

Open-Ended Sentences

In groups of three or four, students are asked to briefly discuss their answers to the following open-ended sentences related to their own families of origin:

- The family I come from could best be described as . . .
- In my family, my mother was always the one who . . .

- In my family, my father was always the one who . . .
- In my family, I was always the one who . . .
- If there was a topic that couldn't be discussed in my family, it was . . .
- The greatest strength about my family was . . .
- Disagreement in my family was handled by . . .
- I learned from my mother that . . .
- I learned from my father that . . .
- My siblings taught me . . .
- To me, family "events" (birthdays, holidays, etc.) were . . .
- An emotion rarely expressed in my family was . . .
- In my family, I usually felt closest to . . .
- In my family, I usually felt most distant from . . .
- When I was out in public with my family, I usually felt . . .
- A myth my family perpetuated was . . .
- If I were to title a book about living with my family, it would be titled . . .
- What I like best about my family is . . .
- If I could change anything about my family, it would be . . .

(This exercise is adapted from Janine Roberts, personal communication, 1984.)

Family Myths

1. Students/trainees may be asked to write down stories about their families of origin for each of these categories:
   a. Interactional scenarios of events that were repetitive.
   b. Legends that have been passed down from generation to generation.
   c. A story commonly told to outsiders about the family.
2. Then students/trainees are asked to write down and/or discuss rules of communication within their family highlighting the following:
   a. What could be discussed within the family?
   b. What could be discussed outside the family?
   c. What could not be discussed directly?
3. Students/trainees then identify family-of-origin themes emerging from the preceding information:
   a. Themes that can be discussed and challenged.
   b. Themes, or family myths, that are not discussed or challenged openly (i.e., people tend to share the same "party line").

(This exercise is also adapted from Janine Roberts, personal communication, 1984.)

RESEARCH ISSUES

Charismatic figures such as Murray Bowen and James Framo have identified some important concepts that have considerable clinical utility. Unfortunately, they defend their therapies with more vigor than rigor. While
family-of-origin issues are beginning to be examined empirically (e.g., Bray,
Williamsom, & Malone, 1984; Hovestadt, Anderson, Piercy, Cochran, &
Fine, 1985), virtually no experimental research has been conducted on the
effectiveness of transgenerational family therapies. However, these therapies are researchable at both the micro and macro levels, as are their
underpinning theoretical assumptions. The first necessary step is to operationalize such fuzzy concepts as "triangling," "detriangling," and "personal authority." For example, degree of differentiation could be measured
by an appropriately developed self-report scale or operationally defined as
the peripheral skin temperature and/or heart rate of a family member at
the time he/she is criticized by two other family members. Given appropriate
concretization of terms, research questions such as the following could
begin to be addressed:

- Is triangling likely to occur at times of high anxiety?
- Which of the differentiation precedures mentioned by Bowen (1974),
  Williamson (1982a), and Framo (1976) are most likely to result in
  differentiation of self?
- Do people marry partners with the same general level of differen-
  tiation?
- What effects do family-of-origin therapies have on present family
  functioning?
- Is complete separation and isolation from one's family of origin (i.e.,
  "emotional cutoff") detrimental to one's present marriage?
- To what extent is one's degree of differentiation of self related to
  measures of individual, marital, and family health?
- Is level of therapist differentiation positively related to the degree
  of change in differentiation achieved by clients?
- Is therapy training that incorporates family-of-origin activities more
  effective than similar therapy training that does not incorporate such
  activities? (Many outcome measures could be used for such a study.
  An important one, however, would be the extent to which the clients
  of the therapists in each group achieve their goals in therapy.)
- Which of the therapist skills associated with a particular family-of-
  origin therapy (e.g., the contextual family therapy of Boszormenyi-
  Nagy), are most positively related to symptom reduction?
- What is the degree of the relationship between unresolved grief and
  the severity of particular presenting problems? When unresolved
  grief is dealt with in therapy, do presenting problems decrease in
  severity? Are changes maintained over time?

KEY BOOKS AND ARTICLES

Anonymous (1972). Toward the differentiation of a self in one's own family. In J. Framo (Eds.), *Family interaction: A dialogue between family researchers and family therapists*. New York: Springer.

Murray Bowen wrote this classic chapter anonymously, reportedly to prevent possible lawsuits arising from it. In the chapter, Bowen describes his long-term efforts to differentiate from his own family of origin. His account is often moving and provides an excellent example of Bowen's own theory in practice.

Bowlby, J. (1961). Processes of mourning. *International Journal of Psychoanalysis, 42,* 317–340.

This is a major work of a biologist focusing on how man and primate deal with separation at infancy and mourn the loss of a significant love object. The author proposes a three-stage process of mourning including (1) attempts to recapture the lost object; (2) disorganization; and (3) reorganization. This article provides a useful theoretical background for Norman Paul's work.

Boszormenyi-Nagy, I., & Spark, G. M. (1973). *Invisible loyalties: Reciprocity in inter-generational family therapy.* New York: Harper & Row.

In this classic, Boszormenyi-Nagy and Spark describe the powerful influences of loyalty commitments across generations. Presenting problems are understood in terms of "balancing the ledger" within the family. While the obfuscatory style of this book makes for difficult reading, its influence on the field renders it an important text for those interested in transgenerational family therapy.

Bowen, M. (1978). *Family therapy in clinical practice.* New York: Jason Aronson.

This book is a collection of Murray Bowen's most important papers from 1957 to 1977. These papers include reports on his clinical research at NIMH with schizophrenics and their families between 1954 and 1959; important papers on the development of his theory; and the much-discussed "Anonymous" piece in which Bowen chronicles his attempts at differentiation from his own family of origin.

Carter, E. A., & McGoldrick Orfanidis, M. (1976). Family therapy with one person and the family therapist's own family. In P. J. Guerin (Ed.), *Family therapy: Theory and practice.* New York: Gardner Press.

Carter and McGoldrick Orfanidis clearly describe family-of-origin procedures based on the theoretical concepts of Murray Bowen. The authors contend that these procedures are equally appropriate for family therapy with one individual and for the training of family therapists. The value of this chapter is in the identification and clarification of these procedures and in the excellent use of illustrative examples.

Dicks, H. V. (1963). Object relations theory and marital status. *British Journal of Medical Psychology, 36,* 125–129.

In this classic article, Dicks extends the object relations theory of Klein, Fairbairn, and Guntrip to the study of marital relationships. Dicks describes marriage as a mutual process of attribution or projection, with each spouse perceived to a degree as an internal object. This article is well written and provides an excellent general background for viewing marriages in terms of object relations theory, so often mentioned by Framo, Williamson, Bowen, and others.

Dicks, H. V. (1967). *Marital tensions.* New York: Basic Books.

In this important volume, Dicks applies Fairbairn's object relations concepts to the understanding and treatment of marital dysfunction.

Fairbairn, W. R. D. (1952). *An object-relations theory of the personality.* New York: Basic Books.

This seminal work in object relations theory had a significant influence on the later work of Dicks, Bowen, Framo, Williamson, and others. Although it is steeped in ponderous psychoanalytic terminology, its influence on the field makes it required reading for those interested in the role of object relations in psychopathology.

Framo, J. L. (1976). Family of origin as a therapeutic resource for adults in marital and family therapy: You can and should go home again. *Family Process, 15,* 193– 210.

This is a pioneering article on Framo's brand of family-of-origin therapy. Framo clearly describes both the theory and practice of his approach. His theory, based on the object relations concepts of Fairbairn and Dicks, emphasizes the importance of clients confronting their parents face to face in order to "loosen the grip of the internal representatives of these figures" (p. 194). This paper is must reading for any student of family-of-origin therapy.

Framo, J. L. (1982). *Explorations in marital and family therapy: Selected papers of James L. Framo, Ph.D.* New York: Springer.

This book includes some of the most important papers of James Framo, whose approach to therapy includes both intrapsychic and interpersonal dimensions. In this collection of papers, he writes about his theoretical orientation and his methods of working with families, couples, couples groups, divorcing couples, and family of origin. He also discusses personal aspects of being a family therapist. His article on conducting family-of-origin work is destined to become a classic.

Guerin, P. J., & Pendagast, E. A. (1976). Evaluation of family system and genogram. In P. J. Guerin (Ed.), *Family therapy: Theory and practice.* New York: Gardner Press.

The authors describe the use of the genogram (a written symbolic presentation of family structure) in the context of taking a family history. The information garnered from both the interview (i.e., generational and personal boundaries, conflictual issues, triangles) and the genogram are critical in locating toxic issues for discussion. The presentation of examples of genograms is particularly helpful for individuals not familiar with this procedure.

Guntrip, H. (1968). *Schizoid phenomena, object relations, and the self.* New York: International Universities Press.

This classic volume was written to free individuals who do not have an adequate adult self from the onus of adhering to moral obligations that they have been taught but simply cannot meet because of the structure of their personalities. This dilemma is identified as "the schizoid problem." The book is a follow-up to the work of Fairbairn and emphasizes the holistic nature of the individual—a point readers may appreciate for its bridging of psychodynamic and system theories.

Hovestadt, A., Anderson, W., Piercy, F., Fine, M., & Cochran, S. (1985). A family-of-origin scale. *Journal of Marital and Family Therapy, 11*(3), 287–298.

This article presents the development and psychometric properties of a scale for measuring the perceived health of one's family of origin. The scale is easy to administer and has acceptable reliability and validity data. It should prove to be a useful measure for those interested in conducting family-of-origin research.

Kramer, J. R. (1985). *Family interfaces: Transgenerational patterns.* New York: Brunner/Mazel.

This book does an excellent job of presenting the multiple levels of family interactions that exist in therapy. The author examines how transgenerational patterns affect families in therapy, as well as how therapists' families of origin affect their behavior. The final section of the book presents the use of family-of-origin groups as a training format for family therapists.

Lindemann, E. (1944). Symptomatology and management of acute grief. *American Journal of Psychiatry, 101,* 141–148.

The syndrome of acute grief with psychological and somatic symptomatology is presented. Appropriate techniques also are included. This article is cited in much of Norman Paul's work as well as the more current publications examining delayed grief and mourning.

McGoldrick, M. & Gerson, R. (1985). *Genograms in family assessment.* New York: Norton.

This readable book provides a rationale and specific procedures for constructing, interpreting, and using genograms. The usefulness of genograms in family assessment is clearly illustrated in the many examples provided. The authors creatively maintain the reader's interest by providing fascinating illustrative genograms of the families of such notables as Sigmund Freud, Gregory Bateson, John Quincy Adams, Alfred Adler, Jane Fonda, the Bronte sisters, F. Scott Fitzgerald, Virginia Woolf, and John F. Kennedy.

Paul, N. L. (1967). The role of mourning and empathy in conjoint marital therapy. In G. H. Zuk & I. Boszormenyi-Nagy (Eds.), *Family therapy and disturbed families.* Palo Alto, CA: Science and Behavior Books.

This key article discusses how incompletely mourned losses are often hidden in marital difficulties. With his classic "Lewis couple" case study, Paul demonstrates the use of operational mourning combined with therapist empathy in neutralizing the long-term effects of hidden grief.

Paul, N. L. (1972). Effects of playback on family members of their own previously recorded conjoint therapy material. In G. D. Erickson & T. P. Hogan (Eds.), *Family therapy: An introduction to theory and technique.* Monterey, CA: Brooks/Cole.

This chapter espouses the view that parents of children with neurotic or psychotic symptoms must recognize that they are hurting their offspring before they can be expected to change their usual interactions with them. Audiotapes and videotapes are used to facilitate this self-confrontive process on the part of the parents by exposing the parents' behavior to the identified patients.

Paul, N. L. (1973), The need to mourn. In E. J. Anthony (Ed.), *The child in his family*. New York: Wiley.

This brief chapter states the core concept in much of Norman Paul's work: People need to mourn the death of loved ones. Paul discusses how society, literature, and sex-role stereotypes have served to block this important process. Multigenerational case studies are presented to illustrate the effect of unresolved mourning of a son for his father and of parents for their daughter.

Paul, N. L. (1974). The use of empathy in the resolution of grief. In J. Ellard, Volkan, V., Paul, N. L. (Eds.), *Normal and pathological responses to bereavement*. New York: MSS Information Corporation.

This chapter spells out the role of empathy in the resolution of unresolved mourning and grief. Paul articulates how the process of resolving grief ties in with the theoretical work of John Bowlby and separation anxiety research. Broader treatment implications are presented.

Paul, N. L. (1976). Cross-confrontation. In P. J. Guerin (Ed.), *Family therapy: Theory and practice*. New York: Gardner Press.

Paul describes in detail and provides a case example of the use of the technique of cross-confrontation. He uses "stressor stimuli" with clients, who learn that unpleasant feeling states are normal features of living and can thus be shared. The experiences selected for use are designed to encourage clients to empathize with other human beings and then with themselves.

Paul, N. L., & Grosser, G. (1965). Operational mourning and its role in conjoint family therapy. *Community Mental Health Journal, 1*(4), 339–345.

This cornerstone work of Norman Paul is well written and is still not outdated. Paul and Grosser maintain that incompleted mourning is a defense against further losses and is often transmitted unwittingly to other family members, especially offspring. The resulting interaction patterns promote a fixated family equilibrium. The authors describe their technique of operational mourning, which is designed to involve the family in a belated grief reaction. The shared affective experience can create empathy and understanding of the origins of current relational difficulties, and can weaken the maladaptive family equilibrium. A case illustration is furnished.

Paul, N. L., & Paul, B. B. (1975). *The marital puzzle*. New York: Norton.

This book demonstrates the importance of transgenerational themes in affecting present marital interactions. The Pauls' ideas are presented through the use of a full-length transcription of a marital case study, with comments added on diagnosis and treatment procedures. The use of operational mourning and of cross-confrontation is presented within the flow of the therapy process.

Paul, N. L., & Paul, B. B. (1982). Death and changes in sexual behavior. In F. Walsh (Ed.), *Normal family processes*. New York: Guilford Press.

In this fascinating chapter, the Pauls present their concept of the relationship between aborted grief processes and changes in sexual behavior. Three cases are presented in which sexual dysfunction or sexual behavioral change is traced to the unresolved mourning of death. Discussion is also given to the use of family genograms and "stressor" tapes in the treatment process.

Sager, C. J. (1976). *Marriage contracts and couple therapy*. New York: Brunner/Mazel.

The central concept of this book is that each partner in marriage brings to it an individual, unwritten contract, a set of conscious and unconscious expectations and promises based in part on transgenerational influences. Sager presents procedures for helping couples uncover and explore the various written and unspoken terms of their individual contracts. The goal of Sager's approach to therapy is to help partners make *quid pro quo* concessions, working toward a single joint contract that is agreed upon at all levels of awareness.

Stewart, R. H., Peters, T. C., Marsh, S., & Peters, M. J. (1975). An object relations approach to pychotherapy with marital couples, families, and children. *Family Process, 14*(2), 161–178.

In this article, object relations concepts are used to understand marital and family problems, as well as various dynamics between therapist and client. Countertransference, for example, is presented as a legitimate means of helping the therapist understand the projected splits of his/her client. This is a good introduction to the role of object relations concepts in family therapy.

Toman, W. (1961). *Family constellation*. New York: Springer.

This classic deals with the importance of birth order in the development of personality characteristics. While Toman's conclusions are not empirically derived, they have generated a great deal of subsequent research.

White, M. (1983). Anorexia nervosa: A transgenerational system perspective. *Family Process, 22*(3), 225–273.

The author suggests a link between anorexia nervosa and certain rigid and implicit family beliefs that are transmitted from one generation to another. A multistaged treatment based on challenging these beliefs is presented.

Williamson, D. S. (1981). Termination of the intergenerational hierarchical boundary between the first and second generation: A "new" stage in the family life cycle. *Journal of Marital and Family Therapy, 7*, 441–452.

This is the first of Williamson's excellent trilogy on renegotiating the power structures between adults and their older parents. This well-written article presents a compelling rationale for the need to redistribute intergenerational power in the direction of equality.

Williamson, D. S. (1982a). Personal authority via termination of the intergenerational hierarchical boundary: Part II. The consultation process and the therapeutic method. *Journal of Marital and Family Therapy, 8*, 23–37.

The author describes his family-of-origin approach by outlining the successive steps used in helping adult clients renegotiate a more emotionally equal peer relationship with their older parents. These steps culminate in a 3-day in-office consultation between the client and his/her parents. This is one of the most specific, pragmatic, and well-written papers on conducting family-of-origin therapy.

Williamson, D. S. (1982b). Personal authority in family experience via termination of the intergenerational hierarchical boundary: Part III. Personal authority defined, and the power of play in the change process. *Journal of Marital and Family Therapy, 8*(3), 309–323.

Williamson suggests personal authority as a synthesizing construct arising from the Hegelian dialectic of autonomy and intimacy. However, the real contribution of the article is in Williamson's enchanting and clever uses of paradox and play in the application of his transgenerational approach.

ACKNOWLEDGMENTS

We would like to acknowledge the aid of Marcia Brown-Standridge and Joseph L. Wetchler in the writing of selected "Key Concepts" definitions and "Key Books and Articles" annotations. We also appreciate the contributions of Janine Roberts, Mark Hirschmann, and Bunny Duhl to the "Teaching Tools and Techniques" section of this chapter.

REFERENCES

Anonymous (1972). Toward the differentiation of one's self in one's own family. In J. Framo (Ed.), *Family interaction: A dialogue between family researchers and family therapists.* New York: Springer.

Boszormenyi-Nagy, I. (1965). A theory of relationships: Experience and transaction. In I. Boszormenyi-Nagy & J. Framo (Eds.), *Intensive family therapy: Theoretical and practical aspects.* New York: Harper & Row.

Boszormenyi-Nagy, I. (1972). Loyalty implications of the transference model in psychotherapy. *Archives of General Psychiatry, 27,* 374–380.

Boszormenyi-Nagy, I. (1976). Behavior change through family change. In A. Burton (Ed.), *What makes behavior change possible?* New York: Brunner/Mazel.

Boszormenyi-Nagy, I., & Spark, G. M. (1973). *Invisible loyalties: Reciprocity in intergenerational family therapy.* New York: Harper & Row.

Boszormenyi-Nagy, I., & Ulrich, D. N. (1981). *Contextual family therapy.* In A. S. Gurman & D. P. Kniskern (Eds.), *Handbook of family therapy.* New York: Brunner/Mazel.

Bowen, M. (1960). A family concept of schizophrenia. In G. D. Jackson (Ed.), *The etiology of schizophrenia.* New York: Basic Books.

Bowen, M. (1974). Toward the differentiation of self in one's family of origin. In F. Andres and J. Loris (Eds.), *Georgetown Family Symposium papers.* Washington, DC: Georgetown University Press.

Bowen, M. (1978). *Family therapy in clinical practice*. New York: Jason Aronson.

Bray, J. H., Williamson, D. S., & Malone, P. E. (1984). Personal authority in the family system: Development of a questionnaire to measure personal authority in intergenerational family processes. *Journal of Marital and Family Therapy, 10,* 167–178.

Brodey, W. (1959). Some family operations and schizophrenia. *Archives of General Psychiatry, 1,* 379–402.

Dicks. H. (1963). Objects relations theory and marital studies. *British Journal of Medical Psychology, 36,* 125–129.

Dicks, H. (1967). *Marital tensions*. New York: Basic Books.

Duhl, B. S. (1983). *From the inside out and other metaphors: Creative and integrative approaches to training in systems thinking*. New York: Brunner/Mazel.

Fairbairn, W. R. D. (1952). *An object-relations theory of the personality*. New York: Basic Books.

Framo, J. L. (1970). Symptoms from a family transactional viewpoint. In C. J. Sager & H. S. Kaplan (Eds.), *Progress in family therapy*. New York: Brunner/Mazel.

Framo, J. L. (1976). Family of origin as a therapeutic resource for adults in marital and family therapy: You can and should go home again. *Family Process, 15,* 193–210.

Framo, J. L. (1980). Marriage and marital therapy: Issues and initial interview techniques. In M. Andolfi & I. Zwerling (Eds.), *Dimensions of family therapy*. New York: Guilford Press.

Framo, J. L. (1981). The integration of marital therapy with sessions with family of origin. In A. S. Gurman & D. P. Kniskern (Eds.), *Handbook of family therapy*. New York: Brunner/Mazel.

Framo, J. L. (1982). *Explorations in marital and family therapy: Selected papers of James L. Framo*. New York: Springer.

Guerin, P. J., & Pendagast, E. A. (1976). Evaluation of family system and genogram. In P. J. Guerin (Ed.), *Family therapy: Theory and practice*. New York: Gardner.

Hovestadt, A., Anderson, W., Piercy, F., Cochran, S. & Fine, M. (1985). A family of origin scale. *Journal of Marital and Family Therapy, 11*(3), 287–297.

Kramer, J. R. (1985). *Family interfaces: Transgenerational patterns*. New York: Brunner/Mazel.

Paul, N. (1974). The use of empathy in the resolution of grief. In J. Ellard *et al.,* (Eds.), *Normal and pathological responses to bereavement*. New York: MSS Information Corporation.

Paul, N. (1977). Cross-confrontation. In P. Guerin (Ed.), *Family therapy: Theory and practice* New York: Gardner Press.

Paul, N., & Grosser, G. (1965). Operational mourning and its role in conjoint family therapy. *Community Mental Health Journal, 1*(4), 339–345.

Sager, C. J. (1976). *Marriage contracts and couple therapy*. New York: Brunner/Mazel.

Stewart, R. H., Peters, T. C., Marsh, S., & Peters, M. J. (1975). An object relations approach to psychotherapy with marital couples, families, and children. *Family Process, 14*(2), 161–178.

Toman, W. (1961). *Family constellation*. New York: Springer.

Williamson, D. S. (1981). Personal authority via termination of the intergenerational hierarchical boundary: A "new" stage in the family life cycle. *Journal of Marital and Family Therapy, 7,* 441–452.

Williamson, D. S. (1982a). Personal authority in family experience via termination of the intergenerational hierarchical boundary: Part II. The consultation process and the therapeutic method. *Journal of Marital and Family Therapy, 8*, 23–37.

Williamson, D. S. (1982b). Personal authority in family experience via termination of the intergenerational hierarchical boundary: Part III. Personal authority defined, and the power of play in the change process. *Journal of Marital and Family Therapy, 8*(3), 309–323.

2

STRUCTURAL, STRATEGIC, AND SYSTEMIC FAMILY THERAPIES

STRATEGIC FAMILY THERAPY

Strategic family therapy and structural family therapy were born on different coasts of the United States. Strategic family therapy has its roots in the Palo Alto research group led by Gregory Bateson in the early 1950s. As part of his research on family communication, Bateson began to look at schizophrenia as a discrepancy between levels of communication. Jay Haley, John Weakland, and Don D. Jackson joined the Bateson project, and in 1956 their paper, "Toward a Theory of Schizophrenia," influenced therapists throughout the country to examine the double-binding communications of family members.

During the 1960s, many articles were written by Jackson and his associates at the Mental Research Institute (MRI) in Palo Alto, describing communicational strategies as devices for escaping or establishing definitions of intrafamilial relationships (Hoffman, 1981, p.23). Strategic family therapy evolved largely from this work at the MRI. It was also influenced by the work of Milton Erickson, with his emphasis on hypnosis and paradoxical therapeutic strategies. Haley, who also worked at the MRI and was a biographer of Erickson, continues to influence the growth and direction of strategic family therapy today.

Strategic family therapy generally is characterized by its use of specific strategies for addressing family problems (Madanes & Haley, 1977). Therapy is directly geared toward changing the presenting complaint and is typically accomplished by the therapist's first assessing the cycle of family interaction, then breaking that cycle through straightforward or paradoxical directives. Therapy is not growth- but change-oriented, and the therapist is responsible for successful therapeutic outcomes. The therapist focuses on present interaction; he/she does not interpret family members' behavior or explore the past. Therapy is terminated when the presenting problems have ceased.

While these characteristics are common to all strategic family therapies, the ways in which strategic therapy is practiced vary considerably. For example, the two approaches most associated with strategic family therapy, that are collectively described as the Haley/Madanes approach (e.g., Haley, 1976, 1980, 1984; Madanes, 1980, 1981), and the Brief Therapy Model developed at the Mental Research Institute (Watzlawick, Weakland, & Fisch, 1974; Watzlawick, 1978; Fisch, Weakland, & Segal, 1983), have some clear differences in emphasis, as noted below. [Although the approach developed by Mara Selvini Palazzoli and her colleagues (Selvini Palazzoli, Boscolo, Cecchin, & Prata, 1978, 1980) in Milan, Italy, is considered by some to be a strategic therapy (Madanes, 1981; Stanton, 1981b), it is presented separately in this chapter as "systemic" family therapy because of its practical and theoretical distinctions (MacKinnon, 1983).]

Haley/Madanes

Both Haley and Madanes believe that problems are maintained by a faulty hierarchy within the family. The goal of therapy is to alter the family's interactions, thereby changing the family's structure. Also, they contend that the presenting problem is often a metaphor for the actual problem (Haley, 1976; Madanes, 1981).

Haley will often align himself with the parental generation when dealing with child-focused problems (Haley, 1980). Bringing parents together to work on their child's problem can both realign problematic hierarchies and serve to strengthen the couple's relationship. Haley and Madanes alter malfunctioning triangles (Haley, 1976, 1980) and incongruent hierarchies (Madanes 1980, 1981) through such diverse interventions as paradox, reframing, ordeals, "pretending," and unbalancing through creating alternative coalitions.

Mental Research Institute (MRI)

The MRI group operates from a process rather than an organizational model. Issues of hierarchy and power are not as important as those of interactional sequence. It is the family's sequence of behavior around their attempted solution that is assumed to maintain the presenting problem (Watzlawick, Weakland, & Fisch, 1974). The MRI therapist tracks this cycle of behavior within the family by asking questions in the session and then prescribes a homework assignment (either direct or paradoxical) designed to break up the existing sequence of behavior.

Because MRI therapists do not place as much importance on hierarchy as Haley or Madanes, they often exhibit a less direct, more one-down position in dealing with a family in order to gain greater maneuverability (Fisch, Weakland, & Segal, 1983).

STRUCTURAL FAMILY THERAPY

The structural school of family therapy has its roots in a residential institution for ghetto boys in New York. In the 1960s, Salvador Minuchin and his colleagues were working at the Wiltwyck School for boys, serving a population primarily from New York's inner-city ghettos. They found psychoanalytic, long-term, passive, growth-oriented therapy to be extremely ineffective with these children, whose issues were immediate and survival-based. Minuchin and his associates experimented with a more active approach to therapy in which they worked with the boys and their families together (Aponte & VanDeusen, 1981). *Families of the Slums* (Minuchin, Montalvo, Guerney, Rosman, & Schumer, 1967) was written about the Wiltwyck School experiences and is the first book to present the structural approach to family therapy.

Born out of this work with low-socioeconomic-status families, structural family therapy is an active, problem-solving approach to a dysfunctional family context. Although Minuchin's work with psychosomatic families is well known (e.g., Minuchin, Rosman, & Baker, 1978), Minuchin has broadened his theoretical base and has applied his approach to patients of varying socioeconomic classes with a variety of presenting problems (Minuchin & Fishman, 1981).

Structural family therapy generally is characterized by its emphasis on hierarchical issues (Madanes & Haley, 1977). Typical goals of therapy include correcting dysfuntional hierarchies by putting parents in charge of their children and differentiating between subsystems within families. Therapy usually involves changing the family structure by modifying the way people relate to one another. This is done with a focus on the present, using direct, indirect, and paradoxical directives. Therapy is terminated when the family structure is positively altered and is able to maintain itself without the use of the presenting problem (Minuchin, 1974).

SIMILARITIES

Although structural therapy and strategic therapy are presented above as theoretically distinct schools, certain similarities are found to exist upon closer inspection, (see Table 2-1). Some of these similarities may be due to previous interaction among prominent structural and strategic family therapists. For example, Haley, one of the founders of strategic family therapy, greatly influenced Minuchin's structural approach during his tenure at the

Table 2-1
Similarities between Structural and Strategic Family Therapies

1. Behavior is understood in the context of the environment (i.e., the family).

2. Concepts from general systems theory are utilized (e.g., homeostasis, positive feedback).

3. Family life cycle is important in diagnosis and treatment.

4. Individual behaviors change as the family context changes.

5. Families are rule-governed systems.

6. Emphasis is on the present.

7. Therapy attempts to change repetitive behavioral sequences.

8. Process is emphasized over content.

9. The therapist plays a directive role.

10. The therapist uses what "works."

11. Therapy is symptom-oriented.

12. Diagnosis involves hypothesizing, intervening, and examining results.

13. Therapeutic contracts are used.

14. Interpretation is used to "relabel" or "reframe" rather than to produce insight.

15. Behavioral tasks are used.

16. "Joining" a family is important.

17. Therapeutic paradox is employed.

18. Therapy tends to be brief.

Note. Adapted from Stanton (1981a) and Fraser (1982).

Philadelphia Child Guidance Clinic. Haley was also influenced by Minuchin, as evidenced by Haley's (1976, 1980) emphasis on hierarchy and boundaries.

The theoretical similarities between structural and strategic family therapies include their view of families as rule-governing systems that can best be understood in context. For both, the presenting problem often serves a function within the family and can best be understood by examining present family interactions. The family life cycle is considered in both, and both employ general systems concepts (e.g., homeostasis, positive feedback) in their conceptualizations of family functioning.

Both also are similar in practice. For example, both employ assessment in the form of observing the results of therapeutic interventions in order to plan future interventions. While adherents of both therapies maintain that they use whatever "works," techniques obviously common to both include joining, reframing, and therapeutic paradox. Both emphasize process over content and present behavior over past behavior. Both utilize therapeutic contracts and behavioral tasks to change family interactions, believing that if the family context changes, so will individual behaviors. In both, the therapist takes a directive role to relieve the presenting problem. Finally, both approaches tend to be brief, usually between 10 and 20 sessions.

DIFFERENCES

Theoretically, structural and strategic therapies differ regarding the negative- or positive-feedback view of symptom dysfunction (see Table 2-2). In structural family therapy, dysfunction is seen in terms of rigid, homeostatic transactions that must be broken. In terms of general systems theory, a family's resistance to change is negative feedback and is seen as an attempt to maintain the family's status quo (e.g., a daughter's asthma keeps the mother and father together). In constrast, strategic family therapy conceptualizes family dysfunction in terms of positive feedback, or the vicious cycle created when an attempt to solve a problem (e.g., a wife's nagging) inadvertently worsens the symptomatic behavior (e.g., her husband's drinking). Thus, the strategic therapist's view of family problems arising from positive feedback (deviation amplification) necessitates a therapeutic focus on behavioral sequence as the locus of analysis and the target for change. On the other hand, structural family therapy, with its assumption of a rigid, negative-loop, homeostatic family structure, logically sees the therapist's role as breaking up that structure (Fraser, 1982).

The differences in therapeutic interventions between the two approaches are not always clear-cut, but are more a matter of emphasis (see

Table 2-2
Differences between Structural and Strategic Family Therapies

Structural	Strategic
1. Emphasizes negative-feedback cycles.	1. Emphasizes positive-feedback cycles.
2. Emphasizes importance of structure in dysfunction.	2. Emphasizes importance of maladaptive behavioral sequences in dysfunction.
3. More straightforward and confrontive.	3. More indirect and nonconfrontive.
4. Therapist generally works with entire family.	4. Therapist often works with only one or two members of a family system.
5. Focuses on immediate in-session behaviors.	5. Retrospectively focuses on out-of-session behavioral sequences.
6. Emphasizes in-session enactment.	6. Emphasizes out-of-session directives.

Note. Adapted from Stanton (1981a) and Fraser (1982).

Table 2-2). For example, structural family therapy is typically more con-
frontive than strategic, perhaps owing to Minuchin's own personal style.
While both are present-oriented, structural family therapy focuses more
on in-session behaviors and is more likely to employ in-session enactments.
Strategic therapy, on the other hand, generally explores current out-of-
session behavioral sequences and employs directives to be completed outside the session to disrupt these sequences. Strategic therapy (particularly
at the Brief Family Therapy Project of the MRI) is also more likely than
structural therapy to work with only one or two members of a family system
to bring about change in the entire system (Stone Fish & Piercy, in press.)

SYSTEMIC FAMILY THERAPY

Systemic family therapy as practiced by the Milan Associates (Selvini Palazzoli, Boscolo, Cecchin, & Prata, 1978) shares similar roots with both the
MRI and Haley/Madanes versions of strategic family therapy in that they
were all influenced by the work of Gregory Bateson. This has led all three
groups to view problems as being maintained by behavioral sequences.
However, MRI and Haley became further influenced by the work of Milton
Erickson while the Milan group held true to Bateson's original works. While
differences between systemic and strategic therapies appear to be subtle,
they run deeply enough for some to consider them separate forms of
therapy (MacKinnon, 1983).

In both strategic and structural family therapies, the therapist takes
responsibility for observing patterns of behavior and altering the family's
interaction through either direct or indirect interventions. In contrast, systemic therapy takes a more evolutionary perspective. The family is viewed
as a system that is constantly evolving. Problems exist when the family's
old epistemology does not fit its current pattern of behaviors (Tomm,
1984a). The therapist does not develop specific goals for the family or
overtly attempt to alter behavior, but instead helps the family develop an
alternative epistemology by creating an environment in which new information is introduced into the family system, information which invites
spontaneous change.

The Milan Associates explain their in-session behavior in terms of three
themes: hypothesizing, circularity, and neutrality (Selvini Palazzoli et al.,
1980). The therapist is constantly generating hypotheses regarding why
the family behaves as it does. These hypotheses create a map by which
questions can be directed to the family and interventions are made. All
hypotheses including those developed by the family are seen as equally
valid.

Circularity exists in the way the therapist conducts the session. Through
the use of triadic or circular questions, in which one family member is asked

to comment on the interactional behaviors of two others, the therapist develops a systemic picture of the family's behavior (Penn, 1982). By conducting the session in this way, new information is introduced which allows family members to experience themselves in a new context. Selvini Palazzoli *el al.* (1980) contend that simply conducting a session in this way may introduce enough new information to produce change.

Therapist neutrality is the glue that holds this process together. By avoiding issues of hierarchy, power, and side-taking the therapist is free to experience the system in its entirety. This facilitates the generation of new hypotheses and allows the family to develop at its own pace in its own way. Within this sense of neutrality, the family is free to decide whether or not it wishes to change (Tomm, 1984b).

Interventions typically are given through the use of a ritual or through the use of paradoxical prescriptions that call for the family not to change. These interventions differ from those used in strategic therapies in that their aim is simply to infuse new information into the system, not necessarily to alter patterns of interaction. Interventions connect family members' behaviors through an explicit systemic hypothesis, as in the paradoxical prescription, or through implicitly having them act out their behavior through a ritual. Whether the family does the task or accepts the hypothesis is irrelevant. The important thing is that they are exposed to a different way of viewing their problems.

The amount of time allotted between sessions differs between strategic and systemic therapies. In strategic therapies, sessions are generally spaced 1 week to several weeks apart. In systemic therapy, sessions are often spaced 1 month apart. This period, according to the Milan group, allows time for the intervention to take effect. As each family member reacts to the intervention, his/her behavior sets off a chain reaction that alters other members' perceptions and actions, creating a vortex of feedbacks (Tomm, 1984a).

In recent years, the Milan associates have split in their approach to systemic therapy. Selvini Palazzoli and Prata have experimented with the "invariable prescription," one intervention that is used with all families. Boscolo and Cecchin, however, are increasingly emphasizing the interview process itself. The above discussion is more reflective of the current work of Boscolo and Cecchin.

KEY CONCEPTS

Structural Family Therapy

Boundaries. Invisible lines of demarcation in a family, which may be defined, strengthened, loosened, or changed as a result of structural family therapy. Boundaries range from "rigid" (extreme separateness) to "diffuse" (extreme togetherness). Ideally, boundaries are "clear."

Coalition. A (usually) covert alliance between two family members against a third. When one parent joins a child in a rigidly bounded cross-generational coalition against the other parent, this is called a "stable coalition" (Minuchin, 1974) (cf. "detouring," "triangulation").

Detouring. A process whereby stresses between spouses get redirected through a child so that the spouse subsystem gives the impression of harmony (cf. "stable coalition," "triangulation").

Disengaged family. An extreme pattern of family organization where members are so separate they seem oblivious to the effects of their actions on each other. Boundaries among family members are typically rigid (opposite of "enmeshed family").

Enmeshed family. An extreme pattern of family organization in which family members are so tightly locked that autonomy is impossible. Boundaries among family members are typically diffuse (opposite of "disengaged family").

Family mapping. The diagramming of a family's organizational structure, boundaries, and patterns of interaction. Family mapping is useful in hypothesizing family functioning and forming goals for structural change (see Minuchin, 1974, Chapter 3).

Generational boundaries. Invisible lines of demarcation between generations. Healthy generational boundaries allow parents to maintain parental roles and children to maintain child roles.

Parental child. Role played by an overly responsible child who has power and authority that more appropriately belongs to the parents. This typically reflects an inappropriate generational boundary within the family.

Subsystems. Units within a family, based upon characteristics such as sex, age, or interest (e.g., mother and daughter may represent the female subsystem in a family).

Triangulation. A process in which each parent demands that the child side with him/her against the other parent. Siding with one is defined as attacking by the other, and the child feels paralyzed (cf. "stable coalition," "detouring").

Strategic and Systemic Family Therapies

Analogical message. A metaphorical or symbolic message. For example, certain behaviors (fighting over who cleans the bathroom) may have a metaphoric meaning for a couple (who is in charge?).

Circularity. A contextual, cyclic view of behavior, as opposed to linear, cause-and-effect explanations of behavior. For example, a father's withdrawal from arguments is not because of anything the mother has done, but is seen in terms of circularity; that is, it is one point in a repetitive, predictable, circular pattern of behaviors in which the family is engaged.

Double bind. Orginally noted by Bateson and his colleagues; a communication that leaves the responder "damned if you do and damned if you don't." A double bind includes (1) a double message (e.g., saying "I'm glad to see you" while looking away) (2) within an emotionally important relationship (3) where the receiver of the message is unable to comment on the message. Bateson proposed that double-bind messages are important ingredients in the etiology of schizophrenia. Therapeutic paradox may be seen as a therapeutic application of double-bind messages.

Error amplification. See "positive feedback."

Homeostasis. The tendency within a system to seek equilibrium or balance through maintaining the status quo and resisting change. Theorists differ as to whether family pathology is maintained by resisting change (homeostasis or negative feedback) or by engaging in vicious cycles of change-attempting behavior (positive feedback or error amplification).

Homeostatic mechanisms. Measures that a system employs to maintain balance and stability.

Metacommunication. Communication about communication. This term usually refers to the covert, nonverbal message (tone of voice, inflection, body language) that gives additional meaning to an overt, verbal message.

Negative feedback. A process to correct system deviations by reestablishing the previous state of equilibrium. For example, this process is at work in families in which a child acts out in order to bring quarreling parents back together again.

Positive feedback. The morphogenic, change-activating process within systems. Any tactic from a therapist or a family that challenges family homeostasis and changes a family's way of behaving is an example of positive feedback. In strategic family therapy, a dysfunctional family's solution to their problem is assumed to involve positive feedback (i.e., deviation amplification) that exasperates the problem rather than solves it. For example, chiding a nonresponsive spouse (the solution) makes the spouse less responsive rather than more responsive (the problem).

Punctuation. Human interaction is typically complex and cyclical. People often attribute different meanings to events because they arbitrarily bracket or focus on different parts of the cycle. For example, if a son's misbehavior and his parents' restrictiveness have produced a vicious cycle, the parents might say, "We are strict because you misbehave," whereas the son would retort, "If I misbehave, it's because you are so strict."

CLINICAL SKILLS

Structural Family Therapy

Accommodation. A general term referring to the adjustments a therapist may make to a family (e.g., joining, maintenance, mimesis) in order to achieve a therapeutic alliance with the family.

Boundary marking. A strategy in which the therapist reinforces appropriate boundaries and diffuses inappropriate boundaries by modifying transactional patterns (e.g., a therapist may sit between an intrusive mother and her child so that the mother will have difficulty speaking for the child).

Creating a workable reality. A strategy in which the therapist attends to certain family issues, ignores others, and reframes still others to emphasize a family situation that has a solution. For example, a presenting problem of childhood schizophrenia may be de-emphasized, and the need for parental cooperation and control in the family may be emphasized. Thus a "workable reality" is created in which the parents have specific tasks to accomplish in relation to their "misbehaving" child.

Enactment. The acting out of dysfunctional transactional patterns within the family therapy session, encouraged by the therapist. Through setting up these transactions in the present, the therapist learns much about the family's structure and interactional patterns. The therapist is then able to intervene in the process by increasing its intensity, indicating alternative transactions, marking boundaries, and so forth. The therapist may also have the family enact more positive transactional patterns within the therapy session, which will serve as a template for more positive interactions outside therapy.

Intensity. The degree of impact of a therapeutic message, selectively regulated by the therapist. Intensity can be achieved by increasing the affective component of a family transaction, by increasing the length of a transaction, or by frequently repeating the same message in different transactions.

Intervening isomorphically. The therapist's focusing on events that are dissimilar in content, but nevertheless are structurally equivalent. For example, whether an anorectic girl says she doesn't know something, complains about the clothes she wears, or won't eat, the therapist can reframe such statements as disrespect for her parent's authority.

Joining. An accommodating maneuver in which the therapist establishes rapport with family members and temporarily becomes part of the family system. The family accepts the therapist more openly, thus enhancing the therapist's ability to bring about change.

Maintenance. An accommodation technique in which the therapist provides planned support of the family structure while he/she analyzes it. For example, comments like "I see," "Tell me more about . . . ," and "Uh-huh" are noncommittal and give the therapist the time to understand the family better.

Mimesis. The paralleling of a family's mood or behavior, which solidifies a therapeutic alliance. For example, a therapist may talk slowly with a slow-talking family or be animated with an animated family.

Restructuring. Any therapeutic intervention that confronts and challenges a family and facilitates structural changes. Examples of restructuring maneuvers include assigning tasks, shifting power systems, escalating stress, and marking boundaries.

Unbalancing. Any therapeutic intervention that supports one member of the family, thus interfering with the homeostasis of the family system.

Strategic and Systemic Family Therapies

Circular Questioning. Introduced by Selvini Palazzoli and her associates (Selvini Palazzoli, Boscolo, Cecchin, & Prata, 1978), circular questions are interview questions used to learn more about changes and differences in family relationships that might provide clues to recursive family patterns. Circular questions are useful in generating systemic hypotheses and interventions, and in allowing a family to begin viewing themselves systemically. For more on the theory and practice of circular questioning, see Fleuridas, Nelson, and Rosenthal (1986) and Penn (1982).

Directives. Therapeutic tasks aimed at breaking inappropriate sequences of behavior.

Family ritual. Used extensively by Selvini Palozzoli and her associates (1978); an individualized prescription of an action or series of actions that are designed to alter the family's roles. For example, the parents of a family with an intrusive live-in grandmother might be given the following message to read to the grandmother each night: "Thank you for your many suggestions regarding how we should discipline our son. If it wasn't for your loving help we would surely fail." The grandmother is told to read this message in response: "I love you and am willing to completely sacrifice my own life and happiness to make sure you don't fail to discipline your child the right way." Any rejection of the positively connoted messages should shift the family members toward more functional interactions.

Positioning. A class of therapeutic paradox in which the therapist accepts and exaggerates what the client is saying. This often has the effect of underlining the absurdity in the situation and forces the client to take a different position. For example, when parents are complaining at length about their child's irresponsibility, a therapist could say, "Maybe you should put him up for adoption," thereby moving the parents to take a position defending rather than scolding their son.

Positive connotation. Relabeling of family behaviors in a positive light. For example, a mother's nagging could be labeled concern for her child. A teenager's running away could be positively connoted as a need for independence or concern that her family receive treatment. In any case, positive connotation reorients the family to more positive ways of viewing their interactions and allows the therapist to gain entrance into the family.

Pretending. Prescribing that a symptomatic person "pretend" to exhibit his/her symptom reclassifies that symptom as voluntary and not really "real," which may have the effect of altering people's reaction to that symptom. For example, when a depressed husband is told to pretend to be depressed a certain number of times during the week, his wife, assuming he *is* pretending, may begin to respond to him differently. Similarly, the husband is now in charge of "acting" depressed, which is more volitional than powerlessly "being" depressed (see Madanes, 1981).

Relabeling (reframing). Use of language to give new meaning to a situation. The alteration of meaning invites the possibility of change. For example, relabeling a youth's depression as stubbornness or laziness suggests personal responsibility for that behavior, and may change the family's response to that behavior.

Restraining. A class of therapeutic paradox in which the therapist discourages change, usually by outlining the dangers implicit in improving. For example, the therapist might say, "If your son got better, you and your husband might not have anything to talk about."

Symptom prescription (prescribing). A strategy in which the therapist encourages or instructs the client to engage in or practice his/her symptom, usually including a compelling rationale. For example, a depressed spouse may be asked to stay depressed on a particular day and keep notes on his/her depression, supposedly so the therapist can learn more about the depression. The client either rebels against this directive and gives up the symptom, or obeys the therapist and continues the symptom, thus putting the maintenance of the symptom under his/her conscious, voluntary control.

Therapeutic paradox. A strategic intervention that has been defined and implemented in many ways (see Weeks & L'Abate, 1979). Generally, it involves a seemingly illogical intervention to bring about change. This entails maneuvers that are in apparent contradiction to the goals of therapy, yet are actually designed to achieve them (Haley, 1976). Major classes of therapeutic paradox are (1) prescribing, (2) restraining, and (3) positioning (see definitions of each above).

Triadic questioning. See circular questioning.

TEACHING TOOLS AND TECHNIQUES

Training Videotapes

Several excellent videotapes are available that demonstrate structural and strategic approaches to family therapy. Lists and descriptions of available tapes can be secured from these sources:

- Boston Family Institute, 251 Harvard St., Brookline, MA 02146
- Family Therapy Institute, 5850 Hubbard Dr., Rockville, MD 20852
- Nathan W. Ackerman Family Institute, 149 East 78th St., New York, NY 10021
- Philadelphia Child Guidance Clinic, Two Children's Center, 34th St. & Civic Center Blvd., Philadelphia, PA 19104
- Master Videotape series, AAMFT, 1717 K Street, N.W., Suite 407, Washington, D.C. 20006

Journal Days

In order to expose students to as many key journal articles as possible, each month each student chooses two articles form an extensive bibliography to read and summarize to the class. Many of these 5-minute summaries generate provocative discussions regarding the theory, research, and practice of strategic, structural, and systemic family therapies.

Debates and Panels

A debate on "how change occurs" may be set up between students identifying themselves as structural and those identifying themselves as strategic. Also, students may take the role of central figures such as Haley, Minuchin, Bateson, Selvini Palazzoli, Watzlawick, Erickson, Stanton, and Madanes for a panel discussion or debate. Needless to say, a student must know the writings of a central figure quite well to be able to step into his/her shoes.

Choreographic History of Strategic, Structural and Systemic Family Therapies

The instructor writes the names of key individuals in the history of strategic, structural and systemic family therapies on separate 5" × 8" cards. On the back of each card, the instructor writes a saying that captures an essential point of each respective key individual's theory. Names and sayings we have used include the following:

Name	Saying
Norbert Wiener	"Cybernetics explains information flow in systems."
Gregory Bateson	"Don't chop up the ecology."
Don D. Jackson	"Families resist change."
Jay Haley	"But how can I bring about change?"
Paul Watzlawick	"You're absolutely right."
John Weakland	"Go slow."
Richard Fitch	"Change can be dangerous."
Milton Erickson	"My voice will go with you."
Mara Selvini Palazzoli	"The observers have an important message for each of you."
Salvador Minuchin	"Sit over here."
Braulio Montalvo	"I'm a clinician."
Cloe Madanes	"Let's pretend."

The instructor tells the history of strategic, structural and systemic family therapies: He/she begins with the work of Norbert Wiener, explains how Wiener's work affected the thinking of Gregory Bateson, describes how Bateson subsequently moved to California and worked on a research grant on levels of communication with Jay Haley and John Weakland, and so on (for a short history of strategic and structural family therapies, see Stanton, 1981b, or Bodin, 1981). As different names are mentioned, the instructor gives a member of the class a card with that person's name on it, and has him/her read the saying on the back of the card. Also, as people move in and out of the historical overview, the instructor has them physically move around the room. For example, such a historical choreography will trace Haley's travels from Palo Alto, to his consultations with Milton Erickson, to his work with Minuchin in Philadelphia, and finally to his present position in Washington. Similarly, students learn that Watzlawick consulted frequently with Selvini Palazzoli in the development of the systemic approach. This kind of choreographic history brings the key figures alive and underlines the influences these leaders had on one another.

Responding to Ethical Concerns

Haley (1976, Chapter 8) addresses quite well a variety of ethical concerns related to strategic therapy. After students have read Haley's ethical justification of strategic therapy, they are given classroom practice in thinking through and responding to similar ethical concerns. Specifically, they are divided into seven small groups, with each group given a provocative ethical concern to discuss and formulate a response to. After about 20 minutes, the instructor dramatically questions each group about the particular concern that the group has been discussing. A predetermined spokesperson from the group then responds to the concern the instructor raised. The entire class is given the opportunity to discuss each issue after the group response is given.

The ethical concerns discussed in the groups include the following:

1. Strategic therapy seems manipulative and underhanded. Don't you agree?
2. Do the ends justify the means?
3. What place does honesty play in this kind of therapy? How acceptable is lying?
4. Isn't it unethical to change someone outside his/her awareness? Why keep therapeutic techniques secret?
5. If a therapist is "in charge" of change, how is the client supposed to become self-sufficient?
6. Who is the therapist to say what is best for a client to do? Isn't nondirective therapy much more respectful and ethical?
7. What right do you have to consider yourself an expert on how people should live their lives?

Read–Summarize–React Exercise

A read–summarize–react exercise may be used to help students learn the various explanations and rationales of therapeutic paradox (cf. Hoffman, 1981; Raskin & Klein, 1976; Weeks & L'Abate, 1979). Each explanation is typed on a 5" × 7" card. Students are formed into groups of five with 10 cards in the middle of each group. Students are instructed in turn to (1) take a card and silently read the explanation; (2) paraphrase the explanation; (3) give their own reactions to it; and (4) allow any other member of the group to respond. After this exercise, the class comes together, and the instructor answers any questions regarding the various explanations of paradox. (This exercise is drawn from Piercy & Sprenkle, 1984.)

Reframing Exercise

Reframing involves giving a new meaning to a presenting problem in a way that facilitates changes. To practice this skill, students are asked to write down the situations or characteristics in the left-hand column below and attempt to give them new meaning. This may be done individually or in small groups. The alternative realities in the right-hand column are shared by the instructor if students have difficulty reframing the symptom or problem behavior. An alternative exercise is to have each small group responsible for role-playing the reframing of one or more of the symptoms below.

Symptom or Problem Behavior	Alternative Reality
Depression	"You are just a little lazy."
Smothering mother	"You really care about your child."
Distant husband	"You are a very loving family member to take the back seat and give the spotlight to others."
Jealousy	"You really care about your husband and don't want to lose the relationship you have."
Adolescent running away	"I compliment you. This is a very creative way to achieve autonomy."
Nagging	"You want to matter to your family—to be closer—and this is the way you are asking for this closeness."
Disrespectful teenager	"You are telling your folks you want to grow up and be more responsible for yourself."
Alcoholic husband	"Your family needed help and you were selfless enough to sacrifice youself so they could get that help."

Strategic Directives

Problems from Haley's (1976) *Problem-Solving Therapy* (pp. 60–63) are presented to students, who then attempt to brainstorm possible directives for interrupting behavioral sequences. After the brainstorming, the directives Haley uses are shared and discussed.

Family Mapping

Family mapping (see Minuchin, 1974, Chapter 3) is a helpful way of visually depicting the structure of a dysfunctional family. The class is given paragraphs depicting certain dysfunctional family hierarchies and asked to (1) draw a map of the family's present structure; (2) draw a map of the ideal family structure at the termination of therapy; and (3) give the rationale and therapeutic strategy to be used to reach this structuring goal. The following is an example:

> *Question:* The husband criticizes the wife, who then seeks a coalition with the child against the father. Map this structure and map your goal. Also, briefly discuss how you would achieve your goal.

> *Possible Answer:*

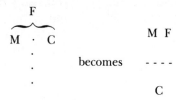

To achieve this, I would see the mother and father alone for therapy and would give a directive that the mother could only speak with the child through the father. I would also provide opportunities in therapy for the mother and father to deal directly with each other without the child.

Milan-Style Messages

Cases are presented to the class, who in groups of five act as therapy teams in developing Milan-style paradoxical messages (see Selvini Palazzoli *et al.*, 1978). Below is an illustrative situation and one possible Milan-style team message (adopted from Mark Hirschman, personal communication, 1984).

> *Situation:* Fabrizio, an encopretic 9-year-old, is the identified patient. The father, usually mild-mannered and withdrawn, has taken major responsibility in trying to discipline and lecture Fabrizio. The mother is a borderline alcoholic, but this fact is not discussed by the family. The mother spends much time at the race track. Rocco, the 11-year-old, is the model child in his parents' eyes, although he is only doing average work in school.

Milan-Style Team Message: "Fabrizio, we are impressed with your self-less gifts to your family and are inclined to suggest no changes at this time. Your soiled pants give your father a reason to be involved in your family. Your messing is also an ingenious way to appear bad, so that your mother can continue to drink and go unnoticed. Your soiling also helps your brother look good. Our team wonders whether Rocco could really be seen as helpful and good without you being so bad. The team, therefore, believes that there could be many negative consequences if you stop soiling your pants. Dad would probably drift away from your family, Mom's drinking would have to be noticed, and Rocco would have to work harder in school to get attention."

RESEARCH ISSUES

Most of the articles and books written about structural, strategic, and systemic therapies are nonempirical and anecdotal in nature. The few data-based research studies that have been conducted (e.g., Minuchin *et al.*, 1978; Stanton, Todd & Associates, 1982) have used relatively specific presenting problems (e.g., psychosomatic illness, drug addiction) and have not employed alternative family therapy control groups. Future research should probe the relative effectiveness of each approach, as well as various components of each approach, with certain presenting problems and/or family types. Researchers should also consider single-case studies utilizing multiple baselines. Examples of research questions that warrant investigation include the following:

- Which structural family therapy interventions account for the greatest change in family therapy outcome?
- Are paradoxical directives more effective than straightforward directives in the removal of specific symptoms (with certain types of families)?
- Which types of paradoxical interventions bring about the greatest degree of change on process and/or outcome levels?
- Are tasks given within the session more effective than those given outside the session?
- Does meeting the supervision team lessen a family's anxiety in therapy?
- Is a "Greek chorus" (Papp, 1980) more effective when the observers side with the family or when they side with the therapist?
- What treatment schedule (e.g., once a week, once a month) is most effective for Milan-style systemic therapy?

KEY BOOKS

Fisch, R., Weakland, J. H., & Segal, L. (1983). *The tactics of change*. San Francisco: Jossey-Bass.

This is perhaps the most pragmatic, useable, compelling book on the MRI approach to "doing therapy briefly." It is clearly written and provides excellent case illustrations. Particularly helpful are the chapters on therapist maneuverability, patient position, and interventions.

Haley, J. (1963). *Strategies of psychotherapy*. New York: Grune & Stratton.

In this early volume, Haley discusses basic systemic assumptions and weaves a compelling rationale for paradoxical therapeutic maneuvers.

Haley, J. (1976). *Problem-solving therapy*. San Francisco: Jossey-Bass.

Haley first coined the term "strategic therapy" in this seminal volume. This book remains one of the clearest expositions of the basic tenets underlying Haley's approach to family therapy. His chapter on ethical issues is particularly timely and compelling, although clearly biased in favor of strategic practices that others have labeled "deception" and "manipulation."

Haley, J. (Ed). (1980). *Advanced techniques of hypnosis and therapy: The selected papers of Milton H. Erickson*. New York: Grune & Stratton.

Some of Milton Erickson's most influential papers are included in this book. The final commentary by Jay Haley summarizes the essence and influence of Erickson's works.

Haley, J. (1980). *Leaving home*. New York: McGraw-Hill.

Haley emphasizes hierarchical issues in this succinct, step-by-step guide to disengaging the disturbed young person from his/her parents. His use of verbatim family therapy transcripts makes this an interesting as well as useful volume. Haley's inclusion of both structural and strategic concepts underlines the overlap of these two family therapy approaches.

Haley, J. (1984). *Ordeal therapy*. San Francisco: Jossey-Bass.

Haley builds upon the work of Milton Erickson by providing a strong and detailed theoretical rationale for the use of ordeals in therapy. Excellent case histories are employed to illustrate the application of ordeal therapy with a variety of clients and presenting problems.

Madanes, C. (1981). *Strategic family therapy*. San Francisco: Jossey-Bass.

Madanes broadens the scope of strategic family therapy with her therapeutic use of pretending and her metaphoric formulations of the role of symptoms. Her case examples are particularly helpful.

Minuchin, S. (1976). *Families and family therapy*. Cambridge, MA: Harvard University Press.

Minuchin clarifies his theory through the use of verbatim therapy transcripts and parallel commentary. Also, his illustrative use of family mapping is particularly helpful. This is a seminal text in structural family therapy and an excellent place to begin reading.

Minuchin, S., & Fishman, H. C. (1982). *Techniques of family therapy*. Cambridge, MA: Harvard University Press.

The techniques of structural family therapy are clearly discussed and exemplified through verbatim excerpts from therapy. Techniques presented include joining, reframing, enactment, restructuring, unbalancing, and the use of paradox. This volume, however, is not simply a manual on the application of techniques; Minuchin and Fishman also articulate the spontaneous, artful side of family therapy.

Minuchin, S., Montalvo, B., Guerney, B. G., Rosman, B. L., & Schamer, F. (1967). *Families of the slums*. New York: Basic Books.

This is the first book to describe the theory and practice of structural family therapy. This volume grew out of the authors' work with disadvantaged children at the Wiltwyck School in New York.

Minuchin, S., Rosman, B. L., & Baker, L. (1978). *Psychosomatic families: Anorexia nervosa in context*. Cambridge, MA: Harvard University Press.

This important volume outlines the theory, research, and practice of structural family therapy with psychosomatic children and their families. Perhaps its greatest contribution is in the suggestions presented for dealing with the parental enmeshment characteristic of these families. Minuchin's research with psychosomatic families is also outlined.

Papp, P. (1983). *The process of change*. New York: Guilford Press.

A well-written book by a creative master clinician. This book grew out of Papp's work with the Ackerman Brief Therapy Project. While the project was inspired by the Milan approach, the Ackerman group also integrates aspects of the work of Minuchin, Haley, and MRI.

Selvini Palazzoli, M., Cecchin, G., Prata, G. & Boscolo, L. (1978). *Paradox and counterparadox*. New York: Jason Aronson.

This classic volume outlines the theory and practice of the Milan group. The group uses a consultation team that observes family therapy sessions and sends in messages tailored to disrupt family patterns. Creative paradoxical messages and rituals such as those presented in this book are being employed by many systemic family therapists today.

Stanton, M. D., Todd, T. C., & Associates. (1982). *The family therapy of drug abuse and addiction*. New York: Guilford Press.

Discussed are the theory, research, and practice of strategic–structural therapy with drug addicts. Stanton and Todd generally believe that addiction serves a homeostatic function within the addict's family. They draw heavily on Haley's model in *Leaving Home* to help parents take charge of their addicted children. The research presented is generally considered to be the best of its kind.

Watzlawick, P., Beavin, J. H., & Jackson, D. (1967). *Pragmatics of human communication: A study of interactional patterns, pathologies and paradoxes*. New York: Norton.

Key aspects of communication are explained and related to cybernetic and general systems concepts. This book is must reading, in that the theoretical underpinnings of much of strategic family therapy are outlined.

Watzlawick, P., Weakland, J., & Fisch, R. (1974). *Change*. New York: Norton.

The basic assumptions of the Palo Alto school are outlined, and innovative interventions are presented that are consistent with these assumptions. The concepts of first- and second-order change and the strategic use of paradox are brought to life with excellent examples from both within and outside of family therapy.

KEY ARTICLES

Andolfi, M. (1980). Prescribing the families' own dysfunctional rules as a therapeutic strategy. *Journal of Marital and Family Therapy, 6*, 29–36.

The use of paradox in therapy is motivated by the fact that many families request help but at the same time seem to reject all offers of help. By prescribing its own dysfunctional rules to the family, the therapist can stimulate the tendencies toward change that are present in the family system.

Aponte, H. J., & VanDeusen, J. M. (1981). Structural family therapy. In A. S. Gurman, & D. P. Kniskern (Eds.), *Handbook of family therapy*. New York: Brunner/ Mazel.

This comprehensive chapter includes a wealth of knowledge about structural family therapy. From theory to therapy to therapist's role to supervision to research, Aponte and VanDeusen project a family therapy whose function is consistent with its underlying structure.

Bateson, G., Jackson, D. D., Haley, J., & Weakland, J. (1956). Toward a theory of schizophrenia. *Behavioral Science, 1*, 251–264.

In this classic article, the authors hypothesize the origin of schizophrenia to be rooted in dysfunctional, double-binding communication between family members. The impact of this article on family therapy has been tremendous. This is must reading!

Coyne, J. C. (1984). Strategic therapy with depressed married persons: Initial agenda, themes, and interventions. *Journal of Marital and Family Therapy, 10*, 53–62.

This excellent article examines the treatment of depression from an interactional perspective. A strategic model of treatment is provided, as well as a case study illustrating the implementation and results of this model.

Coyne, J. C. (1985). Toward a theory of frames and reframing: The social nature of frames. *Journal of Marital and Family Therapy, 11* (4), 337–344.

This largely conceptual article discribes certain critical elements of effective reframes. Coyne discusses the contributions and limitations of "radical constructivism" to the understanding of reframes, and emphasizes their social and inter-subjective nature. Coyne's use of clear examples makes this largely theoretical article surprisingly readable.

Coppersmith, E. (1980). Expanding uses of the telephone in family therapy. *Family Process, 19*, 411–417.

This article describes innovative uses of the telephone by a family therapy training team, including (1) strategic calls to the therapist, (2) calls from the team to family members, and (3) calls between family members. Case examples are given describing the interventions and their impact. Both training and therapeutic benefits are discussed.

Fleuridas, C., Nelson, T., & Rosenthal, D. (1986). The evolution of circular questions: Training family therapists. *Journal of Marital and Family Therapy, 12*(2), 113–127.

This article provides a helpful taxonomy for understanding circular questioning, as well as a variety of useful examples of circular questions. The table of circular questions make particularly good instructional handouts.

Fraser, J. S. (1982). Structural and strategic family therapy: A basis for marriage, or grounds for divorce? *Journal of Marital and Family Therapy, 8* (2), 13–22.

Structural and strategic schools of therapy are examined and compared. Conceptual integration seems possible, but practical integration may be difficult, since the different units of analysis utilized by each logically lead to different interventions.

Fraser, J. S. (1984). Paradox and orthodox: Folie à deux? *Journal of Marital and Family Therapy, 10,* 361–372.

Fraser critiques the contraindications of the use of paradox identified by others, on the grounds that what is paradoxical is dependent on what does or does not make "sense" to the therapist (i.e., what he/she sees as "orthodox"). Fraser contends that what some see as paradoxical may often be elected by therapists with a "systemic orthodox" as a logical and effective first choice in therapy. This is a thought-provoking article.

Greenberg, F. (1977). The family interactional perspective: A study and examination of the work of Don D. Jackson. *Family Process, 16,* 385–410.

This informative article summarizes the work of the late Don D. Jackson, psychiatrist and founder of family interactional psychotherapy. Through this article, the reader is given a glimpse of the names, places, and political influences that gave birth to the MRI and the foundations of strategic family therapy.

Hoffman, L. (1971). Deviation-amplifying processes in normal groups. In J. Haley (Ed.), *Changing families.* New York: Grune & Stratton.

Family theorists tend to agree that the presence of a deviant (dysfunctional) member seems to promote group cohesion. This chapter emphasizes the importance of introducing positive feedback into such a system in order to produce an imbalance that will facilitate change.

Liebman, R., Minuchin, S., & Baker, L. (1974). An integrated treatment program for anorexia nervosa. *American Journal of Psychiatry, 131,* 432–436.

This interesting article discusses a treatment program for anorectics, using behavior conditioning within the context of structural family therapy.

MacKinnon, L. (1983). Contrasting strategic and Milan therapies. *Family Process,* 22(4), 425–438.

MacKinnon does a fine job of clarifying the commonalities and distinctions related to the theory and practice of the MRI, Haley, and Milan models of therapy. The point-by-point comparisons are particularliy helpful, as are the appendices summarizing these comparisons. MacKinnon concludes that the Milan model is sufficiently distinct not to be considered a "strategic" therapy.

MacKinnon, L., Parry, A., & Black, R. (1984). Strategies of family therapy: The relationship to styles of family functioning. *Journal of Strategic and Systemic Therapies,* 3(3), 6–22.

The characteristics of the Milan, MRI, and Haley and Madanes models are examined. The original context and the examples used in the major publications of each model are studied to determine differences in presenting problems, developmental stage, and family characteristics of clientele. The authors suggest some interesting hypotheses regarding the effectiveness of each approach with different problems and family types.

Madanes, C. (1980). Protection, paradox, and pretending. *Family Process,* 19, 73–85.

The paper describes three paradoxical strategies for helping parents solve the presenting problem of their child and the incongruity in the family hierarchy. The therapeutic techniques described are characterized by the use of communication modalities, such as dramatizations, pretending, and make-believe, that are appropriate to children.

Mazza, J. (1984). Symptom utilization in strategic therapy. *Family Process,* 23, 487–500.

Mazza describes how she uses symptoms to put parents back in charge of their children. The key to each of her strategic techniques is to "go with the resistance" and use what the client is most reluctant to give up. Mazza provides clear and concise rationales and examples for each of the techniques she suggests. A useful article.

Minuchin, S., Baker, L., Rosman, B., Liebman, R., Milman, L., & Todd T. (1975). A conceptual model of psychosomatic illness in children. *Archieves of General Psychiatry,* 32, 1031–1038.

The article describes in a detailed and lucid fashion the "open systems" model employed by Minuchin and his associates in their study of the psychosomatogenic family. Three conditions necessary for the development and maintenance of severe psychosomatic problems are discussed, and case examples are given. An excellent bibliography and literature review combine to make this an invaluable article on the subject.

Papp, P. (1980). The Greek chorus and other techniques of paradoxical therapy. *Family Process,* 19, 45–57.

This interesting paper describes the creative use of a consulting group. The group views the therapeutic process with the family from outside a one-way mirror and periodically sends in messages.

Penn, P. (1982). Circular questioning. *Family Process, 21*(3), 267–280.

Penn liberally draws from Bateson, Keeney, and others in describing circular questioning from the perspective of a cybernetic epistemology. Her categories of circular questions help to demystify the process, as does her fascinating case study (which includes an on-going commentary/explanation).

Penn, P. (1985). Feed-forward: Future questions, future maps. *Family Process, 24*(3), 299–310.

This article extends the theory and practice of Milan-style "future questions." As Penn describes the process, "feed-forward" is used in conjunction with positive connotation and encourages families to imagine possible patterns of their relationships in the future. A case study is used to clearly underline the power of this procedure.

Pirrota, S. (1984). Milan revisited: A comparison of the two Milan schools. *Journal of Strategic and Systemic Therapies, 3*(4), 3–15.

This article clarifies the recent differences in the work of the members of the original Milan group. Specifically, the orientation of Selvini Palazzoli and Prata is contrasted with that of Boscolo and Cecchin. Two case studies of anorexia are utilized to highlight the differences, while interesting questions are raised regarding how models evolve over time.

Raskin, D. E, & Klein, Z. E. (1976). Losing a symptom through keeping it: A review of paradoxical treatment techniques and rationale. *Archives of General Psychiatry, 33*, 548–555.

This article describes the use of symptom prescription by various schools of psychotherapy. Raskin and Klein suggest that symptom prescription has been and is being used (under different names) by experimental psychologists, behavior therapists, psychoanalysts, logotherapists, and directive therapist.

Rohrbaugh, M., Tennen, H., Press, S., & White, L. (1981) Compliance, defiance, and therapeutic paradox: Guidelines for strategic use of paradoxical interventions. *American Journal of Orthospsychiatry, 51*, 454–467.

The authors draw from Brehm's reactance theory and the Palo Alto model of brief therapy in their development of one of the few sets of guidelines for using paradoxical interventions.

Selvini Palazzoli, M. (1985). The problem of the sibling as the referring person. *Journal of Marital and Family Therapy, 11*(1), 21–35.

This is a fine example of the theoretical and clinical artistry of Mara Selvini Palazzoli. She provides systemic insight into problems where a sibling is the referring person. The clinical example is particularly illuminating and representative of the Milan approach.

Selvini Palazzoli, M., Boscolo, L., Cecchin, G. F., & Prata, G. (1977). Family rituals: A powerful tool in family therapy. *Family Process, 16*, 445–453.

This article describes, using a case history, the therapeutic intervention of prescribing a family ritual for the purpose of eradicating a destructive family myth. The authors give a glimpse of the historical, cultural, and political context in which they work.

Selvini Palazzoli, M., Boscolo, L., Cecchin, G. F., & Prata, G. (1980). Hypothesizing–circularity–neutrality: Three guidelines for the conductor of the session. *Family Process, 19,* 3–12.

Instead of simply gathering information about the presenting problem, the authors use the interview process to increase information about the system. Since each family member comments on the others, the therapist is able to gain leverage with the whole family through impartiality.

Sluzki, C. E. (1978). Marital therapy from a systems theory perspective. In T. J. Paolino & B. S. McGrady (Eds.), *Marriage and marital therapy: Psychoanalytic, behavioral, and systems theory perspectives.* New York: Brunner/Mazel.

Sluzki provides a well-written series of suggestions for when to use specific strategic interventions with couples. Also, useful examples of each intervention are presented. This is a helpful chapter for the clinician looking for concrete guidelines for when to use a particular intervention.

Stanton, M. D. (1981). An integrated structural/strategic approach to family therapy. *Journal of Marital and Family Therapy, 7,* 427–439.

This article reviews the basic concepts of both the structural and the strategic approaches, with a proposed model for their integration. This interplay presents three general rules of application: (1) One should initially deal with a family through a structural approach; (2) one should switch to a predominantly strategic approach when structural techniques either are not successful or are unlikely to succeed; and (3) following success with strategic methods, it may be advisable to revert once again to a structural approach.

Stanton, M. D., & Todd, T. C. (1981). Engaging "resistant" families in treatment: II. Principles and techniques in recruitment. *Family Process, 20,* 261–280.

Stanton and Todd present 21 principles and a number of strategies and techniques that have been developed for successfully recruiting resistant family members of drug addicts.

Todd, T. C. (1984). Strategic approaches to marital stuckness. *Journal of Marital and Family Therapy, 10,* 373–381.

In this practical article, Todd discusses several useful strategic procedures for accepting and amplifying the status quo in marital therapy. Unlike many authors, Todd identifies potential problems with each intervention and discusses contraindications for the use of his procedures.

Tomm, K. (1984). One prespective on the Milan systemic approach: Part II. Description on session format, interviewing style and intervention. *Journal of Marital and Family Therapy, 10,* 253–271.

Karl Tomm clearly summarizes the basic interviewing principles and interventions associated with Selvini Palazzoli and her colleagues. While this is not a primary source in that it is not written by the Milan group, Tomm's succinct overview of the Milan procedures and his excellent clinical illustrations make this article particularly useful.

Weakland, J. H. (1976). Communication theory and clinical change. In P. J. Guerin (Ed.), *Family therapy: Theory and practice.* New York: Gardner Press.

The argument presented by Weakland questions the typical labeling of so-called illogical, irrational behavior as "mad" or "bad," and offers instead a systemic viewpoint that labels such behavior and communication "metaphorical" in character. Weakland recommends that metaphorical communication be answered metaphorically rather than trying to get a person to talk "in reality."

Weakland, J., Fisch, R., Watzlawick, P., & Bodin, A. M. (1974). Brief therapy: Focused problem resolution. *Family Process, 13,* 141–168.

This article is a good introduction to the MRI's approach to brief, problem-focused therapy. Their approach includes (1) a focus on observable behavioral interaction in the present; (2) deliberate intervention to alter the system; and (3) a maximum of 10 sessions.

Weeks, G. R., & L'Abate, L. (1979). A compilation of paradoxical methods. *American Journal of Family Therapy, 7,* 61–76.

This article presents a history and classification of types of therapeutic paradox, exemplifying interactional and transactional levels of paradox. The various dichotomies include (1) individual versus systemic; (2) prescriptive versus descriptive; (3) directly insight-producing versus indirectly insight-producing; (4) direct versus cryptic; (5) time-bound versus time-random; (6) reframing versus relabeling; and (7) specific versus general.

Wood, B., & Talmon, M. (1983). Family boundaries in transition: A search for alternatives. *Family Process, 22,* 347–357.

This paper develops the concepts of proximity and hierarchy to elaborate on Minuchin's original concept of boundaries. In developing these concepts, the authors remove connotations of pathology inherent in the current concept of "blurred" and "rigid" boundaries. Since the health or pathology of a particular type of boundary is related to such issues as context and life cycle stage, the authors' ideas represent a step in the right direction.

ACKNOWLEDGMENTS

We would like to acknowledge the aid of Linda Stone Fish and Joseph L. Wetchler in the writing of portions of the introduction to this chapter. Also, the following individuals contributed to the writing of the "Key Books" and "Key Articles" annotations; Nick Aradi, Marcia Brown-Standridge, Dan Bowen, Roz Cantrell, Cricket Steinweg, Linda Stone Fish, Paul Sherman, David Tate, and Joseph Wetchler.

REFERENCES

Aponte, H. J., & VanDeusen, J. M (1981). Structural family therapy. In A. S. Gurman & D. P. Kniskern (Eds.), *Handbook of family therapy.* New York: Brunner/Mazel.

Bateson, G., Jackson, D. D., Haley, J., & Weakland, J. (1956). Toward a theory of schizophrenia. *Behavioral Science, 1,* 251–264.

Bodin, A. B. (1981). An interactional view: Family therapy approaches of the Mental Research Institute. In A. S. Gurman & D. P. Kniskern (Eds.), *Handbook of family therapy.* New York: Brunner/Mazel.

Fraser, J. S. (1982). Structural and strategic family therapy: A basis for marriage or grounds for divorce? *Journal of Marital and Family Therapy, 8*(2), 13–22.

Gurman, A. S., & Kniskern, D. P. (Eds.), (1981). *Handbook of family therapy.* New York: Brunner/Mazel.

Haley, J. (1976). *Problem-solving therapy.* San Francisco: Jossey-Bass.

Haley, J. (1980). *Leaving home.* New York: McGraw-Hill.

Hoffman, L. (1981). *Foundation of family therapy.* New York: Basic Books.

Madanes, C. (1981). *Strategic family therapy.* San Francisco: Jossey-Bass.

Madanes, C., & Haley, J. (1977). Dimensions of family therapy. *Journal of Nervous and Mental Disease, 165,* 88–98.

Minuchin, S. (1974). *Families and family therapy.* Cambridge, MA: Harvard University Press.

Minuchin, S., & Fishman, H. C. (1981). *Family therapy techniques.* Cambridge, MA: Harvard University Press.

Minuchin, S., Montalvo, B., Guerney, B. G., Rosman, B. L., & Schumer, F. (1967). *Families of the slums.* New York: Basic Books.

Minuchin, S., Rosman, B. L., & Baker, L. (1978). *Psychosomatic families: Anorexia nervosa in context.* Cambridge, MA: Harvard University Press.

Papp, P. (1980). The Greek chorus and other techniques of paradoxical therapy. *Family Process, 19,* 45–57.

Piercy, F., & Sprenkle, D. (1984). The process of family therapy education. *Journal of Marital and Family Therapy, 10*(4), 399–407.

Raskin, D. E., & Klein, Z. E. (1976). Losing a symptom through keeping it: A review of paradoxical treatment techniques and rationale. *Archives of General Psychiatry, 33,* 548–555.

Selvini Palazzoli, M., Boscolo, L., Cecchin, G. F., & Prata, G. (1978). *Paradox and counterparadox.* New York: Jason Aronson.

Stanton, M.D. (1981a). An integrated structural/strategic approach to family therapy. *Journal of Marital and Family Therapy, 7,* 427–439.

Stanton, M.D. (1981b). Strategic approaches to family therapy. In A. S. Gurman & D. P. Kniskern (Eds.), *Handbook of family therapy.* New York: Brunner/Mazel.

Stanton, M. D., Todd, T. C., and Associates. (1982). *The family therapy of drug abuse and addiction.* New York: Guilford Press.

Stone Fish, L., & Piercy, F. P. (in press). The theory and practice of structural and strategic family therapy: A Delphi study. *Journal of Marital and Family Therapy.*

Tomm, K. (1984). One perspective on the Milan systemic approach: Part II. Description of session format, interviewing style and interventions. *Journal of Marital and Family Therapy, 10,* 253–271.

Weeks, G. R., & L'Abate, L. (1979). A compilation of paradoxical methods. *American Journal of Family Therapy, 7,* 61–76.

3

EXPERIENTIAL FAMILY THERAPIES

Popular humanistic, existential therapies of the 1960s, such as Gestalt therapy, psychodrama, client-centered therapy, logotherapy, and the encounter group movement, have all influenced the theory and technique of various experiential family therapies. And, like individual, humanistic psychotherapies, experiential family therapies challenge the positivistic tenets of some of the current problem-focused schools of family therapy.

A founder and leading catalyst in the evolution of experiential family therapies is undoubtedly Virginia Satir. Satir (1967, 1972) has blended Gestalt techniques, psychodrama, encounter techniques, and communications training into a dynamic family therapy that continues to influence the field today (Sprenkle, Keeney, & Sutton, 1982). Beyond the skillful execution of technique, Satir encourages direct, honest communication among family members through the considerable support and warmth she shows them. She risks and shares herself to encourage risking and sharing from family members. In being fully human through direct, present-centered encounters, Satir demonstrates several of the most vital tenets of experiential family therapy.

Carl Whitaker is another charismatic and influential experiential family therapist (Napier & Whitaker, 1978; Neill & Kniskern, 1982; Whitaker & Keith, 1981). In fact, Whitaker may have been the first to have used the term "experiential psychotherapy" (Whitaker & Malone, 1953). While Whitaker's approach is unconventional and idiosyncratic, the basic assumptions underlying his therapy are largely consistent with existential, humanistic thought.

Other experiential family therapists include Walter Kempler (1973, 1981), a proponent of Gestalt family therapy; Fred and Bunny Duhl (B. S. Duhl, 1983; B. S. Duhl & Duhl, 1981; F. J. Duhl & Duhl, 1979), the developers of "integrative family therapy"; and Ronald Levant (1978), who has proposed a client-centered family therapy approach.

Each of these experiential family therapists conducts therapy in a uniquely different way. However, certain theoretical tenets are common to each. Below are several of the major theoretical assumptions held by most experiential family therapists.

PRIMACY OF EXPERIENCE

Sartre's (1946) classic philosophical assertion, "Existence precedes essence," is basic to experiential family therapy. Our thoughts and intellectualizations ("essence") are our attempts to decipher meaning from our experiences ("existence"), but the experience of living comes first.

A person who only lives intellectually is not in touch with or reflecting on his/her own life experience. Consequently, important nonrational experiential data are ignored. This person would not know himself/herself and thus would have no authentic self to offer others in relationships. As Whitaker (1976) suggests, such a person is "doing" to avoid the anxiety of nonbeing. Kempler (1973) describes it this way:

> There is the risk of becoming the victims of our own logical minds, living lives guided, at best, by sensitive intelligence and practical reality. . . . family is essential to sustaining, in the deepest sense, the happening we call living; and without whom life is reduced to an intelligent reflex arc. (p. 79).

Experiential family therapy succeeds in reminding us of the importance of firsthand experiential data, which is often underemphasized by other schools of family therapy. The experiential family therapist asserts that there is more to life than what can be observed and measured. The "more" is the human, creative, life-and-breath dimension of family. As B. S. Duhl and Duhl (1981) state, "It is hard to kiss a system" (p. 488).

Since experiential family therapists are interested in the direct experience of families, they employ a variety of procedures to facilitate here-and-now experiences, whether in the form of dreams, fantasies, feelings, or sensations.

AFFECT

Families not in touch with their present experiencing are thought to be emotionally dead. Experiential family therapists use evocative procedures to unblock honest emotional expression in such families. Their goal is to open individuals to their inner experience, thus helping them to be more fully human. In this sense, affect is, in itself, therapeutic and growth-producing. Experiential family therapy helps family members begin to feel, to experience each other as real people, and to directly attack the emotional sterility that has enveloped the family. As Carl Whitaker is fond of saying, "One hug from a family member is worth a hundred from a therapist."

THE PERSON OF THE THERAPIST

Experiential family therapists participate actively and personally in therapy sessions; they do not attempt to hide behind a therapeutic mask. This means at times being vulnerable with family members and at other times being angry or upset. If the therapist expects the family to have the courage to be real, the therapist must also demonstrate that courage.

Such self-disclosure has therapeutic benefit for both family and therapist. The therapist's realness and present-centered encounters often stimulate expanded experience and intimate encounters within the family. Likewise, the therapist wants and needs real human contact during the therapy hour. Whitaker and Keith (1981) state that if the therapist gets nothing for himself/herself during therapy, chances are that the family members are not getting much either.

SPONTANEITY AND CREATIVITY

Since creative, nonrational experiencing is an important goal of experiential family therapy, spontaneity is desired for both therapist and family. In fact, Whitaker and Keith (1981) advocate "craziness—nonrational, right-brain experiencing—as a measure of health in both therapist and family.

Any techniques that the experiential therapist might use are meant to foster creative experiencing. Techniques such as family sculpting (F. J. Duhl, Kantor, & Duhl, 1973), family art therapy (Geddes & Medway, 1977; Kwiatkowska, 1967) puppetry (B. S. Duhl & Duhl, 1981), conjoint family drawings (Bing, 1970), psychodramatic techniques (Satir, 1967, 1972), and Gestalt ground rules (Kempler, 1973, 1981) are all applied to free the family members to experience each other and life more creatively and personally.

Techniques, however, are not central to experiential family therapy. Whitaker, for example, believes that the best interventions, particularly in later sessions, are those that arise out of the therapist's own creativity in the moment, rather than any preplanned interventions (Neill & Kniskern, 1982). As Whitaker and Keith (1981) state,"The objective of all techniques is to eliminate techniques" (p. 218).

FREEDOM, HOLISM, AND EXISTENTIAL ANXIETY

Experiential family therapists follow in the tradition of the existential philosophers, in that their views may be regarded as a sustained protest (Kaufman, 1956) against the reduction of human existence to mere behaviors, cognitions, or theories. Whitaker, for example, emphasizes many of the traditional themes of existentialism: freedom; not fate but choices; anxiety; and awareness of death (Napier & Whitaker, 1978). Whitaker emphasizes these themes in therapy, not because they are strategically useful, but because he believes that they are central to the experience of human living.

Experiential family therapists assume the personal freedom of the family members with which they work. But with freedom comes choice, and as Bunny Duhl (1983) states, "We are not accustomed to reaching inward for our answers" (p. 37). Whether through Gestalt techniques, evocative challenges, or silence, the therapist encourages self-responsibility within the family. As Whitaker (in Neill & Kniskern, 1982) states, "the integrity of the family must be respected. They must write their own destiny" (p. 329).

"I–THOU" RELATIONSHIP

Experiential family therapists want to do more than help family members experience their inner reality; they want to encourage an "I–Thou" (Buber, 1970) encounter among family members and perhaps with themselves. Such an existential encounter has sometimes been described as resulting in an "existential shift," a change in referent point, or a "carrying-forward effect" among family members, which leads to a change in how family members experience and relate to one another (Gendlin, 1973). Experiential family therapists believe in the healing nature of human relationships. I–Thou encounters have therapeutic value, in that they set into motion the growth potential of family members.

PRESENT-CENTEREDNESS

Immediate experiencing and person-to-person encounters can take place only in the present. When the past or future is discussed, family members are taken away from direct experience. Such intellectualizations, therefore, are typically seen as counterproductive to the experiential family therapist. As Whitaker states, "Life isn't mind over matter, it's present over past and present over future" (in Neill & Kniskern, 1982, p. 372).

GLOBAL VERSUS SPECIFIC GOALS

Experiential family therapists typically describe their goals in general terms, such as a heightened sense of competence, well-being, and self-esteem (B. S. Duhl & Duhl, 1981); role flexibility (Whitaker & Keith, 1981); awareness and self-responsibility (Kempler, 1973, 1981); and "leveling" communication (Satir, 1972). Such vague, nonoperationalized goals have been criticized by many family therapy researchers. However, experiential family therapists give these criticisms relatively little weight, since, after all, internal experience is seen as infinitely more valid than external, intellectual, nonexperiential data.

KEY CONCEPTS

Alienation. The condition of being shut off from one's true feelings. Most experiential therapists agree that dysfunctional family members are alienated, thus making family intimacy difficult to achieve. Kempler (1981) calls this alienation "astigmatic awareness."

Awareness. Considered by Kempler (1973) to be the "process of processes," which involves a "re-minding, a realization, a bringing into consciousness of the mind's own inherent mechanism for orienting" (p. 61). New awarenesses potentially lead to self-responsibility and growth. For example, if a person becomes aware of his/her need for support or independence, he/she is then better able to act on that need.

Battle for initiative. After the therapist has won the "battle for structure" (see next definition), Carl Whitaker emphasizes the importance of allowing the family the freedom to determine the course of therapy. While Whitaker is concerned and active, he is respectful of the family's right to choose its own destiny, both in the therapy room and in its life outside.

Battle for structure. Carl Whitaker's term for the therapist's task of establishing workable administrative control with a family at the beginning of therapy. Whitaker does this, for example, by clearly being in charge of when the sessions will be held, who will come, and what the process will be.

Communication. The way in which people share meaning with one another. Direct, clear, person-centered communication is generally considered healthy by experiential family therapists, and is particularly emphasized by Satir (1967, 1972), Kempler (1973, 1981), and B. S. Duhl and Duhl (1981).

"Craziness." Whitaker's concept for nonrational, right-brain, creative functioning that he believes is appropriate and healthy for both therapist and family to be able to establish access and to engage in.

Existential shift. A change in referent point or "carrying forward" (Gendlin, 1973) that occurs in a relationship when two people have a moving, present-centered, person-to-person encounter. Such a powerful experience goes beyond one's ability to describe it, and often results in a marked change in how one perceives and acts in the world.

Experience. According to Kempler (1973), the "key to growth and re-growth and to the therapeutic process" (p. 62). By this, Kempler means intimate experience that brings with it new awareness. Gestalt experiential family therapy facilitates experiences that stimulate awareness, thus helping family members get in touch with and reintegrate parts of themselves, which in turn fosters greater self-responsibility.

Flight into health. The tendency of many families, according to Carl Whitaker, to terminate therapy prematurely when family stress is reduced. Whitaker defines this as a positive growth effort that should not be prevented. Moreover, if the family should again seek therapy at a later time, members are often more united and resolved to get the most out of therapy.

Gestalt family therapy. An experiential therapy that use present-centered experience to help the family (1) locate current awareness; (2) explore how awareness is blocked; (3) facilitate the discovery and expression of hidden experiences; and (4) experiment with self-responsibility in the family context (Kaplan & Kaplan, 1978).

Self-awareness. A goal of experiential family therapies (particularly Gestalt family therapy), in which the rigid cycles of automatic behaviors are unblocked. As a person becomes more self-aware by exploring his/her present experience, he/she moves to a position of recognizing choices and responsibility for behavior. Futhermore, self-awareness often brings about an integration of fragmented or "unfinished" aspects of the self that have been outside awareness.

Self-worth. The feelings (self-esteem) and ideas (self-concept) one has about one's self (Satir, 1972). Most experiential family therapists maintain that increased self-worth in family members is an important process and outcome of family therapy.

Unfinished business. A term coined by Fritz Perls, the founder of Gestalt therapy, and frequently used by Gestalt family therapists such as Walter Kempler (1973, 1981) to mean unresolved feelings and/or disowned parts of one's self. Through present-centered Gestalt therapy, such unfinished business can come into awareness and be integrated and responsibly handled.

CLINICAL SKILLS

While the use of techniques is minimized in experiential family therapy, we have included below several ways in which experiential family therapists facilitate present-centered, person-focused contact with client families.

Encounter. A powerful personal experience that occurs when two people drop defenses and interact with one another honestly. Even when a therapist is being authentically angry with a family member, such a powerful personal encounter is thought to encourage a potentially more caring, person-to-person relationship in the future.

Family drawing. An experiential family therapy technique in which family members draw their conception of how their family is organized, in order to stimulate new learnings and insights (see Bing, 1970; Geddes & Medway, 1977; Rubin & Magnussen, 1974).

Gestalt techniques. A wide variety of techniques used by Gestalt family therapists to encourage present-centered family interaction and interpersonal awareness. For example, ground rules such as "No gossiping" and "Statements, not questions," as well as facilitative therapist responses such as "Tell him that, not me," encourage person-to-person communication and interpersonal awareness (cf. Kaplan & Kaplan, 1978; Kempler, 1973, 1981).

Personal involvement. As stated earlier, a critical factor in the successes of experiential family therapy. The therapist must have the courage to be involved in a real caring way with the client family. According to Whitaker, if the therapist is not personally involved there is no real learning.

Sculpture (also known as "space sculpture," "family sculpture," "relationship sculpture," "spatialization"). A technique developed initially by David Kantor, in which symbolic processes and events are portrayed through spatial analogies (e.g., distancing and posturing of various family members. Constantine, 1978; Duhl, 1983). Some family therapists use sculpture to disengage the clients from emotional experience and thus facilitate insight into the past and present situations (Constantine, 1978). Others (e.g., Satir, 1972) use sculpture to bring about an affective experience that will unblock unexpressed emotions.

Self-disclosure. The sharing of aspects of one's self with one's clients, in which virtually all experiential family therapists engage. Self-disclosure is thought to increase trust, provide alternatives through metaphor, facilitate person-to-person encounters, and allow the therapist to be known to the family as an accessible person rather than a distant professional.

Symbolic drawing of the family life space. An expressive activity initially developed by Damuta Mostwin, in which family members graphically represent emotional distance and communication patterns among one another through symbolic drawings on a blackboard. It is thought to be a non-threatening task that facilitates meaningful family interaction, provides a wealth of information about the family in therapy (Geddes & Medway, 1977).

TEACHING TOOLS AND TECHNIQUES

Small-Group Discussion: Theoretical Tenets of Carl Whitaker

The class is broken down into small groups, with each group given a statement or question to discuss that Carl Whitaker has dealt with in his writings. After each group discusses personal opinions related to its respective statement, a spokesperson from each group summarizes the major issues of the group discussion to the entire class. After each summary, the instructor discusses with the class what Carl Whitaker has said about that particular topic (see Neill & Kniskern, 1982). Often lively discussions ensue. Below are questions used in this exercise, along with a summary of Whitaker's views on each particular issue.

   1. *What results do you want in working with a family? Describe how you want the family to function at the end of therapy.*
   Whitaker emphasizes role flexibility, as well as an increased sense of unity and autonomy as appropriate goals of therapy. Whitaker prizes the individuality of families and their freedom to determine their own lives. He does *not* want them to fit some therapist's narrow definition of "well-functioning." By and large, he hopes that therapy will expand a family's options.
   2. *We, as people helpers, are professional parents. Do you agree or disagree? Why?*
   Whitaker would agree with this. A therapist, like a parent, allows more and more responsibility, as time progresses. The therapist also goes through stages with the families analogous to family life cycle stages (e.g., "terrible twos," psychosexual stages, rebellious adolescents, "empty nest" syndrome).
   3. *The therapist must use power in his/her work with families. What are some specific ways of claiming your power during the therapy process?*
   Whitaker's "battle for structure" (Whitaker & Keith, 1981, p. 204) starts with the first phone call, when he tells all family members to come to the first session. He also decides when the session will be, who will speak, what the process will be, and so forth. As therapy proceeds and his administrative control is assured, he then supports the freedom and initiative of the family in setting the direction of therapy.

4. If "love is not enough" and "techniques are not enough," what is? Discuss the basic ingredients in being an effective therapist. Include love and techniques in your discussion.

Whitaker would agree that both love and techniques (to a lesser extent) are important ingredients. According to Whitaker, the therapist should ideally care deeply about the client family. While Whitaker emphasizes the therapeutic value of the therapist–client relationship, he also has identified various therapeutic techniques (cf. Whitaker & Keith, 1981; Whitaker & Napier, 1977). However, as Whitaker and Napier (1977) state, "the objective of technique is the development of . . . the therapist . . . beyond 'using' techniques." (p. 5).

5. When cotherapy is used, should it involve a male and female?

Whitaker believes that it is not essential to have a male and female cotherapist so long as the cotherapists can establish themselves as symbiotic parents to the whole family. What really helps is that both are ageless and sexless, free "to play all the keys." Whitaker, for example, can be a tender mother and a tough grandfather.

6. Families should not leave a session with confusion or unfinished feelings. Do you agree or disagree?

Whitaker would disagree. Confusion is good—the beginning of creativity. Napier and Whitaker (1978, p. 77) tell families, "Don't try to sort it out. Let it cook in you, and don't talk about this stuff at home. The things that are valuable will sort themselves out and begin to make sense to you as we go on."

7. The therapist's contribution comes primarily out of his/her own person, not out of his/her professional skill. Do you agree or disagree?

Whitaker would agree. The therapist's intuitive and deeply personal involvement in a "reparenting" process characterizes his approach, as does his goal of establishing a caring, person-to-person relationship with the members of the family. Through the therapist's allowing his/her own personhood into therapy, an existential shift can occur that results in positive family growth.

Read–Summarize–React Exercise: Provocative Statements of Carl Whitaker

Many of Carl Whitaker's provocative statements are included by Neill and Kniskern (1982) in a chapter entitled "Gatherings." Statements related to the therapeutic process and theoretical tenets of Whitaker are typed on separate 5″ × 7″ cards. Students are formed into groups of five with 10 cards in the middle of each group. Students are instructed in turn to (1) take a card and silently read Whitaker's statement, (2) paraphrase the statement; (3) give their own reactions to it, and (4) allow any other member of the group to respond. This exercise, plus any discussion that follows, provides students opportunities to clarify their own theoretical suppositions as they learn more about those of Carl Whitaker.

Several examples of provocative statements made by Carl Whitaker include the following:

- "Professionalism can be a serious problem."
- "Insight is a by-product of growth or change rather than a precursor or a cause of growth or change."
- "My theory is that all theories are bad except for preliminary game playing with ourselves until we get the courage to give up theories and just live."
- "You can fall in love but you can't fall out."
- "Psychotherapy is like yearning to play the piano. How much, how long, how deeply depends on what you want as an experience—to play hymns or to play Bach or Beethoven."
- "You don't really know somebody until you know their parents."
- "Real hatred is probably never destructive—we don't want to lose the object of our hatred; hatred has a unifying effect."
- "The best way to avoid psychotherapy is to have regular interviews with a therapist."

Position Paper

The following assignment for a five-page position paper is made after a thorough reading of Kempler (1973, 1981). It should be noted that this assignment could be adopted easily to cover any experiential family therapist.

> Kempler (1973) discusses Hegel's contention that any thought (thesis) implies its own equal and opposite thought (antithesis), and when these two specific points are confronted they unite (synthesis) to become a single point (thesis) in a new spiral of thesis–antithesis–synthesis. Based on your assigned readings, what major thoughts (theses) of Kempler are directly confronted by your own thinking (antithesis)? From this dialectic tension and resulting synthesis, what theses, if any, emerge for you?

Satir Communications Exercise

In many of her workshops, Virginia Satir employs an experiential activity that demonstrates the personal and interpersonal impact of five types of communication (Satir, 1972). This exercise may also be used as a training

activity that familiarizes students/trainees with Satir's contentions related
to these styles of communication. In the exercise, groups of four are formed
into "families." A mother, a father, an oldest child, and a youngest child
are chosen in each "family." Then the following five communications styles
are presented in a minilecture (see Satir, 1972):

1. *Placating*—pacifying, smoothing over differences, being nice, protective, defending others gently, covering up.
2. *Avoiding* (distracting)—being quiet, pretending not to understand,
   changing the subject, playing weak, playing helpless.
3. *Blaming*—judging, bullying, comparing, complaining.
4. *Computing*—using logic, lecturing, using outside authority.
5. *Leveling*—"real" responding (i.e., integrated, flowing, and alive; appropriate to the situation; verbally and nonverbally consistent).

After the minilecture, each family is instructed to "plan where you will
go and what you will do on your vacation." Each of five 5-minute family
discussions takes place in which family members act out one of Satir's
communication styles. The assignment of styles we have employed is as
follows:

	Mother	Father	Oldest child	Youngest child
Role play #1	3	4	1	2
Role play #2	1	3	2	4
Role play #3	2	1	4	3
Role play #4	(Student chooses his/her own role)			
Role play #5	5	5	5	5

After each role play, there is an opportunity for each group to debrief.
A large-group discussion typically follows the completion of the small-
group exercises. It is our experience that students get very involved in these
small-group exercises and that the personal insights shared are considerable.

Films/Videotapes

The following representative films or videotapes provide useful examples
of experiential family therapy:

- *Virginia Satir Teaching Tapes*. Available from Golden Triad Films,
  Inc., 100 Westport Square, 4200 Pennsylvania, Kansas City, MO
  64111.
- *Making the Invisible Visible* (family sculpture, with Peggy Papp). Avail-

able from Nathan W. Ackerman Family Institute, 149 East 78th St., New York, NY 10021.

- *Affinity* (with Carl Whitaker). Available from Philadelphia Child Guidance Clinic, Two Children's Center, 34th St. & Civic Center Blvd., Philadelphia, PA 19104.
- Films with Walter Kempler. Available from The Kempler Institute, P.O. Box 1692, Costa Mesa, CA 92626.
- Boston Family Institute Videotape Series on Family Therapy (videotapes with Fred and Bunny Duhl, Charles and Jan Kramer, Virginia Satir, and Carl Whitaker). Available from Boston Family Institute, 251 Harvard St., Brookline, MA 02146.

RESEARCH ISSUES

Experiential family therapists are generally uninterested in empirical research, largely because any "objective" reality is considered to be at best an imperfect reflection of lived human experience. Also, global, nonspecific goals such as "growth," "self-responsibility," and "self-worth" are difficult to operationalize, and to operationalize any such concept as scores on a self-report test is felt to be taking a life-and-blood experience and reducing it to a sterile, intellectual concept far different from the experience itself.

However, research is at best inferential. Just because the mystical aspects of the therapeutic experience cannot be completely comprehended or described by current research methodology does not mean that research should not be conducted on experiential family therapies. Not to examine therapeutic process is to allow experiential family therapy to develop as an unguided cult. We have much to learn about experential family therapies at both the micro and the macro levels that could potentially lead to more effective therapy. Below are examples of possible research questions:

- Does Gestalt experiential family therapy lead to more responsible behavior (e.g., more first-person pronouns, completion of personal goals) than does a more nondirective, client-centered experiential family therapy?
- What family behavior occurs immediately after certain experiential therapeutic interventions (e.g., Gestalt awareness exercises, therapist self-disclosure, therapist encounter)? What are the family members' reactions to these therapist interventions?
- Is there a correlation between the quality and quantity of therapist self-disclosure and family self-disclosure?
- Are the therapist's goals for family members consistent with the family members' goals for themselves? When the goals are not consistent, is therapy as effective as when they are?

- How does the personality of an experiential family therapist differ from the personalities of therapists from other schools of family therapy? Do certain personality traits of experiential family therapists successfully predict outcome?
- Are cotherapy teams more creative in therapy than solo family therapists (as suggested by Whitaker & Keith, 1981), and does this translate into more creativity on the part of client families?
- What are the short- and long-term effects of therapist confrontation? More specifically, what type of confrontation is beneficial for what type of family with what presenting problems?
- Is there a correlation between the therapist's psychological health and the extent of family improvement in family therapy (as suggested by Whitaker & Keith, 1981, p. 217)?

KEY BOOKS AND ARTICLES

Constantine, L. (1978). Family sculpture and relationship mapping techniques. *Journal of Marriage and Family Counseling, 4*(2), 13–23.

This article provides an overview of family sculpture and a variety of illustrative ways it may be used. The examples of sculpture techniques should prove helpful to clinicians wishing to expand their use of spatialization procedures.

Duhl, B. S. (1983). *From the inside out and other metaphors: Creative and integrative approaches to training in systems thinking.* New York: Brunner/Mazel.

This is a book about teaching nonlinear concepts in a nonlinear manner. Duhl teaches through metaphor, movement, analogy, play, imitation, and more. She engagingly explains the process of learning through doing, experiencing, and debriefing—that is, learning from the inside out.

Duhl, B. S. & Duhl, F. J. (1981). Integrative family therapy. In A. S. Gurman & D. P. Kniskern (Eds.), *Handbook of family therapy.* New York: Brunner/Mazel.

This is the most comprehensive description to date of the Duhls' integrative approach to family therapy. The Duhls present an approach devoid of dogma, which emphasizes therapeutic flexibility, creativity, and above all, an appreciation of the humanness of all family members.

Duhl, F. J., & Duhl, B. S. (1979). "Structured spontaneity": The thoughtful art of integrative family therapy at BFI. *Journal of Marital and Family Therapy, 5,* 59–76.

This delightful paper describes the integrative training program at the Boston Family Institute. The authors provide an adequate overview of their goals and procedures, as well as a sense of their enthusiasm for their program. This is one of the best articles available describing an integrative, humanistic family therapy training program.

Duhl, F. J., Kantor, D., & Duhl, B. S. (1973). Learning, space, and action in family therapy: A primer of sculpture. In D. A. Bloch (Ed.), *Techniques of family psychotherapy: A primer*. New York: Grune & Stratton.

Family sculpturing provides the kind of insight that makes it impossible to return to a previously implicit way of functioning, thereby encouraging new behavioral patterns. The association provided between sculpturing and learning is interesting. Instructions on debriefing are included, which other writers on the subject have neglected to clarify.

Geddes, M., & Medway, J. (1977). The symbolic drawing of family life space. *Family Process, 16*, 219–228.

The authors review expressive techniques used by other family therapists and present the symbolic drawing of the family life space as a simple and effective activity for lowering anxiety and reducing blocks to communication. The activity involves family members' graphically representing emotional distances and communication patterns among one another through a drawing on a blackboard. Several examples are given.

Gendlin, E. T. (1973). Experiential psychotherapy. In R. Corsini (Ed.), *Current psychotherapies*. Itasca, IL: F. E. Peacock.

This chapter traces the roots of experiential psychotherapy and outlines the author's present conception of it. Gendlin sees this approach as having arisen from existentialism as a protest against the partitioning of human beings into measurable units. Healing or change in psychotherapy takes place within the context of a holistic relationship between client and therapist. What is important to be changed is one's process of interacting with the world. This chapter is a good introduction to experiential psychotherapy, although it does not specifically discuss experiential *family* therapy.

Kaplan, M. L., & Kaplan, N. R. (1978). Individual and family growth: A Gestalt approach. *Family Process, 17*(2), 195–205.

This article provides a good background to Gestalt family therapy. Basic concepts are discussed and distinctions between Gestalt family therapy and other experiential family therapies are clarified.

Kempler, W. (1968). Experiential psychotherapy with families. *Family Process, 7*, 88–99.

Kempler uses a clear, poetic style to discuss the basic principles of his approach to Gestalt experiential family therapy. The value of this piece is in the excellent illustrative dialogue Kempler sprinkles throughout, bringing life to his description of the therapy process.

Kempler, W. (1973). *Principles of Gestalt family therapy*. Salt Lake City: Deseret Press.

Kempler illustrates many Gestalt family therapy principles in this short, crisply written, eminently readable book. His excellent use of self and ability to facilitate meaningful person-to-person communications are illustrated in a variety of fascinating examples.

Kempler, W. (1981). *Experiential psychotherapy with families*. New York: Brunner/ Mazel.

This is Kempler's latest and fullest explication of Gestalt experiential family therapy. As in his other works, Kempler makes excellent use of illustrative dialogue and emphasizes the powerful effects of person-to-person encounter, therapist involvement, and present-centered family interaction.

Kwiatkowska, H. Y. (1967). Family art therapy. *Family Process, 6*, 37–55.

The author discusses a family approach to art therapy used by researchers at NIMH. Illustrative case material is presented and clinical research data are discussed. While psychiatric nomenclature is employed in this article to a greater degree than experiential assumptions, the article does have value in its compelling rationale for the diagnostic, research, and therapeutic advantages of this expressive mode of family treatment.

Levant, R. F. (1978). Family therapy: A client centered approach. *Journal of Marriage and Family Counseling, 4*(2), 35–42.

The author contrasts the pessimistic assumptions of psychodynamic and systems therapies to the growth orientation of a client-centered approach to family therapy. Theoretical assumptions of client-centered family therapy are clearly presented, but the author appears to sidestep the issue of how such a nondirective approach might deal with rigid, manipulative, and other difficult family systems.

Napier, A. Y. & Whitaker, C. (1978). *The family crucible*. New York: Harper & Row.

This engaging book is about one family's struggles and growth in long-term therapy with Napier and Whitaker. The reader is given a rare bird's-eye-view of how Carl Whitaker, a family therapy pioneer, conducts his brand of experiential family therapy from beginning to end. This book is an eminently readable "true-story" novel.

Neill, J., & Kniskern, D. (Eds.). (1982). *From psyche to system: The evolving therapy of Carl Whitaker*. New York: Guilford Press.

This book presents the vintage writings of Carl Whitaker and is as provocative an experience as the experiential therapy he espouses. The first section of the edition provides a useful biographical sketch of the life experiences that contributed to his work. The writings span over 40 years, allowing the reader to examine Whitaker's evolution "from psyche to system." Those expecting an instruction manual will be disappointed, but Whitaker's writings are guaranteed to challenge basic assumptions about therapy, marriage, and life in general.

Papp. P. (1976). Family choreography. In P. J. Guerin (Ed.), *Family therapy: Theory and practice*. New York: Gardner Press.

Papp substitutes the word "choreography" for family sculpturing in this chapter in order to more accurately describe its "fluid state." She emphasizes that the technique is not theory-bound and can accomplish a myriad of possible goals. The purpose of family choreography is to help lift family members out of their context by experiencing it in a new way. This is a good introductory article on family choreography.

Papp, P., Silverstein, O., & Carter, E. (1973). Family sculpting in preventive work with "well families." *Family Process, 12*(2), 197–212.

This ground-breaking, highly readable article introduces preventive possibilities for using family sculpting in groups for nonclinical families. The authors maintain that change need not be based on desperation. This rather innovative project shares its paradoxical discoveries regarding limiting group interaction and enhancing structure via sculpting to release emotion and bring about change.

Satir, V. (1967). *Conjoint family therapy.* Palo Alto, CA: Science and Behavior Books.

In this classic, Satir illustrates her approach to family therapy, which includes an integration of Gestalt, psychodramatic, communicational, and historical techniques. While few family therapists are as charismatic as Satir, this book is helpful in its illustration of procedures she uses to facilitate family communication and to unlock the affective resources of family members.

Satir, V. (1972). *Peoplemaking.* Palo Alto, CA: Science and Behavior Books.

Satir, writing for a lay audience, discusses the basic concepts she believes are tied to individual and family health. Her discussions of self-esteem and communication styles are particularly clear and may be useful as reading assignments for certain client families.

Whitaker, C. A., & Keith, D. V. (1981). Symbolic-experiential family therapy. In A. S. Gurman & D. P. Kniskern (Eds.), *Handbook of family therapy.* New York: Brunner/Mazel.

This is perhaps the most comprehensive, well-organized, and well-written article that Carl Whitaker has authored on his approach to family therapy. While Whitaker's charm and "craziness" are reflected in certain case examples, the real contribution of this article is in its demystification of Whitaker's brand of experiential family therapy.

Woods, M. D., & Martin, D. (1984). The work of Virginia Satir: Understanding her theory and technique. *American Journal of Family Therapy, 12*(4), 3–11.

The authors do a fine job of summarizing the philosophical assumptions, principles, goals, and basic techniques of Virginia Satir. This is a good introductory source.

Wright, S. E. (1985). An existential perspective on differentiation/fusion: Theoretical issues and clinical applications. *Journal of Marital and Family Therapy, 11*(1), 35–46.

This article calls for a recognition of existential issues in family therapy. The author provides a good background to the subject and, as one example, discusses differentiation/fusion from an existential perspective. Her guidelines for clinical application are also worthwhile.

ACKNOWLEDGMENTS

We would like to acknowledge the aid of Cleveland Shields in the preparation of portions of the introduction of this chapter. We also appreciate Marcia Brown-

Standridge's help with some of the annotations in the "Key Books and Articles" section.

REFERENCES

Bing, E. (1970). The conjoint family drawing. *Family Process, 9*, 173–194.

Buber, M. (1970). *I and thou.* New York: Scribner's.

Constantine, L. (1978). Family sculpture and relationship mapping techniques. *Journal of Marriage and Family Counseling, 4*(2), 13–23.

Duhl, B. S. (1983). *From the inside out and other metaphors: Creative and integrative approaches to training in systems thinking.* New York: Brunner/Mazel.

Duhl, B. S., & Duhl, F. J. (1981). Integrative family therapy. In A. S. Gurman & D. P. Kniskern (Eds.), *Handbook of family therapy.* New York: Brunner/Mazel.

Duhl, F. J., & Duhl, B. S. (1979). "Structured spontaneity": The thoughtful art of integrative family therapy at BFI. *Journal of Marital and Family Therapy, 5*, 59–76.

Duhl, F. J., Kantor, D., & Duhl, B. S. (1973). Learning, space and action in family therapy: A primer of sculpture. In D. A. Bloch (Ed.), *Techniques of family therapy: A primer.* New York: Grune & Stratton.

Geddes, M., & Medway, J. (1977). The symbolic drawing of family life space. *Family Process, 16*, 219–228.

Gendlin, E. T. (1973). *Experiential psychotherapy.* In R. Corsini (Ed.), *Current psychotherapies.* Itasca, IL: F. E. Peacock.

Kaplan, M. L., & Kaplan, N. R. (1978). Individual and family growth: A Gestalt approach. *Family Process, 17*, 195–205.

Kaufman, W. (Ed.). (1956). *Existentialism from Dostoevsky to Sartre.* New York: World.

Kempler, W. (1973). *Principles of Gestalt family therapy.* Salt Lake City: Deseret Press.

Kempler, W. (1981). *Experiential psychotherapy with families.* New York: Brunner/Mazel.

Kwiatkowska, H. Y. (1967). Family art therapy. *Family Process, 6*, 37–55.

Levant, R. F. (1978). Family therapy: A client centered approach. *Journal of Marriage and Family Counseling, 4*(2), 35–42.

Napier, A. Y., & Whitaker, C. (1978). *The family crucible.* New York: Harper & Row.

Neill, J., & Kniskern, D. (Eds.). (1982). *From psyche to system: The evolving therapy of Carl Whitaker.* New York: Guilford Press.

Rubin, J., & Magnussen, M. A. (1974). A family art evaluation. *Family Process, 13*, 185–200.

Sartre, J. P. (1946). *Existentialism and humanism.* London: Methuen.

Satir, V. (1967). *Conjoint family therapy.* Palo Alto, CA: Science and Behavior Books.

Satir, V. (1972). *Peoplemaking.* Palo Alto, CA: Science and Behavior Books.

Sprenkle, D. H., Keeney, B. P., & Sutton, P. M. (1982). Theorists who influence clinical members of AAMFT. *Journal of Marital and Family Therapy, 8*(3), 367–370.

Whitaker, C. A. (1976). The hindrance of theory in clinical work. In P. J. Guerin, Jr. (Ed.), *Family therapy: Theory and practice.* New York: Gardner Press.

Whitaker, C. A., & Keith, D. V. (1981). Symbolic–experiential family therapy. In

A. S. Gurman, & D. P. Kniskern (Eds.), *Handbook of family therapy*. New York: Brunner/Mazel.

Whitaker, C. A., & Malone, T. P. (1953). *The roots of psychotherapy*. New York: Blakiston.

Whitaker, C. A., & Napier, A. Y. (1977). Process techniques of family therapy. *Interaction*, *1*(1), 4–19.

BEHAVIORAL FAMILY THERAPIES

Behavior modification is associated with principles of learning derived from extensive laboratory research examining the effects of environmental events on the frequency of behavior. The discovery that behavior can be predictably increased or decreased by the manipulation of antecedent and consequent events (usually in the form of punishments and rewards) has led to a far-reaching behavioral technology evident in virtually every area of our lives.

Predictably, behaviorists use the terminology of operant and classical conditioning to explain family dynamics. For example, marital satisfaction is sometimes defined as a relatively high rate of rewards to punishers. Supporting this view, research has found that distressed couples exchange relatively higher rates of displeasing behavior and lower rates of pleasing behavior than nondistressed couples (Birchler, Weiss, & Vincent, 1975; Gottman, Markman, & Notarius, 1977; Gottman *el al.*, 1976; Vincent, Weiss, & Birchler, 1975).

The concepts of coercion and reciprocity also are used frequently by behavioral family therapists. "Coercion" is the general use of negative events to control family interaction. "Reciprocity," on the other hand, involves partners' tendency to reward and punish each other at approximately equal rates over time. Lederer and Jackson (1968) were referring to reciprocity when they stated that "nastiness begets nastiness" (p. 269). However, every interchange among couples is not reciprocal. Gottman *et al.* (1976) discuss a "bank account" model of marital exchange, in which a spouse's rewarding behavior may be considered an investment over time. This concept accounts for a husband's responding to his sick wife's anger with a loving remark. Over the long haul, however, both partners expect an equitable rate of positive return on their positive investments.

Behavioral family therapists increasingly recognize the importance of cognitions (Mahoney, 1974; Meichenbaum, 1977) as events mediating family interactions. For example, Patterson (1982) states that parents of aggresive children tend to attribute negative intentions to their children's behavior. Such attributions serve to maintain negative response cycles. Similarly, Jacobson and Margolin (1979) state that a young spouse's overall feeling of marital satisfaction (i.e., a cognition) may influence his/her immediate response to his/her partner.

In sum, then, behavioral marital and family therapists generally assume that family interactions are maintained and changed by enviornmental events preceding and following each family member's behavior. These environmental events, or contingencies, along with mediating cognitions, influence the form and frequency of each family member's behaviors.

While behavioral family therapies often are not considered systems therapies, they do take into consideration the interactive qualities of family relationships. Discussing marriage, Jacobson and Margolin (1979) state:

> Since each spouse is providing consequences for the other on a continuous basis, and since each partner exerts an important controlling influence on the other's behavior, the marital relationship is best thought of as a process of circular and reciprocal sequences of behavior and consequences, where each person's behavior is at once being affected by and influencing the other. (p. 13)

In other words, each family member's behavior is intertwined in various stimulus–response–reinforcement cycles. What is a response for one family member (e.g., a crying child) may be a reinforcement for another (i.e., a teasing sibling) and a stimulus for still another (i.e., a parent). Endless chains such as these make up what we call family interaction. The interactional sequences typical of families with problems are often characterized by reciprocal patterns of coercion and pain control (Patterson, 1982).

Since skill deficits and inappropriate uses of positive reinforcement and punishment tend to charcterize families with problems, two broad sets of skills—parenting skills and problem-solving/communication skills—are employed by many behavioral marital and family therapists.

PARENT SKILLS TRAINING

Parent skills training involves teaching behavioral skills to parents so that they can employ them with their own children. The initial focus of therapy is on the parents themselves, who learn how to apply behavior change procedures to increase the prosocial behavior and decrease the maladaptive behavior of their children. In essence, the behavioral parent trainer functions as a "consultant" to the parents, who then become the primary therapists or behavior change agents for their children (Tharp & Wetzel, 1969).

A variety of theoretical and practical arguments supporting behavioral parent training are presented in detail elsewhere (Cone & Sloop, 1974; Graziano, 1977; O'Dell, 1974). Suffice it to say here that the simplicity and straightforwardness of specific learning theory principles (Gordon & David-

son, 1981) allow them to be tau
(Wiltz & Gordon, 1974) or gro
erally, behavioral parent trainin
ing theory; (2) the pinpointing
antecedent and consequent beha
recording behaviors (e.g., freque
baseline data; and (6) the training
The procedures most often taught in behavioral parent training include
the definition and enforcement of rules and the use of positive reinforcement, time out, behavioral contracting, and home token economies (Gordon & Davidson, 1981).

While more needs to be learned about behavioral parent training (see
"Research Issues," below), research to date generally has been encouraging
in both quantity and quality. Behavioral parent training has been employed
to successfully modify children's presenting problems as varied as asthma
(Neisworth & Moore, 1972), toilet training (Foxx & Azrin, 1973), nocturnal
enuresis (Paschalis, Kimmel, & Kimmel, 1972), encopresis (Edelman, 1971),
self-injurious behavior (Graziano, 1974), thumbsucking (Tahmisian &
McReynolds, 1971), seizures (Zlutnick, 1972), eating problems (Bernal, Williams, Miller, & Reagor, 1972), autism (Wolf, Risley, Johnson, Harris, &
Allen, 1967), and childhood aggression (Patterson, 1982). In fact, Graziano
(1977) has stated that "parent behavior training, as a child psychotherapy
approach, is a highly promising area that might prove to be one of the
most important developments in the child mental health field" (p. 287).

PROBLEM-SOLVING/COMMUNICATION SKILLS TRAINING

Problem-solving/communication skills training is employed under the assumption that some communication patterns are more adaptive and useful
than others. This assumption is supported by research examining communication patterns of groups of distressed and nonstressed couples and
families (e.g., Alexander, 1973; Billings, 1979; Gottman, 1979; Robin &
Weiss, 1980). The goals of problem-solving/communication skills training
usually include (1) defining problems in a nonblaming way, (2) listening
empathically (3) formulating "I want" statements, (4) generating solutions,
(5) deciding upon a solution, and (6) implementing the solution (see Jacobson & Margolin, 1979).

ROLE OF THE THERAPIST

The role of the behavioral marital or family therapist is that of a teacher
who often employes instructions, coaching, modeling, and behavioral rehearsal in order to impart the skills necessary for couples or families to

begin interacting more effectively. Generally, the therapist assesses the contingencies influencing problematic behaviors, then develops intervention strategies aimed at changing these contingencies. Popular interventions include parent skills training and problem-solving/communication skills training, as mentioned above, as well as contingency contracting, cognitive restructuring, assertion training, and home token economies. Specific interventions employed to increase positive interchanges between spouses include "caring days" (Stuart, 1980) and "love days" (Jacobson & Margolin, 1979). Also, behavioral marital and family therapists are increasingly emphasizing the importance of issues previously neglected by behaviorists, such as the therapist–client relationship (Alexander & Parsons, 1982) and the therapist's ability to establish a "collaborative set" with the couple or family (Jacobson & Margolin, 1979).

Behavioral family therapists tend to stress the importance of procedures such as charting, homework, and follow-up assessment, which promote and evaluate the maintenance and generalization of positive changes in therapy. The presumed necessity of long-term maintenance procedures in behavioral family therapies contrasts sharply with the assumption of strategic and structural therapies that homeostatic processes will maintain family behavior once it is changed.

AN EXAMPLE OF RECENT RESEARCH

Falloon's Behavioral Family Therapy for the Management of Schizophrenia

The work of Ian Falloon and his colleagues in California (Falloon, Boyd, & McGill, 1984; Falloon, Boyd, McGill, Bazani, Moss & Gilderman, 1982) has been the most comprehensive of the recent attempts to examine the effects of behavioral family interventions on relapse rates in schizophrenic patients. This work represents a dramatic departure from attempts to posit family dynamics as the major etiological factor in schizophrenia. The theoretical foundation of Falloon's method is the stress–vulnerability (i.e., medical) view of this disorder. Family therapy is employed (along with psychotropic medication) to manage the identified patient and his/her family.

Falloon's group compared home-based family treatment with supportive individual psychotherapy at a community clinic. The family intervention consisted of education about schizophrenia and several behaviorally oriented interventions including training in problem solving and communication. A behavioral analysis of each family was completed to assess its strengths and deficits. The major goal of treatment was to enhance the family's ability to cope with stress (Magee, 1985).

The two treatment conditions were compared at baseline, 3 months, 9 months, and 24 months. All patients met a stringent research diagnosis of schizophrenia and resided with or had close contact with one or both biological parents. All but three of these parents were rated high on Expressed Emotion (EE), a highly reliable rating of the number of critical comments and levels of hostility and over-involvement of family members toward the schizophrenic patient (Leff & Vaughn, 1985; Miklowitz, Goldstein, Falloon, & Doane, 1984). Thirty-six (of 39 eligible patients) were randomly assigned to one of the treatment groups. They were seen weekly during the first 3 months, bi-weekly during the next 6 months and on a monthly basis thereafter. Patients were also monitored monthly for "clinically optimal" drug dosage and evaluation of symptoms.

At the 9-month assessment, major symptom exacerbation had occurred among 44% of those in individual treatment, but only among 6% of patients in family treatment. Relatives of the index patient also showed a reduction in EE-like behaviors among the family treatment group. Finally, Faloon showed that even with the additional cost of home visits, the family method resulted in 20% less cost than individual treatment. Family treatment patients, even though more compliant to taking drugs, actually required less medication than the patients in the non-family condition (Magee, 1985).

Regretfully, this study did not employ a no-treatment control group. Also, the principal investigators did therapy for both conditions and the individual sessions were less regularly attended. Fortunately, other researchers and clinicians interested in the model can examine the detailed treatment protocol (Falloon et al., 1984).

KEY CONCEPTS AND INTERVENTIONS

Since the key concepts in behavioral family therapies are inextricably linked to and often overlap with specific behavior intervention procedures, both are presented together in this section.

Baseline. The initial recorded observations of behaviors that are intended to be changed once different treatment conditions are introduced. For example, a child's hitting behaviors between 4:00 p.m. and 6:00 p.m. may be counted for a week prior to initiating an intervention program, so that baseline data will be available to determine whether or not the intervention program, when it is begun, actually decreases the frequency of hits.

Behavioral exchange theory. A theory that explains relationship behaviors in terms of costs and benefits. A distressed relationship, for example, is one in which there is a scarcity of benefits or rewards relative to costs or aversive events. According to Jacobson and Margolin (1979), marital distress can be described both in terms of reduced reward–punishment ratios and in terms of increased reactivity to the partners' aversive behavior.

Caring days. A structured method of concurrently increasing the caring behaviors of spouses. Each spouse identifies various behaviors that the partner finds enjoyable, and commits himself/herself to increasing these behaviors (Stuart, 1980). A daily record is kept by the couple of the extent to which each partner initiates caring behaviors for the other. In social exchange terms, the family therapist who uses caring days is attempting to increase the reward within the relationship, thus increasing the perceived value of the relationship.

Classical conditioning. The process by which a stimulus takes on the ability to elicit certain behaviors or emotions by being associated with a behavior-eliciting stimulus. For example, a song that was played at times a couple was romantic may eventually in and of itself elicit romantic emotions for the couple.

Coaching. The process of structuring interaction by providing verbal instructions. For example, a family therapist may coach a wife who is having trouble getting her husband's attention when she talks by saying, "This time when he turns his head away, I want you to squeeze his hand gently and tell him you really want him to listen."

Coercion. An interaction in which a person uses aversive stimuli or responses to control the behavior of others. Negative reinforcement explains the maintenance of coercive behavior; that is, the use of coercion to terminate an aversive stimulus increases the likelihood of the use of coercion in the future. For example, if a husband's shout terminates a wife's nagging, the husband has used a coercive response that will probably be repeated in similar circumstances.

Contingency contract. A written agreement between spouses that specifies expectations of behavior and consequences for either meeting or not meeting those expectations. Contracts may either be *quid pro quo*, where the behavior of one spouse is contingent on another, or parallel, where one spouse's behavior is independent of another's (Jacobson & Margolin, 1979).

Discriminative stimulus (cue). A signal indicating that a likely and positive set of results will occur contingent upon a particular behavior's being performed (Jacobson & Margolin, 1979). For example, if a mother and daughter have agreed that the daughter has 5 minutes to start her household chores once the mother holds up her five fingers as a cue (the discriminative stimulus), then the daughter knows she can avoid her mother's nagging if she begins to work within the 5-minute time frame.

Extinction. The procedure by which previously reinforced behaviors are no longer reinforced. For example, a father who has been attentive to his daughter only when she makes funny noises may start to ignore her antics. Since the funny noises are no longer reinforced by the father's attention, the daughter eventually stops making them (i.e., they are extinguished).

Functions. According to Alexander and Parsons (1982), symptoms typically serve the "function" or purpose of creating interpersonal closeness or distance (i.e., dependence or autonomy) relative to other family members. For example, a child's symptom of stealing may serve the function of bringing the child in closer contact with his/her parents (i.e., a "closeness" function).

Home token economy. A contingency-contracting procedure in which secondary reinforcers (e.g., points, poker chips) are earned by accomplishing appropriate tasks. Home token economies can include both rewards and fines for behaviors, and are instituted in order to modify the contingencies and frequency of behaviors within the family.

Love days. A structured procedure in which on a given day one spouse noncontingently increases behavior that the other spouse finds pleasurable (Jacobson & Margolin, 1979). For instance, on an assigned day one spouse may try to be especially pleasing to the other (regardless of the other's behavior) by offering breakfast in bed, a surprise gift, a shower of kisses, and other rewarding behaviors and comments.

Modeling. In social learning theory, a term for acquiring *new* behavior or strengthening/weakening *previously* learned responses on the basis of noticing rewarding or punishing consequences for observed behavior (Bandura, 1971). For example, if a young child observes that his older brother's whining behavior results in rewards, the younger child will be more likely also to engage in whining behavior in the future.

Negative reinforcement. The procedure by which a behavior is strengthened when it results in the removal of a certain stimulus (usually aversive). For example, if a child's lie stops a parent's angry questioning, lying behavior may increase in the future (i.e., it is "negatively reinforced" by the cessation of an aversive stimulus, the angry questioning). If telling the truth also results in a decrease of the parent's angry questioning, negative reinforcement still occurs (given that telling the truth increases in the future). In other words, the term "negative" refers to a taking away or decrease of a subsequent event, and not to a negative valence of the preceding behavior.

Operant conditioning. The process by which the frequency of a behavior is altered by its consequences. Consequences may be variably introduced as either positively reinforcing, negatively reinforcing, or punishing stimuli.

Parallel (good faith) contract. A contingency contract in which the behavior of one person is independent of that of the other. For example, a husband may receive the reward of playing golf after doing the laundry, while the wife earns the reward of going shopping for herself after she vacuums the house.

Positive reinforcement. The procedure by which the appearance of an event strengthens the behavior that precedes it. For example, if a husband self-discloses more frequently when his self-disclosures are followed by appreciative statements from his wife, those appreciative statements are considered positive reinforcers.

Punishment. The procedure by which the appearance of a stimulus decreases the behavior that precedes it. For example, if (and only if) a child's misbehavior decreases after a spanking is the spanking considered a punishment.

Quid pro quo contract. A contingency contract in which the behavior of one person is contingent on that of another. For example, a husband may agree to do the dishes each evening in exchange for the wife taking the children to school and picking them up again. Likewise, her driving the children is contingent upon his doing the dishes.

Reciprocal inhibition (counterconditioning). A process in which specific behaviors may be weakened by establishing antagonistic behaviors. For example, a father's anxiety may be decreased by teaching him to be more assertive. Likewise, systematic desensitization, which teaches one to relax while imagining increasingly anxiety-provoking situations, is another example of reciprocal inhibition.

Reciprocity. The likelihood that two people will reinforce each other at approximately equitable rates over time.

Successive approximation (shaping). The reinforcing of gradual changes in behavior toward a desired goal. For example, the process of toilet training may be broken down into successively more complicated steps (e.g., walking to the potty, pulling down pants, sitting down, etc.). Completion of each step is rewarded in the step-by-step shaping of appropriate toileting behavior.

Time out. A means of extinguishing inappropriate behavior by removing·the reinforcing consequences of that behavior. Typically, in time out a child is immediately removed from a situation that reinforces unproductive behavior (e.g., a class of giggling children) and placed in a solitary location (e.g., an empty room) where the behavior is likely to decrease. Time-out procedures may be literally thought of as "time out" from reinforcement.

TEACHING TOOLS AND TECHNIQUES

Minilecture: Similarities and Differences between Behavioral and Strategic–Structural Therapies

A short lecture comparing and contrasting behavioral and strategic–structural therapies can be given, based on the following points made by Foster and Hoier (1982).

SIMILARITIES

1. The same behaviors and interpersonal interactions are monitored.
2. The focus is on behavioral sequences versus subjective experiences.

3. Problems are conceptualized interactionally within the environ- ment or system, rather than in terms of individual pathology.
4. Problems serve some function.
5. Problems are maintained by family processes.
6. "Here and now" rather than past history is emphasized.
7. The focus is on changing target behaviors and/or behavioral se- quences.
8. The goal of therapy is to restructure interactions via behavioral or cognitive change in order to change a presenting problem.
9. Instruction, cognitive restructuring (reframing), and coaching in sessions are employed.
10. Homework is assigned to generalize change.
11. Behavioral parent training is like restructuring family hierarchies.

DIFFERENCES

Behavioral	Strategic–Structural
The main interest is in observables, operationalizability, and a molecular view.	Systems descriptions are inferred from observables and represent motor constructs (e.g., enmeshment.
Therapy is more likely to engage in subsystem analysis.	Therapy begins with descriptions of family system.
Causal factors that can be tested are hypothesized.	Circular causality and homeostasis, which are *not* tested, are assumed.
Resistance is rejected.	Resistance is expected.
There is a concern with long-term maintenance.	The asumption is that homeostatic processes will maintain change.

Experiential Assignments

Students may be given assignments that encourage their firsthand appli- cation of behavioral principles. Below is such an assignment that our stu- dents have found particularly worthwhile:

Jacobson and Margolin (1979) state that negative cycles of behavior "can be abated if spouses learn to maintain consistently high levels of pleasing behaviors" (p. 176). Similarly, they discuss the positive affects that may occur when one spouse independently increases his/her pleasing behaviors toward the other. Your task is to experientially examine the validity of independently increasing positive behaviors in a relationship.

Without telling him/her about this assignment, choose a person you have sustained contact with, and count the number of pleasing behaviors you emit toward that individual in a week's time. During the second week, at least double your reinforcing or pleasing behaviors toward this individual. Notice the results. Does the quality of his/her behaviors toward you change? And what about the quality of your relationship? Describe the effects of this experiment both on you and on your chosen subject. What implications do your findings have for your practice of marital therapy? Also, how would you explain these results in behavioral terms?

Journal Days

The extensive literature related to behavioral marital and family interventions is overwhelming to assign to students in its totality. Students may be exposed to many of the key journal articles in behavioral marital and family therapy by scheduling occasional "journal days." On these days, each student summarizes and critiques for the class two articles assigned from an extensive bibliography. Many of these 5-minute summaries/critiques generate provocative discussions regarding the theory, research, and practices of the particular behavioral family therapy being studied. Students are also asked to write short annotations to their assigned articles. These annotations are later combined to form an annotated bibliography for the class. (This suggestion is taken from Piercy & Sprenkle, 1984.)

Behavioral Rehearsal

When behavioral (as well as other) skills are taught, we attempt to follow these sequential steps: (1) to discuss the skill's theoretical rationale; (2) to demonstrate the skills through a role play or videotape; (3) to provide simulated opportunities for skill practice; and (4) to provide instructor or peer feedback to encourage skill improvement. We have used this theoretical rationale–modeling–behavioral rehearsal–reinforcement paradigm to teach family therapy skills such as communication skills training (Jacobson & Margolin, 1979), positive connotation (Constantine, Stone Fish, & Piercy, 1984), and behavioral contracting (Piercy & Sprenkle, 1984).

Position Papers

The student is assigned to read certain articles by authors holding behavioral and nonbehavioral theoretical views on specific issues related to family therapy. Each position paper should reflect the student's own view on the issue in question, in light of the assigned articles and the student's own professional training and background. A position paper is typically three to five double-spaced typewritten pages in length.

The examples below illustrate several possible assignments for position papers that contrast behavioral and nonbehavioral theoretical orientations (from Piercy & Sprenkle, 1984, pp. 401–402).

Minuchin (1974) includes as possible goals of family therapy the involvement of an uninvolved parent and the disengagement of an overinvolved parent. However, Alexander and Parsons (1982) would probably see the function of the uninvolved parent's behavior as distancing and the function of the overinvolved parent's behavior as merging, and would consequently not try to change these functions. Your question is: Can and should a therapist change the degree of involvement of family members, assuming that their behavior is serving a distancing or merging function? Give a rationale for your answer and examples, if appropriate.

Jacobson and Margolin's (1979) approach to behavioral marital therapy emphasizes the importance of clear, straightforward communications among married couples. Consequently, they teach communications skills as part of their therapy. Carl Whitaker, on the other hand, contends that marriage should be an intense relationship where normal rules of social interaction are suspended. According to Whitaker, couples are not fair or polite to one another, nor should they try to be. As Whitaker is fond of saying, "telephones are great, but they shouldn't be expected to heat the house!" (See Neill & Kniskern, 1982). React to this statement and outline the role and importance you give to communications training in your own approach to marital therapy.

Films and Videocassettes

Several films and videocassettes on behavioral marital and family therapies are available from Research Press, Box 31773, Champaign, IL 61821. Titles include the following:

- *Parents and Children: A Positive Approach to Child Management*
- *Behavioral Principles for Parents*
- *Childhood Aggression: A Social Learning Approach to Family Therapy*
- *Behavioral Interviewing with Couples*
- *Three Styles of Marital Conflict*

Concept Papers

Papers may be assigned that will encourage students to grapple with behavioral concepts as they relate to therapy. For example, while no behavioral terms are actually mentioned in the following assignment, it is intended to encourage students to think about the reinforcement qualities of isolated acts, as well as the potential for such reinforcers to initiate a cycle of additional reinforcers in behavioral marital therapy.

> In the movie *Back to the Future*, Marty McFly returns to the past, where his wimpish, ineffectual father, Geroge McFly, is courting Marty's future mother, Lorraine, who seems more interested in *Marty* than in George. Marty sets up a situation that results in George's successfully protecting Lorraine from the school bully, Bif. This important event sets in motion a series of events that changes George McFly's view of himself, other people's interactions with him, and, subsequently, his future relationship with his wife. (It also profoundly affects Bif, but that's another story!)
>
> Your job is to explain and critique this "key event" idea of change in behavioral terms. How does it work? Can it only happen in the movies, or can family therapists create new futures through initiating small changes? Can changing one event or (behavior) make a difference? And what is the ideal role of the behavioral marital therapist in maintaining new behaviors? In essence, then, is a "back to the future" kind of change worth considering in behavioral marital therapy? Regardless of your answer, give examples to illustrate your thinking.

RESEARCH ISSUES

More methodologically sound research has been conducted on behavioral marital and family therapies than on other family therapies, perhaps because of their emphasis on operationalization of treatment components and assessment of change. However, many questions regarding efficacy and the assumptions underlying behavioral interventions with couples and families remain to be answered. Here are some examples:

- Does "egalitarian" behavioral contracting subtly support the more powerful or articulate spouse at the expense of the other (as suggested by Jacobson, 1983)?
- What are the most effective components of communication skills training in bringing about change in couples? Can these components be explained in nonbehavioral terms (as suggested by Gurman, Knudson, & Kniskern, 1978)?
- What sequence of interventions for specific behavioral family ther-

apies will produce the most favorable outcome? (This question should be addressed for different subject populations and different presenting problems.)

- Should behavioral marital therapy, if indicated, precede behavioral parent training or vice versa? Do concurrent treatments improve effectiveness?
- Do certain types of clients benefit more from behavioral family therapies than others? What are the critical client variables?
- To what extent does behavioral parent training positively affect marital adjustment? Conversely, to what extent does behavioral marital therapy affect parent–child relationships?
- To what extent do the effects of behavioral family therapies generalize to behaviors not targeted in treatment? For example, what generalization occurs to the sibling of an identified patient?
- Some approaches to behavioral parent training have employed "refresher courses." How effective are these additional treatments in increasing and/or maintaining treatment effects?
- What factors contribute to attrition in behavioral family therapies?
- To what extent do elaborate assessment procedures contribute to change in couples and/or families (above and beyond the treatment itself?)
- To what extent are behavioral family therapies effective relative to specific nonbehavioral family therapies (see Jacobson & Weiss, 1978, p. 158)?
- Do closeness and distancing functions of interpersonal behavior change with behavioral and/or nonbehavioral family therapies? Is it more efficacious to attempt to change function in therapy, or, as suggested by Alexander and Parsons (1982), to change behavior in ways consistent with family members' present interpersonal functions?
- To what extent do therapists' conceptual set, relationship skills, and structuring skills predict family change on a variety of outcome measures?

KEY BOOKS AND ARTICLES

Alexander, J. F., & Barong, C. (1980). Systems–behavioral intervention with delinquent families: Clinical, methodological, and conceptual considerations. In J. D. Vincent, (Ed.), *Advances in family assessment and theory* (Vol. 1). Greenwich, CT: JAI Press.

This chapter outlines the research supporting the functional family therapy of Alexander and his associates. The outcome results are compelling. The authors also draw tentative conclusions about the effect of therapists' abilities and characteristics on the outcome of therapy.

Alexander, J. F., Barton, C., Schiaro, R. S., & Parsons, B. V. (1976). Systems behavioral intervention with families of delinquents: Therapist characteristics, family behavior, and outcome. *Journal of Consulting and Clinical Psychology, 44*, 656–
774.

In order to study the relationship of therapist characteristics to outcome, the
authors studied 21 families with delinquent adolescents. The possession of good
relationship skills by the therapist was the variable most predictive of positive outcome (it accounted for 45% of outcome variance). Good relationship skills, according to the authors, need to be accompanied by a well-structured therapeutic framework in order to be optimally successful.

Alexander, J. F., & Parsons, B. V. (1973). Short-term behavioral intervention with
delinquent families. *Journal of Abnormal Psychology, 81*, 219–225.

This article describes the results of a short-term behaviorally oriented family
intervention program designed to increase family reciprocity, clarity of communication, and contingency contracting for delinquent teenagers. These families were
trained to communicate more effectively and to set up token economies. The program was compared with a client-centered family group program, a psychodynamic
family program, and a no-treatment control group. The program showed significantly reduced recidivism at follow-up and significant changes in family interaction
at the end of therapy, compared to the alternative treatment groups and the control
group.

Arnold, J. E., Levine, A. G., & Patterson, G. R. (1975). Changes in sibling behavior
following family intervention. *Journal of Consulting and Clinical Psychology, 43*,
683–688.

This article reports on sibling delinquency in families that were previously
treated for adolescent delinquency. The authors found that delinquency rates were
significantly lower for the families treated as a system than for delinquent families
treated individually or for the no-treatment control group. The authors, therefore,
suggest that families function as an interactional unit.

Atkeson, B. M., & Forehand, R. (1978). Parent behavioral training for problem
children: An examination of studies using multiple outcome meaasures. *Journal
of Abnormal Child Psychology, 6*, 449–460.

This article is a review of 24 studies that utilized three outcome measures: (1)
independent observer-collected data, (2) parent-collected data, and (3) parent-completed questionnaire data. The data from the three outcomes were compared. All
yielded positive results, but parent-collected data and parent-completed questionnaire data were associated with more positive outcome results than the independently collected data.

Barton, C., & Alexander, J. F. (1977). Therapists' skills as determinants of effective
systems–behavioral family therapy. *Interantional Journal of Family Counseling, 5*(2)
11–19.

This useful nonempirical article identifies therapists' technical, conceptual, and
interpersonal skills as variables that may be highly related to family treatment

success. Also noteworthy is the recommendation that therapists focus their attention on three components of family behavior: specific behaviors, interactional patterns, and interpersonal payoffs.

Berkowitz, B. P., & Graziano, A. M. (1972). Training parents as behaviour therapists: A review. *Behaviour Research and Therapy, 10,* 297–317.

This article is a critical review of 34 studies ranging from single-case studies to large-scale, multifamily training programs. Of primary concern is the nature of family involvement and the responsibility the family has in planning and implementing the intervention program. The sophistication of research methods is also critically analyzed.

Bernal, M. E., Klinnert, M. D., & Schultz, L. A. (1980). Outcome evaluation of behavioral parent training and client-centered parent counseling for children with conduct problems. *Journal of Applied Behavioral Analysis, 13,*677–691.

The central question of this study was whether a behaviorally oriented parent training approach for 5- to 12-year-olds with conduct problems would produce more effective results than either a client-centered parent counseling approach or a waiting-list control group. Parent reports and paper-and-pencil test of child deviance and parent satisfaction indicated superior results for the behavioral group over the client-centered and waiting-list control groups, and no differences between the latter two groups. These superior results were not maintained at follow-up: Home observation showed no advantage among groups. The authors raise some provocative questions about whether parents can be taught to be effective change agents for their conduct-problem children—a view contrary to that of other studies, which promote behavioral approaches with parents.

Birchler, G. R., & Spinks, S. H. (1980). Behavioral–systems marital and family therapy: Integration and clinical application. *American Journal of Family Therapy, 8,* 6–28.

In this integration of behavioral (social learning) and family systems (communication theory) therapy, the authors present a detailed behavioral treatment plan that is also sensitive to process issues within the system. A good example of their conceptual integration is their discussion of the development of family rules from a behavioral point of view.

Conway, J. B., & Bucher, B. D. (1976). Transfer and maintenance of behavior change in children: A review and suggestions. In E. J. Mash, L. A. Hamerlynck, & L.C. Handy (Eds.), *Behavior modification and families.* New York: Brunner/Mazel.

This overview of child-oriented behaviorist literature focuses on the use of parents, teachers, peers, and even the subject's own cognitions as "mediators" in the modification process. A unique contribution is offered in the distinction between effects of supportive and nonsupportive environments following treatment. Like other reviewers, the authors applaud advances in specifying behavioral changes under certain conditions, but appear to find efforts to maintain and generalize change weak by comparison. References at the end of the chapter are replete with sources that emphasize problems in generalization and methods for facilitating response transfer.

Falloon, I. R. H., Boyd, J. L., & McGill, C. W. (1984). *Family care in schizophrenia.*
New York. Guilford.

This book describes the most comprehensive of the recent attempts to utilize
family interventions in the management of schizophrenic patients and their families.
The investigation compares a home-based family treatment with individual psychotherapy conducted at a community clinic. The former includes behavioral training in problem solving and communication, as well as education about schizophrenia. The volume offers not only dramatic evidence for the efficacy of the family
approach but also offers a detailed description of the treatment protocol.

Forehand, R., & Atkeson, B. M. (1977). Generality of treatment effects with parents
as therapists: A review of assesment and implementation procedures. *Behavior
Therapy, 8*(4), 575–593.

This review focuses on studies in which parents are trained to generalize treatment of a child's behavior over time, across settings, to other behaviors, and to
other siblings. Generally, while parent training has been found effective with targeted behaviors, its effect on generalization has yet to be impressive. One exception
is the contagion effect of one child's improvement on that of siblings. The authors
concede that many of the studies cited are weak in methodology, and assert that
studies examining methods for implementing generalization are needed.

Forehand, R., Wells, K. C., & Griest, D. L. (1980). An examination of the social
validity of a parent training program. *Behavior Therapy, 11,* 488–502.

This study evaluated the impact of a parent training program for children with
behavior problems in the home. The program consisted of training the children's
mothers in the use of behavioral child management techniques. These mother–
child dyads were compared with normal mother–child dyads at pretest, posttest,
and follow-up. Pretest results indicated significant differences in these children's
behavior, while posttest and follow-up showed no significant difference. A 15-
month folow-up of the clinic groups showed continued treatment satisfaction on
the mothers' part.

Foster, S. L., & Hoier, T. S. (1982). Behavioral and systems family therapies: A
comparison of theoretical assumptions. *American Journal of Family Therapy, 10*(3),
13–23.

This article highlights several areas of similarity and difference between behavioral and systems therapies. The potential integration of two are discussed.
Advantages of such integration would include greater use of molar-level descriptors
by behavioral therapists and a greater focus on specific units of interaction by
systems therapists.

Gordon, S. B., & Davidson, N. (1981). Behavioral parent training. In A. S. Gurman
& D. P. Kniskern (Eds.), *Handbook of family therapy.* New York: Brunner/Mazel.

This excellent review includes a rationale and procedures forbehavioral parent
training. Its major strength, however, is in the distillation of the large body of
literature in this area. The authors also do a fine job of identifying important issues
related to research, training, and future directions for behavioral parent training.

Gottman, J. M. (1979). *Marital interaction: Experimental investigations.* New York: Academic Press.

This volume pulls together the theory and research of the author, drawing upon previous works from sociological, family systems, social learning, and developmental theories. The book is noteworthy for its analysis of patterns and sequence in marital interaction and is must reading for those interested in process research in couple communication. The culmination of the author's work is in the Couples Interaction Scoring System (CISS). The procedure is thorough but expensive and likely to be more practical for researchers than clinicians.

Graziano, A. M. (1977). Parents as behavior therapists. In M. Hersen, R. M. Eisler, & P. M. Miller (Eds.), *Progress in behavior modification* (Vol. 4). New York: Academic Press.

The author's compendium of literature regarding parents as behavior modifiers is extended to these child problem categories: somatic symptoms, mental deficiency or disturbance, aggressive behaviors, fears, language and speech disorders, and behavioral problems in the home. In addition, methods of training parents and evaluating change in a child's performance are identified. An extensive and useful set of references follows this chapter.

Greer, S. E., & D'Zurilla, T. J. (1975). Behavioral approaches to marital discord and conflict. *Journal of Marriage and Family Counseling, 1*(4), 299–315.

The authors assert in this article that the adaptation of behavioral techniques to marital conflict stems from the realization that a child's problems cannot be treated in a vacuum. The social learning concepts of reciprocity and coercion are utilized to compare positive reinforcement with aversive exchange. This article cites important early behaviorist-oriented marital therapy research incorporating assessment tools, apparatus, individual case studies, and nonfactorial single-group designs.

Griest, D. L., & Wells, K. C. (1983). Behavioral family therapy with conduct disorders in children. *Behavior Therapy, 14,* 37–53.

This article stresses the point that behavioral family therapy for childhood conduct disorders should move beyond the parent training model of treatment and incorporate a "multimodal" focus in which several areas of family functioning are assessed and treated. This idea is supported by several studies showing that behavioral disorder in children may be linked to parental cognitions regarding a child, parental mental health, marital stability, and the degree of positive–negative parental social relationships.

Gurman, A. S., & Kniskern, D. P. (1978). Behavioral marriage therapy: II. Empirical perspective. *Family Process, 17,* 149–163.

The authors discuss the state of the art in behavioral marital therapy from the perspective of outcome research as presented in published reviews. Gurman and Kniskern summarize the results of 23 additional studies of behavioral couples therapy; they conclude that these additional data on controlled and comparative studies do little to enhance the current empirical status of the efficacy of behavioral marriage therapy, and in no case do they establish the superiority of social learning approaches.

Gurman, A. S., & Knudson, R. M. (1978). Behavioral marriage therapy: I. A psychodynamic-systems analysis and critique. *Family Process, 17,* 121–138.

This article should be required reading for family therapists wishing to better understand the potential shortcomings of behavioral marital therapy. The authors list and critically examine five major clusters of implicit assumptions in behavioral marital therapy (e.g., "Repression is good for your marital mental health"), and this touches off a heated debate with Jacobson and Weiss, proponents of behavioral marital therapy in this issue of *Family Process.* The lively interchange that ensues raises important issues and makes for interesting reading.

Gurman, A. S., Knudson, R. M., & Kniskern, D. P. (1978). Behavioral marriage therapy. IV. Take two aspirin and call us in the morning. *Family Process, 17,* 165–180.

This paper is a response to the spirited Jacobson–Weiss critique of the Gurman–Kniskern and Gurman–Knudson discussions of behavioral marital therapy. The authors contend that Jacobson and Weiss have failed to comprehend the essence of the theoretical and empirical criticisms of behavioral marital therapy. Also, the authors state that research cited by Jacobson and Weiss in support of the therapy is equivocal and exaggerates its success.

Hahlweg, K., & Jacobson, N. S. (Eds.). (1984). *Marital interactions: Analysis and modification.* New York: Guilford Press.

This volume has been edited from the 1981 proceedings of an international conference (held in Germany) on behavioral marital therapy. While it suffers from the unevenness characteristic of most edited volumes, this book provides a good sense of the present status and future directions of behavioral marital therapy. Chapters are divided into the following three sections: "Treatment Outcome Research," "Assessment and Analysis," and "Clinical Extensions and Innovations."

Jacobson, N. S. (1978). A stimulus control model of change in behavioral marital therapy: Implications for contingency contracting. *Journal of Marriage and Family Counseling, 4*(3), 29–35.

Jacobson proposes a model for change that dispenses with contingency contracting. He states that the quality of the negotiation session determines the success or failure of the *quid pro quo.* Attribution theory and extrinsic motivation theory suggest that with couples, if stimuli are identified or a written statement is formulated, a successful outcome is less likely.

Jacobson, N. S. (1979). Behavioral treatments for marital discord: A critical appraisal. In M. Hersen, R. M. Eisler, & P. M. Miller (Eds.), *Progress in behavior modification* (Vol. 8). New York: Academic Press.

This review covers the first 10 years (1969–1979) of applying behaviorist principles to couples. Specifically, it maps the course of increasing reciprocity and the exchange of rewards between spouses to bring about a collaborative set for skill building. Jacobson emphasizes the importance of assessing the complexity of dyadic interaction via multiple measures, including self-reports, spouse observations, and more objective behavioral observations. However, he questions the ability of paper-and-pencil instruments to capture the complexity of couples' interactions.

Jacobson, N. S. (1981). Behavioral marital therapy. In A. S. Gurman & D. P. Kniskern (Eds.), *Handbook of family therapy*. New York: Brunner/Mazel.

This is a fine introductory overview. Jacobson discusses the basic social learning theory, as well as the basic components of this therapy. Gurman and Kniskern's notes throughout this chapter are provocative and insightful, and add to the reader's understanding of important issues to consider.

Jacobson, N. S., & Margolin, G. (1979). *Marital therapy: Strategies based on social learning and behavioral exchange principles.* New York: Brunner/Mazel.

This is a clear and comprehensive presentation of the authors' social learning approach to couple therapy. Its strength is in its detail regarding the initial interview, increasing couples' positive exchanges, communication and problem-solving training, and contingency contracting. The authors also discuss at length the importance of such intangibles as persuasion and the "collaborative set."

Jacobson, N. S., & Martin, B. (1976). Behavioral marriage therapy: Current status. *Psychological Bulletin, 83*(4), 540–556.

This article reviews progress up to 1976 on the use of social learning and exchange principles to enhance rewards and reciprocity in marriage while minimizing punishing, coercive behaviors. In addition, it documents studies that lend support to the use of behavioral techniques to enhance reciprocity in both distressed and nondistressed couples. An advantage of the synopsis is its outline of intervention strategies and corresponding research.

Jacobson, N. S., & Weiss, R. L. (1978). Behavioral marriage therapy: III. The contents of Gurman *et al.* may be hazardous to our health. *Family Process, 17,* 139–148.

This article is a reply to the spirited critiques of behavioral marital therapy by Gurman, Kniskern, and Knudson in the same issue of the journal. Jacobson and Weiss attempt to correct and clarify what they consider misconceptions by their critics, and they restate some of the basic ideological principles in the behavioral model. The literature investigating the therapeutic efficacy of behavioral marital therapy is reviewed, and the authors conclude that the therapy is demonstrably effective.

Kelley, M. L., Embry, L. H., & Baer, D. M. (1979). Skills for child management and family support: Training parents for maintenance. *Behavior Modification, 3,* 373–396.

This article presents a one-family case study in which both parents were trained in child management skills and in improving parental support and consistency in order to deal effectively with their noncompliant child. In-home observations showed improvement in all treatment areas at termination, with continued maintenance of results at follow-up 6 months later.

Klein, N. C., Alexander, J. F., & Parsons, B. V. (1977). Impact of family systems intervention on recidivism and sibling delinquency: A model of primary prevention and program evaluation. *Journal of Consulting and Clinical Psychology, 45*(3), 469–479.

This study of families of juvenile delinquents compared a behavioral, short-term family systems approach (now known as "functional family therapy") with a client-centered family approach, an eclectic–dynamic approach, and a no-treatment control group. The behavioral systems approach, as compared to the other treatment conditions, was found to produce significant improvement in terms of family process and rate of recidivism. Results support the contention that client-centered family therapy alone is not as effective as a combination of behavioral and systems approaches. The study is exemplary for its sound methodology.

Lieberman, R. P. (1970). Behavioral approaches to family and couple therapy. *American Journal of Orthopsychiatry, 40*(1), 106–118.

This article explains how social reinforcement employed in families balances aversive behavior from one family member with gratifying consequences for all members involved. Changing the contingencies by which attention and concern are shared is considered the crucial determinant for success in treatment. The reading is historically pivotal, in that it brought social learning theory to the treatment of whole families, rather than using it to target and treat deviant individuals.

Lester, G. W., Beckman, E., & Baucom, D. H. (1980). Implementation of behavioral marital therapy. *Journal of Marital and Family Therapy, 6*, 189–199.

This article describes three behavioral interventions used in marital therapy. These are (1) problem solving, which consists of three stages (selecting and stating a problem, listing possible alternative solutions, and agreeing on a final solution; (2) communication skills, where the authors give therapist responses to 12 dysfunctional communication styles and describe 7 functional styles; and (3) contracting, which is divided into good-faith and *quid pro quo* contracting. The authors then discuss other therapeutic techniques, homework, and maintenance. This is a good introductory discussion of these behavioral interventions.

Margolin, G., Fernandez, V., Talovic, S. & Onorato, R. (1983). Sex role considerations and behavioral marital therapy. *Journal of Marital and Family Therapy, 9*, 131–145.

This article examines sex-role issues related to behavioral marital therapy. Specific issues include (1) underlying assumptions of relationship equality; (2) failure to recognize external causes of stereotypical behavior; and (3) action orientation in skills training without consideration of the role of socialization in inhibiting behaviors. Specific behavioral marital therapy procedures (goal setting, behavioral exchange for gender bias, and recommendations are given to help therapists become more sensitive to sex-role issues.

McGovern, K., Kirkpatrick, C., & Lo Piccolo, J. (1976). A behavioral group treatment program for sexually dysfunctional couples. *Journal of Marital and Family Counseling, 2*, 397–404.

This article describes a group behavioral treatment program for sexually dysfuctional couples presenting with problems of primary inorgasmic dysfunction and premature ejaculation. The authors report improvement of ejaculatory latency, increased rate of orgasm, and a significant rise in the couples' satisfaction with sex at termination. Follow-up showed some regression in the physical gains achieved, but not in the couples' sexual satisfaction.

O'Dell, S. (1974). Training parents in behavior modification: A review. *Psychological Bulletin, 81*(7), 418–433.

This article reviews 70 studies of parents trained to apply behavioral principles to the discipline of their children, dating back to 1965. The author's conclusion notes that most of the studies have focused on changes in the children while ignoring the necessary phases of maintenance and generalization of the parents' behavior. This is a hefty and useful resource for early articles on behavioral parent training.

Parsons, B. V., & Alexander, J. F. (1973). Short-term family intervention: A therapy outcome study. *Journal of Consulting and Clinical Psychology, 41*, 195–201.

This well-designed study was conducted to investigate the effectiveness of a family intervention program in shaping adaptive patterns of communication among delinquent families. Results indicate that the treatment (differentiating roles from requests, use of a token economy, reinforcement, and bibliotherapy) was effective in helping dysfunctional families develop adaptive interactional patterns.

Patterson, G. R. (1974). Interventions for boys with conduct problems: Multiple settings, treatments, and criteria. *Journal of Consulting and Clinical Psychology, 42*, 471–481.

A group of 27 boys with a "conduct disorder" label received treatment in their homes; 14 of these also received treatment in school. Treatment consisted of training the parents and teachers in behavior modification techniques to use in their respective settings. Deviant behavior was found to be signifcantly reduced at the end of treatment and at follow-up for both settings. The breakdown showed that two out of three cases were improved, with an average expenditure of 61.9 hours per family.

Patterson, G. R. (1975). *Families: Applications of social learning to family life.* Champaign, IL: Research Press.

Although this book was first published in 1971, it is still an excellent source for helping parents learn to apply social learning theory to family problems. Patterson's presentations of contracting and time out are particularly clear, and are well illustrated with a variety of examples.

Patterson, G. R. (1983). *Coercive family process.* Eugene, OR: Castalia.

In this large volume, Patterson presents a wealth of empirical data and clinical observations that undergird an evolving coercion theory based upon the observed behavior of antisocial children and their families. This book is more descriptive and data-based than his earlier "how-to" books for parents. As a comprehensive integration of research findings, it stands alone in its thoroughness in clarifying the dynamics of coercive families from a social learning theory perspective.

Patterson, G. R., & Fleischman, M. J. (1979). Maintenance of treatment effects: Some considerations concerning family systems and follow-up data. *Behavior Therapy, 10,* 168–185.

This article summarizes and critically reviews empirical studies examining the persistence of treatment effects in families with aggressive children who received behavioral therapy. Authors include key results of each study along with an analysis of strengths and weaknesses. The extensive bibliography is particularly useful.

Patterson, G. R., Reid, J. B., Jones, R. R., & Conger, R. E. (1975). *A social learning approach to family intervention: Vol. 1. Families with aggressive children.* Eugene, OR: Castalia.

This treatment manual, based on the work of the Oregon Research Institute, reports on the noncoercive behavioral methods used to reduce aggressive behavior in children. A child's behavior is controlled primarily through behavioral contracting and time out, not only by parents but also by school personnel who are regularly involved with the child. The author's attention to procedural details and to data-based assessment makes this a particularly useful volume.

Spinks, S. H., & Birchler, G. B. (1982). Behavioral systems marital therapy: Dealing with resistance. *Family Process, 21*(2), 169–183.

A behavioral systems marital therapy approach is presented as an integrative therapeutic model. The authors state that it is sometimes necessary to depart from the behavioral marital therapy model when resistance is not due to the design, timing, or appropriateness of assignment. Six basic options for interventions are presented, with a rational for the departure from the behavioral framework.

Stuart, R. B. (1969). Operant interpersonal treatment for marital discord. *Journal of Counseling and Clinical Psychology, 33,* 675–682.

This classic paper represents the first published application of a behavioral change contract to marital problems.

Stuart, R. B. (1971). Behavioral contracting within the families of delinquents. *Journal of Behavioral Therapy and Experimental Psychiatry, 2,* 1–11.

Stuart describes in readable detail the procedure for developing a behavioral contract with an adolescent. Portions of this article are suitable to give to parents.

Stuart, R. B. (1980). *Helping couples change.* New York: Guilford Press.

This well-documented book outlines a structured program for couples consistent with learning theory principles. Stuart's role as scholar/clinician is evident throughout. His specific descriptions of contracting, caring days, and procedures for containing conflict will be particularly useful to the practicing family therapist.

Weiss, R. L. (1978). The conceptualization of marriage and marriage disorders from a behavioral perspective. In T. J. Paolino, Jr., & B. S. McCrady (Eds.),

Marriage and marital therapy: Psychoanalytic, behavioral, and systems theory perspectives.
New York: Brunner/Mazel.

This chapter provides a detailed summary of behavioral principles as they relate to marriage and marital interaction. This is an excellent introduction to marriage from a learning theory perspective. While based upon cited research findings, Weiss's points are clearly presented without being overly reliant on the specifics of individual studies.

ACKNOWLEDGMENTS

We would like to acknowledge Marcia Brown-Standridge for her important and sustained contributions in the "Key Concepts and Interventions" and the "Key Books and Articles" sections. Also, the following individuals contributed to the writing of several annotations: Nick Aradi, Judy Myers Avis, Roz Cantrell, Maria Flores, Mark Hirschmann, Cleve Shields, Tom Shubeck, Cricket Steinweg, Linda Stone Fish, Paul Sherman, David Tate, Nondus Walls, and Joseph L. Wetchler.

REFERENCES

Alexander, J. F. (1973). Defensive and supportive communications in normal and deviant families. *Journal of Consulting and Clinical Psychology, 40,* 223–231.

Alexander, J. F., & Parsons, B. V. (1982). *Functional family therapy.* Monterey, CA: Brooks/Cole.

Bandura, A. (1971). *Psychological modeling: Conflicting theories.* Chicago: Aldine/Atherton.

Bernal, M. E., Williams, E. D., Miller, W. H., & Reagor, P. A. (1972). The use of videotape feedback and operant learning principles in training parents in management of deviant children. In R. D. Rubin, H. Festerheim, J. D. Henderson, & L. P. Ullmann (Eds.), *Advances in behavior therapy.* New York: Academic Press.

Billings, A. (1979). Conflict resolution in distressed and nondistressed married couples. *Journal of Consulting and Clinical Psychology, 47,* 368–376.

Birchler, G. R., Weiss, R. L., & Vincent, J. P. (1975). A multimethod analysis of social reinforcement exchange between maritally distressed and nondistressed spouse and stranger dyads. *Journal of Personality and Social Psychology, 45,* 494–495.

Cone, J. D., & Sloop, E. W. (1974). Parents as agents of change. In W. W. Spradlin & A. Jacobs (Eds.), *The group as agent of change.* New York: Behavioral Publications.

Constantine, J., Stone Fish, L. S., & Piercy, F. (1984). A procedure for teaching positive connotation. *Journal of Marital and Family Therapy, 10*(3), 313–316.

Edelman, R. I. (1971). Operant conditioning treatment of encopresis. *Journal of Behavior Therapy and Experimental Psychiatry, 2,* 71–73.

Falloon, I. R. H., Boyd, J. L., & McGill, C. W. (1984). *Family care in schizophrenia.* New York: Guilford.

Falloon, I. R. H., Boyd, J. L., McGill, C. W., Bazani, J., Moss, H. B., & Gilderman, A. H. (1982). Family management in the prevention of exacerbations of schizophrenia: A controlled study. *New England Journal of Medicine, 306*, 1437–1440.

Foster, S. L., & Hoier, T. S. (1982). Behavioral and systems family therapies: A comparison of theoretical assumptions. *American Journal of Family Therapy, 10*(3), 13–23.

Foxx, R. M., & Azrin, N. H. (1973). Dry pants: A rapid method of toilet training children. *Behaviour Research and Therapy, 11*, 435–442.

Gordon, S. B., & Davidson, N. (1981). Behavioral parent training. In A. S. Gurman & D. P. Kniskern (Eds.), *Handbook of family therapy*. New York: Brunner/Mazel.

Gordon, S. B., Lerner, L. L., & Keefe, F. J. (1979). Responsive parenting: An approach to training parents of problem children. *American Journal of Community Psychology, 7*, 45–56.

Gottman, J. M. (1979). *Marital interaction: Experimental investigations*. New York: Academic Press.

Gottman, J. M., Markman, H., & Notarius, C. (1977). The topography of marital conflict: A sequential analysis of verbal and nonverbal behavior. *Journal of Marriage and the Family, 39*, 461–477.

Gottman, J. M., Notarius, C., Markman, H., Bank, S., Yoppi, B., & Rubin, M. (1976). Behavior exchange theory and marital decision making. *Journal of Personality and Social Psychology, 34*, 14–23.

Graziano, A. M. (1974). *Child without tomorrow*. New York: Pergamon Press.

Graziano, A. M. (1977). Parents as behavior therapists. In M. Hersen, R. M. Eisler, & P. M. Miller (Eds.), *Progress in behavior modification*. New York: Academic Press.

Gurman, A. S., Knudson, R. M., & Kniskern, D. P. (1978). Behavioral marriage therapy: IV. Take two aspirin and call us in the morning. *Family Process, 17*, 165–180.

Jacobson, N. S. (1983). Beyond empiricism: The politics of marital therapy. *American Journal of Family Therapy, 11*, 11–24.

Jacobson, N. S., & Margolin, G. (1979). *Marital therapy*. New York: Brunner/Mazel.

Jacobson, N. S., & Weiss, R. L. (1978). Behavioral marriage therapy: III. The contents of Gurman *et al.* may be hazardous to our health. *Family Process, 12*, 149–164.

Lederer, W. J., & Jackson, D. D. (1968). *Mirages of marriage*. New York: Norton.

Leff, J., & Vaughn C. (1985). *Expressed emotion in families*. New York: Guilford Press.

Magee, R. (1985). Current developments in the family treatment of schizophrenia. Unpublished manuscript.

Mahoney, M. J. (1974). *Cognitive and behavior modification*. Cambridge; MA: Ballinger.

Meichenbaum, D. H. (1977). *Cognitive behavior modification*. New York: Plenum.

Miklowitz, D. J., Goldstein, M. J., Falloon, I. R. H., & Doane, J. A. (1984). Interactional correlates of expressed emotion in the families of schizophrenics. *British Journal of Psychiatry, 144*, 482–487.

Minuchin, S. (1974). *Families and family therapy*. Cambridge, MA: Harvard Press.

Neill, J. R., & Kniskern, D. P. (Eds.). (1982). *From psyche to system: The evolving therapy* of Carl Whitaker. New York: Guilford Press.

Neisworth, J. T., & Moore, F. (1972). Operant treatment of asthmatic responding with the parent as a therapist. *Behavior Therapy, 3,* 95–99.

O'Dell, S. (1974). Training parents in behavior modification: A review. *Psychological Bulletin, 81,* 418–433.

Paschalis, A. P., Kimmel, H. D., & Kimmel, E. (1972). Further study of diurnal instrumental conditioning in the treatment of enuresis nocturna. *Journal of Behavior Therapy and Experimental Psychiatry, 3,* 253–256.

Patterson, G. R., (1982). *Coercive family process.* Eugene, OR: Castalia.

Piercy, F., & Sprenkle, D. (1984). The process of family therapy education. *Journal of Marital and Family Therapy, 10*(4), 399–407.

Robin, A. L., & Weiss, J. G. (1980). The criterion-related validity of observational and self-report measures of problem-solving communications skills in distressed and nondistressed parent–adolescent dyads. *Behavioral Assessment, 2,* 339–353.

Stuart, R. B. (1980). *Helping couples change.* New York: Guilford Press.

Tahmisian, J. A., & McReynolds, W. T. (1971). Use of parents as behavioral engineers in the treatment of a school-phobia girl. *Journal of Consulting and Clinical Psychology, 18,* 225–228.

Tharp, R. G., & Wetzel, R. J. (1969). *Behavior modification in the natural environment.* New York: Academic Press.

Vincent, J. P., Weiss, R. L., & Birchler, G. R. (1975). A behavioral analysis of problem solving in distressed and nondistressed married and stranger dyads. *Behavior Therapy, 6,* 475–487.

Wiltz, N. A., & Gordon, S. B. (1974). Parental modification of a child's behavior in an experimental residence. *Journal of Behavior Therapy and Experimental Psychiatry, 5,* 107–109.

Wolf, M. M., Risley, T., Johnson, M., Harris, R., & Allen, E. (1967). Application of operant conditioning procedures to the behaviour problems of an autistic child: A follow-up and extension. *Behaviour Research and Therapy, 5,* 103–111.

Zlutnick, S. (1972). *The control of seizures by the modification of preseizure behavior: The punishment of behavioral chain components.* Unpublished doctoral dissertation, University of Utah.

5

SEX THERAPY

Sex therapy is generally considered to have come of age with the publication of Masters and Johnson's *Human Sexual Inadequacy* in 1970. While certainly not the first work in this area, it did a great deal to establish the legitimacy of this form of intervention and helped spur the rapid growth of a variety of sex clinics and programs (Annon, 1975, 1976; Fisher & Gochros, 1977; Hartman & Fithian, 1972; Kaplan, 1974, 1979; Maddock, 1976).

Prior to 1970, people with sexual dysfunctions relied primarily on folk cures or saw psychodynamically oriented therapists who offered long-term insight-oriented treatment with questionable results (Heiman, LoPiccolo, & LoPiccolo, 1981).

EARLY PIONEERS

Masters and Johnson, however, owe a considerable intellectual debt to earlier pioneers. Their behavioral–learning–cognitive approach was predated by the application to sexual problems of systematic desensitization (Wolpe, 1958), assertiveness training (Lazarus, 1965), and cognitive restructuring (Ellis, 1962). J. LoPiccolo (1978) has written about the "quiet revolution in American psychotherapy," beginning in the late 1950s, which emphasized short-term techniques based on learning theory and present-centered direct retraining of behavior. Two earlier sex therapists deserve special note: James Semans developed an effective, direct behavioral method for the treatment of premature ejaculation in the mid-1950s (Semans, 1956), and Donald Hastings (1963) described programs to retrain couples to function better sexually, such as through using direct clitoral stimulation for female anorgasmia (Heiman *et al.*, 1981). The monumental sex research of Alfred Kinsey (Kinsey, Pomeroy, & Martin, 1948; Kinsey, Pomeroy, Martin, & Gebhard, 1953) probably also did much to create a climate in which Masters and Johnson's work could be carried out and accepted. Kinsey and his University of Indiana associates also observed male and

94

female responses in the laboratory during coitus and masturbation, even though they remained much more circumspect than Masters and Johnson concerning how such data were obtained.

MASTERS AND JOHNSON

Though not totally original, Masters and Johnson's work has nonetheless been monumental. Their contributions include the following:

1. The duo's clinical work has been based upon the previous laboratory observation of the sexual response of 694 individuals, including 75 married couples. In *Human Sexual Response* (Masters & Johnson, 1966), they have delineated four phases of sexual response (excitement, plateau, orgasm, and resolution) and have clarified the parallel nature of male and famale response by describing the analogous changes in each gender in each phase. The cause of female sexuality has also been enhanced by their attention to the multiorgasmic capacity of many women, and especially by their refutation of the physiological distinction between vaginal and clitoral orgasms. (Freud asserted that a mark of female maturity was having vaginal, as opposed to the more infantile clitoral, orgasms.) This finding has led to relief for many women who were labeled, or who labeled themselves, immature or inadequate because they were not able to have orgasms through vaginal intercourse alone. Another myth that has been exploded in this work is the alleged importance of having a large penis in satisfying a woman.

2. Masters and Johnson have stressed the importance of learning, both in the etiology of dysfunction and also in its remediation. The ordinary processes of socialization (upbringing, role models, experiences, information/misinformation), and not just neurotic conflict, contribute substantially to an individual's capacity to perform in a sexual situation. Also, simple information (e.g., that direct clitoral stimulation may be necessary) and the relearning that is the by-product of new experiences (e.g., sensate focus exercises) are often curative.

3. Masters and Johnson have demonstrated that direct behavioral techniques can often be effective even in the absence of much attention to etiology or "underlying causes." For example, their treatment for premature ejaculation, the "squeeze technique," has proven to be generally effective in brief, present-centered, problem-focused treatment.

4. Masters and Johnson have also emphasized the role of anxiety in dysfunction and demonstrated that it need not be related to remote or historical causes. Simple "performance anxiety," which leads to "spectatoring" (or anxiously watching one's own sexual performance), may be a significant contributing factor. (Performance anxiety can also be a by-product of dysfunction.) The development of their sensate focus program (de-

scribed below) has done a great deal to provide couples with a low-anxiety setting where relearning could take place in an atmosphere in which demands for performance were minimal.

5. Finally, Masters and Johnson have stressed the systemic nature of dysfunction and emphasized that there is no such thing as an uninvolved party. For this reason they have stressed conjoint treatment, and for a time they utilized surrogate sex partners when a patient was not in an ongoing relationship. While the relational component of dysfunction is something generally accepted today, it was quite innovative at the time it was first introduced. Masters and Johnson have been able to grasp, in a profoundly humane way, the interpersonal and emotional components of sexual interaction and have capitalized on this in their treatment approaches. Their use of a dual-sex therapy team and their emphasis on a couple's interaction have helped to defocus the identified patient and to diminish emphasis on blame.

HELEN S. KAPLAN

Following Masters and Johnson, the next "giant" in the field is Helen Singer Kaplan. Her work can be seen in part as an answer to the question, "What is sex therapy and how is it different from and similar to other forms of therapy?" This has become an important issue, since many people have entered the field with disparate backgrounds and sometimes with minimal training in other forms of psychotherapy.

Kaplan argues that sex therapy cannot be reduced to a series of techniques that can be practiced by persons untrained in intrapsychic or interpersonal dynamics. On the other hand, she also rejects the notion that these dynamics must *necessarily* play a role in progress or even cure.

Rejecting either a strict behavioral or psychodynamic orientation, Kaplan integrates these approaches, along with an emphasis on interpersonal processes, into what she calls "psychosexual therapy." Like most behaviorists, she is concerned with symptomatic relief and uses sexual and communication tasks as an integral part of treatment. However, in many cases the use of these methods alone will not produce adequate results. To understand why, one must examine Kaplan's beliefs about the etiology of sexual dysfunctions.

Kaplan conceptualizes such dysfunctions as psychosomatic (excluding, of course, those with an organic cause) problems. At one level they are caused by a single factor—anxiety. This anxiety may be due, however, to causes that are immediate or remote, mild or serious, intrapsychic or interpersonal. She calls this the concept of "multicausal levels."

In treating a dysfunction, it is always necessary to attack the "specific immediate cause," which is similar for most individuals with the same dysfunction. Premature ejaculators, for example, regardless of whatever else may cause their problem, experience high anxiety during times of intense sexual arousal and suppress or repress their erotic sensations, which are sufficient cues to control ejaculation. Premature ejaculators can be taught to control this anxiety through methods such as the "stop–start" procedure (see "Key Clinical Terms," below).

What varies is the extent to which there are other causes and whether addressing these causes is necessary. Certain dysfunctions (especially desire disorders) generally have more serious and remote causes, and Kaplan believes that success is unlikely unless these causes are uncovered through longer-term insight-oriented therapy. Mild anxieties, such as performance anxiety, overconcern for the partner, and anxieties related to unrealistic expectations, can typically be dealt with through standard sex therapy procedures. Midlevel anxieties include success and pleasure anxieties and fears of intimacy and commitment, all of which are less amenable to simple behavioral intervention. The most serious causes include hostile and neurotic relationship patterns as well as "Oedipal" conflicts. These are unconscious, deeply threatening, and not responsive to nonpsychodynamic sex therapy.

Kaplan does what is necessary to obtain relief for the presenting problem. Following initial assessment (a client's responses to interventions are a part of ongoing assessment), she introduces behavioristic interventions such as sensate focus. As sessions progress, she helps clients to have an awareness of the immediate cause of the problem and of relationship patterns that affect or are affected by the problem. To the extent necessary, or if the clients request it, she will explore more serious or remote causes. Her techniques are an eclectic blend of Masters-and-Johnson-type strategies, family systems interventions, miscellaneous behavioral prescriptions, and psychodynamic psychotherapy. Unlike Masters and Johnson, she believes that a single therapist can work effectively with sexual dysfunctions on an outpatient basis.

Kaplan's other major contributions include the following:

1. She has developed a triphasic concept of sexual response (Kaplan, 1979), which has supplanted her earlier biphasic concept of "excitement" and "orgasm" (Kaplan, 1974). She has added the "desire" phase in response to the numbers of persons presenting with desire problems and nonresponsiveness to treatment. Kaplan posits that "immediate" anxiety is experienced earliest in the sexual response cycle by those with desire problems. Persons with excitement difficulties experience this anxiety somewhat later. Those with orgasm difficulties experience it the latest (e.g., a premature ejaculaor only feels debilitatingly anxious after he has already experienced desire and excitement).

2. Her concern with disorders of desire has not only generated a significant book on this theme (Kaplan, 1979), but has also inspired other

clinicians/researchers to investigate this problem (Fish, Fish, & Sprenkle, 1984; Levine, 1984; McCarthy, 1984; Regas & Sprenkle, 1983; Schover & LoPiccolo, 1982).

3. Kaplan has alerted the therapeutic community to the problem of phobic avoidance of sex, which may be distinct from disorders of desire, excitement, or orgasm (there may be nothing wrong with the client's sexual response). She has demonstrated that if panic accompanies the phobia, 80–85% of such patients will improve if antipanic medication is included in the treatment (Kaplan, 1983, p. 35).

4. She has developed a systematic plan for assessment and evaluation (Kaplan, 1983) and has given special attention to the organic basis of many disorders. While at one time it was believed that 95% of all sexual disorders had a psychological base, Kaplan believes this figure is much too high. Especially for clients over the age of 40, illness and drugs must be ruled out, especially for those disorders that carry a high risk of organicity (Kaplan, 1983, p. 23). Several books (Kolodny, Masters, & Johnson, 1979; Munjack & Oziel, 1980; Wagner & Green, 1981) and articles (Buffum, 1982; Kaplan, Fyer, & Novick, 1982) in the "Key Books" and "Key Articles" sections also attest to a renewed interest in sexual medicine and the organic etiology of many disorders.

OTHER DEVELOPMENTS IN SEX THERAPY

Self-Help Procedures

Long before the new sex therapy, couples turned to books and popular magazines for sexual advice and counsel. The phenomenal success of Alex Comfort's (1972) *The Joy of Sex* and the sexual and marital "aids" industry (offering a smorgasbord of products through glossy catalogues and even boutiques in the local mail) attest to the continuing demand for such material.

Reputable and noted sex therapists have produced materials designed to be used with limited therapeutic assistance. Examples include sexual growth programs for women (Barbach, 1975; Heiman, LoPiccolo, & LoPiccolo, 1976); help for impotence (Brooks & Brooks, 1981); and treatment for premature ejaculation (Lowe & Mikulas, 1975). The degree to which people comply with these programs and their efficacy are, with few exceptions, largely unknown.

Group Therapy

The group therapy format has been used successfully to treat a variety of dysfunctions. Mills and Kilmann (1982) offer a thorough review of the empirical literature on this modality.

Assessment Instruments

Assessment has been done through direct observation of sexual behavior (see the entry for "sexological exam" in the "Key Clinical Terms" section, below), through clinical history taking (see the entry for "sex history"), or through assessment instruments, predominantly of the paper-and-pencil variety. The development of empirically reliable and valid instruments has been part of the trend (see below) to emphasize accountability through research. Ideally, measures should assess change from multiple perspectives (client, therapist, partner). Instruments should also address both the presenting sexual problem as well as the individual's and the couple's more general functioning and satisfaction. Among paper-and-pencil instruments, the Marital Satisfaction Inventory (Snyder, 1981) and Prepare–Enrich (Olson, 1982) are examples of general marital instruments that have sexual satisfaction subscales. Among the more widely used instruments that more specifically target sexual functioning are the Sexual Interaction Inventory (J. LoPiccolo & Steger, 1974), which focuses on 17 specific activities and asks each partner questions about frequency and enjoyment, as well as perceptions of the other partner's responses to these activities; and the Derogatis Sexual Functioning Inventory (Derogatis & Melisaratos, 1979), a 245-item questionnaire that measures individual functioning in the areas of information, experience, drive, attitudes, symptoms, affect, gender-role definition, fantasy, body image, and satisfaction.

The reader may also find valuable a compendium of instruments used in the assessment of sexual function and marital interaction found in Schiavi, Derogatis, Kuriansky, O'Connor, and Sharpe (1979).

For physiologically oriented tools, see the entries for "psychophysiological assessment of vasocongestion" and "penile strain gauge" in "Key Clinical Terms," below.

Research Accountability

Like all new clinical disciplines, the field of sex therapy is empirically underdeveloped. Zilbergeld and Evans (1980) began the present decade with a vigorous attack on the methodological "inadequacy" of Masters and Johnson's *Human Sexual Inadequacy*. These critics' interest was first piqued when they began to notice that other therapists did not seem to be getting results as good as those claimed by the St. Louis researchers.

Zilbergeld and Evans (1980) have asserted that Masters and Johnson have withheld, or have presented in unclear ways, important information on their patient population as well as on the criteria and measures used to assess treatment effects initially and at follow-up. Their using the term "failure rate," while seemingly conservative, is no more inherently objective than reporting success rates; also, what constitutes failure is poorly operationalized, especially for the female dysfunctions. Furthermore, Masters and Johnson do not report how many applicants for treatment were rejected or give any information about dropouts. The follow-up data are also criticized because of Masters and Johnson's policy of not following up on initial treatment failures and because the researchers do not sufficiently describe the nature and extent of follow-up contacts.

Kolodny (1981), the training director at the Masters and Johnson Institute, has offered a spirited defense in which he documents that few cases were screened out. He also operationalizes treatment "failure" in a more careful way than is done in *Human Sexual Inadequacy*. In addition, new data are presented that Kolodny asserts support the outcome claims of the basic volume. Kolodny has also argued that unless other researchers are willing to go to the expense of truly replicating Masters and Johnson's procedures (e.g., dual-gender teams, intensive residential experience), they should not facilely criticize the St. Louis outcomes.

Whatever the relative merits of these arguments, the debate demonstrates the concern in this decade for research evidence for the field. In the "Key Articles" section below, the reader will note several reviews that focus on methodological issues in sex therapy research (Kilmann, 1978; Mills & Kilmann, 1982), as well as a variety of controlled studies that are beginning to research the relative efficacy of the various components of sex therapy (e.g., Fichten, Lobman, & Brender, 1983; Takefman & Brender, 1984). Outcome research is also an international concern (Dekker & Everaerd, 1983).

Emphasis on Psychological/Experiential Components of Response

Sex researchers have been criticized for placing an undue emphasis on the physiological component of sexual response. Kinsey, for example, used female orgasm as the primary indicator of female sexual satisfaction. Masters and Johnson's response cycle is composed of physiological stages, and they have tended to emphasize physical intensity of orgasm at the expense of more qualitative indices.

Recently, there has been a shift from narrow notions of performance to broader models that emphasize psychological/experiential components. This has been reflected in (1) emphasis on cognitive models of sexual functioning (Ellis, 1980; Lazarus, 1980; Walen, 1980); (2) attention to the role of attribution in sexual experience (e.g., Zilbergeld's [1980] attention to the role of labeling and relabeling of internal experience as a curative factor in treatment); and (3) concern for qualitative dependent variables in outcome research (Levine, 1980), such as a person's ability to enjoy sex and a couple's ability to enjoy sex together.

Ecosystemic Orientation

Although Masters and Johnson and Kaplan have given serious attention to interpersonal factors in the etiology and treatment of dysfunction, several authors have taken a more radically ecosystemic view by developing models that give proportionately much less attention to intrapsychic and personal history variables and more emphasis to the role of one's current relationship contexts. For example, Regas and Sprenkle (1983) challenge Kaplan's notion that inhibited sexual desire (ISD) necessarily reflects deep intrapsychic blocks that are only amenable to long-term insight-oriented therapy. Alternatively, ISD often serves important functions in the current relationship context; for example, it may be a means for regulating closeness and distance. In a related paper, Fish *et al.* (1984) utilize principles of structural family therapy to show how ISD may be a means whereby a couple can work out issues related to inclusion and boundaries, hierarchy and power, and intimacy. Both papers suggest that ISD may be indirectly dealt with through relatively brief present-centered therapies.

A more general model of an interactional approach to sexual dysfunctions is offered by Verhulst and Heiman (1979).

KEY TERMS AND CONCEPTS

Absolute global dysfunction. A dysfunction experienced in all situations with all partners of "situational dysfunction").

Anorgasmia. Another term for "inhibited female orgasm."

Clitoris. The female homologue to the male penis. It is the transmitter and conductor of erotic sensations, even though it is often stimulated indirectly via pressure from the pubic bone and from the labia minora. Masters and Johnson (1970) have shown that all orgasms are physiologically similar, laying to rest Freud's belief that clitoral orgasms were less "mature" than those produced by vaginal stimulation. In those rare instances where orgasm does come from vaginal stimulation alone, it has a psychological and not a physiological base (Kaplan, 1974). Orgasm is triggered by clitoral stimulation but is located and experienced in the circumvaginal muscles.

Deeper causes. In Kaplan's (1974, 1979, 1983) model, sometimes immediate causes of dysfunction operate in the service of deeper causes, which may be intrapsychic or relational. These typically are outside of the client's awareness and must be inferred from descriptions of current and past romantic relationships, family history, and so on. Intrapsychic causes might include Oedipal conflicts and fears of intimacy or success. Relationship causes might include power struggles or differing marital contracts. (See also "immediate causes.")

Dyspareunia (functional). The third edition of the *Diagnostic and Statistical Manual of Mental Disorders* (DSM-III; American Psychiatric Association, 1980) restricts this term to pain in coitus and gives the following definition: "recurrent and persistent genital pain in either the male or female" (p. 280). The term is derived from the Greek terms for "bad" or "painful" (*dys*) and for "lying in bed" (*pareunia*). It may be caused by a collection of dysfunctional conditions that have painful intercourse as the final common symptomatic presentation (Kaplan, 1983).

Ejaculatory incompetence. See "retarded ejaculation."

Emission. The contraction of the smooth muscles (contained in the walls of the internal male reproductive organs) that collects ejaculate in the posterior urethra (Kaplan, 1983, p. 19). The sensation experienced may be perceived as the sensation of ejaculatory inevitability.

Excitement phase disorder. A term referring to impotence in males and vaginal dryness leading to painful coitus in females. It is due to deficiencies in genital vasocongestion (see "vasocongestion," "inhibited sexual excitement in females," "impotence").

Frigidity. An often misused term that should only be applied to "inhibited sexual excitement in females." Because of its negative connotations, many sex therapists avoid its use.

General sexual dysfunction. See "inhibited sexual excitement in females."

Immediate causes. Kaplan's (1974, 1979, 1983) term for immediate psychological causes or antecedents of sexual symptoms. These include ineffective sexual behavior, destructive interaction with the partner, obsessive thoughts, or fearful and angry emotions, which the patient experiences just prior to the occurrence of the dysfunction. (See also "deeper causes.")

Impotence. The DSM-III definition "inhibited sexual excitement in males," is this: "Recurrent and persistent inhibition of sexual excitement during sexual activity, manifested by . . . partial or complete failure to attain or maintain erection until completion of the sexual act" (American Psychiatric Association, 1980, p. 279). Masters and Johnson (1970) included the condition of failing in more than 25% of one's attempts at intercourse. Levine and Agle (1978) developed a scale of 0–6 for erectile functioning.

Kaplan (1974, p. 255) says that about one-half of the male population has experienced at least occasional transient episodes of impotence. The immediate causes include performance anxiety, pressure from the partner, and overconcern with pleasing the partner (Kaplan, 1983). It is the dysfunction most likely to have an organic basis.

Inhibited female orgasm (also called "impaired female orgasm," "orgasmic or orgastic dysfunction," or "anorgasmia"). The DSM-III definition (302.73) is as follows: "Recurrent and persistent inhibition of the female orgasm as manifested by a delay in or absence of orgasm following a normal sexual excitement phase during sexual activity that is judged by the cl be adequate in focus, intensity, and duration" (American Psych sociation, 1980, p. 279).

Kaplan (1974) says that 8–10% of women never experience orgasm under any circumstances and that perhaps 50% do not experience orgasm in coitus without additional stimulation. Hence, not having orgasm in coitus should be considered a common sexual variant and not a dysfunction. The incidence of secondary or situational anorgasmia is difficult to determine, since there are types of partners, types of stimulation, and certain settings that may lead to difficulties for perhaps half of all women (Munjack & Oziel 1980). Immediate causes include obsessive observation during sex, the inability to let go, and insufficient stimulation (Kaplan, 1983, p. 19).

Inhibited male orgasm. See "retarded ejaculation."

Inhibited sexual desire (ISD). "Persistent and pervasive inhibition of sexual desire. The judgment of inhibition is made by the clinician's taking into account factors that affect sexual desire such as age, sex, health, intensity and frequency of sexual desire, and the context of the individual's life" (DSM-III, 302.71; American Psychiatric Association, 1980, p. 278). This dysfunction is common in both males and females; it is described extensively by Kaplan (1979), and has been summarized earlier in this chapter.

Inhibited sexual excitement in females (also called "general sexual dysfunction" or "frigidity"). The DSM-III definition (302.72) is this. "A recurrent and persistent inhibition of sexual excitement during sexual activity, manifested by partial or complete failure to attain or maintain the lubrication–swelling response of sexual excitement until completion of the sexual act" (American Psychiatric Association, 1980, p. 279). It is relatively uncommon as an isolated clinical syndrome (if there is sufficient stimulation) except as a result of physiological factors like estrogen deficiency. Having sex with a dry and nondistended vagina will probably lead to secondary inhibition of desire. The immediate cause is unknown, other than that it is any emotional state that interferes with the dilating of the genital vasculature in response to a sexual stimulus (Kaplan, 1983).

Inhibited sexual excitement in males. See "impotence."

Orgasm. In the male, the 0.8-second contractions of the striated perineal muscles that propel semen out of the urethra; in the female, the 0.8-second contractions of striated perineal muscles (Kaplan, 1983, p. 19).

Orgasm phase disorders. A term referring to premature, retarded, or partially retarded ejaculation in males and to inhibited, delayed, or absent orgasm in females.

Orgasmic or orgastic dysfunction. See "inhibited female orgasm."

Paraphilias (perversions, deviations, variations). DSM-III states, "The essential feature of disorders of this subclass is that unusual or bizarre imagery acts are necessary for sexual excitement" (American Psychiatric Association, 1980, p. 266). Common paraphilias include fetishism (use of nonliving objects for sexual excitement), transvestism (cross-dressing), pedophilia (use of prepubertal children), exhibitionism (exposing the genitals), and voyeurism ("peeping"). These disorders are found almost exclusively among males.

Partially retarded ejaculation. A relatively rare variation of retarded ejaculation in which the emission phase of the ejaculatory response is normal but the pleasant ejaculatory phase is inhibited. Semen seeps out, but there are neither contractions nor pleasure (Kaplan, 1983, p. 219).

Performance anxiety. The anxiety that accompanies concern about performance. It is most often related to fear of failure, partner's demand for performance, or the excessive need to please one's partner.

Premature ejaculation. Inadequate control of the ejaculatory reflex (Kaplan, 1983, p. 19). Premature ejaculation is the most common dysfunction among men and is especially common among the sexually inexperienced. The immediate cause is the suppression of pre-ejaculatory sensations during periods of high sexual excitement (Kaplan, 1983).

Phobias (sexual). The essential feature of a sexual phobia is the persistent and irrational fear of and compelling desire to avoid sexual feelings and/or experiences (Kaplan, 1983, p. 264). According to DSM-III, the fear is recognized by the individual as excessive and unreasonable (American Psychiatric Association, 1980, p. 225). The distinction between "simple" sexual phobia and phobia associated with panic disorder is of the utmost importance, since panic disorders are not amenable to psychological therapies alone. Antipanic medication is usually necessary (Kaplan, 1983, pp. 266–267). Kaplan *et al.* (1982) describe the difficulties in distinguishing between true inhibited sexual desire and the phobic avoidance of sex.

Primary dysfunction. A dysfunction that has always been present; that is, there has never been a time of adequate functioning (cf. secondary dysfunction").

Response cycle. The psychophysiological phases through which an individual progresses during the sex act. Masters and Johnson (1966) have posited a fourfold cycle of excitement, plateau, orgasm, and resolution. Kaplan (1974), because of conceptual difficulties with the plateau and resolution stages, developed a biphasic concept of excitement and orgasm. In a later book (1979), she has posited a triphasic model that adds desire. Other authors (e.g., Walen, 1980; Zilbergeld & Ellison, 1980) have proposed more complex schemes that include more cognitive and subjective variables.

Retarded ejaculation (also called "inhibited male orgasm". Masters and Johnson (1970) employ the term *"ejaculatory incompetence."* The DSM-III definition (302.74) is this: "Recurrent and persistent inhibition of the male orgasm as manifested by delay in or absence of ejaculation following an adequate phase of sexual excitement" (p. 280). The immediate causes often include obsessive self-observation during sex and the inability to "let go" (Kaplan, 1983, p. 19). In addition, secondary retarded ejaculation carries a significant risk of organicity.

Retrograde ejaculation. A "dry orgasm" due to semen entering the urinary bladder rather than the urethra following the ejaculatory response. This is always due to organic causes. It should not be confused with retarded ejaculation, in which the physiological process of ejaculation itself is inhibited.

Secondary dysfunction. A dysfunction that follows a period of normal functioning (cf. "primary dysfunction").

Situational dysfunction. A dysfunction experienced with certain partners and/or under certain circumstances (cf. "absolute dysfunction"). This distinction is important in making a differential diagnosis; if the symptom is clearly situational, psychogenicity is established and disease and drugs can be ruled out as causative factors (Kaplan, 1983).

Spectatoring. The tendency to watch oneself and monitor one's own sexual performance. It both causes and is caused by performance anxiety.

Testosterone. The primary sex ("libido") hormone for both genders. Testosterone levels are affected by mood. High anxiety or depression will lower levels of the hormone, and it may be best to postpone sex therapy until these conditions are remedied (Kaplan, 1974).

Vaginismus. According to DSM-III (306.5), "recurrent and persistent involuntary spasm of the musculature of the outer third of the vagina that interferes with coitus" (American Psychiatric Association, 1980, p. 280). The contractions are usually painful and the woman is typically unable to have intercourse, even though she may be aroused, may lubricate, or may even experience multiple orgasms. In milder forms, it may cause dyspareunia rather than prevent intercourse. The immediate cause is a fear reaction evoked by vaginal penetration (Kaplan, 1979).

Vasocongestion. In the male, the dilation of penile arteries, which increases the inflow of blood while the outflow is diminshed. It creates a high-pressure system in the cavernous sinuses of the penis, which produces erection. In the female this term describes the diffuse dilation of blood vessels in the labia and around the vagina, which produces genital swelling and vaginal lubrication (Kaplan, 1983, p. 20).

KEY CLINICAL TERMS

Antipanic medication. Typically, tricyclic or tetracyclic antidepressants. When there is a phobic avoidance of sex, accompanied by a panic response,

Kaplan (1983) believes the problem may be made worse by sex therapy unless clients are protected from panic attacks by antipanic medication.

Bridge maneuvers. Maneuvers that are utilized for stimulation of the clitoris during intercourse when the female is unable to have orgasm during intercourse alone. Kaplan (1974, pp. 404, 406, 408) offers illustrations of these techniques to "bridge" manual stimulation of the clitoris and coitus. If these are successful, direct stimulation should cease progressively earlier before orgasm.

Co-therapy. In sex therapy, the use of a dual-gender team of therapists. Masters and Johnson (1970) believe that successful sex therapy is enhanced by such cotherapy. Their reasons include (1) that partners will be initially more self-disclosing of their beliefs, values, and attitudes with someone of their own gender; (2) that partners each need someone of the same gender to fully understand those aspects of sexual response unique to males and females; and (3) that a dual-gender team avoids potential pitfalls related to interpreting patients' complaints on the basis of gender bias. Although Kaplan (1974) and others claim similar results utilizing solo therapists, to the best of our knowledge there has been no carefully controlled research to settle the question of the relative efficacy of cotherapy. Hence, the issue remains controversial.

Desensitization. Some means of gradually reducing anxiety-arousing stimuli. Since anxiety is associated with almost all forms of sexual dysfunction, treatment typically includes some type of desensitization. This may take the form of imagining progressively more anxiety-arousing situations or of experiencing them *in vivo* while remaining relaxed. The very structure of sex therapy itself, which typically begins with low-anxiety tasks and progressively moves to more threatening ones, is based on the principle of desensitization (Heiman *el al.*, 1981).

Differential diagnosis. The term used to describe the differentiation between organicity (caused by genetics, disease, or drugs) and pychogenicity (caused by psychological impairment) of a sexual dysfunction. If a dysfunction has already been determined to be situational, one can usually rule out organicity.

Dilators. A series of objects of increasing size, inserted by the husband under the wife's control into the wife's vagina for the purpose of gradual desensitization. Masters and Johnson (1970) pioneered the use of dilators in the treatment of vaginismus. Kaplan utilizes the finger instead—beginning with the female's own, followed by her partner's.

Group therapy. A format that has been used successfully to treat a variety of dysfunctions. Mills and Kilmann (1982) offer a thorough review of the empirical literature on this modality. Advantages include a format to meet the needs of individuals without partners, the opportunity to improve social skills and gain social reinforcement, and potential savings in therapist's fees. Potential problems include maintaining change after the group has disbanded and the generalization of changes made in the group to other significant relationships (Heiman *et al.*, 1981).

Homework assignments. See "structured sexual tasks or sigs."

Masturbation or self-stimulation (as a part of treatment). The most widely used and effective method for the treatment of primary inhibited female orgasm (anorgasmia). It may be preceded by genital self-examination, various types of body awareness, use of erotic stimuli, and so forth. The client often uses lubrication or a vibrator as an aid. Self-stimulation in the presence of a partner may be used as a step preceding manual stimulation by the partner. For clients with coital anorgasmia, self-stimulation during intercourse may be recommended.

Orgasmic reconditioning. A process in which therapists direct clients' fantasies in conjunction with masturbation in order to modify the types of stimuli that are associated with arousal (Leiblum & Pervin, 1980). It has been used to treat concerns about object choice, such as fetishes or homosexuality; it is also used to enhance attraction in heterosexual relations (e.g., thinking about one's partner prior to orgasm). A classical conditioning paradigm is often used to explain the results.

Organicity. See "differential diagnosis."

Pause technique. See "stop–start."

Penile strain gauge. This mercury-filled or mechanical device can be used to test for organicity of impotence when attached to the penis overnight. During the four or five periods of rapid eye movement (REM) sleep, penile tumescence (erection) frequently occurs. As the penis erects, the stretching of the gauge is recorded like an electrocardiogram and can be read by the physician the following morning.

P-LI-SS-IT model. Devised by Jack Annon (1976) as an acronym for the process of sex therapy, which should ordinarily begin with "Permission," followed by "Limited Information," then "Specific Suggestions," and finally "Intensive Therapy," if necessary. The first three components constitute brief therapy.

Psychogenicity. See "differential diagnosis."

Psychosexual evaluation. Kaplan's (1983) term for an evaluation that integrates the psychological and medical aspects of diagnosis of dysfunction. A cornerstone of this approach is the "sexual status examination" (see below).

Psychophysiological assessment of vasocongestion. For females, measurement of vaginal vasocongestion with a vaginal photoplethysmograph, a tampon-like acrylic tube that uses a photocell to measure blood volume and pressure pulse change in the vagina. Heiman (1978) suggests the utility of this measure of arousal for research and treatment. The male counterpart (see "penile strain gauge") is significant in the diagnosis of impotence.

Sensate focus. A procedure originally developed by Masters and Johnson to create an atmosphere whereby performance anxiety and spectatoring can be minimized. Couples are initially encouraged to be sensual (rather than sexual) through body exploration/massage of each other. While one person receives, the other massages/explores while encouraging feedback from the former concerning what feels good. The "giver" is also asked to get in touch with his/her own sensations. The process is designed to inter- rupt the current destructive sexual system of anxiety, expectation, and pressure, and couples are initially informed *not* to caress genitals or breasts in Sensate focus I). In Sensate Focus II, partners may also pleasure each other's primary erotic areas, but not to the point of orgasm. In Sensate Focus III, orgasm may be included.

Sex history. Many sex therapists believe that an in-depth history of clients' behavior is important, as well as knowledge of current attitudes and behaviors. Masters and Johnson advocate extensive interviews lasting about 7 hours, with male and female partners separated and interviewed by a same-sex therapist for the majority of the time. Other authorities (e.g., Annon, 1976) advocate a simpler approach. The efficacy of extensive his- tory taking has not been empirically validated.

Sexological exam. A variety of direct observations of the couple's sexual relationship, whereby (most typically) one member of a dual-gender team stimulates the breasts and genitals of the opposite-sex client in order to assess and demonstrate physiological responsiveness (Hartman & Fithian, 1972; Heiman *et al.*, 1981, p. 602). The procedure is generally considered of dubious value, due to limited generalizability and ethical considerations.

Sexual status examination. Kaplan's (1983) term for an important aspect of her psychosexual evaluation. It is a highly detailed description of the couple's current sexual experience through their self-reports. It is the clos- est one can ethically get to observing the couple and has the advantage of offering information about subjective experience and cognitive processes.

Stop–start. A method (the alternative to the "squeeze technique"; see below) pioneered by James Semans (1956) for the treatment of premature ejaculation. The client's partner is asked to stimulate his penis until he begins to feel premonitory sensations of orgasm. He then instructs her to "stop" and the cycle is repeated. The method encourages concentrating on preorgastic sensations rather than suppressing them (Kaplan, 1974). This procedure is used in a series of graduated sexual assignments culminating in intercourse.

Structured sexual tasks or SIGS. The specific behavioral strategies assigned by the therapist to modify the specific and immediate causes of the various dysfunctions. These differ, since the immediate causes of the dysfunctions differ. An excellent brief summary of these *sigs* is found in Kaplan (1979, Chapter 3). Most involve the client couple in some form of gradual *in vivo* systematic desensitization procedure. Many begin with or include sensate focus.

Squeeze technique. A method pioneered by Masters and Johnson (1970) for the treatment of premature ejaculation. The client's partner is asked to stimulate his penis until he begins to feel premonitory sensations of orgasm. He then cues her to grasp his penis between the thumb and first finger of both hands and to squeeze the shaft just below the coronal ridge for about 3–4 seconds. While most authorities now prefer the stop–start method, the advantage of the squeeze is that it more rapidly diminishes erection and therefore the potential for ejaculation. Like the stop–start method, this technique is used in a series of graduated sexual assignments culminating in intercourse.

TEACHING TOOLS, TECHNIQUES, AND RESOURCES

Class "Icebreakers" and Introductions

If the class is small, this exercise can be done individually. If large, it can be carried out in dyads. Each class member introduces himself/herself through describing the sex socialization and education he/she received in his/her family of origin. These issues are generally far enough removed from the present to make this task relatively unthreatening: yet the exercise also sets the tone for openness in the class.

What is Sexual "Health"?

The class is divided into triads. The groups are asked, "Given that this is a course on sexual dysfunction, is there some kind of standard or 'ideal' from which one is dysfunctional?" Alternately, one can prepare a handout or overhead display on "sexual health" based on Maddock's (1976) definition. This suggests that a sexually healthy individual has, first, a certain amount of cognitive knowledge about sexual phenomena; second, a degree of self-awareness about his/her own atitudes toward sex; third, a well-developed, usable value system that provides input into sexual decisions; and, finally, some degree of emotional comfort and stability in relation to sexual activities in which the individual and others engage.

Phase–Etiology Grid

A overhead display or sheet is prepared that includes a blank 3 × 3 grid. Across the horizontal axis are the three phases of the sexual response cycle: desire, excitement, and orgasm. On the vertical axis on the left are three etiological explanations of dysfunction: situational, relational, and intra-psychic. Students are asked to think of dysfunctions that might be placed in each of the nine cells. For example, in the upper left-hand corner, a desire-situational problem may arise when, for example, a person does not feel sexual desire when sleeping with his/her spouse at either partner's parents' home.

Practice in History Taking

Various models of sex history taking (already discussed to some extent; see also "Key Books" and "Key Articles") include at least the following major components: (1) questions that enable one to make a differential diagnosis between a dysfunction of organic etiology, and one of psychogenic etiology; (2) questions about the duration and course of the dysfunction; and (3) questions about the current sexual behavior of the client. Since modeling and practice of a complete sexual history can often be too time-consuming, these components can be modeled/practiced in different class sessions.

Student Reports on Dysfunctions

Students can be asked to make oral presentations or write term papers on the most current information regarding the major dysfunctions. A suggested outline includes: (1) definitions, (2) incidence, (3) etiology, (4) consequences of the dysfunction for the individual or couple, (5) treatment, and (6) prognosis and outcome as suggested by research.

Multiple Conceptualization Exercise

The students should be familiar with Kaplan (1974, 1979, 1983), as well as with Leiblum and Pervin (1980). The latter affords them the opportunity to conceptualize dysfunctions from a variety of viewpoints. In small groups, student can be assigned a specific sexual dysfunction and challenged to indicate how it would be conceptualized and treated by Kaplan, Zilbergeld, Ellis, and Lazarus. Also, the students can be asked how their own conceptualizations and treatment programs would differ from those of these recognized experts.

Sensate Focus Instructions

Since sensate focus is a common element in many treatment plans, students need to learn to practice giving the rationale and specific instructions for this task. Examples of verbatim instructions are found in Kaplan (1974) and Munjack and Oziel (1980).

Exercise in Specific Treatment Strategies

Although treatment must, of course, be tailored to the individual client or couple, there is some advantage in knowing (perhaps even memorizing) a basic sequence one might typically follow for treating each of the major dysfunctions. Kaplan (1979, Chapter 3) offers a succinct outline of treatment steps for each dysfunction. The class is divided into triads. The instructor calls out the name of a particular dysfunction and asks person A, B, or C to delineate the steps. The two individuals in each triad who are not being targeted help out if the first person gets stuck. The triads can then discuss the circumstances under which this treatment strategy might *not* be appropriate.

Ethics Exercise

The instructor prepares a handout containing a list of 12 behaviors actually engaged in by some sex therapists. All of these behaviors might be considered ethically objectionable by some therapists, while others might be quite comfortable with them. Individually, students are asked to rank-order the behaviors from 1 (least objectionable to them personally) to 12 (most objectionable to them personally). The results are then discussed in small groups. Examples of such therapist behaviors might include (1) using sexually explicit materials as part of therapy; (2) counseling a person who wants the therapist to facilitate a sexual activity that the therapist considers unethical for himself/herself although not necessarily unethical for others (e.g., a client who wants help in working through jealousies related to "swinging," which the therapist does not personally endores); or (3) having sexual relations with a client, sincerely believing that this will be helpful to him/her.

Training and Research Centers

- Masters and Johnson Institute, 4910 Forest Park Boulevard, St. Louis, MO 63108.

- Center for Marital and Sexual Studies, 5199 E. Pacific Coast Highway, Long Beach, CA 90804.
- Program in Human Sexuality, The Medical School, University of Minnesota, Department of Family Practice & Community Health, Research East Building, 2630 University Avenue, S.E., Minneapolis, MN 55414.
- Institute for Sexual Research (Kinsey Institute), 416 Morrison, Indiana University, Bloomington, IN 47401.
- Institute for Advanced Study in Human Sexuality, 1523 Franklin Street, San Francisco, CA 94109 (Offers Masters and Doctorates in Human Sexuality).
- Human Sexuality Program, Mount Sinai Medical Center, Madison Avenue and Ninety-Ninth Street, New York, NY 10029.
- The Marriage Counsel of Philadelphia, 4025 Chestnut Street, Second Floor, Philadelphia, PA 19104.
- New York University Human Sexuality Program, South Building, 5th Floor, New York, NY 10003.

Producers of Films and Videotapes on Sex Therapy

- Multi-Focus, Incorporated, 1525 Franklin Street, San Francisco, CA 94109 (800-821-0514).
- Med-Pro Productions, P.O. Box 275, Palisades Park, NJ 07650 (201-461-4216).
- Edcoa productions, 310 Cedar Lane, Teaneck, NJ 07666 (201-692-1200).

Journals Related to Sex Therapy

- *Alternative Lifestyles*, See Publications, 275 Beverly Drive, Beverly Hills, CA 90212.
- *Archives of Sexual Behavior*, Plenum Publishing Co., 227 West 17th Street, New York, NY 10011.
- *Current Research Updates in Human Sexuality*, P.O. Box 2577, Bellingham, WA 98227 (206-647-1588).
- *Journal of Homosexuality*, Haworth Press, 149 Fifth Avenue, New York, NY 10010.
- *The Journal of Sex Education, Counseling, and Therapy*, American Association of Sex Educators, Counselors, and Therapists, One East Wacker Dr., Suite 2700, Chicago, IL 60601.
- *The Journal of Sex and Marital Therapy*, Brunner/Mazel, 19 Union Square, New York NY 10003.
- *The Journal of Sex Research*, Society for the Scientific Study of Sex, Inc., 208 Daffodil Rd., Glen Burnie, MD 21061.

- *Medical Aspects of Human Sexuality,* Hospital Publications, 360 Lexington Avenue, New York, NY 10017.
- *Sexuality and Disability,* Human Sciences Press, 72 Fifth Avenue, New York, NY 10011.
- *Sexuality Today,* Atcom, Inc., 2315 Broadway, New York, NY 10024.
- *SIECUS Report,* Sex Information and Education Council of the United States, 8 Fifth Ave., New York NY 10011.

National Organizations Concerned with Human Sexuality

- (AASECT) American Association of Sex Educators, Counselors, and Therapists, One East Wacker Dr., Suite 2700, Chicago, Il 60060.

   In addition to publishing a journal (see above), the organization conducts many national and regional workshops and certifies sex educators and therapists.
- (SIECUS) Sex Information and Education Counsel of the United States, 8 Fifth Avenue, New York, NY 10011.

   This organization publishes the *SIECUS Report,* an excellent bimonthly newsletter telling what is happening in the field and offering both book and audio–visual reviews. It also publishes excellent study guides and pamphlets such as an updated film resource guide. You may write them and ask for a list of publications.

RESEARCH ISSUES

Although a number of voices have called for better research in sex therapy, and the "Key Books" and "Key Articles" sections contain some examples of good research, clinical folklore rather than a solid empirical base still dominates the field. Samples, with some exceptions, tend to be small. Most of the research studies, including Masters and Johnson's work, have been uncontrolled. A considerable amount of the "research" has been case studies. Much of what we "know" about the relationship of client variables to outcome is speculation. There is almost no research on therapist variables in sex therapy.

   Concerning treatment variables, it is difficult to determine the curative value of various techniques, since therapy usually consists of a combined-technique approach. Two techniques do seem to be fairly robust; they are the "squeeze" or "stop–start" for premature ejaculation, and the "dilation" procedure for vaginismic women. In addition, the general therapeutic technique of anxiety reduction is clearly beneficial for the large number of clients whose sexual dysfunction is bound up with tension and anxiety. However, since the treatment interventions reported are generally broad-spectrum combinations, there are a few attempts to differentiate the "active ingredients" from the "inert fillers" in the total package (Heiman *et al.*, 1981). There is, in sum, little evidence to support the differential effectiveness of various modalities of therapy.

The problem of dependent variables may be the most serious issue in the sex therapy research literature. There are clearly no well-operationalized and generally accepted standards as to what constitutes a "success" or a "failure," and measurement techniques are in their infancy. As in other areas of family therapy outcome literature (Gurman & Kniskern, 1981), it will be necessary to have multiple measures from multiple vantage points. One could utilize patient, partner, or therapist reports. Data could include questionnaries, physiological evidence, or behavioral indices.

An excellent list of prominent questions and issues for future research (adapted from Heiman *et al.* 1981, p. 622) is as follows:

- What treatments are best for the currently treatment-resistant dysfunctions (primary erectile failure and low sex drive being two prominent examples)?
- What is the differential effectiveness of sex therapy with various dysfunctions?
- What are the patient and therapist characteristics corelated with success or failure of treatment?
- Which are the "active ingredients" and which the "inert fillers" in multifaceted treatment packages such as Masters and Johnson's (1970)?
- What are the effects of sex therapy upon other areas of patient functioning, such as marital happiness, psychiatric status, and so on?
- How can we develop more objective diagnostic and treatment outcome measures?
- What techniques are helpful in treating the "resistant" patient couple?
- What are the long-term effects of sex therapy?
- What is the role of biological/physiological factors in the treatment of sexual dysfunction?

KEY BOOKS

Araoz, D. L. (1982). *Hypnosis and sex therapy.* New York: Brunner/Mazel.

This relatively short book (178 pages) is a remarkably comprehensive and truly integrative treatise on these two disciplines. The result of this synthesis is a "hypnobehavioral model" that incorporates principles of cognitive therapy, imagery conditioning, and behavior modification within an interactional perspective.

Arentewicz, G., & Schmidt, G. (1983). *The treatment of sexual disorders: Concepts and techniques of couple therapy.* New York: Basic Books.

The hallmark of this text is its use of basic Masters and Johnson behavioral sex therapy techniques with special attention to the couple system. Case transcripts illustrate how marital conflict is deftly handled without detracting from the focus on sexual dysfunction. Seasoned therapists will be more likely to appreciate the suggested interventions in light of the complicated symptomology presented in the case studies.

Barbach, L. G. (1975). *For yourself: The fulfillment of female sexuality.* Garden City, NY: Doubleday.

This very readable book presents a step-by-step approach designed to help women achieve orgasm and greater fulfillment of their sexual potential. The author discusses sources of sexual confusion, describes female anatomy and physiology, examines the psychological aspects of reaching orgasm, and presents a set of exercises for individuals and couples designed to enhance their sexual expression. This clear and intimately written book can be recommended with little reservation to either preorgasmic women or couples seeking greater sexual satisfaction.

Barbach, L. (1980). *Women discover orgasm: A therapist guide to a new treatment approach.* New York: Free Press

This is an excellent book for therapists who are leading or want to lead sex therapy groups for preorgasmic women. It includes discussions of forming a group, therapy methods, homework assignments, dealing with resistance, working with the client's partners, cotherapists' problems, and the limitations of the group method.

Bell, A. P., & Weinberg, M. S. (1978). *Homosexualities: A study of diversity among men and women.* New York: Simon & Schuster.

Based on data obtained from in-depth interviews with some 1,500 persons, the authors identify and describe five types of homosexual men and women, comparing them to one another in terms of their social and psychological adjustment and to similar heterosexual samples. The authors posit a view of homosexuality as a complex phenomenon involving quite varied life styles.

Brewer, J. S. (1979). *Sex research: Bibliographies from the Institute for Sex Research* Phoenix, AZ: Oryx Press.

This reference was written by the reference librarian at the Institute for Sex Research at Indiana University in Bloomington. One of the major categories in the bibliography is sex therapy.

Brooks, M. B., & Brooks, S. W. (1981). *Lifelong sexual rigor: How to avoid and overcome impotence.* Garden City, NY: Doubleday.

Here is a book written for the educated layperson who wishes to learn about the causes and treatments for sexual impotence. This work explains the medical and surgical aspects of impotence in clear, understandable language. The psychological causes are presented with archetypal conversations associated with marital discord and other psychogenic causes. The strength of the volume is in its discussion of sensate focus, prostheses, and ways to obtain professional help.

Gebhard, P., & Johnson, A. (1979). *The Kinsey data: Marginal tabulations of the 1938–*

1963 interviews conducted by the Institute for Sex Research. Philadelphia: W. B. Saunders.

This work is an important revision of and supplement to the previously published Kinsey data. It includes 45 pages of text with 580 statistical tables and thus offers a valuable opportunity for researchers to compare their current findings with Kinsey's figures from an earlier generation.

Hansen, J. C. (General Ed.). (1983). *Family therapy collections: Vol. 5. Sexual issues in family therapy* J. D. Woody, & R. H. Woody, (Volume Eds.) Rockville, MD: Aspen Systems Corporation.

This book links sexual issues to family behavior throughout the family life cycle. It is systemic in its approach and is written largely for the beginning clinician. The chapter on "Incest and Sexual Violence" is especially illuminating.

Heiman, J., LoPiccolo, L., & LoPiccolo, J. (1976). *Becoming orgasmic: A sexual growth program for women.* Englewood Cliffs, NJ: Prentice-Hall.

This article outlines a detailed growth program for women who have problems in experiencing orgasm. The book also includes a section relating to male partners. The emphasis is on orgasm as a part of, rather than the only or primary goal of, sexuality and sexual experience.

Kaplan, H. S. (1974). *The new sex therapy.* New York: Quadrangle Books.

This classic work is an interesting synthesis of psychoanalytic, behavioral, and systems approaches to sex therapy. The first 116 pages cover the physiology of sexual response. Then the author turns to general approaches to treatment, with six very detailed chapters on the six major dysfunctions. In addition, the book has sections on the results of sex therapy, sexual therapy with psychiatric patients, the relationship of sexual therapy and marital therapy, and so on.

Kaplan, H. S. (1979). *Disorders of sexual desire.* New York: Brunner/ Mazel.

A ground-breaking work, in which the author articulates her triphasic model of sexual response that includes "desire." After reviewing the physiology, etiology, and treatment guidelines for the basic dysfunctions, Kaplan devotes four chapters specifically to desire phase disorders of males and females. She posits that desire disorders are typically related to deeper, often unconscious causes, and are therefore less amenable to brief behaviorally oriented sex therapy. She believes their treatment often requires longer insight-oriented approaches.

Kaplan, H. S. (1983). *The evaluation of sexual disorders: Psychological and medical aspects.* New York: Brunner/Mazel.

The latest of Kaplan's impressive books focuses on the diagnosis and evaluation of sexual disorders, with a special emphasis on the differential diagnosis of psychogenic and organic etiology. In the first section, Kaplan describes her general process of psychosexual evaluation of dysfunctional patients. In the second section, a group of colleagues detail the medical evaluation of the major dysfunctions. In the final section, Kaplan details her specific assessment criteria (both medical and social-psychological) for gender identity disorders, the major psychosexual dysfunctions, sexual phobias and avoidance, and unconsummated marriage. The volume is an excellent resource on the latest information concerning differential diagnosis.

Kolodny, R. C., Masters, W. H., & Johnson, V. E (1979). *Textbook of sexual medicine.* Boston: Little, Brown.

The pioneers in the treatment of sexual dysfunction have written this text to meet the needs of instructors of sexual dysfunction who teach medical and nonmedical health care providers. The overall result is a well-referenced, comprehensive text covering a breadth of topics. There are some weaknesses; notably, the chapter on sex therapy discusses only the Masters and Johnson model of rapid treatment. Those searching for a textbook in this area will find this book a good foundation to be supplemented with other references and educational materials.

Leiblum, S. R. & Pervin, L. A. (Eds.) (1980). *Principles and practice of sex therapy.* New York: Guilford Press.

This volume is more useful than the typical edited work, in that the authors have been asked to describe treatment failures as well as successes. The volume attempts to identify some of the factors leading to varying degrees of success with different clients and problems. Contributors constitute a "who's who" of sex therapy (L. LoPiccolo, Zilbergeld, Barbach, Lazarus, Ellis, etc). The book demonstrates the enormous diversity of both conceptualization and treatment in sex therapy. Valuable introductory and closing chapters by the editors describe the development of the field and critical issues facing it.

LoPiccolo, J., & LoPiccolo, L. (Eds.). (1978). *Handbook of sex therapy.* New York: Plenum.

This is a collection of articles covering a wide range of topics in both sexology and sex therapy. The anthology is of uneven quality and, unfortunately, contains reprints of a number of rather old articles. Nonetheless, some of the selections are excellent, such as the introductory chapter by J. LoPiccolo.

Masters, W. H., & Johnson, V. E. (1970). *Human sexual inadequacy.* Boston: Little, Brown.

On the basis of 11 years of careful clinical research, Masters and Johnson present findings for the treatment of impotency, ejaculatory disorders, inadequate female response, vaginismus, dyspareunia, and sexual problems of aging. The book is a basic and essential resource for all therapists and counselors, as well as for others seriously interested in human sexuality. The publishing of this book was perhaps the single most important milestone in the history of sex therapy.

Masters, W. H., & Johnson, V. E. (1979). *Homosexuality in perspective.* Boston: Little, Brown.

This is Masters and Johnson's third landmark work on human sexuality. This volume includes a section on the treatment of dysfunctional homosexual couples, as well as their report of a 10-year study on individuals who requested to be either reverted or "converted" to heterosexuality. This book has been the subject of considerable debate and critical analysis. See the *SIECUS Report* (Vol. 8, No. 1, September, 1979) for extensive reviews.

Masters, W. H., Johnson, V. E., & Kolodny, R., (Eds.). (1977). *Fundamental ethical issues in sex therapy.* Boston: Little, Brown.

This volume includes a collection of essays and transcribed conversations at a 1976 conference sponsored by the Reproductive Biology Research Foundation (now the Masters and Johnson Institute). The purpose of the conference was "identifying and discussing the fundamental ethical issues in therapeutic and investigative approaches to human sexuality."

Munjack, D. J., & Oziel, L. J. (1980). *Sexual medicine and counseling in office practice.* Boston: Little, Brown.

This treatment-oriented manual has been written to present sexual information for the office practitioner in digestible and usable form. It is clearly written by a physician and a psychologist, with step-by-step instructions for the treatment of each major dysfunction.

Offit, A. K. (1981). *Night thoughts: Reflections of a sex therapist.* New York: Congdon & Lattes.

This book has been recommended not only to therapists but also to clients for its clarity and simplicity in explanation. The content is specific, with a variety of suggested sexual activities. Nonmedical practitioners may find the descriptions of physiology to be particularly enlightening.

Wagner, G., & Green, R. (1981). *Impotence (erectile failure): Physiological, psychological, surgical diagnosis and treatment.* New York: Plenum.

If ever there was a complete volume on impotence, this is the one. in concise, clear, professional language, erectile function and dysfunction are given a thorough presentation with helpful pictures, graphs, and diagrams. Published studies provide the substance for several chapters describing the influence of major diseases on erectile function. The book is outstanding in its description of many advanced diagnostic techniques, as well as surgical and psychotherapeutic interventions.

KEY ARTICLES

Buffum, J. (1982). Pharmacosexology: The effects of drugs on sexual function. A review. *Journal of Psychoactive Drugs, 14,* 5–44.

Many drugs reviewed here have positive and negative effects on human sexual performance. After a brief summary of sexual physiology, studies describing the sexual effects of drugs in common use for high blood pressure, mental disturbances, depression, and other disorders are summarized and evaluated. An extensive bibliography and a summarizing table make this a useful article for researchers and clinicians.

Chapman, R. (1982). Criteria for diagnosing when to do sex therapy in the primary relationship. *Psychotherapy: Theory, Research and Practice, 19,* 359–367.

Chapman conducted a retrospective study of case notes from 30 cases of sex therapy. Success cases were ones in which the couples had *bona fide* sexual dysfunction, with a good relationship, no other significant problems, and a positive attitude toward therapy. Deviations from this profile even on a single component could confound success of treatment. Chapman suggests that the computation of success rates should be limited to cases that are diagnosed to fit this profile.

Cotten-Huston, A. L., & Wheeler, K. A. (1983). Preorgasmic group treatment: Assertiveness, marital adjustment, and sexual function in women. *Journal of Sex and Marital Therapy, 9*(4), 296–302.

Women in a treatment group for primary and secondary orgasmic dysfunction increased the frequency of orgasm from self-stimulation significantly more than women in a control group. Their improvements in self-esteem and in communication with their partners were also superior to those of their control counterparts. No significant results were found for dyadic adjustment or assertive behavior. A major methodological problem that weakens the study, however, is the lack of consistency in data collection. Data were collected both in small groups and by mail, which may have biased the treatment group because of the presence of group pressure to succeed.

de Bruijun, G. (1982). From masturbation to orgasm with a partner: How some women bridge the gap—and why others don't. *Journal of Sex and Marital Therapy, 8*(2), 151–167.

A large nonclinical population of women in the Netherlands responded to a questionnaire in which they described their methods of masturbation and sex with their partners. The various masturbation techniques they used are discussed at length. A satisfactory experience with masturbation does not appear to assure orgasm during coitus. The reasons for this, based on the quetionnaire, are as follows: (1) Some women may not be interested in orgasm; (2) some women may not engage in sexual play that promotes excitement; and (3) couples may not spend enough time in the type of foreplay that causes excitement. Implications for the treatment of anorgasmic women are discussed.

Dekker, J., & Everaerd, W. (1983). A long-term follow-up study of couples treated for sexual dysfunctions. *Journal of Sex and Marital Therapy, 9*, 99–113.

This paper reports the results of a 5- to 8-year study conducted in the Netherlands on 140 couples treated for a variety of nonsomatic sexual dysfunctions. The study consisted of administering a questionnaire designed to assess eight aspects of couples' past (pretherapy and posttherapy) and current sexual relationships. The paper reports a myriad of results broken down by sample (e.g., intact, separated, divorced), time (e.g., pretherapy, posttherapy, follow-up), activity (e.g., affection, coitus, communication), and extent of therapy.

Derogatis, L. R., & Melisaratos, N. (1979). The DSFI: A multidimensional measure of sexual functioning. *Journal of Sex and Marital Therapy, 5*(3), 224–281.

The Derogatis Sexual Functioning Inventory (DSFI) is a multidimensional assessment tool of human sexual functioning. Ten areas of assessment, including sexual experience, fantasies, and satisfaction, are described, together with the rationale for constructing each part of the test. Reliability and validity measures such as factor analysis, predictive validation, and discriminant-function analyses are discussed. Clinical profiles are provided for the more typical sexual dysfunctions. This article is a useful introduction to the DSFI for both researchers and clinicians.

Fichten, C. S., Lobman, E., & Brender, W. (1983). Methodolgical issues in the study of sex therapy: Effective components in the treatment of secondary orgasmic dysfunction. *Journal of Sex and Marital Therapy* , *9*, 191–202.

This experimental study attempted to examine the effects of three components of treatment (Sensate Focus I, Sensate Focus II, and ban on intercourse) on therapy outcome. The sample (N = 23) consisted of couples with the problem of secondary orgasmic dysfunction in the wife. The research design involved three treatment groups, pretest measures, 14 weeks of treatment, posttest measures, and a 3-month follow-up. The treatment groups consisted of standard couples therapy, group therapy, and minimal-contact bibliotherapy. Outcome measures included questionnaires and daily behavioral reports on (1) frequency, (2) level of enjoyment, and (3) whether orgasm was attained. Results indicated no significant differences in outcome for either males or females during Sensate Focus I or Sensate Focus II. However, for females, sensate focus exercises coupled with the ban on intercourse produced a significant increase in level of enjoyment of noncoital sexual activity. This result is inconsistent with Takefman and Brender's (1984) findings on the effects of banning intercourse.

Gagnon, J. H., Rosen, R. C., & Leiblum, S. R. (1982). Cognitive and social aspects of sexual dysfunction: Sexual scripts in sex therapy. *Journal of Sex and Marital Therapy, 8*, 44–56.

Cognitive and social aspects of sexual dysfunction are conceptualized in terms of sexual scripts (i.e., routine patterns of thought and behavior in the sexual domain). Such scripts are learned as socially acceptable sexual behavior. Sexual scripts at the cognitive level include fantasies, plans, guidelines for interactive behavior, and memories. The authors use two clinical examples to demonstrate how sexual scripts are reviewed and then modified to reduce sexual dysfunction.

Graber, B. (1981). Demystifying "sex therapy." *American Journal of Psychotherapy, 35*(4), 481–488.

The author of this paper questions the development of a separate discipline of "sex therapy" and encourages therapists from the established mental health professions, especially psychiatry, to take a more active role in treating sexual disorders. His typology of problem areas is useful for both evaluation and treatment and encompasses these four areas: (1) physical, (2) intrapsychic, (3) interpersonal, and (4) learning. The article suggests what skill training techniques clinicians will have to add to their repertoire for treatment of sexual dysfunctions.

Heiman, J. R., LoPiccolo, L., & LoPiccolo, J. (1981). The treatment of sexual dysfunction. In A. S. Gurman & D. P. Kniskern (Eds.), *Handbook of family therapy*. New York: Brunner/Mazel.

This chapter is an excellent overview of the sex therapy field. The work includes a historical overview, a discussion of the differences between health and dysfunctional sexual relationships, suggestions for assessment and treatment, a review of research, and recommendations for training in the field. Its clarity, organization, and scope make this an excellent introductory reading for anyone interested in sex therapy.

Kaplan, H. S., Fyer, J., & Novick, A. (1982). The treatment of sexual phobias: The combined use of antipanic medication and sex therapy. *Journal of Sex and Marital Therapy, 8,* 3–28.

Theories and treatment of anxiety disorders are reviewed. Klein's psychophysiological theory of anxiety and the phobia–anxiety syndrome are used to explain sexual phobias. This clear and comprehensive paper represents an excellent example of the integration of theory and practice, physiology and psychology, chemotherapy and sex therapy.

Kilmann, P. R. (1978). The treatment of primary and secondary orgasmic dysfunction: A methodological review of the literature since 1970. *Journal of Sex and Marital Therapy, 4,* 155–176.

The studies in this literature review are evaluated in terms of subjects, therapist, time format, treatment, and outcome criteria. Although the studies being assessed do not support definite conclusions, there is the suggestion that the primary orgasmic dysfunction responds better than the secondary to sexual and nonsexual communication treatment. Secondary nonorganismic women respond better than primary when treated with desensitization procedures and sexual technique training. Desensitization appears to be appropriate for women with secondary sexual anxiety.

Kolodny, R. C. (1981). Evaluating sex therapy: Process and outcome at the Masters and Johnson Institute. *Journal of Sex Research, 17*(4), 301–318.

This author defends the research published by Masters and Johnson (1970) involving brief treatment of sexual dysfunction by a male–female cotherapy team. The article is written in response to a number of critiques, most notably that of Zilbergeld and Evans (1980). Kolodny justifies the Masters and Johnson data, operationalizes what cases constituted statistical "failure," and emphasizes that only 1 case in 50 was denied sex therapy due to screening. The tone of the article is understandably defensive and should probably not be read unless one also reads Zilbergeld and Evans (1980) counterpart.

Levine, S. B. (1984). An essay on the nature of sexual desire. *Journal of Sex and Marital Therapy, 10*(2), 83–96.

This highly readable and informative paper emphasizes that sexual desire is not a quantifiable phenomenon, but rather is produced by the complex interaction of biological drive, psychological motivation, and cognitive aspiration. The author uniquely focuses not only on inhibited sexual desire, but also on sexual desire that is relentless. The paradigm he offers helps organize terms used by laypersons and sexologists alike to describe the propensity for sexual behavior.

Levine, S. B., & Agle, D. (1978). The effectiveness of sex therapy for chronic secondary psychological impotence. *Journal of Sex and Marital Therapy, 4*,(4), 235–258.

This article challenges suppositions that alleviation of psychogenic impotence is tantamount to restoring complete sexual health. The authors report their study of 16 couples, which indicated that there was a degeneration over a 1-year follow-up of the improvement gained in treatment for 11 of the 16 men. The recurrence of the symptom is linked to the complexity of the interplay between intrapsychic and interpersonal issues within a marriage.

McCarthy, B. W., (1984). Strategies and techniques for the treatment of inhibited sexual desire. *Journal of Sex and Marital Therapy, 10*, 97–104.

This paper presents a cognitive–behavioral model for conceptualizing and treating ISD. The dysfunction is seen as a self-defeating cycle of negative anticipation, aversive experience, and avoidance. Treatment involves a sequence of individual-specific and couple-specific strategies.

Mills, K. H., & Kilmann, P. R. (1982). Group treatment of sexual dysfunctions: A methodological review of the outcome literature. *Journal of Sex and Marital Therapy, 8*(4), 259–296.

This paper presents a thorough overview of the empirical literature involving group treatment of sexual dysfunctions. It is a major source for anyone planning research in the area of sex therapy, since gaps in the current literature as well as methodological deficiencies are highlighted. Because it is essentially a reference article, researchers and academicians will probably find it more useful than clinicians. Group treatment for clients with sexual problems is supported by the literature cited, but few studies actually isolate treatment components.

Norton, B. R., & Jehu, D. (1984). The role of sexual anxiety in sexual dysfunctions: A review: *Archives of Sexual Behavior, 13*, 165–183.

This paper reviews three types of studies that investigate the role of anxiety in sexual dysfunctions: (1) studies comparing anxiety reactions of normals with those of people who have sexual dysfunctions; (2) studies reviewing the efficacy of anxiety reduction procedures in the treatment of sexual dysfunction; and (3) studies investigating the specific mechanisms through which anxiety impairs sexual dysfunction. Due to methodological limitations relating to the operationalization of anxiety, specification of subject characteristics, and outcome measures, few conclusive findings emerge. The review, nevertheless, is thorough, organized, and concise.

Nowinski, J. K., & LoPiccolo, J. (1979). Assessment of sexual behavior in couples. *Journal of Sex and Marital Therapy, 5*, 225–243.

This article describes the assessment battery of the Stony Brook Sex Therapy Center, which includes the General Information Form, the Locke–Wallace Marriage Inventory, the Sexual Interaction Inventory, and the Marriage and Sex Defensiveness Scales. Two case studies exemplify the process of integrating this information into a pretreatment clinical picture. The article is a fine presentation of the use of self-report assessment techniques in sex therapy.

Price, S. C., Reynolds, B. S., Cohen, B. D., Anderson, A. J., & Schochet, B. V. (1981). Group treatment of erectile dysfunction for men without partners: A controlled evaluation. *Archives of Sexual Behaviors, 10,* 253–268.

This experimental study investigates the effectiveness of group therapy in the treatment of erectile difficulty. Results indicate that treatment groups improved significantly more than the waiting-list group on measures of sexual attitudes. However, groups did not differ significantly on behavioral measures of erection difficulty. This study is clearly and thoroughly reported and generates salient questions for further study.

Reynolds, B. S. (1980). Biofeedback and facilitation of erection in men with erectile dysfunction. *Archives of Sexual Behavior, 9,* 101–113.

The role of biofeedback in the treatment of psychogenic erectile dysfunction was examined in this study, where the increase in penile diameter of 30 men was measured. One group received erotic film stimulation contingent on increases of penile size, along with continuous biofeedback (auditory and visual) of the same response. A second group received contingent films without biofeedback, and a third received noncontingent films at intervals similar to those in the first two groups. Measures made during the treatment and at a 1-month follow-up showed no significant differences among groups. The contingent-film group demonstrated greater responsivity than the group with contingent films and biofeedback. This study is elegantly designed and discussed in detail.

Schover, L. R., & LoPiccolo, J. (1982). Treatment effectiveness for dysfunctions of sexual desire. *Journal of Sex and Marital Therapy, 8,* 179–197.

Retrospective data from 747 cases seen at the Sex Therapy Center at Stony Brook were reassessed for low sexual desire and sexual aversion. (The total of cases actually rediagnosed came to 152.) Both men and women were considered to have low sexual desire; however, only women were diagnosed as having sexual aversion. Outcome measures of marital satisfaction, sexual satisfaction, and sexual performance were largely positive over the 3-month treatment period and were maintained at the 3-month follow-up. Gains after treatment were rated as minimally adequate, not optimal. The analysis is thorough and expressed clearly.

Shull, G. R., & Sprenkle, D. H. (1980). Retarded ejaculation reconceptualization and implications for treatment. *Journal of Sex and Marital Therapy, 6*(4), 234–246.

The authors of this article take the position that the conceptualization of retarded ejaculation has been "too narrowly defined." A thorough review of the relevant historical literature puts this stance into perspective. What is proposed is to put retarded ejaculation on a continuum with premature ejaculation, while at the same time emphasizing that the former may be the result of a lack of psychological and/or physical stimulation.

Snyder, D. K., & Berg, P. (1983). Predicting couples' response to brief directive sex therapy. *Journal of Sex and Marital Therapy, 9*(2), 114–120.

In this study, the Marital Satisfaction Inventory (MSI) was administered pre- and posttreatment for couples entering sex therapy. Six of the 11 scales at pretreatment predicted dissatisfaction with frequency of intercourse upon termination, while five scales predicted lack of affection for the partner. The purpose of the study was to confirm marital distress as a mediating factor in outcome.

Takefman, J., & Brender, W. (1984). An analysis of the effectiveness of two components in the treatment of erectile dysfunction. *Archives of Sexual Behavior, 13*, 321–340.

This experimental study examined (1) the effectiveness of a specific treatment component, the temporary banning of coitus, in relation to a second component, couples' communication of sexual preferences; and (2) the ability of initial hormone levels to predict treatment outcome. Results indicating no significant differences in sexual and marital functioning between groups suggested that the widely accepted practice of banning intercourse did not add to the improvement produced by communication. Since all males had testosterone levels within the normal range, this variable could not be used with confidence to predict outcome. However, findings indicate that males with lower testosterone levels had less successful outcomes.

Thompson, A., & Cranewell, F. (1984). Frequently cited sources in human sexology. *Journal of Sex and Marital Therapy, 10*, 63–70.

Three widely recognized journals of sexology were surveyed over a 2-year period (mid-1981 to mid-1983) to identify the most frequently cited authors, books, and articles in the field. Of the 4,400 references examined, Masters and Johnson and Alfred Kinsey ranked first and second, respectively, in the categories of both authors and books. Unlike the categories of authors and books, no clear leader(s) emerged in the category of most frequently cited articles. This paper is useful in that it provides a comprehensive synopsis of significant references in the field of sexology.

Trudel, G., & Saint-Laurent, S. (1983). A comparison between the effects of Kegel's exercises and a combination of sexual awareness relaxation and breathing on situational orgasmic dysfunction in women. *Journal of Sex and Marital Therapy, 9*(3), 204–209.

This experimental study compared women with situational orgasmic dysfunction who were trained to practice a combination of sexual awareness, relaxation, and breathing (SARB group) to women trained in pubococcygeal muscle exercises (PC group). This is an important study, since Kegel's genital muscle exercises are often prescribed as part of a treatment regimen. The investigation resulted in no significant differences between groups over the 12-week practice period. Significant differences were reported for certain questionnaire items, and these differences favored the SARB group. Unfortunately, the lack of a control group, the limited sample size of six women per group, and the lack of controls on the degree to which women actually practiced the exercises all serve to weaken the methodology and the conclusions of the study.

Vandereycken, W. (1982). Paradoxical strategies in a blocked sex therapy. *American Journal of Psychotherapy, 36*(1), 103–108.

The success rate of the Masters and Johnson approach to sexual dysfunction is used as the context in which to discuss the use of strategic adjuncts to sex therapy. In two case studies reported here, the inhibiting patterns were disrupted through the use of paradoxical strategies, enhancing clinical success. Though not a comprehensive discussion of strategic therapy, this article nicely demonstrates the role of paradox in sex therapy.

Verhulst, J., & Heiman, J. R. (1979). An interactional approach to sexual dysfunctions. *American Journal of Family Therapy, 7,* 19–36.

The authors employ a systemic perspective to conceptualize sexual dysfunction. The model includes an explication of the basic sexual interaction cycle, individual and interactional variables that modify the cycle, and a conceptualization of sexual patterns as continuously changing figure–ground configurations. Although somewhat turbid, this paper represents a significant step in understanding sexual dysfunction from an ecosystemic perspective.

Zilbergeld, B. (1980). Alternatives to couples counseling for sex problems: Group and individual therapy. *Journal of Sex and Marital Therapy, 6*(1), 3–18.

In this article, the author challenges Masters and Johnson's standard treatment model of two therapists working with a couple for sexual problems. He emphasizes reasons why many clients may not be appropriate for couples therapy. Rather than rule out treatment for these individuals, Zilbergeld suggests either group or individual therapy. The article is especially useful for therapeutic situations wherein one partner seeks therapy and the other is not interested.

Zilbergeld, B., & Evans, M. (1980, August). The inadequacy of Masters and Johnson. *Psychology Today,* pp. 29–43.

This critical analysis of Masters and Johnson's sex therapy research indicates that "the research is so flawed by methodological errors and slipshod reporting that it fails to meet customary standards for evaluation (p. 29). Major flaws cited include inadequately defined criteria for success–failure, incomplete description of the sample of subjects, poorly defined follow-up procedures, incomplete delineation of treatment duration, and inadequate attention paid to negative effects of treatment. In addition to these serious limitations, the authors assert that both landmark works, *Human Sexual Inadequacy* and *Homosexuality in Perspective,* suffer from a vague writing style and inaccuracy in reporting data. See Kolodny (1981) for a rebuttal of this article.

ACKNOWLEDGMENTS

We wish to acknowledge the contributions of the following individuals in the writing of an earlier draft of the "Key Books and Articles" section: Marcia Brown-Standridge, Nicholas Aradi, and Mark Hirschmann.

REFERENCES

American Psychiatric Association. (1980). *Diagnostic and statistical manual of mental disorders* (3rd ed.). Washington, DC: Author.

Annon, J. (1975). *The behavioral treatment of sexual problems: Intensive therapy.* Honolulu: Enabling Systems.

Annon, J. (1976). *The behavioral treatment of sexual problems: Brief therapy.* New York: Harper & Row.

Barbach, L. (1975). *For yourself: The fulfillment of female sexuality.* Garden City, NY: Doubleday.

Brooks, M. B., & Brooks, S. W. (1981). *Lifelong sexual rigor: How to avoid and overcome impotence.* Garden City, NY: Doubleday.

Buffum, J. (1982). Pharmacosexology: The effects of drugs on sexual function. A review. *Journal of Psychoactive Drugs, 14,* 5–44.

Comfort, A. (1972). *The joy of sex.* New York: Crown.

Dekker, J., & Everaerd, W. (1983). A long-term follow-up study of couples treated for sexual dysfunctions. *Journal of Sex and Marital Therapy, 9,* 99–113.

Derogatis, L., & Melisaratos, N. (1979). The DSFI: A multidimensional measure of sexual functioning. *Journal of Sex and Marital Therapy, 5,* 244–281.

Ellis, A. (1962). *Reason and emotion in psychotherapy.* New York: Lyle Stuart.

Ellis, A. (1980). Treatment of erectile dysfunction. In S. R. Leiblum & L. A. Pervin (Eds.), *Principles and practice of sex therapy.* New York: Guilford Press.

Fichten, C. S., Lobman, E., & Brender, W. (1983). Methodological issues in the study of sex therapy: Effective components in the treatment of secondary orgasmic dysfunction. *Journal of Sex and Marital Therapy, 9,* 191–202.

Fish, L., Fish, R., & Sprenkle, D. (1984). Treating inhibited sexual desire: A marital therapy approach. *American Journal of Family Therapy, 12,* 3–12.

Fisher, J., & Gochros, H. (1977). *A handbook of behavior therapy with sexual problems* (Vols. 1 & 2). New York: Pergamon Press.

Gurman, A. S., & Kniskern, D. P. (Eds). (1981). Handbook of family therapy. New York: Brunner/Mazel.

Hartman, W., & Fithian, M. (1972). *Treatment of sexual dysfunction.* Long Beach, CA: Center for Marital and Sexual Studies.

Hastings, D. W. (1963). *Impotence and Frigidity.* Boston: Little, Brown.

Heiman, J. R. (1978). Use of psychophysiology in the assessment and treatment of sexual dysfunction. In J. LoPiccolo & L. LoPiccolo (Eds.), *Handbook of sex therapy.* New York: Plenum.

Heiman, J. R., LoPiccolo, L., & LoPiccolo, J. (1976). *Becoming orgasmic: A sexual growth program for women.* Englewood Cliffs, NJ: Prentice-Hall.

Heiman, J., LoPiccolo, L., & LoPiccolo, J. (1981). The treatment of sexual dysfunction. In A. Gurman & D. Kniskern (Eds.), *Handbook of family therapy.* New York: Brunner/Mazel.

Kaplan, H. S. (1974). *The new sex therapy.* New York: Quadrangle Books.

Kaplan, H. S. (1979). *Disorders of sexual desire.* New York: Brunner/Mazel.

Kaplan, H. S. (1983). *The evaluation of sexual disorders: Psychological and medical aspects.* New York: Brunner/Mazel.

Kaplan, H. S., Fyer, J., & Novick, A. (1982). The treatment of sexual phobias: The combined use of antipanic medication and sex therapy. *Journal of Sex and Marital Therapy, 8*, 3–28.

Kilmann, P. R. (1978). The treatment of primary and secondary orgasmic dysfunction: A methodological review of the literature since 1970. *Journal of Sex and Marital Therapy, 4*, 155–176.

Kinsey, A. C., Pomeroy, W. B., & Martin, C. E. (1948). *Sexual behavior in the human male.* Philadelphia: W. B. Saunders.

Kinsey, A. C., Pomeroy, W. B., Martin, C. E., & Gebhard, P. H. (1953). *Sexual behavior in the human female.* Philadelphia: W. B. Saunders.

Kolodny, R. C. (1981). Evaluating sex therapy: Process and outcome at the Masters and Johnson Institute. *Journal of Sex Research, 17*(4), 301–318.

Kolodny, R. C., Masters, W. H., & Johnson, V. E. (1979). *Textbook of sexual medicine.* Boston: Little, Brown.

Lazarus, A. (1965). The treatment of a sexually inadequate man. In L. P. Ullmann & L. Krasner (Eds.), *Case studies in behavior modification.* New York: Holt, Rinehart & Winston.

Lazarus, A. (1980). Psychological treatment of dyspareunia. In S. R. Leiblum & L. A. Pervin (Eds.), *Principles and practices of sex therapy.* New York: Guilford Press.

Leiblum, S. R., & Pervin, L. A. (Eds.). (1980). *Principles and practice of sex therapy.* New York: Guilford Press.

Levine, S. B. (1980). Conceptual suggestions for outcome research in sex therapy. *Journal of Sex and Marital Therapy, 6*, 102–108.

Levine, S. B. (1984). An essay on the nature of sexual desire. *Journal of Sex and Marital Therapy, 10*, 83–96.

Levine, S. B., & Agle, D. (1978). The effectiveness of sex therapy for chronic secondary psychological impotence. *Journal of Sex and Marital Therapy, 4*, 235–258.

LoPiccolo, J. (1978). Direct treatment of sexual dysfunction. In J. LoPiccolo & L. LoPiccolo (Eds.), *Handbook of sex therapy.* New York: Plenum.

LoPiccolo, J., & Steger, J. C. (1974). The Sexual Interaction Inventory: A new instrument for assessment of sexual dysfunctions. *Archives of Sexual Behavior, 3*, 585.

Lowe, J. C., & Mikulas, W. L. (1975). Use of written material in learning self-control of premature ejaculation. *Psychological Reports, 37*, 295–298.

Maddock, J. (1976). Sexual health: An enrichment and treatment program. In D. H. Olson (Ed.), *Treating relationships.* Lake Mills, IA: Graphic.

Masters, W. H., & Johnson, V. E. (1966). *Human sexual response.* Boston: Little, Brown.

Masters, W. H., & Johnson, V. E. (1970). *Human sexual inadequacy.* Boston: Little, Brown.

McCarthy, B. (1984). Strategies and techniques for the treatment of inhibited sexual desire. *Journal of Sex and Marital Therapy, 10*, 97–104.

Mills, K. H., & Kilmann, P. R. (1982). Group treatment of sexual dysfunctions: A methodological review of the outcome literature. *Journal of Sex and Marital Therapy, 8*(4), 259–296.

Munjack, D. J., & Oziel, L. J. (1980). *Sexual medicine and counseling in office practice.* Boston: Little, Brown.

Olson, D. H. (1982). *Prepare–Enrich: Counselor's manual.* Minneapolis: Prepare–Enrich.

Regas, S., & Sprenkle, D. (1983). Functional family therapy and the treatment of inhibited sexual desire. *Journal of Marital and Family Therapy, 10,* 63–72.

Schover, L. R., & LoPiccolo, J. (1982). Treatment effectiveness for dysfunctions of sexual desire. *Journal of Sex and Marital Therapy, 8,* 179–197.

Schiavi, R., Derogatis, L., Kuriansky, J., O'Connor, D., & Sharpe, L. (1979). The assessment of sexual function and marital interaction. *Journal of Sex and Marital Therapy, 5,* 169–224.

Semans, J. H. (1956). Premature ejaculation: A new approach. *Southern Medical Journal, 49,* 353–357.

Snyder, D. (1981). *Marital Satisfaction Inventory (MSI): Manual.* Los Angeles: Western Psychological Services.

Takefman, J., & Brender, W. (1984). An analysis of the effectiveness of two components in the treatment of erectile dysfunction. *Archives of Sexual Behavior, 13,* 321–340.

Verhulst, J., & Heiman, J. (1979). An interactional approach of sexual dysfunctions. *American Journal of Family Therapy, 7,* 19–36.

Wagner, G., & Green, R. (1981). *Impotence (erectile failure): Physiological, psychological, surgical diagnosis and treatment.* New York: Plenum.

Walen, S. (1980). Cognitive factors in sexual behavior. *Journal of Sex and Marital Therapy, 6,* 87–101.

Wolpe, J. (1958). *Psychotherapy by reciprocal inhibition.* Stanford, CA: Stanford University Press.

Zilbergeld, B. (1980). Alternatives to couples counseling for sex problems: Group and individual therapy. *Journal of Sex and Marital Therapy, 6*(1), 3–18.

Zilbergeld, B., & Ellison, C. (1980). Desire discrepancies and arousal problems in sex therapy. In S. R. Leiblum & L. A. Pervin (Eds.), *Principles and practice of sex therapy.* New York: Guilford Press.

Zilbergeld, B. & Evans, M. (1980, August). The inadequacy of Masters and Johnson. *Psychology Today,* pp. 29–43.

6

DIVORCE THERAPY

The 1970s gave birth to a new form of family intervention—divorce therapy. It was necessitated not only by the large increase in the number of divorces, but also by an increased awareness that divorcing people need help uncoupling (Olson, Russell, & Sprenkle, 1980).

The family field, however, was somewhat reluctant to accept this new emphasis. As Emily Brown (1985), a pioneer in divorce intervention, has written,

> Historically, the marriage centers wanted no part of divorce. Success meant keeping couples together, not helping them end their marriage. Those who saw a need for divorce counseling and tried to interest the established marriage and family agencies received a chilly response until very recently. Therefore, as with many new ideas, the innovative work in developing divorce services was done outside the mainstream, usually in small, private organizations which focused on one or more aspects of divorce. (p. 159)

Hence, the interventions described in this chapter have gained public as well as professional respectability only recently. This might help us to understand why, although there is an enormous body of literature on divorce in general, attention to divorce therapy has been both late and underdeveloped. We may hope that the field has moved past the association of divorce with pathology and the belief that divorce therapy is "antifamily" or "antimarriage" (Sprenkle, 1985).

By 1986, there were only two published general texts on divorce therapy (Sprenkle, 1985; Rice & Rice, 1986). Books had been written about certain special topics such as mediation (Coogler, 1978; Haynes, 1981; Irving, 1980) and treating postdivorce families (Hansen, 1982; Sager *et al.*, 1983; Visher & Visher, 1979). In addition, overview articles and book chapters on divorce therapy began appearing in the literature (E. M. Brown, 1976; Kaslow, 1981; Storm, Sprenkle, & Williamson, 1985).

DEFINING DIVORCE THERAPY

In its strictest sense, marital therapy can be defined as relationship treatment that focuses on maintaining, enhancing, and strengthening the marital bond. Conversely, divorce therapy can be defined as relationship treatment that focuses on decreasing the function of the marital bond with the eventual goal of dissolving it.

Unfortunately, however, such a clear-cut dichotomy is not often found in clinical practice. Marital and divorce therapy are not so much distinct clinical entities as they are segments of a continuum that cannot be easily demarcated. One or both partners who present themselves for marital therapy frequently have desires and often behave in ways suggesting that they want out of their relationship. Conversely, divorce therapy clients are often ambiguous about uncoupling. Establishing and redefining therapeutic contracts are often major aspects of this work.

We favor a broad definition of the term "divorce therapy" and consider those definitions found in the literature, even only a few years ago, to be too narrow. For example, Gurman and Kniskern (1978) have defined the goals of divorce therapy as limited to "aiding the divorced and separated partner to deal with his/her loss, resolving ambivalence, fostering autonomy, and self-esteem as a separate person" (p. 881). We conceptualize divorce therapy more broadly as helping couples and families through the stages of (1) predivorce decision making, (2) divorce restructuring, and (3) postdivorce recovery.

In the first stage, therapists help couples to look at divorce as one alternative to relationship difficulties and help them appraise the consequences of such a major decision. The therapist also encourages nondestructive communication about the decision so that family members are better prepared for the major changes that will follow. In the second stage, the therapist helps family members make the legal, emotional, financial, social, and parental arrangements necessary for the transition from marriage to the postmarriage family. During the third stage, the therapist facilitates the growth of the divorced spouses as autonomous individuals with stable life styles and helps them to develop social relationships independent of the former love relationship (goals similar to Gurman and Kniskern's definition as noted above). Continuing difficulties related to parent–child relationships, sibling relationships, and custody/visitation issues often occupy the therapist during this postdivorce stage. Preparation for remarriage and facilitating the remarriage process can also be included here. Alternatively, remarriage can be considered a fourth stage, since the majority of divorcing families will experience remarriage of one or both spouses (Sprenkle, 1985).

It is important to note that these stages are more heuristic than literally descriptive of all divorces, since divorces vary widely and issues cycle and recycle among the various stages. Some individuals, for example, have no time or even the option to think about the decision to divorce, since they are abruptly abandoned (Sprenkle & Cyrus, 1983). Other persons, far into the second stage, re-evaluate their decision and reconcile. Nonetheless, these stages are generally accurate and serve as useful benchmarks of the divorce process.

Below, we describe types of interventions carried out in each of the stages.

THERAPY FOR PREDIVORCE DECISION MAKING (STAGE 1)

The first stage in our conceptualization is the least developed of the areas. Nathan Turner (1980, 1985) is one of the few scholars who has written specifically on the intricacies of predivorce decision making and ways in which therapists can facilitate the process. Turner has drawn upon the social-psychological decision-making theories of Janis and Mann (1977) to make some sense of the often puzzling decisional behavior of clients contemplating divorce—frequently marked by seeming irrationality, extraordinary ambivalence, regressive behavior, decisional reversals, and impulsive behavior (Turner, 1985). Turner delineates stages of predivorce decision making, as well as typical coping patterns and common problems of people undergoing decisional stress. Turner recommends stress inoculation (Janis, 1983), emotional role playing (Janis, 1983), and the decisional balance sheet (Janis & Mann, 1977) as useful techniques for therapists during this stage of the divorce process.

Building on the work of Storm and Sprenkle (1982), who recommend that this stage calls for a high emphasis on conjoint therapy and a low emphasis on both individual and family therapy, Salts (1985) offers a variety of helpful suggestions for couples' work. She demonstrates how techniques of circular questioning can be utilized to clarify the clients' commitment to the marriage. For couples with serious doubts about continuing the relationship, Salts recommends a decision-making contract that enables them to determine whether their needs can be met *within* the marriage (not necessarily *by* the marriage).

Structured separation is sometimes used with couples who do not appear to be benefiting from marriage counseling but who are doubtful that divorce is the best alternative. Different models of structured separation are reviewed by Granvold (1983). Most require a written contract that specifies the ground rules of the separation. Time limits are set (typically 6 weeks to 3 months), and interaction is structured in such a way as to maintain a balance between "absence makes the heart grow fonder" and "out of sight, out of mind" (Granvold, 1983, p. 407). All of the models require couples to attend therapy, usually once a week, and the therapist attempts to create a more rational environment for decision making.

Since the few follow-up studies of this method suggest a high rate of marital termination (Greene, Lee, & Lustig, 1973; Toomin, 1972), it is important to match the technique to the needs of the couple. Granvold (1983) offers some guidelines for assessing whether this technique is either premature or too late for a couple.

THERAPY FOR DIVORCE RESTRUCTURING (STAGE 2)

Ideally, if the couple's decision to divorce has been facilitated by a therapist who has created a mutually acceptable decision and hence has toned down the intensive emotions surrounding the divorce, then the couple is ready to explore alternative ways to carry out this decision (Salts, 1985). The decision to divorce entails the legal, emotional, financial, social, and parental arrangements necessary to make the shift from marriage to single status (Storm & Sprenkle, 1982). This is a time of inordinate stress because of the multitude of changes that often occur—moving, lowering standards of living, shifting parental arrangements, changing social networks, and so on. The difficulty in this stage depends, in part, on the process used to arrive at the decision to divorce. If one spouse feels callously "dumped" and is desperately "holding on," restructuring will be more difficult. Ideally, conjoint couples therapy, with family therapy to deal with children's issues, is preferable here. Of course, people who have been "left" will often first seek help at the time of physical separation, and even the most engaging therapist will have difficulty getting the other spouse to participate (Salts, 1985).

Often, children are neglected emotionally during this period because parents are overwhelmed by their own needs (Salts, 1985). Since there is research evidence that children's postdivorce adjustment is directly related to the parents' own adjustment (Wallerstein & Kelly, 1980), therapists may gain leverage to encourage partners to continue working on their own emotional issues by informing them of the benefits for the children (Kaslow, 1984; Salts, 1985). Fortunately, there are a variety of resources for the professional (Cantor & Drake, 1983; Gardner, 1976; Hetherington, Cox, & Cox, 1981; Kurdek, 1983; Nichols, 1984, 1985; Stuart & Abt, 1981; Wallerstein & Kelly, 1980) and for parents themselves (Francke, 1983; Newman, 1981; Oakland, 1984) to help with parenting and children's issues. There are also several excellent books written for children (Gardner, 1971, 1978, 1982; Rofes, 1982).

The form of intervention most directly related to restructuring is divorce mediation. While mediation has been widely accepted in other aspects of life (e.g., labor disputes), it has been only recently applied to divorce, as Cohen (1985) notes in his interesting history of divorce mediation. The movement arose as a reaction to the destructive dimensions of the adversary legal system and was made possible by a confluence of social, economic, and legal changes, including the widespread acceptance of no-fault divorce. Mediation does not replace the legal system, but attempts to circumvent its more negative aspects. The mediation process is typically present-centered and time-limited, and focuses on the goal of reaching agreement on such crucial issues as custody, visitation, and finances. Typically, the end product is a nonlegal written agreement by the couple, which must then be formalized by the attorneys.

Early mediation services developed as an extension of ongoing services provided by professionally staffed counseling units, called "conciliation courts," that were attached administratively to a judicial jurisdiction. Originally, these services were designed to provide marriage counseling, focusing on the reconciliation of couples who had filed for divorce or were considering it (Cohen, 1985). As divorce rates began to climb, conciliation courts expanded their services to include the mediation of custody and visitation disputes. Non-court-related mediators are more likely to include financial mediation among their services. There are only a small number of full-time private practice mediators; more typically, mental health professionals provide divorce mediation in addition to other services. Lawyers also provide this service, but typically continue to practice more traditional law while offering mediation to selected clients (Cohen, 1985). An interdisciplinary team approach involving attorneys and therapists has also been advocated (Bernstein, 1977; Kaslow & Steinberg, 1981). The rationale is that therapists cannot keep up with the complex issues related to property, pensions, taxes, support and the like, while attorneys are often not trained to deal with the complex emotional issues surrounding divorce. Fortunately, therapists desiring to learn more about mediation have a variety of books to consult (Coogler, 1978; Haynes, 1981; Irving, 1980; Saposnek, 1983; Shapiro & Caplan, 1983).

The role of the mediator or therapist in facilitating custody decisions has received considerable attention in recent years. Typically, mediated divorces are much more likely to result in joint custody arrangements than nonmediated divorces, and valuable resources are now available for mediator/therapists who wish to learn more about such options. Howell and Toepke (1984) summarize the joint custody laws for the 50 states. Folberg (1984) offers the most recent comprehensive collection of papers on this theme. Volgy and Everett (1985) offer five criteria that may be used to determine whether couples are adaptive enough to make joint custody work. These authors stress that joint custody, like mediation, is not to be viewed as a panacea, and therapists cannot be blind to contraindications to these approaches.

THERAPY FOR POSTDIVORCE RECOVERY AND REMARRIAGE (STAGE 3)

Following initial restructuring, the therapist can begin to focus more on individual issues, such as coping with loneliness, regaining self-confidence, and rebuilding social relationships (Storm & Sprenkle, 1982).

Unless there are continuing problems with parent–child relationships or custody/visitation issues, or unless remarriage issues are the focus, the individual is the unit of treatment during this stage (Storm & Sprenkle, 1982). The therapist's goals include helping the individual to develop an autonomous life style, altering self-destructive cognitions about the divorce and the self, and mobilizing resources to achieve personal goals and ambitions. M. D. Brown (1985) demonstrates how a structural–strategic approach may be utilized with such individuals to help create "new realities" for the recently divorced.

More has been written about group and educational approaches than about techniques for therapists working with individuals. A variety of such programs and their goals are reviewed by Storm et al. (1985). Typically, a group format is used to normalize the divorce experience and to generate support and acceptance. Groups are also typically less expensive than individual therapy. Formats include short didactic educational emphases, skills training, group therapy, or combinations of these (Storm et al., 1985).

Group leaders, as well as individual therapists, often suggest bibliotherapy for divorcees at this time. Among the most popular self-help books are those by B. Fisher (1981) and Bernard and Hackney (1983). Older but still well-received works are those by Johnson (1977), Krantzler (1974), Smoke (1976), and Weiss (1975).

The single-parent phase following divorce is often problematic, and Weiss (1979) offers a text that is valuable for mental health professionals and the single parent. Both Weltner (1982) and Isaacs (1982) offer structural family therapy models for dysfunctional single-parent families. Eno (1985) addresses a greatly neglected area of divorce therapy literature— sibling relationships in families of divorce and ways in which these relationships can be affected therapeutically.

Perhaps the most impressive divorce intervention literature is in the area of the transition from divorce to remarriage. Crosbie-Burnett and Ahrons (1985) offer therapists a detailed guide for the issues and problems families face at this time. Ahrons (1979) has coined the term "binuclear family" to describe the context in which remarriage occurs. Therapists must frequently dispel courtship expectations and the myth that the remarried family will replace the nuclear family. One of Ahron's theoretical tenets is the boundary ambiguity inherent in remarried families and the greater need for boundary permeability than is the case for nuclear families. Such issues as movement between households, exchange of money, and shared decision making between "coparents" (ex-spouses) reflect this need for permeability and also underscore the potential for difficulty. Role ambiguity in remarried families is often the "twin" of boundary ambiguity. Therapists must help clients define roles while at the same time encouraging them to be flexible (Sprenkle, 1985).

The classic text on treating the remarried family is that by Sager *et al.* (1983). These authors prefer the term "remarried (REM) family" and examine it on three levels: "family systems," "life cycle," and "intrapsychic." Other important recent texts include those by Hansen (1982) and Visher and Visher (1979, 1982). The important area of the impact of divorce on the extended family is explored in a collection of articles by E. O. Fisher (1982).

DIVORCE THEORY

Kaslow (1981) has written that what therapists need is not simply a new technique for doing divorce therapy (as virtually any existing therapeutic modality may be applied), but a deeper understanding of the phenomenon of divorce. Similarly, Gurman and Kniskern (1981) have written that there is little that is strategically or technically unique to divorce therapy itself. This section briefly reviews the major theoretical approaches that have been taken to understand the phenomenon of divorce, in the hope that they will increasingly affect the work of practitioners.

The theory most widely used to explain the causes of divorce (on the individual as opposed to the societal level) has been social exchange theory. It has been used by Levinger (1976), Spanier and Lewis (1980), and other scholars to explain how individuals assess the costs and rewards associated with both staying in and terminating a relationship. In Levinger's (1976) highly influential formulation, people remain in a relationship on the basis of an unconscious accounting of three factors: (1) their attractions to the relationship, (2) barriers they perceive to divorce, and (3) comparisons they make between their current relationship and the alternatives they perceive are available to them. If internal attractions to the marriage and barrier forces to divorce become distinctly weaker than alternative attractions, the consequence is marital breakup.

The sociological version of crisis theory, originally developed by Hill (1949) and others, has been used by family stress researchers to describe, predict, and explain when a stressor event will cause a crisis or disorganization in a family, and also to predict the extent of the crisis (Raschke, 1982). Hill's (1949) "ABCX" theory posits that A, the stressor or event, is mediated by B, the crisis meeting resources of the family, and C, the definition of the situation by the family, to produce X, the crisis (Raschke, 1982). Sprenkle and Cyrus (1983), for example, have utilized this basic scheme to predict the relative level of stress experienced by persons abruptly abandoned by their spouses.

Other forms of crisis theory were developed during the 1970s by clinically oriented researchers to describe the developmental process of adjustment to divorce. These writers generally view divorce as a series of overlapping stages based on the psychological/emotional consequences of separation and divorce (Raschke, 1982). For example, several writers (Froiland & Hozeman, 1977; Weisman, 1975) describe the divorce process as analogous to the grief process articulated by Kübler-Ross (1969). Smart (1977) has used Erikson's (1963) "eight stages of man" typology as a model for the divorce process. Other frequently cited stage theories are those of Bohannan (1970), Kessler (1975), Weiss (1975), and E. M. Brown (1976).

These crisis theories that conceive of divorce in stages must be envisaged more as theoretical models than as full-fledged theories with interrelated propositions. Nonetheless, they do have considerable descriptive and explanatory power for the process of adjustment (Raschke, 1982). Several useful tables that compare the various models are found in Price-Bonham and Balswick (1980) and Salts (1979).

KEY CONCEPTS

Adjustment. Basically, the process of adapting to the difficulties and challenges both of ending a marriage and of beginning a new life style (Spanier & Casto, 1979). Beginning with Goode (1956, p. 19) and Waller (1967, p. xxi), and continuing to Kitson and Raschke (1981, p. 16), there have been a variety of influential definitions of divorce adjustment. Divorce adjustment is considered constructive when a divorced person is able to develop a life style and identity independent of the previous marriage and the ex-spouse and to function satisfactorily in the new identity and life style (Kitson & Raschke, 1981). Sutton and Sprenkle (1985) have postulated 10 criteria for long-term constructive adjustment to divorce and have developed a scale that is being used to measure the perceptions of therapists (Sutton, 1983), divorced people (Cantrell, 1985), attorneys (Sprenkle & Cantrell, 1986), and clergypersons (Wong, 1986) about constructive divorce. Holley (1980) has prepared an analysis of existing divorce adjustment measures.

Attachment. The bond that frequently persists between partners following separation and divorce, even after the "erosion of love" (Weiss, 1975). Kitson (1982) believes that attachment is the primary cause of emotional distress experienced by those divorcing and believes that the failure to "let go" can hinder adjustment. Ahrons (1980) indicates, however, that one needs to differentiate between "normal" attachment based on realistic caring and friendship, and "pathological" holding on. Thompson and Spanier

(1983) have developed an 11-item scale for attachment (Acceptance of Marital Termination, or AMT), developed on the basis of previous work by Kitson (1982).

Binuclear family. A term coined by Ahrons (1979) to describe the organization of the nuclear family after divorce into two interrelated households or two nuclei. Ahrons argues that although there are two households, there is one family system and the term holds whether or not the households have equal importance in the child's life experience. The term is more inclusive than "remarried (REM) family" or "stepfamily" but less inclusive than "REM suprasystem" (see entries for these terms, below).

Blended family. A synonym, along with "reconstituted family," for the postdivorce family. These terms are less widely used today because they do not make sufficiently clear the distinction between the postdivorce and the nuclear family. The connotation that parts of two previous nuclear families can be "blended" or "reconstituted" into something approximating the nuclear family is misleading. (See also "binuclear family," "remarried (REM) family," and "stepfamily.")

Custody. A term used by the courts to describe a variety of arrangements for the raising and rearing of children after divorce. The most common custody arrangement has been and continues to be "sole custody," which typically means that the children live with a "custodial" parent, and the other ("noncustodial") parent has "visitation" time. With this arrangement, the custodial parent has full authority and full responsibility to make medical, educational, and religious decisions, as well as to give consent for a minor child to marry or enter the armed forces (Association of Family and Conciliation Courts, 1982). Until recently, most other arrangements were called "divided custody" or "alternating custody." In such arrangements, each parent has physical custody and legal authority for a specified period of time (e.g., alternate years, or school year vs. summer). "Divided custody" (or, more commonly, "split custody") is also used to describe the arrangement whereby one parent has custody of some of the children and the other parent has custody of the remaining children. Although the term "joint custody" is sometimes used to describe a divided custody arrangement, the term typically goes beyond it. The typical hallmark of joint custody is that both partners have *shared decision-making authority* regarding all important matters concerning the children, such as educational, medical, and religious decisions. The term also implies that both parents have the *responsibility* for raising the children and carrying out such tasks as guiding and disciplining them. The mother and father are often referred to as "coparents" and the process as "coparenting" (Galper, 1978). The granting of joint custody does *not* imply a fixed arrangement for physical custody. Typically, it allows parents to plan creatively for the residential arrangements that they think make the most sense. Sometimes the court will determine physical custody arrangements, and joint custody may *de facto* not be that much different from sole custody with visitation. Nonetheless, the nonresidential parent in a joint custody arrangement even of this nature typically feels less demeaned and more "involved." The term "shared custody" has been offered to describe the arrangement whereby parents share major decisions, but the residential parent makes day-to-day decisions.

Divorce rates. A number of different methods are used to report on the incidence of divorce. One can, of course, simply count the number of couples divorcing each year. For example, this figure, in 1984, was 1,200,000. Because the population is increasing, however, this figure alone does not give one a "rate" that can be compared with previous years. The least satisfactory divorce "rate" is that frequently offered by the popular press, which gives a ratio of divorces decreed in a particular year to marriages performed in that year. For example, in 1978, there were about 1.1 million divorces and 2.2 million marriages, and hence the marriage–divorce ratio was 50%. This is a misleading "rate" because few of those divorces came from the marriages contracted in 1978. The vast majority came from marriages started in earlier years (Reiss, 1980). The "crude" divorce rate is a better alternative. It is the number of divorces occurring each year for each 1,000 persons in the population. The crude divorce rate for 1984 was 5.0, which means that 5 out of every 1,000 men, women, and children in the United States divorced in 1984. The "refined" divorce rate was 22. This means that if a random sample were taken of any 1,000 marriages in the United States in 1984, approximately 22 of them would have ended in divorce.

The difficulty with both the crude and refined divorce rates is that they do not make any assumptions about future years. For this reason, demographers have also devised a "cohort" approach, which tracks the percentage of marriages that have actually ended in divorce for marriages that began each year (e.g., for marriages beginning in 1964, 29.7% of these marriages had resulted in divorce by 1980). Using the technique called "demographic projection," the cohort approach also predicts the percentage of these marriages that will eventually end in divorce. For example, 42.2% of marriages commencing in 1964 are projected to eventually end in divorce (Weed, 1980). Utilizing these techniques, Glick (1984) projects that 49% of those born between 1946 and 1955 will dissolve their first marriage.

Leaver and left. The perceptions individuals have of themselves concerning whether they are the initiators or noninitiators of the divorce. In his popular text, B. Fisher (1981) uses the terms "dumper" and "dumpee." These terms are described here as "perceptions," since the individual who thinks he/she is being left at the time of the divorce may have been involved in subtle or not-so-subtle "leaving" behavior for many years. Nonetheless, typically, the experience at the time of divorce is more painful for the one "left," since he/she feels out of control or emotionally abandoned. Utilizing his Divorce Adjustment Scale, B. Fisher (1976) found that after 1 year, "left" spouses attained a level of adjustment equal to that of "leavers" at the time of the overt breaks in their relationships. Typically, however, a "leaver" experiences more pain during a marriage, or at least during the period prior to the decision to terminate the relationship (Sprenkle & Cyrus, 1983).

Mediation. A specific type of intervention by a trained therapist designed to help divorcing couples in conflict over custody, visitation, spouse and child support, and issues related to the economic settlement. It also can be utilized to address postdivorce disputes related to remarriage, visitation, and child support issues (Cohen, 1985). Described in more detail elsewhere in this chapter, mediation can be viewed as an alternative to self-help on the one hand and litigation on the other. Rather than being an advocate for a particular point of view, the mediator (or mediators) is a neutral facilitator who helps the couple reach a consensual agreement around disputed issues. The process does not circumvent the legal system, since mediated agreements are often subsequently written up in legal language by lawyers. Nonetheless, it is envisaged as a constructive alternative to the adversarial nature of the legal process.

No-fault divorce laws. Basically, laws that obviate the necessity for establishing a "guilty" and "innocent" party in a divorce and allow divorce on the basis of "irreconcilable differences" or following a separation for a specified period of time. Beginning with California's ground-breaking legislation in 1970, some form of no-fault divorce legislation has been adopted by almost all the states. No-fault divorce has not eliminated the adversarial process, since custody and property settlements can still be contested. Nonetheless, no-fault laws have resulted in a savings of time and legal expense, as well as eliminating a degree of sham from the courtroom.

Remarried (REM) family. The term of choice in the classic work *Treating the Remarried Family* (Sager *et al.*, 1983). It is defined as a family created by the marriage (or living together in one domicile) of two partners, one or both of whom have been previously married, then divorced or widowed. There may or may not be children from prior marriages who visit or reside with them. The adult couple and the children comprise the REM family system (Sager *et al.*, 1983, p. 3). Since children are not *required*, an REM family presumably need not be a stepfamily, even if one or both of its members are stepparents. As defined, the REM family could be a part of a binuclear family. (See also "binuclear family" and "stepfamily.")

REM suprasystem. Another term used by Sager *et al.* (1983) to describe the network of people and relationships created through a prior divorce and remarriage. It includes the former spouses of one or both the REM adults (alive or dead), the families of origin of all of the adults, the REM couple themselves, and the children of each of these adults. Hence, grand-parents, aunts, uncles, cousins, and stepgrandparents are included. Bo-hannan (1971) has used the term "divorce chains" to describe this entourage (Sager *et al.*, 1983, p. 3).

Separation. A term that is used in a variety of ways. In its most informal sense, a couple is considered to be "separated" when they are not living together due to conflict or dissatisfaction. The term is typically not applied to couples living apart because of vocational choice (as in commuter mar-riages) or because of hospitalization, military service, or the like. The term "legal separation" applies to a formalized legal agreement that regulates such matters as custody, visitation, finances, and residential access. Most legal separations are preliminaries to divorce, although a small minority are entered into in lieu of divorce by persons for whom divorce is not a viable alternative. The extent of informal separations is not known, al-though, of course, they are more frequent than divorces. Weiss (1975) has written that "almost certainly not more than half of all separations go on to divorce" (p. 11).

The term "structured separation" refers to a therapeutic technique used for couples who are undecided about divorce. It has been described previously in this chapter.

Single-parent family. Once a popular term for the postdivorce family prior to remarriage; however, it is now being criticized because it connotes noninvolvement of the nonresidential, generally noncustodial parent (Ah-rons, 1979; Bernard & Hackney, 1983). Ahrons believes that while the term "single parent" is appropriate, the "family" of the children following a divorce should be conceptualized as a "binuclear family" (see above).

Stages of divorce. A number of authors have postulated that divorce is typically experienced as the unfolding of certain stages. A number of major theories have been noted previously in this chapter (see section entitled "Divorce Theory"). Although stages underlying these theories have con-siderable descriptive appeal and are heuristic for the therapist, stage cat-egories have not been empirically confirmed.

Stepfamily. According to Visher and Visher (1979, p. 4), a family in which at least one partner of a couple is a stepparent. The only difference of a stepfamily from an REM family is that the REM construct does not necessarily assume that either partner previously had children. Like the REM family, the stepfamily could be a part of a binuclear family. Visher and Visher (1979, p. 19) emphasize that the stepfamily has five structural characteristics distinguishing it from the nuclear family: (1) There is a biological parent elsewhere; (2) virtually all members have recently sus-tained a primary relationship loss; (3) the relationship between one adult (parent) and a child predates the marriage; (4) a child is a member of more than one household; and (5) one adult (stepparent) is not legally related to a child (stepchild). (See also "binuclear family" and "remarried family.")

TEACHING TOOLS AND TECHNIQUES

Values Clarification Exercises

Divorce is a topic that is replete with value implications for both the instructor and the students. There are a variety of values clarification exercises that also serve as excellent "warm-up" tasks for classes or groups. On an overhead projector or in a handout, an instructor can do a sentence completion exercise with the following sentence stems: "Divorce means . . . "; "The best thing about divorce is . . . "; "The worst thing about divorce is . . . "; "My children will react to my divorce by . . . "; My parents, other relatives, church, friends, employer, and colleagues will react to my divorce by . . . "; and so on.

Another exercise is to say a series of statements about divorce and ask class members to go to one of four corners in the room designated "strongly agree," "agree," "disagree," and "strongly disagree." The statements might include such opinions as "I believe that divorce is a sensible solution to many unhappy marriages," or "Divorce is harder on children than on the divorcing parents." Once the group is divided into these categories, the instructor can also stimulate debates by asking people in the opposite corners to give rationales for their "strongly agreeing" or "strongly disagreeing."

Still another exercise is to draw an imaginary line across the room that represents a continuum of opinions about divorce. Class members are then asked to position themselves on the line between two opposites, such as "acceptable–sinful," "selfish–caring," "failure–success," "relief–trauma." Once class members have positioned themselves on the continuum, they are asked to discuss with another person why they placed themselves at the point they did. They may then be asked to move to the point on the continuum where they would "like to be." This move may be debriefed by asking them to discuss what would have to happen to make this change possible.

Grid Balance Sheet

The grid balance sheet is one of the techniques described by Turner (1985) in his discussion of divorce decision making and is adapted from the work of Janis (1983, p. 171). Students are asked to imagine that they themselves are anticipating divorce. Either on an overhead projector or through a handout, they are asked to consider two columns called "positive anticipations" and "negative anticipations." A grid is formed utilizing the following "rows": "tangible gains and losses for self"; "tangible gains and losses for others"; "self-approval or disapproval"; and "social approval or disapproval." A separate sheet is made out for each major alternative, such as "remaining married" or "trial separation." The procedure requires the decision maker to investigate carefully all alternatives and systematically consider the major gains and risks that might be otherwise overlooked (Turner, 1985).

Outcome Psychodrama

The instructor can model the psychodrama procedure for the class through either the use of a videotape or a role-play simulation with class volunteers. A person simulating decisional conflict concerning divorce is asked to assume one side of the ambivalence: for example, "Let us say you have decided to get a divorce." Turner (1985) describes the procedure:

> The therapist leads the person through all of the consequences of that decision. "You are now telling your husband/children. What are you saying? How does that feel?" The client is led further. "You are now in the court. What are you feeling as you look over at your partner across the room/as you leave the courtroom as a newly single person?" The sequence progresses. "It is now six months after the divorce. What are you doing? What do you feel? How much support are you receiving?"
>
> The process is then repeated taking the other polarity. You have decided to stay in your marriage. You are telling your husband of that decision. "What are you saying? How does that feel?"
>
> By giving the client the freedom to fantasize about the consequences of both outcomes, there is the opportunity to clarify thoughts and feelings and to assess the emotional readiness for a given decision. (pp. 35–36)

Following the second drama, the instructor can debrief the experience with the volunteers and then with the class itself.

We have also adapted this exercise for use in divorce therapy. Ambivalent clients are asked to "picture" (fantasize) themselves acting out each decision, being aware of their feelings as they do so. Through this focused fantasy, clients are encouraged to get in touch with their affect related both to choosing divorce and to staying married.

Model of the Divorce Process

Class members are presented with various models of the divorce process, such as those by E. M. Brown (1976), Kessler (1975), and Salts (1979). Class members are then challenged to develop a diagram of their conceptualization of the process and to produce a written commentary explaining it. They are free to draw upon the models developed by others, but are also encouraged to add something that is original. While this task is challenging, many report it to be the highlight of their course in divorce therapy. Class members also are asked to explicate therapeutic implications of the various components of the model.

B. Fisher's (1981) Building Blocks

In his popular and highly readable self-help book for persons going through divorce, *Rebuilding: When Your Relationship Ends,* B. Fisher (1981) presents a series of building blocks that one must "assemble" on the "ascent" to divorce recovery. Each of these blocks constitutes a chapter in his book. Each chapter ends with a quiz that a divorcing person can use to assess his/her own progress. While this is not a book for therapists, each of these chapters has many therapeutic implications. Class members can be asked to make a presentation that describes a particular building block, and can also be asked to explicate the therapeutic implication of the topic under consideration, (e.g., dealing with anger, friendships, sexuality, one's self-concept).

Divorce Interviews

Class members are assigned to interview one or more persons who have experienced divorce. Prior to the interview, they are warned that sometimes such interviews elicit powerful emotions, and are given steps to take should this occur. If two interviews are possible, students can be encouraged to interview one person who was the "leaver" in the marriage and another who perceives himself as the "left." In the case of the former, questions can be asked about the decision to divorce, utilizing the Levinger (1976) model described earlier (see the "Divorce Theory" section). If students have developed their own model of the divorce process (see teaching strategy on "Model of the Divorce Process," above), the interview can be structured around the model. It is important for the interviewer to ask whether the interviewee was engaged in divorce therapy and what was useful or not useful about the experience. If the interviewee did not seek therapy, what was his/her rationale, and what kinds of help (if any) facilitated his/her adjustment?

Visits to and from Representatives of the Legal System

Following an orientation, students can be asked to visit divorce court—preferably during a contested custody hearing. If possible, interviewing a divorce judge can be instructive. Inviting a divorce lawyer and/or a divorce mediator to class is often helpful and can be stimulating if they appear simultaneously on a panel.

"Ripple Effects" Exercise

Another exercise is designed to show the number of people who are affected by each divorce. A series of concentric circles is drawn on a blackboard or presented on an overhead projector or handout. The innermost circle contains the word "individual," and in progressive concentric circles are the terms (one in each circle) "marital couple," "nuclear family," "extended family," "friends," "work associates," and "professional helpers."

Members of the class are to list the numbers of people affected by each "typical" divorce as its "ripple effect" is felt. The exercise demonstrates that although there are approximately 1,200,000 divorces each year, the percentage of people affected directly or indirectly by these divorces constitutes a fairly large percentage of the population of the United States.

RESEARCH ISSUES

Sprenkle and Storm (1983) have reviewed 22 empirical investigations of divorce intervention. They report studies in the areas of mediation ($n = 6$), conciliation courts counseling ($n = 4$), consumer evaluation studies ($n = 2$), divorce groups ($n = 6$), structured separation techniques ($n = 2$), and marriage counseling with divorce as an unintended outcome ($n = 2$). Only the first two of these groups of studies utilized sound methodological procedures. Hence, results outside the areas of mediation and conciliation courts counseling must be considered quite tentative. Fortunately, 13 studies did use replicable standardized treatments.

The mediation studies used the most impressive designs and had equally impressive results. Unfortunately, however, all but one investigation (Kressel, Jaffee, Tuchman, Watson, & Deutsch, 1980) focused exclusively on child custody and/or visitation conflicts, and therefore there is little research on the mediation of financial settlements and child support. In all but one of the studies (Irving, Benjamin, Bohm & MacDonald, 1981), mediation was compared with the traditional adversary method of resolving disputes.

In these direct comparisons, mediation produced the following results: (1) a considerably higher rate of pretrial stipulations or agreements; (2) a significantly higher level of satisfaction with the agreements reached; (3) a dramatic reduction in the amount of litigation following the final order; (4) an increase in joint custody arrangements; and (5) a decrease in public expenses, such as custody studies and court costs. However, one study (Pearson & Thoennes, 1982) suggests that attorney fees may not be reduced by mediation (Sprenkle & Storm, 1983, p. 140).

The studies of conciliation court counseling utilized reconciliation as the major dependent variable. They showed a significantly greater number of reconciliations in experimental groups than no-treatment control groups, but the follow-ups were completed at only 3, 4, and 9 weeks posttreatment. Hence, although these studies were otherwise generally well designed, only short-term results have been reported.

The two studies of consumers of court-related counseling centers (P. Brown & Manela, 1977; Lee, 1979) indicated global satisfaction rates roughly similar to those in other uncontrolled studies of marital and family therapy.

The studies of divorce education–adjustment groups indicated that such groups appeared to be helpful in aiding divorcing individuals to feel greater mastery of their environment and to gain more self-confidence (Sprenkle & Storm, 1983). In addition, at least short-term gains in measures of self-esteem and divorce adjustment were common outcomes. Typically ranging from 4 to 10 sessions, these group approaches included didactic and experiential components.

Finally, two studies (Greene et al., 1973; Toomin, 1972) investigated structured separation techniques. Of the couples in these investigations, 44% and 67%, respectively, went on to divorce following structured separation. However, severe methodological problems in the two studies, and the fact that there is no "base divorce rate" for those who are participating in conjoint marital therapy (Gurman, Kniskern, & Pinsof, 1986), makes meaningful interpretation of these results difficult.

The field of divorce intervention is still woefully empirically underdeveloped. Aside from the firm conclusion that the mediation of custody and visitation disputes is preferable to the traditional adversary process, there is no strong data base on which to conclude that any other form of divorce intervention is superior to no treatment. Aside from the mediation investigations, and the conciliation courts counseling studies (which were not really of divorce therapy per se), there are only two studies (of divorce adjustment groups) that used random assignments to treatment and no-treatment conditions. There is no controlled research about what is probably the most widely practiced form of divorce therapy—namely, individuals' or couples' going to therapists for help in getting through the trauma of divorce. In short, basic controlled research on the process and outcome of divorce therapy has yet to be done (Sprenkle & Storm, 1983, p. 255).

It is also unfortunate that none of the studies of divorce therapy have investigated the effects of treatment on the children of divorce. Nor has a single study included children as participants in the therapy experience. Such investigations are crucial for public policy as well as clinical reasons (Gurman *et al.*, 1986).

Divorce mediation research needs to include examinations of the mediation of property settlement and child support, since private mediators, in particular, frequently facilitate agreements on such matters.

To the best of our knowledge, there is no research on interventions related to remarriage or single-parent families, in spite of the excellent books on theory and technique in this area.

Finally, there is a need to control for client variables that theoretically may have relationships with divorce outcome. Specifically, the stages of the dissolution process should be controlled in future research, since it is unwise to lump together persons in crises immediately following separation with subjects who are many months into the single life. It is also conceivable that there will be significant differences in the nature of adjustment experience between those who perceive themselves as the "leaver" and those who see themselves as the "left" in the divorce (Sprenkle & Storm, 1983).

Finally, it will behoove investigators to compare various forms of treatment. For example, no one has examined the results of individual versus conjoint versus family treatment for persons going through divorce. On theoretical grounds, Storm and Sprenkle (1982) have argued that specific units of treatment (individual, conjoint, family and group) are most appropriate for persons in certain stages of the dissolution process, but research is urgently needed to verify such speculation.

KEY BOOKS AND ARTICLES[1]

Adjustment for the Divorced Person

Bernard, J. M., & Hackney, H. (1983). *Untying the knot: A guide to civilized divorce.* Minneapolis: Winston Press.

The central thesis of this book is that divorce need not necessarily be destructive. Written for the layperson, it offers wise counsel on such topics as dealing with the legal system, coparenting, and teaching children about marriage. The authors seek

1. This section is an expanded version of "Divorce and Divorce Therapy: An Annotated Bibliography" by R. G. Cantrell, 1985, in D. H. Sprenkle (Ed.), *Divorce Therapy*. New York: Haworth Press. Used by permission.

to dispel a variety of myths about divorce that parallel society's myths about marriage.

Fisher, B. (1981). *Rebuilding: When your relationship ends.* San Luis Obispo, CA: Impact.

This is an excellent handbook for those going through the divorce process. Using the metaphor of climbing a mountain, Fisher divides the process into 16 rebuilding blocks. This most readable book normalizes what divorced people go through and gives suggestions on how to deal with each rebuilding block.

Gettleman, S., & Markowitz, J. (1974). *The courage to divorce.* New York: Ballantine Books.

The authors offer divorce as an alternative to a bad marriage. They profess that marriage is only one of many satisfying and normal options available in life. An excellent job has been done to show that divorce can be a healthy, constructive, fulfilling beginning for both parents and children.

Grollman, E. A., & Sams, M. L. (1978). *Living through your divorce.* Boston: Beacon Press.

This is a nicely illustrated book of poetry-like prose that describes the pain, struggle, and potential growth of divorce in ways with which most clients can identify. This book is very suitable as a gift to a divorcing person.

Krantzler, M. (1974). *Creative divorce.* New York: Signet.

Using his own experience and those of divorced persons going through his seminars, Krantzler describes the steps one goes through when divorced. He defines divorce as a new beginning in which one can learn to use his/her untapped resources. Krantzler includes in the book nine emotional traps faced by divorced people and ways to deal with each. This is a good book for people right after the physical separation.

Smoke, J. (1976). *Growing through divorce.* Irving, CA: Harvest House.

For those wanting a Christian perspective, this is a helpful book for those adjusting to divorce. The main focus is whether an individual wants just to go through a divorce or is willing to grow through one. Each chapter ends with personal growth and discussion questions. Areas covered include letting go, assuming responsibility, finding a "family," new relationships, and remarriage. Personal growth experiences from members of a Christian singles group make up two of the chapters. A list of resources is included at the end of the book.

Weiss, R. S. (1975). *Marital separation.* New York: Basic Books.

Here is a book both for those going through a divorce and for the professional. Weiss describes the process of divorce and separation. He includes many accounts of those who are in the process, to give the flavor of what it is like. Areas covered in the book include why separation takes place; the emotional impact of separation; various aspects of relationships between the separating spouses and with friends and relatives of each; difficulties that are likely to come up with children; and establishing a new life. Weiss does a good job of explaining and demonstrating the attachment felt between separating spouses.

Children's Books

Gardner, R. A. (1971). *The boys and girls book about divorce.* New York: Bantam Books.

Gardner, R. A. (1978). *The boys and girls book about one-parent families.* New York: Bantam Books.

Gardner, R. A. (1982). *The boys and girls book about stepfamilies.* New York: Bantam Books.

Each of these books is written for both children and parents to read. Each is written at the third- to fourth-grade level, although younger children can understand as parents read. Each book includes an introduction for parents and one for children. An excellent description of each situation is given, including feelings that a child may expect and suggestions for how to deal with individual situations. It is highly recommended for parents and children to discuss issues covered in the books.

Rofes, E. (Ed.). (1982). *The kids' book of divorce: By, for and about kids.* New York: Vintage Books.

This book is written by 20 youngsters aged 11 to 14 who have either experienced divorce personally or through a friend or relative. (Professionals are also interviewed.) The contributors explain what happens during the divorce process and give many suggestions on how to deal with divorce. Some topics included are: how parents should tell kids; legal issues; counseling; "weekend Santa"; stepparents; and gay parents. This book is appropriate for both parents and children.

Custody

Folberg, H. (Ed.). (1984). *Joint custody and shared parenting.* Portland, OR: Association of Family and Conciliations Courts.

Included in this book is a comprehensive, well-organized collection of articles dealing with joint custody. The first section provides a historical perspective, definitions, different living arrangements, and a review of the literature. Chapters in the second part examine factors that may influence the decision to implement joint custody and the success of shared parenting. Research findings are discussed in Part III, including what we know and what we have yet to learn. The last section deals with issues and trends in the law. Appendices include an excellent chart of state-by-state custody statutes and judicial interpretations, and a sample joint custody agreement with alternative provisions.

Galper, M. (1978). *Co-parenting: Sharing your child equally.* Philadelphia: Running Press.

Here is a source book for the separated and divorced family on the issue of coparenting. To gather her material, Galper drew from her own experience and corresponded with and interviewed professionals and others who are successfully coparenting. Topics covered in the book include a definition of coparenting, how actually to do it, the coparents' (ex-spouses') relationship, and what the professionals say. Variations of handling different situations according to what is best for the individual family are stressed.

Howell, R. J. & Toepke, K. E. (1984). Summary of the child custody laws for the fifty states. *American Journal of Family Therapy, 12*, 56–60.

The contribution of this article lies in its chart, which summarizes the child custody laws for each state. The chart indicates whether the following situations occur in each state: whether psychological investigation may be ordered by the court; whether either parent is preferred due to parent's sex; whether joint custody is specifically allowed; whether the noncustodial parent has access to a child's records; whether similar relevant factors are used to determine custody; whether a child's wishes are considered by the court; whether parental conduct not affecting relationship with the child is considered; and whether grandparent visitation rights are allowed.

Leupnitz, D. A. (1982). *Child custody.* Lexington, MA: Lexington Books.

The study reported in this book indicates better overall results for joint custody than for sole custody. Specifically, parents with joint custody were more likely to maintain contact with each other; the fathers were more likely to support the children financially; and parents were less likely to feel overwhelmed by child care responsibilities. The major disadvantages of joint custody found in this investigation were that the parents felt too tied to each other and that some complained of lack of geographical mobility.

Roman, M., & Haddad, W. (1978). *The disposable parent: The case for joint custody.* New York: Holt, Rinehart & Winston.

Writing from the male point of view, Roman and Haddad argue their case for joint custody. They begin with a historical view of custody and continue by looking at the impact of divorce on the whole family. As suggested by research, they show how contact with the father, who is usually the noncustodial parent, is important. Moreover, they reflect the difficulty of the mother in maintaining the role of a single parent. They demonstrate how parenting is a human, not a gender, trait. Roman and Haddad give excellent arguments to counter those objecting to joint custody. Case studies are included. The authors realize that culturally induced attitudes are most difficult to change and give ideas on what can be done.

Extended Family

Fisher, E. O. (Ed.). (1982). *Impact of divorce on the extended family.* New York: Haworth Press.

The impact of divorce on the extended family is explored in this collection of articles. Some of the topics examined include the dynamics of relationships within the extended family after divorce and remarriage; the role of extended kin in the adjustment to divorce/separation; effects of those in the role of grandparents and parents of an adult son or daughter; visitation rights of grandparents; the beneficial impact of divorce on the extended family; and services and interventions for this population.

Mediation

Coogler. O. J. (1978). *Structured mediation in divorce settlement.* Lexington, MA: Lexington Books.

This is a handbook for marital mediators. Coogler provides definitions and clear directions for divorce mediation. Qualifications for mediators are also discussed. All forms used are included in the books.

Haynes, J. M. (1981). *Divorce mediation: A practical guide for therapists and counselors.* New York: Springer.

Haynes believes that mediation involves the roles of both therapist and mediator. Part I discusses the divorce process and indicates how to deal with each stage as a mediator. The mediation process itself, is covered in the second part. Analysis of nine mediation case studies is included in Part III. The last section looks at the implications for practice. Sample forms used are included at the end of the books.

Irving, H. H. (1980). *Divorce mediation: A rational alternative to the adversary system.* New York: Universe Books.

This book covers what divorce mediation is, describes how it came about, and uses case studies to show how it can be used. At the end of the book Irving tells how a couple interested in mediation might proceed and where to go to find a mediator.

Saposnek, D. T. (1983). *Mediating child custody disputes.* San Francisco: Jossey-Bass.

Written from a systems perspective, this is a comprehensive guide for the professional who wants to mediate child custody disputes. Saposnek explains each step in the mediation process, with an excellent description of the beginning phase. Discussed are strategies used by children and parents that play into the custody dispute. The author describes interventions for eliciting cooperation and managing conflict. Both successful and unsuccessful case studies are given. Appendices include descriptions of California laws on joint custody, mandatory mediation, and family conciliation courts; confidentiality forms; and sample mediation agreements.

Shapiro, J. J., & Caplan, M. S. (1983). *Parting sense: A couple's guide to divorce mediation.* Lutherville, MD: Greenspring.

Shapiro and Caplan offer a book that fills the void for the layperson. Written by a lawyer and a psychotherapist, this book acquaints the reader with the concept and practice of divorce mediation, describes how joint custody works, and suggests that the family relationship is restructured rather than terminated with divorce.

Areas covered are (1) division of marital property, (2) spousal support, (3) child custody and parental access, (4) child support, and (5) tax considerations. Vignettes are used to help illustrate certain aspects of the mediation process. The authors include guidelines and forms used in mediation.

Parenting and Children

Cantor, D. W., & Drake, E. A. (1983). *Divorced parents and their children: A guide for mental health professionals.* New York: Springer.

Here is a book that familiarizes the reader with the current literature and research, while providing a sourcebook for mental health professionals who are working with divorcing families. Cantor and Drake give a wealth of information to help mental health professionals deal with the following areas: the effects of divorce on children; different approaches for working with both children and parents; ways to minimize the negative impact of divorce on children; custody arrangements; visitation; and parental dating and remarriage.

Francke, L. B. (1983). *Growing up divorced.* New York: Linden Press.

Through interviews with children and experts in the field, the author describes the effects of divorce on children according to their age level: babies and toddlers, preschoolers, 6- to 8-year-olds, 9- to 12-year-olds, and teenagers. At the end of each chapter is a section on what parents can do to help. The latter part of the book looks at the roles that the institutions (e.g., schools, courts, government) can and cannot fill.

Gardner, R. A. (1976). *Psychotherapy with children of divorce.* New York: Jason Aronson.

Gardner describes various reaction patterns of children to divorce and therapeutic approaches to dealing with them. An excellent chapter is included on special techniques, such as the mutual storytelling approach. Two chapters are devoted to advising parents. A lengthy chapter on litigation includes how to conduct a custody evaluation and recommendations for the therapist in court. There are many clinical examples throughout the book.

Hetherington, E. M., Cox, M., & Cox, R. (1981). The aftermath of divorce. In E. M. Hetherington & R. D. Parke (Eds.), *Contemporary readings in child psychology.* New York: McGraw-Hill.

This chapter describes one of the best-designed studies to date on the effects of divorce on mothers, fathers, and children. In this study, continued involvement of the noncustodial father proved to be most important. The study demonstrates that a conflict-ridden intact home is more detrimental to all members of the family than a stable home where the parents are divorced.

Kurdek, L. A. (Ed.). (1983). *New directions for child development: Children and divorce.* San Francisco: Jossey-Bass.

The unifying theme of this collection of articles is the child's view of divorce.

Each author has addressed some aspect of the question "What is the child's view of the divorce?" Rather than relying on parent reports, these authors have gone directly to the children themselves. Areas covered are children's understanding of their parents' divorces; young adolescents' responses; exploration of father-custody and mother-custody homes; correlates of children's adjustment; and a divorce adjustment project.

Newman, G. (1981). *101 ways to be a long distance super-dad*. Mountain View, CA: Blossom Valley Press.

This book is for the noncustodial father who does not live close to his children. It is a series of ideas to make the relationship special through ordinary means. This idea book includes ways to liven up phone calls and ways to let the children know that their lives and what they do are important. Examples include using a different type of postage stamp on each letter for stamp collecting, playing long-distance chess, and sending clippings from the newspaper that will interest the children.

Oakland, T. (1984). *Divorced fathers: Reconstructing a quality life*. New York: Human Sciences Press.

This book is written as a primer to help divorced fathers to understand what they are going through, how their children are affected, and how to reconstruct their lives. Topics covered include psychological and social changes faced by fathers; understanding children and the effects of divorce; how to anticipate children's problems and how to deal with them; custody; legal issues; and managing a household.

Stuart, I. R., & Abt, L. E. (Eds.). (1981). *Children of separation and divorce: Management and treatment*. New York: Van Nostrand Reinhold.

This book, divided into four parts is a collection of articles that deal with matters of child management and treatment of children of divorce. The first section examines the legal rights and responsibilities regarding children of divorced parents and the attitude of courts and their staff. Part II explores the emotional and psychological factors involved in understanding and providing for these children. The third part includes chapters on different child management problems growing out of divorce and separation. The final section examines treatment within the family unit.

Wallerstein, J. S., & Kelly, J. B. (1980). *Surviving the breakup: How children and parents cope with divorce*. New York: Basic Books.

The California Children of Divorce Project is described in this book. Findings at the time of initial separation, 1 year later, and 5 years later are discussed in detail. The authors look at the reactions of parents, children, and school personnel at all three time periods. The chapter on how children responded to their parents' divorces is an exceptionally good one. Using developmental theory, Wallerstein and Kelly describe the reactions of the children in their study according to their developmental stage. Another excellent chapter to help understand the process of divorce and its ramifications is the one on the implications of their findings.

Postdivorce Families

Hansen, J. C. (Ed.) (1982). *Therapy with remarriage families.* Rockville, MD: Aspen Systems Corporation.

Information and techniques are provided for the therapist who is working with family members going through the remarriage cycle. Articles have been arranged according to the temporal sequence of this process. Several articles look at the concerns and needs of children and adults in dealing with the losses they encounter in the separation process. Others explore concepts and techniques to assist the remarried family in resolving problems.

Sager, C. J., Brown, H. S., Crohn, H., Engel, T., Rodstein, E., & Walker, L. (1983). *Treating the remarried family.* New York: Brunner/Mazel.

This comprehensive book is a must for the mental health professional who is working with remarried families. The authors examine the remarried (REM) family on three levels: family systems, life cycle, and intrapsychic. This well-organized volume discusses in great detail the theory, structure, treatment, special issues, and prevention in dealing with this population. Case examples are well utilized. An appendix of forms and checklists for the clinician to use is included.

Visher, E. B., & Visher, J. S. (1979). *Stepfamilies: A guide to working with stepparents and stepchildren.* New York: Brunner/Mazel.

The Vishers help those in the mental health field realize the uniqueness of stepfamilies and how to help them. The first three chapters discuss the cultural and structural characteristics of stepfamilies and the research done on them. The rest of the book looks at different constellations of family members in stepfamilies. The authors explore what difficulties to expect and how to deal with them as a therapist.

Visher, E. B., & Visher, J. S. (1982). *How to win as a stepfamily.* New York: Dembner Books.

In this book, the Vishers cover mainly the same material as in *Stepfamilies: A Guide to Working with Stepparents and Stepchildren.* The difference lies in the audience for which the book has been written—stepfamilies themselves. The authors do an excellent job of explaining stepfamilies and the difficulties they face. Included in these difficulties are dealing with former spouses; grandparents of remarriage; legal issues; and helping children adjust. The Vishers have succeeded in normalizing stepfamily interactions. Information and suggestions are given on how to make a stepfamily work. References for stepparents and children are included at the end of the book.

Weiss, R. S. (1979). *Going it alone: The family life and social situation of the single parent.* New York: Basic Books.

Through interviews of over 200 single parents and about 40 children of single parents, Weiss describes what it is like to be raising children alone. Much information is given; at the same time, a real understanding of the single-parent situation is shown. The following topics are covered: how one becomes a single parent; the way the household is structured and how it operates; relationships with children and ex-spouses; organization of social lives; the strengths and vulnerabilities in being a single parent; and ways in which single parents manage. The book is filled with quotations and examples from Weiss's interviews. This is a good book for both the mental health professional and the single parent.

Schools

Allers, R. D. (1982). *Divorce, children, and the school.* Princeton, NJ: Princeton Books.

If the therapist plans on involving the school as part of the therapeutic program, this book will prove to be most helpful. The first half of the book describes both the child's and parents' experience of divorce. The role of the school is described in the last half. The role of the teacher is explored in relation to what would be helpful and what wouldn't. Allers also describes a program to be led by mental health professionals to help children of divorce in the school. A bibliography for children and adults is included.

Theory, Therapy, and Research

Ahrons, C. R. (1983). Divorce: Before, during, and after. In H. I. McCubbin & C. R. Figley (Eds.), *Stress and the family: Coping with normative transitions.* New York: Brunner/Mazel.

Divorce is conceptualized as a normal family transition in this chapter. Ahrons introduces the concept of the binuclear family as a useful family model. Through a case example, the author reviews the stressors involved with each phase in the divorce process and suggests functional and dysfunctional coping patterns at each stage. The five transitions are (1) individual cognition, (2) family metacognition, (3) separation, (4) family reorganization, and (5) family redefinition. The chapter ends with implications for counselors and therapists.

Albrecht, S. L. (1980). Reactions and adjustments to divorce: Differences in the experiences of males and females. *Family Relations, 29,* 599–68.

Albrecht reviewed the reactions of 500 male and female divorced individuals to the divorce experience and the adjustments made. Differences due to gender were found, especially in the areas of stress, property settlement, changes in social participation, and effects on income.

Cherlin, A. J. (1981). *Marriage, divorce, remarriage.* Cambridge, MA: Harvard University Press.

The author examines overall trends in the United States over the last several decades in relation to marriage, divorce, and remarriage. He first examines the demographic data and then outlines the trends. Cherlin continues with explanations for these trends for each decade from the 1950s to the 1980s. Consequences of these trends for spouses, parents, and children are then explored. In his last chapter, Cherlin looks at differences in family patterns of black families and white families.

Espenshade, T. J. (1979). The economic consequences of divorce. *Journal of Marriage and the Family, 41*, 615–625.

Espenshade does an excellent job of summarizing the recent research on the economic consequences of divorce for husbands, wives, and children. One important finding is that the economic status of wives typically gets worse after divorce, while that of the husbands improves. The children's economic well-being is dependent upon which parent they live with. The author analyzes why this is so and discusses policy implications of the findings.

Frederico, J. (1979). The marital termination period in the divorce adjustment process. *Journal of Divorce, 3*(2), 93–106.

This articles explores the dynamics of a couple during the period immediately prior to the decision to divorce. The author's contribution to the field lies in his concept of a marital "point of no return" in relation to deciding to divorce. An excellent discussion of this concept is included.

Goetting, A. (1981). Divorce outcome research: Issues and perspectives. *Journal of Family Issues, 1*, 350–378.

This is a review of the recent research findings on the effects of divorce on divorcing men and women and their children. The importance of this review lies in using only well-designed studies employing "normal," rather than clinical, subjects and appropriate control groups. One major observation from this article is that family discord may be a more important predictor of divorce than marital structure.

Goldsmith, J. (1982). The postdivorce family system. In F. Walsh (Ed.), *Normal family processes*. New York: Guilford Press.

Using general systems theory, Goldsmith identifies the processes and patterns in postdivorce families. The main contribution of this chapter lies in viewing the postdivorce family as one that is normal, functional, and reorganizing. The author breaks down the family into structural subsystems and discusses working with each one.

Isaacs, M. (1982). Helping mom fail: A case of a stalemated divorcing process. *Family Process, 21*, 225–234.

This article describes a systems approach to the problem of a symptomatic child whose parents are separated. Background material is given, followed by a case example elucidating a systemic intervention.

Jacobson, G. F. (1983). *The multiple crisis of material separation and divorce*. New York: Grune & Stratton.

Following a review of the literature, the author describes a study of 159 females and 79 males subdivided into three groups: married/discussing separation; separated and divorced within the previous 14 months; separated and divorced more than 14 months. Subjects had all sought professional help. Data are reported on the relationship of gender, time, age, the presence of children, relationships with ex-spouses, and social relationships to the mental health of the subjects.

Kaslow, F. W. (1981). Divorce and divorce therapy. In A. S. Gurman & D. P. Kniskern (Eds.), *Handbook of family therapy*. New York: Brunner/Mazel.

In this chapter, Kaslow gives an overview of divorce. Topics covered include divorce statistics; factors that lead to divorce; various models of stages of the divorce process; the impact of divorce on children; intervention strategies; research on divorce therapy; and training of the divorce therapist.

Kaslow, F. W. (1984). Divorce: An evolutionary process of change in the family system. *Journal of Divorce, 7*(3), 21–39.

Kaslow explores divorce from a combination of perspectives: family systems, the individual life cycle, and stage theories of development. The choice of treatment varies according to where one is in the divorce process, one's ego strength, one's cognitive functioning, and available social and resource networks. Kaslow includes an excellent chart of stages, feelings, actions and tasks, and the most appropriate therapeutic interventions. Case vignettes are also presented to elaborate Kaslow's thinking further.

Kitson, G. C., & Raschke, H. J. (1981). Divorce research: What we know; what we need to know. *Journal of Divorce, 4*(3), 1–37.

Kitson and Raschke explore the divorce process through an extensive review of the literature. The main focus is on antecedents and consequences of divorce. They examine the sociological and psychological factors, the causes, and various theoretical perspectives of divorce. Much information is shared in this clearly written review, with an excellent bibliography at the end.

Kitson, G. C., & Sussman, M. B. (1982). Marital complaints, demographic characteristics, and symptoms of mental distress in divorce. *Journal of Marriage and the Family, 44*, 87–101.

This articles describes a study examining divorced persons' perceptions of their reasons for divorcing. Results are compared to those of Goode's (1956) study. Goode's study identified more reasons as instrumental, while more expressive reasons were given in the current study. Major differences between men and women are also reported.

Kressel, K., & Keutsch, M. (1977). Divorce therapy: An in-depth survey of therapists' views. *Family Process, 16*, 413–443.

With the use of in-depth interviews, the authors discuss therapists' views on the criteria for a constructive divorce, obstacles that get in the way of constructive divorce, and strategies used in divorce therapy. Techniques fall into one of three categories. Reflexive strategies are those used to help the therapist better understand the clients' situation and to join with them. Contextual interventions are those used to create the climate needed for decision making. Substantive interventions include those that are intended to produce a resolution. Different strategies under each of the three categories are discussed.

Levinger, G., & Moles, O. C. (Eds.). (1979). *Divorce and separation: Context, causes, and consequences.* New York: Basic Books.

This book is a comprehensive collection of often-cited articles to help one better understand divorce and its ramifications. The wide range of topics in this volume include perspectives on marital dissolution; social and psychological determinants of breakup; economic determinants; consequences and effects on the ex-spouses; and effects on families and children.

Raschke, H. J. (in press). Divorce. In M. Sussman & S. Steinmetz (Eds.), *Handbook of marriage and the family.* New York: Plenum.

Here is a review and analysis of the "state of the art" of the separation/divorce literature as of the early 1980s. This comprehensive chapter covers the contexts, correlates, and causes; consequences for and adjustment of both adults and children; legal aspects; and policy implications. This work is an excellent place to start in order to find where to read further in the key areas of divorce. The extensive bibliography, as well as the thorough literature review, makes this chapter a must to read.

Rice, Joy K., & Rice, D. G. (1986). *Living through divorce: A developmental approach to therapy.* New York: Guilford Press.

Although written by practicing therapists, this book stresses theory as well as technique. The authors believe that divorce needs to be integrated theoretically in the individual, marital, and family life cycles. They also stress that ". . .a therapist [who] thoroughly understands the processes of narcissistic injury and role disorientation accompanying divorce. . .is in a better position to help the client accomplish the related therapeutic and developmental tasks: ego reparation and role restructuring" (p. xi). This is one of the most comprehensive texts on divorce therapy.

Salts, C. (1979). Divorce process: Integration of theory. *Journal of Divorce, 2*(3), 233–240.

In this paper, Salts compares several models of the divorce process, including those of Kessler, Bohannon, Wiseman, Froiland and Hozeman, Levy and Joffe, Waller, and Weiss. Salts concludes that the models are not in conflict with one another. Implications for counseling are discussed. A chart showing the comparisons is included.

Sprenkle, D. H. (Ed.). (1985). *Divorce Therapy.* New York: Haworth.

This collection of articles is organized around therapeutic interventions related to the following stages of divorce: (1) divorce decision-making; (2) restructuring-therapy for children, mediation, and custody; and (3) postdivorce recovery and remarriage. This book also contains a helpful overview article, a paper on criteria for a constructive divorce, and a comprehensive annotated bibliography. The book is one of the few general texts on divorce therapy.

Sprenkle, D. H., & Cyrus, C. L. (1983). Abandonment: The stress of sudden divorce. In C. R. Figley & M. I. McCubbin (Eds.), *Stress and the family: Coping with catastrophe.* New York: Brunner/Mazel.

As illustrated in this chapter, the sudden divorce has its own unique circumstances with which one must deal. The authors examine, both theoretically and practically, one specific type of divorce—abandonment. Areas covered include (1) the meaning of emotional abandonment, (2) why this stressor is so painful for all involved, (3) factors determining the level of stress experienced, (4) constructive and destructive coping methods, (5) useful interventions, (6) the constructive potential for the survivor, and (7) gaps in our knowledge and recommendations for future research.

Sprenkle, D. H., & Storm, C. L. (1983). Divorce therapy outcome research: A substantive and methodological review. *Journal of Marital and Family Therapy, 9,* 239–258.

The authors provide a substantive and methodological review of 22 empirical studies related to divorce therapy. The studies are divided into the following six areas: (1) mediation, (2) conciliation courts counseling, (3) consumer evaluation, (4) divorce groups, (5) separation techniques, and (6) marriage counseling with divorce as an unintended outcome. An excellent chart comparing the studies is included. There is strong evidence for the superiority of mediation to traditional adversary methods in custody and visitation disputes. There appears to be an increase in the number of reconciliations in the short term for those using conciliation counseling. Due to the weakness of the methodologies of many of the studies, other conclusions remain tentative.

Storm, C. L., & Sprenkle, D. H. (1982). Individual treatment in divorce therapy: A critique of an assumption. *Journal of Divorce, 6,* 87–97.

The authors critically examine the commonly held maxim that the treatment of choice in divorce is working with the individual. Conjoint and family treatment are explored as alternatives. A model of divorce therapy using all three modes of treatment is offered. Storm and Sprenkle propose conjoint and/or family treatment as most effect in the decision-making and restructuring stages. Individual treatment is the most appropriate for the recovery phase.

Weltner, J. S. (1982). A structural approach to the single-parent family. *Family Process, 21,* 203–210.

This article focuses on the problems implicit in the structure of a family unit that includes one parent and at least one child. Specific therapeutic approaches are discussed. Two priorities examined are support of the executive system's functioning and establishment of generational boundaries.

Women's Issues

Colleta, S. D. (1983). Stressful lives: The situation of divorced mothers and their children. *Journal of Divorce, 6*(3), 19–31.

In this study, 72 divorced and married mothers were interviewed. The results suggest that the negative situations of divorced mothers and children are largely due to the low income of divorced mothers, rather than the fathers' absence.

Langelier, R., & Deckert, P. (1980). Divorce counseling guidelines for the late divorced female. *Journal of Divorce, 3*(4), 403–411.

Based on research, this article offers divorce counseling guidelines for females who divorce after being married a minimum of 20 years. Guidelines are given in the six following areas: emotions, divorce grounds, finances and budgeting, children, life style changes, and independence.

Robertson, C. (1980). *Divorce and decision making: A woman's guide.* Chicago: Follett.

This is an excellent how-to book for women going through the divorce process. It is full of information, activities, and questions that a woman needs to ask as she goes through a divorce. Part I deals with emotional supports, values, plans for the future, and decision-making ability. Part II deals with specific decisions that need to be made in the following areas: legal help, the divorce settlement, children, money, careers, and social life. The last chapter discusses the use of assertiveness in implementing decisions. An excellent bibliography and list of resources are included at the end of the book.

Women in Transition. (1975). *Women in transition: A feminist handbook on separation and divorce.* New York: Scribner's.

Here is another how-to book for women in transition, including divorcées. It is geared to middle- and working-class women. Although in a few areas it is outdated, it is packed with down-to-earth information on the following areas: emotional support, children, the law, financial resources, living space, and taking care of oneself. The section on the law gives much needed information. The section on financial resources is another excellent one; it includes what to do if on welfare, how to get a job, sexism at work, educational resources, and financial resources (such as savings, loans, and insurance). At the end of the book is a national list of centers where women may go for help.

REFERENCES

Ahrons, C. R. (1979). The binuclear family: Two households, one family. *Alternative Lifestyles, 2*, 499–515.

Ahrons, C. R. (1980). Divorce: A crisis of family transition and change. *Family Relations, 4*, 533–540.

Association of Family and Conciliation Courts (1982). *Joint custody: A new way of being related.* (Available from Association of Family and Conciliation Courts, % Nova University Law Center, 3100 S.W. Ninth Ave., Fort Lauderdale, FL 33315.)

Bernard, J. M., & Hackney, H. (1983). *Untying the knot: A guide to civilized divorce.* Minneapolis: Winston Press.

Bernstein, B. (1977). Lawyer and counselor as an interdisciplinary team: Preparing the father for custody. *Journal of Marriage and Family Counseling, 3*, 29–40.

Bohannan, P. (1970). The six stations of divorce. In P. Bohannan (Ed.), *Divorce and after.* Garden City, NY: Doubleday.

Bohannan, P. (1971). Divorce chains, households of remarriage, and multiple divorces. In P. Bohannan (Ed.), *Divorce and after: An analysis of the emotional and social problems of divorce.* New York: Anchor Books.

Brown, E. M. (1976). Divorce counseling. In D. H. Olson (Ed.), *Treating relationships.* Lake Mills, IA: Graphic.

Brown, E. M. (1985). The comprehensive divorce treatment center: the divorce and marital stress clinic model . In D. H. Sprenkle (Ed.), *Divorce therapy.* New York: Haworth Press.

Brown, M. D. (1985). Creating new realities for the newly divorced: A structural strategic approach for divorce therapy with an individual. In D. H. Sprenkle (Ed.), *Divorce therapy.* New York: Haworth Press.

Brown, P. & Manela, R. (1977). Client satisfaction with marital and divorce counseling. *Family Coordinator, 26,* 294–303.

Cantor, D. W., & Drake, E. A. (1983). *Divorced parents and their children: A guide for mental health professionals.* New York: Springer.

Cantrell, R. (1985). *Defining constructive adjustment to divorce: I. Comparison between groups of divorcees; II. Comparison of therapists and divorcees.* Unpublished doctoral dissertation, Purdue University.

Cohen, S. N. (1985). Divorce mediation: An introduction. In D. H. Sprenkle (Ed.), *Divorce therapy.* New York: Haworth Press.

Coogler, O. J. (1978). *Structural mediation in divorce settlement.* Lexington, MA: Lexington Books.

Crosbie-Burnett, M., & Ahrons, C. R. (1985). From divorce to remarriage: Implications for therapy with families in transition. In D. H. Sprenkle (Ed.), *Divorce therapy.* New York: Haworth Press.

Eno, M. M. (1985). Sibling relationships in families of divorce. In D. H. Sprenkle (Ed.), *Divorce therapy.* New York: Haworth Press.

Erikson, E. K. (1963). *Childhood and society.* (2nd ed.). New York: Norton.

Fisher, B. (1976). *Identifying and meeting needs of formerly married people through a divorce adjustment seminar.* (Available from Family Relations Learning Center, 450 Ord Drive, Boulder, CO 80303.)

Fisher, B. (1981). *Rebuilding: When your relationship ends.* San Luis Obispo, CA: Impact.

Fisher, E. O. (Ed.). (1982) *Impact of divorce on the extended family.* New York: Haworth Press.

Folberg, J. (Ed.). (1984). *Joint custody and sharing parenting.* Portland, OR: Association of Family and Conciliation Courts.

Francke, L. B. (1983). *Growing up divorced.* New York: Linden Press.

Froiland, D. J., & Hozeman, T. L. (1977). Counseling for constructive divorce. *Personnel and Guidance Journal, 55,* 525–529.

Galper, M. (1978). *Co-parenting: Sharing your child equally.* Philadelphia: Running Press.

Gardner, R. A. (1971). *The boys and girls book about divorce.* New York: Bantam Books.

Gardner, R. A. (1976). *Psychotherapy with children of divorce.* New York: Jason Aronson.

Gardner, R. A. (1978). *The boys and girls book about one-parent families.* New York: Bantam Books.

Gardner, R. A. (1982). *The boys and girls book about stepfamilies.* New York: Bantam Books.

Glick P. (1984). Marriage, divorce, and living arrangements: Prospective changes. *Journal of Family Issues, 5,* 7–26.

Goode, W. J. (1956). *After divorce.* Glencoe, IL: Free Press.

Granvold, D. K. (1983). Structured separation for marital treatment and decision-making. *Journal of Marital and Family Therapy, 9,* 403–412.

Greene, B. L., Lee, R. R., & Lustig, N. (1973). Transient structured distance as a maneuver in marital therapy. *Family Coordinator, 20,* 15–22.

Gurman, A. S. & Kniskern, D. P. (1978). Research on marital and family therapy: Progress, perspective and prospect. In S. Garfield & A. Bergin (Eds.), *Handbook of psychotherapy and behavior change* (2nd ed.). New York: Wiley.

Gurman, A. S., & Kniskern, D. P. (1981). Editor's note to "Divorce and divorce therapy." In A. S. Gurman & D. P. Kniskern (Eds.), *Handbook of family therapy.* New York: Brunner/Mazel.

Gurman, A., Kniskern, D., & Pinsof, W. (1986). Research on the process and outcome of marital and family therapy. In S. Garfield & A. Bergin (Eds.), *Handbook of psychotherapy and behavior change* (3rd ed.). New York: Wiley.

Hansen, J. C. (Ed.). (1982). *Therapy with remarriage families.* Rockville, MD: Aspen Systems Corporation.

Haynes, J. M. (1981). *Divorce mediation: A practical guide for therapists and counselors.* New York: Springer.

Hetherington, E. M., Cox, M., & Cox, R. (1981). The aftermath of divorce. In E. M. Hetherington & R. D. Parke (Eds.), *Contemporary readings in child psychology.* New York: McGraw-Hill.

Hill, R. (1949). *Families under stress.* New York: Harper Press.

Holley, P. (1980). *An analysis of divorce adjustment measures.* (Available from Department of Social Sciences, Southwestern Oklahoma State University, Weatherford, OK 73096.)

Howell, R. J., & Toepke, K. E. (1984). Summary of the child custody laws for the fifty states. *American Journal of Family Therapy, 12,* 56–60.

Irving, H. H. (1980). *Divorce mediation: A rational alternative to the adversary system.* New York: Universe Books.

Irving, H. H., Benjamin, M., Bohm, P., & MacDonald, G. (1981). *A study of conciliation counseling in the Family Court of Toronto: Implications for socio-legal practice.* Toronto: Department of National Health and Welfare and the Ontario Ministry of the Attorney General.

Isaacs, M. (1982). Helping mom fail: A case of a stalemated divorcing process. *Family Process, 21,* 225–234.

Janis, I. L. (1983). Short-term counseling: Guidelines based on recent research. New Haven, CT: Yale University Press.

Janis, I. L., & Mann, L. (1977). *Decision making: A psychological analysis of conflict, choice, and commitment.* New York: Free Press.

Johnson, S. M. (1977). *First person singular.* Philadelphia: J. B. Lippincott.

Kaslow, F. W. (1981). Divorce and divorce therapy. In A. S. Gurman & D. P. Kniskern (Eds.), *Handbook of family therapy.* New York: Brunner/Mazel.

Kaslow, F. W. (1984). Divorce: An evolutionary process of change in the family system. *Journal of Divorce, 7,* 21–39.

162   Divorce Therapy

Kaslow, F. W., & Steinberg, J. (1981). Ethical divorce therapy and divorce proceedings: A psycho-legal perspective. In L. L'Abate (Ed.), *Values, ethics, legalities, and the family therapist*. Rockville, MD: Aspen Systems Corporation.

Kessler, S. (1975). *The American way of divorce: Prescriptions for change*. Chicago: Nelson-Hall.

Kitson, G. C. (1982). Attachment to the spouse in divorce: A scale and its applications. *Journal of Marriage and the Family, 44*, 379–393.

Kitson, G. C., & Raschke, H. J. (1981). Divorce research: What we know; what we need to know. *Journal of Divorce, 4*(3), 1–37.

Krantzler, M. (1974). *Creative divorce*. New York: Signet.

Kressel, K., Jaffee, N., Tuchman, B., Watson, C., & Deutsch, M. (1980). A typology of divorcing couples: Implications for mediation and the divorce process. *Family Process, 19*, 101–116.

Kübler-Ross, E, (1969). *On death and dying*. New York: Macmillan.

Kurdek, L. A. (Ed.). (1983). *New directions for child development: Children and divorce*. San Francisco: Jossey-Bass.

Lee, B. E. (1979). Consumer evaluation of a family court service. *Conciliation Courts Review, 17*, 49–54.

Levinger, G. (1976). A social psychological perspective on divorce. *Journal of Social Issues, 32*, 21–47.

Newman, G. (1981). *101 ways to be a long distance super-dad*. Mountain View, CA: Blossom Valley Press.

Nichols, W. C. (1984). Therapeutic needs of children in family system reorganization. *Journal of Divorce, 7*, 23–44.

Nichols, W. C. (1985). Family therapy with children of divorce. In D. H. Sprenkle (Ed.), *Divorce therapy*. New York: Haworth Press.

Oakland, T. (1984). *Divorced fathers: Reconstructing a quality life*. New York: Human Sciences Press.

Olson, D. H., Russell, C. S., & Sprenkle, D. H. (1980). Marital and family therapy: A decade review. *Journal of Marriage and the Family, 42*, 973–993.

Pearson, J., & Thoennes, N. (1982). The benefits outweigh the costs. *Family Advocate, 4*, 26–32.

Price-Bonham, S., & Balswick, J. O. (1980). The noninstitutions: Divorce, desertion, and remarriage. *Journal of Marriage and the Family, 42*, 959–972.

Raschke, H. J. (1982). *Divorce and marital separation*. Unpublished manuscript, Department of Psychology and Sociology, Austin College, Sherman, TX.

Reiss, I. L. (1980). *Family systems in America*. New York: Holt, Rinehart & Winston.

Rice, J. K., & Rice, D. G. (1986). Living through divorce: A developmental approach to divorce therapy. New York: Guilford Press.

Rofes, E. (Ed.). (1982). *The kid's book of divorce: By, for and about kids*. New York: Vintage Books.

Sager, C. J., Brown, H. S., Crohn, H., Engel, T., Rodstein, E., & Walker, L. (1983). *Treating the remarried family*. New York: Brunner/Mazel.

Salts, C. J. (1979). Divorce process: Integration of theory. *Journal of Divorce, 2*, 233–240.

Salts, C. J. (1985). Divorce stage theory and therapy: Therapeutic implications throughout the divorcing process. In D. H. Sprenkle (Ed.), *Divorce therapy*. New York: Haworth Press.

Saposnek, D. T. (1983). *Mediating child custody disputes*. San Francisco: Jossey-Bass.

Shapiro, T. J. & Caplan, M. S. (1983). *Parting sense: A couple's guide to divorce mediation*. Lutherville, MD: Greenspring.

Smart, L. S. (1977). An application of Erikson's theory to the recovery-from-divorce process. *Journal of Divorce, 1*, 67–79.

Smoke, J. (1976). *Growing through divorce*. Irving, CA: Harvest House.

Spanier, G. B. & Casto, R. F. (1979). Adjustment to separation and divorce: An analysis of 50 case studies. *Journal of Divorce, 2*, 241–253.

Spanier, G. B., & Lewis, R. A. (1980). Marital quality: A review of the seventies. *Journal of Marriage and the Family, 42*, 825–839.

Sprenkle, D. H. (1985). Introduction: divorce therapy. In D. H. Sprenkle (Ed.), *Divorce therapy*. New York: Haworth Press.

Sprenkle, D. H., & Cantrell, R. G. (1986). *Attorney conceptions of constructive divorce*. Unpublished manuscript, Purdue University.

Sprenkle, D. H., & Cyrus, C. (1983). Abandonment: The sudden stress of divorce. In C. R. Figley & H. I. McCubbin (Eds.), *Stress and the family* (Vol. 2). New York: Brunner/Mazel.

Sprenkle, D. H., & Storm, C. L. (1983). Divorce therapy outcome research: A substantive and methodological review. *Journal of Marital and Family Therapy, 9*, 239–258.

Storm, C. L., & Sprenkle, D. H. (1982). Individual treatment in divorce therapy: A critique of an assumption. *Journal of Divorce, 5*, 87–97.

Storm, C. L., Sprenkle, D. H., & Williamson, W. (1985). Innovative divorce approaches developed by counselors, conciliators, mediators, and educators. In R. Levant (Ed.), *Psychoeducational approaches to family therapy*. New York: Springer.

Stuart, I. R., Abt, L. E. (Eds.). (1981). *Children of separation and divorce: Management and treatment*. New York: Van Nostrand Reinhold.

Sutton, P. (1983). *Defining divorce adjustment: A study of marriage and family therapists' criteria for constructive long-term adjustment to divorce*. Unpublished doctoral dissertation, Purdue University.

Sutton, P., & Sprenkle, D. (1985). Criteria for a constructive divorce: Theory and research to guide the practitioner. In D. H. Sprenkle (Ed.), *Divorce therapy*. New York: Haworth Press.

Thompson, L., & Spanier, G. (1983). The end of marriage and acceptance of marital termination. *Journal of Marriage and the Family, 45*, 103–113.

Toomin, M. K. (1972). Structured separation with counseling: A therapeutic approach for couples in conflict. *Family Process, 11*, 299–310.

Turner, N. W. (1980). Divorce in mid-life: Clinical implications and applications. In W. Norman & T. J. Scaramella (Eds.), *Mid-life: Developmental and clinical issues*. New York: Brunner/Mazel.

Turner, N. W. (1985). Divorce: Dynamics of decision therapy. In D. H. Sprenkle (Ed.), *Divorce therapy*. New York: Haworth Press.

Visher, E. B., & Visher, J. S. (1979). *Stepfamilies: A guide to working with stepparents and stepchildren*. New York: Brunner/Mazel.

Visher, E. B., & Visher, J. S. (1982). *How to win as a stepfamily*. New York: Dembner Books.

Volgy, S. S., & Everett, C. A. (1985). Systemic assessment criteria for joint custody. In D. H. Sprenkle (Ed.), *Divorce therapy*. New York: Haworth Press.

Waller, W. W. (1967). *The old and the new: Divorce and adjustment* (3rd ed.). Carbondale, IL: Southern Illinois University Press.

Wallerstein, J. S., & Kelly, J. B. (1980). *Surviving the breakup: How children and parents cope with divorce.* New York: Basic Books.

Weed, J. A. (1980). *National estimates of marriage dissolution and survivorship: United States.* Vital and Health Statistics: Series 3, Analytical Studies, No. 19 (Department of Health and Human Services publication number 81-1403) Hyattsville, MD: National Center for Health Statistics.

Weiss, R. S. (1975). *Marital separation.* New York: Basic Books.

Weiss, R. S. (1979). *Going it alone: The family life and social situation of the single parent.* New York: Basic Books.

Weisman, R. S. (1975). Crisis theory and the process of divorce. *Social Casework, 56,* 205–212.

Weltner, J. S. (1982). A structural approach to the single-parent family. *Family Process 21,* 203–210.

Wong, R. (1986). *Defining constructive adjustment to divorce: Comparison of Protestant, Catholic and Jewish clergy.* Unpublished doctoral dissertation, University of Washington.

7

PREMARITAL COUNSELING

DENNIS A. BAGAROZZI

In 1932, the first premarital education program was established at the Merrill-Palmer Institute (Mudd, Freeman, & Rose, 1941). Since then, premarital counseling programs have proliferated throughout the United States in order to meet the needs of various populations, such as dating couples (Schlein, 1971), couples living with their parents (Rolfe, 1977b), the handicapped and disabled (Stallings, 1968; Walker, 1977), couples where one of the partners is a minor (Shonick, 1972), teenage couples (Reiner & Edwards, 1974; Rolfe, 1976; Rue, 1972), West Point cadets (Glendening & Wilson, 1972), members of particular religious denominations (Apple, 1970; Boike, 1977; Gangsei, 1971; Microys & Bader, 1977; Oates & Rowatt, 1975; Rolfe, 1977a; Wright, 1977), college students (D'Augelli, Deyss, Guerney, Hershenberg, & Sbordfsky, 1974, Hinkle & Moore, 1971; Jackson, 1972; Meadows & Taplin, 1970; Miller, 1971; Van Zoost, 1973), and the general public (Bernstein, 1977; Bienvenu, 1974; Freeman, 1965; Holoubek & Holoubek, 1973; Holoubek *et al.*, 1974; Levine & Brodsky, 1949; Mace, 1972; McRae, 1975; Ridley, Avery, Harrell, Leslie, & O'Connor, 1979; Rolfe, 1973; Ross, 1977).

While the long-term effects of premarital counseling have yet to be determined, some states have passed laws requiring all couples with a member under the age of 18 who are applying for marriage licenses to receive some type of premarital counseling (Ehrentraut, 1975; Elkin, 1977; Leigh, 1976; Shonick, 1972).

Recently, a comprehensive review of contemporary premarital counseling programs in the United States has been published (Bagarozzi & Rauen, 1981). Although over 50 published programs are surveyed, only 13 of these studies have used standardized procedures and appropriate outcome measures.

THEORETICAL CONSIDERATIONS

If one conceptualizes the family as a continually developing, goal-directed living system, the premarital dyad can be thought of as the foundation upon which the family system is built. In order for any system to remain viable, it must develop mechanisms to regulate the flow of information that crosses its boundaries. It also must manage the information that is exchanged within the family system itself (i.e., between and among its component members). The system must be able to use positive- and negative-feedback processes to its advantage, if it is to survive. Positive feedback enables the system to change outmoded structures and processes that have outlived their usefulness. Negative feedback, on the other hand, is used to preserve those structures and functions that are necessary to maintain stability. Both feedback processes are essential and can be thought of as acting in concert to help the system achieve its desired ends.

The premarital dyad has been shown to progress through six stages of development (Lewis, 1972):

1. *The process of perceiving similarities.* During the first stage of relationship development, prospective mates are attracted to the relationship because similarities along certain salient dimensions are perceived. In addition to perceiving similarities in the areas of age, race, religion, social factors, and economic factors, the empirical literature cited by Lewis (1972) supports his contention that perceiving similarities in values, interests, and personality also facilitates the relationship's progression.

2. *The process of achieving pair rapport.* As the relationship develops, rapport between the members of the dyad should increase. This is evidenced by the ease with which the couple communicates, the reciprocal exchange of positive evaluations, and the perceived validation of each individual by the partner.

3. *The process of inducing self-disclosure.* This process is seen both as an outcome of increased pair rapport and as an essential prerequisite for later stages of dyadic development.

4. *The process of role taking.* Role taking is comprised of the following components: the ability to decenter, to reverse perspectives, and to experience the world as does one's partner. Role taking consists of both affective components (empathy) and cognitive components (decentering and perspective reversal).

5. *The process of achieving interpersonal role fit.* Lewis (1972) states that the meshing of two distinct persons (e.g., individual personalities, social roles, and marriage-specific need hierarchies) into one interpersonal system is probably the most obvious requirement that confronts the premarital dyad. Lewis (1972) conceptualizes this process as operating within three related yet distinct modes: observed similarity of personalities, role complementarity, and need complementarity. In all three of these areas, it is

incumbent upon the couple to assimilate and accommodate their roles in some mutually satisfying way.

6. *The process of achieving dyadic crystallization.* Dyadic crystallization is a process involving the following components: (a) progressive involvement, (b) dyadic functioning, (c) boundary establishment, (d) pair commitment, and (e) couple identity formation.

Each stage of the process outlined by Lewis (1972) consists of specific developmental tasks that must be completed successfully if the couple is to continue as a unit.

Lewis's (1972) presentation is schematic and does not allow one to gain an intimate view of the internal dynamics of the evolving relationship, especially those aspects of dyadic functioning having to do with the development of rules that are to govern the marital system. Systems' rules usually evolve through nonverbal behavioral negotiations, which are rarely, if ever, openly discussed between the prospective spouses.

KEY CONCEPTS AND THEORETICAL ISSUES

There are a variety of ways to conceptualize marital choice and mate selection. Some of the more common theories used to explain the mate selection process in Western society include theories of complementary needs (Winch, 1974), value consensus and homogamy (Kerckhoff, 1974), process (e.g., Bolton, 1961; Rapoport & Rapoport, 1968; Reiss, 1971), development (Lewis, 1972) and stimulus–value–role theories of marital choice (Murstein, 1976). In this section, the mate selection process is outlined according to a cognitive–behavioral–systems model that I use in my own work with couples.

The Ideal Spouse

According to this cognitive–behavioral–systems viewpoint, mate selection is seen as a cognitive matching process wherein individuals actively seek out and attempt to marry persons who they believe will behave in accordance with an internal cognitive image or model of their ideal spouse. This matching process takes place at both conscious and unconscious levels of awareness. Associated with this ideal image are various affective states and role behaviors that the ideal is expected to enact. When a prospective mate's behavior is perceived to be in accord with one's ideal, intrapersonal and dyadic equilibria are simultaneously maintained. However, when one's partner's behavior deviates too drastically from one's internal representation, disequilibrium results. When this occurs, the person will behave in ways designed to restore congruence between the partner's behavior and the internal ideal. Frequently, coercion is used by a partner to force his/her mate to behave in ways that conform to the ideal. The internal cognitive ideal can be thought of as a composite structure that evolves over time. The ideal has both conscious and unconscious components. It is a result of the person's perceptions, interpretations of events, attributions, and reconstructions of affectively laden experiences and relationships with significant others that have been internalized. These experiences give rise to prototypical models for future relationships (e.g., man–woman, husband–wife, father–son, father–daughter, mother–son, mother–daughter, sibling–sibling, etc.). It is important to keep in mind that it is the relationships between the person and significant others (who serve as models for identification) that are introjected, not merely the models themselves.

For most people, the parent of the opposite sex usually serves as a model for the ideal mate, and the parent of the same sex becomes the model for how one is to behave toward his/her mate-to-be. Sometimes, however, parents become negative models. When this occurs, a person may seek an ideal who does not consciously represent the opposite-sex parent. Similarly, one may consciously avoid treating one's partner in the same way that he/she perceived his/her same-sex parent to have treated the parent of the opposite sex. While the most potent models for the ideal spouse come from one's parents, there are a variety of real and fictional persons who can serve as models for the ideal.

The term "ideal" is used here to refer to the composite model that is built from each person's experiences. This ideal represents an enduring model that becomes the standard against which all prospective mates are judged. The ideal represents a more or less complete model, but does not represent perfection. This sought-after ideal possesses predominantly positive and desirable qualities and traits. Negative qualities, when consciously acknowledged, are minimized.

In addition to the cognitive matching that takes place at both conscious and unconscious levels of awareness, another important process takes place throughout the courtship period, which I call "mutual shaping toward the ideal." In this process, both individuals tend to selectively reinforce those behaviors, characteristics, traits, and roles of their mates-to-be that are consistent with their ideals. However, behaviors, characteristics, traits, and roles that are not perceived to be consistent with this ideal are ignored, denied, and defended against if they cannot be assimilated into the ideal. Since these discrepant behaviors are not reinforced, they frequently become extinguished. However, behaviors that are periodically reinforced become resistant to extinction. Behaviors that persist are defended against if they cannot be assimilated into the ideal. Any behaviors, characteristics, traits, or roles will create problems in the relationship if they (1) are resistant to extinction, (2) cannot be assimilated into the ideal, and (3) cannot be defended against because doing so would require reality distortions that are too great. Frequently, punishment and coercion are used to modify these undesirable behaviors and traits. However, punishment tends to be reciprocated (Patterson & Hops, 1972), and the excessive use of coercion may lead to termination of the courtship if more attractive and less punishing alternatives are available. However, if no alternatives are perceived, the punished behavior will be suppressed temporarily. Punishment is not an effective solution, because when the threat of punishment is removed (e.g., after the couple is married), the undesirable behaviors and traits will resurface in more exaggerated form.

In sum, mutual shaping toward the ideal consists of four related processes:

1. Reward for those behaviors, traits, characteristics, and roles that are congruent with one's ideal spousal image.
2. Extinction of behaviors, traits, characteristics, and roles that are not consistent with the ideal.
3. The use of defenses to avoid dealing with behaviors, traits, characteristics, and roles that cannot be assimilated into the ideal.
4. Punishment of behaviors, traits, characteristics, and roles that cannot be assimilated into the ideal or defended against, because doing so would require gross distortions of reality.

It is important to keep in mind that one's ideal is not a static or rigid structure. The ideal is malleable and capable of changing over time by assimilating into itself behaviors and characteristics that are not discrepant from the ideal and by accommodating to external realities.

Internalized Relationship Rules and the Matching Process

Not only do people seek out spouses whom they perceive will closely approximate their internal ideals; they also attempt to find mates who they believe share the same internalized rules concerning husband–wife relationships. Several types of rules have been identified. These include (1) rules of distributive justice governing the exchange process between spouses (Bagarozzi & Wodarski, 1977); (2) rules defining power relationships between spouses in various areas of marriage (Haley, 1963; Watzlawick, Beavin, & Jackson, 1967); and (3) rules for sending and receiving value messages (Strayhorn, 1978). Each of these sets of rules is discussed below.

RULES OF DISTRIBUTIVE JUSTICE AND EXCHANGE

Social exchange formulations about sharing in marital relationships (Bagarozzi & Wodarski, 1977) assume that marital behavior is governed by fixed rules of justice. Exchange theorists assume that spouses evaluate the fairness of conjugal exchanges according to the norms of equitable sharing and distributive justice, and that prolonged perceptions of inequity between spouses lead to marital dissatisfaction. It is important to note that a dissatisifed spouse responds to what he/she perceives to be a violation of the fair exchange system. However, the rules for fair exchange may never have been negotiated explicitly, and it is possible that spouses hold vastly different views about the types of exchange rules that are to govern their system. Recent empirical investigations suggest that equity in interpersonal sharing represents only one form of distributive justice, and that other types of exchange rules (e.g., equality, Marxist sharing, and sharing according to fixed laws) also may be used, depending upon how one perceives the relationship (Bagarozzi, 1983; Lerner, 1974; Shapiro 1975).

Several difficulties can arise between spouses in the area of relationship rules. First, in the early stages of relationship development (e.g., dating, courtship), the type of sharing and exchange engaged in by the couple may be determined by the stage of relationship development as well as by the context of the relationship itself. How each person shares and exchanges during this stage of the relationship may not be a valid predictor of how he/she will behave after marriage.

A shift in spouses' exchange behavior after marriage can be explained in several ways:

1. Premarital exchanges initially are strategically (consciously or unconsciously) designed maneuvers used to "win over" the prospective mate. In this case, the spouse's true exchange orientation is masked.
2. With the change in context and relationship development (from premarried to married), each spouse may begin to apply different rules of exchange. Here, no deception, conscious or unconscious, is planned. Spouses simply hold different expectations for exchanges after marriage.
3. Spouses' exchange orientation may change with the passage of time.

A second class of problems involves difficulties that arise not because spouses apply different rules of exchange to their relationship, but because they perceive their mates not to be sharing according to the rules. For example, a spouse may (1) disagree about the value of his/her inputs relative to those of his/her partner, or (2) disagree about the value of the resources that are being exchanged.

The final class of difficulties arises when spouses are no longer able to provide resources that are valued by their mates or when the resources that spouses have traditionally exchanged are no longer experienced as valued and satisfying, and they are unable to acquire new resources that can be used as exchange commodities.

RULES DEFINING POWER IN THE RELATIONSHIP

The second set of rules governing the relationship between husbands and wives has received much attention from systems theorists (Haley, 1963; Watzlawick *et al.*, 1967). These rules have to do with defining power relationships between spouses in various areas of marriage. The rules of a given relationship can be determined by observing the behavioral interaction patterns between spouses. There are basically three types of interaction patterns: complementary, symmetrical, and parallel.

When a couple is unable to agree upon which set of rules is to govern their relationship, the marriage is restricted (Haley, 1963). According to this viewpoint, marital conflicts center around the following:

1. Disagreement about the rules for living together as a couple—that is, what type of rules the couple will follow in central areas of their relationship (e.g., marital roles, finances, relationships with friends, neighbors, relatives, child rearing, sexual practices, religion, etc.).

2. Disagreement about who is to set the rules for the type of relationship the couple is to have in central areas of their marriage.

3. Conflict over the incompatibility between the first two levels of the relationship—that is, a relationship that is defined in one way on the first level conflicts with the relationship as it is defined on the second level. For example, both husband and wife agree that the husband is to be the dominant figure in the relationship, but the wife continually berates the husband, because he is insufficiently dominant and assertive with her.

4. Conflicts between the metarules that a couple has established for resolving differences between them and the actual rules that the couple uses to resolve these differences. For example, a couple may agree that when there is a problem that cannot be resolved, the husband will make the decision. However, the husband's decision is that his wife should decide how their differences are to be resolved. In this case, conflict arises because the couple is attempting to enforce incompatible rules. The relationship between the spouses is defined in one way at one level, but this conflicts with the definition of the relationship at another level.

RULES FOR SENDING AND RECEIVING VALUE MESSAGES
BETWEEN SPOUSES

Strayhorn (1978) has shown how behaviors exhibited by spouses carry important messages concerning the sender's evaluations of the receiver. For Strayhorn (1978), these messages convey much more to one's mate than the actual pleasurable or displeasurable value of the behaviors themselves. Problems arise whenever the sender's rules and receiver's rules for the same behavioral message do not correspond. Three types of difficulties are identified:

1. *Noncorrespondent rules for value messages.* Here, the receiver's rule for the value message implied in a specific behavior does not correspond to the sender's rule and intention. Therefore the receiver does not get the intended message. For example, the sender's rule may be this: "If you love me, you will show it by being concerned about my personal safety and whereabouts whenever I am late for an appointment." By contrast, the receiver's rule may be this: "If you love me, you will always be prompt for appointments. Whenever I have to wait for you, it is proof that I really don't mean very much to you."

2. *Reliance upon painful channels for communicating value messages.* In this situation, the sender's rules and the receiver's rules do correspond, but the channels necessitate pain on the part of one or both spouses. For example, the sender's rule may be this: "If you love me, you will show it by being concerned when I am sick or hurt and by being jealous of other men/ women when I flirt with them. I, in turn, will show my love for you by being concerned when you are hurt or ill and by being jealous of other men/women." The corresponding receiver's rule may be this: "I will show my love for you by being concerned when you hurt yourself or when you are ill and by being jealous of other men/women. I know that you will show your love for me whenever I am sick or hurt and by being jealous of other men/women."

3. *One spouse's extreme sensitivity to receiving "devalue" messages and inordinate fear of losing value messages that convey love.* For example, a spouse may respond immediately with coercion and retaliation for what he/she perceives to be a devalue message, or a spouse's intense fear of loss of love may drive him/her to resort to ever-increasing and dangerous, painful channels in order to receive value messages.

By this time, the reader has become aware of the complexities involved in the matching process. Not only does one have to find a spouse who fits his/her ideal image; one must find a spouse who shares the same rules for exchange, for power in relationships and for the transmission of value messages that convey love and affection.

Intrapersonal and Interpersonal Homeostasis: The Delicate Balance

The active quest for and ultimate selection of a mate who closely resembles one's ideal is an example of cybernetic goal seeking and mapping. This behavior serves a homeostatic function, because the closer the match is between one's actual spouse and the ideal, the less one is required to modify his/her ideal image. Similar matching along the behavioral and interactional dimensions outlined above also occurs. However, perfect matching rarely occurs, and conflicts develop whenever spouses attempt to impose their own rules or to coerce their mates into behaving in accordance with an internalized ideal.

The redundant interaction patterns that result in connection with such issues, in part, give the couple system its unique character. However, it would be erroneous to conclude that the interaction process that one observes is merely the joint product of each spouse's attempt to impose his/her will. Dicks (1967) has shown through object relations theory how spouses often enter into unconscious collusion in order to protect each other. Collusion begins with the defensive splitting of introjected objects and the self (ego). This is followed by projections of the hated object and repudiated aspects of the self onto the spouse, who unconsciously cooperates by playing out the role ascribed to him/her. (Object relations theory is explained in greater detail in Chapter 1 of this volume.)

IMPLICATIONS FOR PREMARITAL INTERVENTION

Based upon the theoretical discussion of premarital and marital behavior outlined above, assessment of couples seeking premarital counseling should entail a number of steps. First, it is important to determine which of the developmental tasks couples have completed in the process of achieving dyadic crystallization. Frequently, premarital couples initially give the outward appearance of having achieved dyadic crystallization, because they are intimately involved, function as a dyad, have established strong (if not rigid) boundaries around the couple system, are deeply committed as a pair, and have formed a solid identity as a couple. However, many couples have not successfully completed some crucial tasks that are thought to be essential (e.g., achieving pair support, developing role-taking skills, and achieving interpersonal role fit).

After determining which developmental tasks have not been resolved satisfactorily, the counselor should attempt to gain an understanding of each partner's internalized rules for distributive justice and exchange. This can be achieved by administering the Exchange Orientation Inventory (Murstein & MacDonald, 1977). In order to learn each mate's idiosyncratic set of rules for sending and receiving value messages, individual and conjoint interviews should be conducted. Finally, to learn how couples negotiate issues of power and control, each dyad should be observed while it attempts to resolve a relationship conflict.

Essentially, the model of courtship behavior presented above assumes that both partners use negative-feedback processes to maintain intrapersonal and interpersonal stability. Therefore, assessment procedures should be designed to evaluate the degree to which both partners can utilize positive feedback to change their expectations and behaviors in the three crucial areas of relationship rules: distributive justice and exchange; sending and receiving value messages; and power and control. Another promising method of assessment which offers premarital counselors a computer printout of relevant information on a couple is the PREPARE instrument (Olson, Fournier, & Druckman, 1982) Once assessment is completed, couples can be taken through a structured learning program such as the Premarital Education and Training Sequence (PETS) (Bagarozzi & Bagarozzi, 1982; Bagarozzi, Bagarozzi, Anderson, & Pollane, 1984). This program is outlined below.

PREMARITAL EDUCATION AND TRAINING SEQUENCE (PETS): ONE PREMARITAL THERAPY MODEL

The Content Areas of PETS

In addition to achieving dyadic crystallization, a number of developmental tasks must be mastered and overcome in the initial stages of the relationship if the newly forming marital system is to remain viable. The broad content areas of the PETS program are based upon the ideas of a number of family developmentalists (Duvall, 1977; Hill, Foote, Aldous, Carlson, & MacDonald, 1970; R. Rogers, 1973). Each content area can be thought of as being comprised of structural and process subtasks that both partners must negotiate and resolve if they are to build a successfully functioning dyadic system. The eight content areas couples consider are as follows:[1]

1. Marital Roles and Tasks
2. Financial Management and Financial Decision Making
3. Religion and Religious Practices
4. Sexual Relations and Sexual Practices
5. Children and Child-Rearing Practices
6. In-Laws and Intergenerational Relationships
7. Friendships and Extramarital Interpersonal Relationships and Associations
8. Recreation

The PETS program consists of six weekly, 2-hour training sessions. Participants are seen in groups of three of four couples. Each group is led by a husband–wife cotraining team that has undergone PETS counselor training. The skills taught to couples are hierarchically sequenced and ordered. (This sequence is outlined below.) Live and videotaped models

1. Samples of two of the content areas—Religion and Religious Practices, and Children and Child-Rearing Practices—are presented in Appendix A and Appendix B, respectively.

are used to present the skills to be learned each week. Couples' progress during practice periods is carefully monitored by a cotraining team, which offers positive reinforcement and corrective feedback. Homework and practice exercises are assigned at the conclusion of each session in order to ensure skill maintenance and generalization. At the beginning of each weekly session, all couples are evaluated in order to determine whether they have successfully mastered the skills taught the previous week. Couples who have not achieved competence receive additional training before they are allowed to proceed to the next level of training. This training is done with the couple apart from the group. Additional homework assignments may be used if in-session practice is not sufficient. The PETS program is designed to allow couples to progress and develop at their own pace.

In the first session, couples are taught the fundamentals of functional communication. Following acquisition of these skills, couples are ready to consider, discuss, and negotiate any differences they have in each of the eight content areas of married life where difficulties often arise. The mutually satisfying and equitable resolution of these issues is crucial to the successful resolution of successive developmental tasks that the couple will face later on. Negotiating differences in these eight topic areas is an important part of the PETS program. The preventive task is to help couples resolve differences, if they can, and to recognize where differences cannot be resolved or negotiated equitably. To this end, couples are taught a problem-solving paradigm.

The final stage of the program is devoted to having couples re-evaluate their decision to marry. They are asked to review all issues where they were unable to reconcile their differences, to evaluate the seriousness and importance of these differences, and to speculate about the possible difficulties that these unresolved differences might present in the future. The program concludes with having the couples discuss additional questions, such as these: "Can the marriage be terminated?" "Does the couple wish to write a formal marriage contract?" "How will unresolved differences be settled?" "Do you both plan to have a career? If yes, will one person's career be more important than the other?"

The Dynamic Component of PETS

It is important to keep in mind that the subissues and subtasks that couples are asked to consider for each of the eight spheres of their relationship represent only the surface layer of more deeply rooted relationship issues. For example, when couples are asked to consider subissues in the area of Financial Management and Financial Decision Making (e.g., responsibility for financial support of the couple, the acceptability of dual careers, one's right to have separate funds, etc.), the cotraining team must be aware that the couple is symbolically negotiating more crucial issues of autonomy, power, and control. Similarly, it is important to realize that when couples are negotiating subissues in other content areas (e.g., Sexual Relations and Sexual Practices, or In-Laws and Intergenerational Relationships), they also are dealing with important issues of boundary erection, boundary permeability, boundary maintenance, and so forth.

The PETS program was designed (Bagarozzi et al., 1984) to remedy the major conceptual and methodological inadequacies identified in our comprehensive review and critique of empirically tested premarital counseling programs (Bagarozzi & Rauen, 1981). The cotraining team is primarily concerned with helping couples develop functional processes and flexible structures that promote viability. Content issues are used as vehicles to help couples modify potentially dysfunctional structures and processes. Achieving a delicate balance between morphogenic and morphostatic processes is the ultimate goal.

RESEARCH ISSUES

Previous research on the effectiveness of premarital intervention programs is fraught with methodological inadequacies. These have been highlighted in the opening sections of this chapter. In the future, practitioners will be able to advance our knowledge concerning the effectiveness of premarital counseling programs if they take the time to (1) design experimental studies that are methodologically sound; (2) conduct long-term follow-up evaluations; (3) use reliable and valid instruments and observational procedures that have been developed specifically for use with intimate dyads; (4) assess change at both the individual and dyadic levels of systems functioning; (5) consider both "insider" and "outsider" perspectives when selecting dependent measures; (6) evaluate change from a variety of inference levels; and (7) select instruments that are theoretically meaningful.

Premarital intervention programs can be compared only if all program developers agree to use the same battery of outcome measures, in addition to measures they believe to be sensitive to the unique components of their particular programs. My own choice for a standard battery includes the Dyadic Adjustment Scale (Spanier, 1976), the Hill Interaction Matrix (Hill, 1965), the Relational Communication Coding System (Ericson & Rogers, 1973), and the Marital Interaction Coding System III (Weiss & Summers, 1983).

In addition, program developers must begin to investigate whether their programs are successful in preventing "bad" or "unsuccessful" marriages from taking place. To answer this question, longitudinal studies of program participants who decided not to marry after having participated in a program are necessary. It is important to determine whether these individuals are more satisfied or less satisfied with their eventual spouses and marriages (if they marry at all) than those couples who chose to remain together and marry after having completed premarital counseling.

Another research question has to do with program contents. It has been hypothesized that training in open and functional communication may not be sufficient, in and of itself, to produce long-lasting marital satisfaction, because teaching couples only to communicate does not equip them with the skills required to make structural and process changes in their relationships (Bagarozzi & Rauen, 1981). We contend that couples must learn additional skills, such as joint problem solving, conflict nego- tiation, and noncoercive behavior change strategies, in order for their mar- riages to remain viable. These skills are thought to enable couples to modify dysfunctional relationship structures and process patterns. In order to test this hypothesis, experimental studies must be undertaken to compare pro- grams that offer communication training with those that do not. Similarly, programs that offer communication training plus skills training in conflict negotiation, problem solving, and so on, must be compared with programs offering only communication training. Counterbalancing treatments and component analyses of programs teaching a variety of skills must be used to learn more abut the effects of various training sequences and to discover the active ingredients of multiple-skills intervention packages.

Programs (such as PETS) that focus on specific developmental tasks and issues must be compared with programs that do not target these issues, in order to discover whether negotiating selected topics thought to be crucial to developing a satisfactory marriage is, in fact, essential for de- veloping future relationship satisfaction.

Finally, questions having to do with cognitive matching of the ideal spousal image or model with the perceived spouse-to-be need to be con- sidered. Some of these are as follows:

1. To what extent can premarital counseling help couples reduce the discrepancies between their ideal spousal images and their per- ceived spouses-to-be?
2. Do couples' ideal spousal images change so that they become more congruent with the perceived spouses-to-be as couples get closer to marriage, regardless of whether the couples receive premarital counseling or not?
3. Will couples who develop a more realistic image of their mates-to- be, as a result of premarital counseling, have more satisfying re- lationships than couples who do not reconcile the ideal–perceived spousal image discrepancy?

KEY ARTICLES

Bagarozzi, D. A., & Rauen, P. (1981). Premarital counseling: Appraisal and status. *American Journal of Family Therapy, 9*, 13–30.

This article is the first publication to subject premarital counseling programs to a systematic and critical analysis of their structural components, theoretical soundness, relevance of program goals, and methodological inadequacies. Premarital counseling programs are reviewed only if they outline standardized intervention procedures and have utilized dependent measures to assess their effectiveness. Only 13 programs are found that meet these minimal criteria.

Bernardo, M. L. (1981). Premarital counseling and the couple with disabilities. A review and recommendations. *Rehabilitation Literature, 42*, 213–217.

This clinical article, written by a nurse, offers the reader some insights into the complexities of premarital counseling with the disabled. This article is one of very few published works devoted to premarital counseling with disabled individuals. The author stresses the importance of working with disabled couples in groups composed primarily of couples who have no disabilities. The author asserts that premarital counseling of persons with disabilities differ from other premarital counseling only in its length and breadth. However, she offers no empirical support for this statement.

L'Abate, L. (1981). Screening couples for marital enrichment programs. In A. S. Gurman (Ed.), *Questions and answers in the practice of family therapy*. New York: Brunner/Mazel.

Although this brief chapter deals with screening couples for marital enrichment programs, the author puts forth some important guidelines and considerations concerning the suitability of certain couples for educational and enrichment programs such as premarital counseling. The author outlines some of the factors one must take into consideration in determining which couples can benefit from an enrichment experience. This article offers some very specific guidelines that should prove invaluable to seasoned therapists as well as to counselors who are just beginning to work with couples.

Markham, H. J. (1981). Prediction of marital distress: A five year follow up. *Journal of Consulting and Clinical Psychology, 49*, 760–762.

In this brief longitudinal study, the author conducted a $5\frac{1}{2}$- year follow-up on a sample of 26 couples involved in a study designed to investigate the relationship between communication ratings of dating couples and later marital satisfaction. Couples were tested at four separate time periods. However, only nine intact couples were available to complete paper-and-pencil measures at all four time periods. Significant correlations were obtained between couples' ratings of communication and later marital satisfaction. However, this research suffers from numerous methodological flaws.

Markham, H. J., & Floyd, F. (1980). Possibilities for the prevention of marital discord: A behavioral perspective. *American Journal of Family Therapy, 8*, 29–48.

In this article, the authors stress the need for research on the effects of pre-marital counseling programs. Emphasis is placed upon premarital intervention programs developed by behaviorists, and the authors outline the Premarital Relationship Enhancement Program (PREP), which they developed. Unfortunately, no differences were found between the experimental group (PREP group) and a control group at posttest evaluations.

Norem, R. H., & Olson, D. H. (1983). Interaction patterns of premarital couples: Typological assessment over time. *American Journal of Family Therapy, 11*, 25–37.

This empirical study was undertaken to investigate whether couples' interaction patterns, and couple types based upon these patterns, remained stable over time. The authors identified 13 types of couple interaction patterns at pretesting and 11 types at posttesting. Only 5 of the 74 couples (7%) involved in this study showed the same type of relationship pattern at posttesting. The authors conclude that couples in a premarital relationship have not yet established a stable, homeostatic system.

Ridley, C. A., Avery, A. W., Dent, J., & Harrell, J. E. (1981). The effects of Relationship Enhancement and problem solving programs on perceived heterosexual competence. *Family Therapy, 8*, 59–65.

This study was conducted to investigate the effect of two premarital counseling programs on participants' perceptions of heterosexual competence. The two programs used in this study were the Relationship Enhancement (RE) program and a problem-solving approach developed by the first author. These two groups were compared to a third group, a discussion group. Results indicated the RE group to have made significant gains over the discussion group at posttesting, 8 weeks later. No significant differences between the RE group and the problem-solving group were observed.

Ridley, C. A., Avery, A. W., Harrell, J. E., Leslie, L.A., & Dent, L. (1981). Conflict management: A premarital training program in mutual problem solving. *American Journal of Family Therapy, 9*, 23–50.

This published study is the same study cited as unpublished in the Bagarozzi and Rauen (1981) review. For a detailed analysis of this research see the Bagarozzi and Rauen (1981) article.

Ridley, C. A., Jorgensen, S. R., Morgan, A. D., & Avery, A. W. (1982)., Relationship Enhancement with premarital couples: An assessment of effects on relationship quality. *American Journal of Family Therapy, 10*, 41–48.

This empirical study was designed to assess the effects of the Guerney RE program on relationship adjustment, trust, intimacy, empathy, warmth, genuineness, and communication between members of premarital dyads. However, only self-report measures were used to evaluate the program's effectiveness. Results indicated that, at posttesting, the experimental group made significant gains on all dependent measures when compared with the control group.

Schumm, W. R., & Denton, W. (1979). Trends in premarital counseling. *Journal of Marital and Family Therapy, 5*, 23–32.

This is one of the first articles to attempt to catalogue the existing programs in premarital intervention (as of 1979). Developments in the premarital counseling arena till that time are reviewed, and some of the problems in the field of premarital counseling are highlighted. The authors devote one section to the need for rigorous training of premarital counselors and call for a more systematic approach to evaluating premarital intervention programs.

Schumm, W. R., Figley, C. R., & Jurich, A. P. (1979). Dimensionality of the Marital Communication Inventory: A preliminary factor analytic study. *Psychological Reports, 45,* 123–128.

This is an obscure but important empirical study. The authors subject an abbreviated version of the Bienvenu Marital Communication Inventory to factor analysis to assess the dimensionality of this scale. Results of this analysis indicated that the scale is not unidimensional (as was commonly assumed), which calls its validity into question. This research is important, because the Bienvenu measure has been used in numerous studies of marital communication. The inappropriateness of using paper-and-pencil inventories, tests, and self-report questionnaires as valid indicators of actual behavior is highlighted by this brief report.

Appendix A.   RELIGION AND RELIGIOUS PRACTICES

Discuss each of the following questions about the place of religion in your marriage.

If you are in agreement, write in your decision in the space provided. If you cannot reach an agreement that is acceptable to both of you, write in your reasons in the space provided (e.g., undecided, disagree, etc.)

1. On a scale of 1–10, how important is religion in your marriage?

   Husband-to-be:

Not at all important									Very important
1	2	3	4	5	6	7	8	9	10

   Wife-to-be:

Not at all important									Very important
1	2	3	4	5	6	7	8	9	10

2. Will you both attend church?

3. How frequently will both of you attend church?

4. What religious practices will each of you engage in?

5. Will you give financial support to your church?

6. How much financial support will you give your church?

7. Will both of you be involved in church activities?

8. Which activities will both of you be involved in?

9. Which activities will each of you be involved in without the other?

10. If there are religious differences between you, how great do you consider them to be on a scale of 1–10?

   Husband-to-be:

Not at all great									Very great
1	2	3	4	5	6	7	8	9	10

   Wife-to-be:

Not at all great									Very great
1	2	3	4	5	6	7	8	9	10

11. If you are of different religions, how will you resolve issues such as:
    a. Church attendance?

    b. Frequency of attendance?

    c. Religious practices and rituals?

    d. Financial support?

    e. Involvement in church activities?

    f. Religious upbringing of the children?

    g. Celebration of different holidays?

12. Will there be religious vows taken as a part of your marriage contract? If yes, what will they consist of?

13. Are there any issues in the area of religion that have been overlooked? If the answer is yes, please list them below:

14. Below list those issues and areas where there is not complete agreement, but which you believe *can be* negotiated.

15. Below list those issues and areas where there is not complete agreement and where there is *no possibility for negotiation and compromise.*

Appendix B.   CHILDREN AND CHILD-REARING PRACTICES

Discuss each of the following questions about the role of children in your marriage. If you are in agreement, write in your decision in the place provided. If you cannot reach an agreement that is acceptable to both of you, write in your reasons in the space provided (e.g., undecided, disagree, etc.).

1. Do you plan to have children?

2. How many children do you plan to have?

3. How do you plan to space having your children?

4. If either of you is unable to have children, what alternatives are acceptable?
   a. Adoption?

   b. Artificial insemination?

5. What expectations do you have for your children's education?

6. Who will be responsible for the sex education of your children?

7. Who will be responsible for the religious education of your children?

8. Who will be responsible for the discipline of your children?

9. What type of discipline is acceptable?

10. What type of discipline is unacceptable?

11. What roles will male children be taught?

12. What roles will female children be taught?

13. How much time will each of you spend with your children?

14. How much time will you spend with your children as a family?

15. What types of activities will each of you engage in with your children?

16. How will you handle the birth of a handicapped child?

17. Are there any issues in the area of children and child rearing that have been overlooked? If the answer is yes, please list them below:

18. Please list those issues and areas where there is not complete agreement, but which you believe *can be* negotiated:

19. Please list those issues and areas where there is not complete agreement and where there is *no possibility for negotiation and compromise.*

REFERENCES

Apple, J. (1970, March/April). Premarital counseling techniques. *Your Church*, pp. 30–31, 51–54.

Bagarozzi, D. A. (1983). Contingency contracting for structural and process changes in family systems. In L. A. Wolberg & M. L. Aronson (Eds.), *Group and family therapy 1982: An overview.* New York: Brunner/Mazel.

Bagarozzi, D. A., & Bagarozzi, J. I. (1982). A theoretically derived model of premarital intervention: The making of a family system. *Clinical Social Work Journal, 10*, 52–56.

Bagarozzi, D. A., Bagarozzi, J. I., Anderson, S. A., & Pollane, L. (1984). Premarital education and training sequence (PETS): A three year follow up of an experimental study. *Journal of Counseling and Development, 63*(2), 91–100.

Bagarozzi, D. A., & Rauen, P. (1981). Premarital counseling: Appraisal and status. *American Journal of Family Therapy, 9*, 13–30.

Bagarozzi, D. A., & Wodarski, J. S. (1977). A social exchange typology of conjugal relationships and conflict development. *Journal of Marriage and Family Counseling, 3*, 53–60.

Bernstein, B. (1977). Lawyer and counselor as an interdisciplinary team: Premarital counseling. *Family Coordinator, 26*, 415–420.

Bienvenu, M. J. (1974). *Talking it over before marriage: Exercises in pre-marital communication* (Public Affairs Pamphlet No. 512). New York: Public Affairs Committee.

Boike, D. (1977). *The impact of a premarital program on communication process, communication facilitativeness and personality trait valuables of engaged couples.* Unpublished doctoral dissertation, Florida State University.

Bolton, C. D. (1961). Mate selection and the development of a relationship. *Marriage and Family Living, 23,* 234–240.

D'Augelli, A., Deyss, C., Guerney, B., Hershenberg, B., & Sbordfsky, S. (1974). Interpersonal skills training for dating couples: An evaluation of an educational mental health service. *Journal of Counseling Psychology, 21,* 385–389.

Dicks, N. V. (1967). *Marital tensions: Clinical studies toward a psychological theory of interaction.* London: Routledge & Kegan Paul.

Duvall, E. M. (1977). *Marriage and family development.* Philadelphia: J. B. Lippincott.

Ehrentraut, G. (1975). *The effects of premarital counseling of juvenile marriages on marital communication and relationship patterns.* Unpublished doctoral dissertation, United States International University.

Elkin, W. (1977). Premarital counseling for minors: The Los Angeles experience. *Family Coordinator, 26,* 429–443.

Ericson, P. M., & Rogers, L. E. (1973). New procedures for analyzing relational communication. *Family Process, 12,* 244–267.

Freeman, D. (1965). Counseling engaged couples in small groups. *Social Work, 10,* 36–42.

Gangsei, L. (1971). *Manual for group premarital counseling.* New York: Association Press.

Gledening, S. E., & Wilson, A. (1972). Experiments in group premarital counseling. *Social Casework, 53,* 551–562.

Haley, J. (1963). *Strategies of psychotherapy.* New York: Grune & Stratton.

Haley, J. (1978). *Problem solving therapy.* San Francisco: Jossey-Bass.

Hill, W. F. (1965). *Hill interaction matrix: A method of studying interaction in psychotherapy groups.* Unpublished manuscript, Youth Studies Center, University of Southern California.

Hill, R., Foote, N., Aldous, J., Carlson, R., & MacDonald, R. (1970). *Family development in three generations.* Cambridge, MA: Schenkman.

Hinkle, J. E., & Moore, M. A. (1971). A student couples program. *Family Coordinator, 20,* 153–158.

Holoubek, A., & Holoubek, J. (1973). Pre-marriage counseling. *Journal of the Arkansas Medical Society, 70,* 176–178.

Holoubek, A., Holoubek, J., Bergerson, J., Bacarisse, A., Inaina, J., Sanders, A., & Baker, D. (1974). Marriage preparation: An interdisciplinary approach. *Journal of the Louisiana State Medical Society, 126,* 313–316.

Jackson, R. W. (1972). *Simulation as an adjacent in premarital counseling: A theoretical examination.* Unpublished master's thesis, Purdue University.

Kerckhoff, A. C. (1974). The social context of interpersonal attraction. In T. L. Huston (Ed.), *Foundations of interpersonal attraction.* New York: Academic Press.

Leigh, D. (1976). *An exploration of Ohio's premarital counseling requirement in Ohio Appalachia: A descriptive and comparative analysis of responses.* Unpublished doctoral dissertation, Ohio University.

Lerner, M. J. (1974). Social psychology of justice and interpersonal attraction. In T. Huston (Ed.), *Foundations of interpersonal attraction.* New York: Academic Press.

Levine, L., & Brodsky, J. (1949). Group premarital counseling. *Mental Hygiene, 33*, 577–578.

Lewis R. (1972). A developmental framework for the analysis of premarital dyad formation. *Family Process, 11*, 17–48.

Lewis, R. & Spanier, G. B. (1979). Theorizing about the quality and stability of marriage. In W. R. Burr, R. Hill, F. I. Nye, & I. L. Reiss (Eds.), *Contemporary theories about the family* (Vol 1). New York: Free Press.

Mace, D. (1972). *Getting ready for marriage.* Nashville: Abingdon Press.

McRae, B. (1975). *A comparison of a behavioral and a lecture discussion approach to premarital counseling.* Unpublished doctoral dissertation, University of British Columbia.

Meadows, M. E., & Taplin, J. (1970). Premarital counseling with college students: A promising trend. *Journal of Counseling Psychology, 17*, 516–518.

Microys, G., & Bader, E. (1977). *Do premarital programs really help?* Unpublished manuscript, Department of Family and Community Medicine, University of Toronto.

Miller, S. (1971). *The effects of communication training in small groups upon self disclosure and openness in engaged couples' system of interaction: A field experience.* Unpublished doctoral dissertation, University of Minnesota.

Mudd, E., Freeman, C., & Rose, E. (1941). Premarital counseling in the Philadelphia Marriage Council. *Mental Hygiene, 25*, 98–119.

Murstein, B. L. (1976). *Who will marry whom: Theories and research in marital choice.* New York: Springer.

Murstein, B. L., & MacDonald, M. C. (1977). *The relationship of exchange orientation and commitment: Scales to marriage adjustment.* Unpublished manuscript.

Oates, W., & Rowatt, W. (1975). *Before you marry them: A premarital guidebook for pastors.* Nashville: Broadman Press.

Olson, D. H., Fournier, D. G., & Druckman, J. M. (1982). Prepare Enrich counselor's manual. Minneapolis: Prepare-Enrich, Inc.

Patterson, G. R., & Hops, H. (1972). Coercion, a game for two: Intervention techniques for marital conflict. In R. C. Ulrich & P. Mountjoy (Eds.), *Behavior modification in clinical psychology.* New York: Appleton-Century-Crofts.

Rapoport, R., & Rapoport, R. (1968). Family transitions in contemporary society. *Journal of Psychosomatic Research, 12*, 29–38.

Reiner, B., & Edwards, R. (1974). Adolescent marriage—social or therapeutic problem? *Family Coordinator, 23*, 715–731.

Reiss, I. L. (1971). *The family system in America.* New York: Holt, Rinehart & Winston.

Ridley, C., Avery, A., Harrell, J. E., Leslie, L. A., & O'Connor, J. (1979). *Conflict management: A premarital training program in mutual problem solving.* Unpublished manuscript, Texas Tech University.

Rogers, R. (1973). *Family interaction and transaction: The developmental approach.* Englewood Cliffs, NJ: Prentice-Hall.

Rolfe, D. (1973, October). *Family groups of engaged couples for marriage.* Paper presented at the National Council on Family Relations, Toronto.

Rolfe, D. (1976). Premarital assessment of teenage couples. *Journal of Family Counseling, 4*, 32–39.

Rolfe, D. (1977a). *Marriage preparation manual.* New York: Paulist Press.

Rolfe, D. (1977b). Premarital contracts: An aid to couples living with parents. *Family Coordinator, 26*, 281–285.

Ross, J. (1977). *The development and the evaluation of a group premarital counseling workshop.* Unpublished doctoral dissertation, University of Northern Colorado.

Rue, J. (1972). Premarital counseling for teenagers. *Marriage, 54*, 60–66.

Schlein, S. (1971). *Training dating couples in empathic and open communication: An experimental evaluation of a potential preventive mental health program.* Unpublished doctoral dissertation, Pennsylvania State University.

Shapiro, G. (1975). Effects of expectation of future interaction on reward allocation in dyads: Equity and equality. *Journal of Personality and Social Psychology, 31*, 873–881.

Shonick, H. (1972). Premarital counseling in California. *Health Service Report, 87*, 304–310.

Spanier, G. B. (1976). Measuring dyadic adjustment: New scales for assessing the quality of marriage and similar dyads. *Journal of Marriage and the Family, 38*, 15–28.

Stallings, J. (1968). Premarital counseling with the deaf. *American Annals of the Deaf, 113*, 918–919.

Strayhorn, J. M., Jr. (1978). Social exchange theory: Cognitive restructuring in marital therapy. *Family Process, 17*, 439–448.

Van Zoost, B. (1973). Premarital communication skills education with university students. *Family Coordinator, 22*, 187–191.

Walker, P. (1977). Premarital counseling for the developmentally disabled. *Social Casework, 58*, 475–479.

Watzlawick, P., Beavin, J., & Jackson, D. D. (1967). *Pragmatics of human communication.* New York: Norton.

Weiss, R. L., & Summers, K. J. (1983). Marital interaction coding system—III. In E. E. Filsinger (Ed.), *Marriage and family assessment: A sourcebook for family therapy.* Beverly Hills, CA: Sage.

Winch, R. F. (1974). Complementary needs and related notions about voluntary mate selection. In R. F. Winch & G. Spanier (Eds.). *Selected studies in marriage and the family.* New York: Holt, Rinehart & Winston.

Wright, H. (1977). *Premarital counseling.* Chicago: Moody Press.

8

MARRIAGE AND FAMILY ENRICHMENT

DAVID R. MACE

I have observed many changes in my professional career. My own close association with the marriage counseling movement began in Britain in the late 1930s, and has been continuous and worldwide ever since. I have observed and have been party to many of the changes of the American Association of Marriage Counselors (AAMC), launched in 1942. Moreover, I have also witnessed the beginnings of family therapy in the United States and helped to prepare the way for its later integration with marriage counseling. I have followed this creative union as the resulting American Association for Marriage and Family Therapy (AAMFT) developed into the large and influential organization it is today.

However, the recognition of family therapy as a valid professional discipline came slowly and even painfully. I can recall, in the prestigious Tavistock Clinic in London, the almost violent rejection by psychiatrists of my statement that a husband and wife could be counseled *together*. The only recognized pattern then was that each marriage partner should work separately with a different therapist. I recall, also in Britain, the vigorous rejection by social workers of the idea of being involved in a family relationship, and the opinion of some pastors that marriage counseling was "interfering in the private lives of other people." Our major task in the years during which I organized the AAMC was not to convince the *public*, but to overcome the *professional* prejudice that working with families was not a valid activity. The widespread acceptance of family therapy today must not obscure the fact that we arrived there only after a long, hard struggle.

More recently, I have been looking toward the future. Over the last two decades, I have become more and more convinced that we must add

The "Types of Enrichment Programs," "Teaching Tools and Techniques," and "Research Issues" sections, as well as most of the "Key Books and Articles" section, were added by Fred P. Piercy and Douglas H. Sprenkle.

to our present remedial services, greatly needed and highly effective as they are, by providing corresponding preventive services. I believe that our future goal should be an ultimate 50–50 distribution between remedial and preventive services in terms both of time and money spent and of personnel involved. There will undoubtedly be hurdles in the realization of this goal, just as there were hurdles in the development of family therapy.

THE EMERGING EMPHASIS ON PREVENTION

In 1962, my wife, Vera, and I were asked to lead a retreat for married couples in the mountains of eastern Pennsylvania. We went to this event with some trepidation. The couples concerned were not seeking help about their "problems." They were responsible people who wanted to *avoid* the problems they had seen experienced by others. Hitherto we had seen this kind of task as "education" of the cognitive type—information giving. But these couples, we found, were willing to talk openly about their relationships, and this was a new experience for us. The event proved to be so successful that, in the years that followed, we were asked again and again to lead such weekend retreats; we have continued to do so ever since.

This led us to a startling discovery. While the couples considered that they had what might be called "good" marriages, their hope was to achieve something decidedly better. And as they opened up their relationships in a trusting group exchange, we were able to see again and again clear evidences of maladjustments that, in much more advanced stages of development, we had been accustomed to find in couples we had treated in therapy. In other words, in the retreat setting, we were (we hoped) clearing up troubles that were otherwise likely to become much more serious over time. This, in fact, was *prevention*!

At first we called these events "marriage retreats," but in time we needed a more descriptive term, and settled for "enrichment." We asserted, however, that this didn't mean *adding* something new to those marriages; rather, it meant drawing out "relational potential" that was already there, but had never been developed and used in the growth of these relationships.

I am not suggesting that this had never been done before, or that it was not a process also used in therapy. What was new to us, however, was that the growth process that took place for those couples was the result of couples group interaction, and not "intervention" by us. Our roles were not those of "leaders" in the ordinary sense of the word. We preferred to think of ourselves as "participating facilitators." We found that our primary role was to open up our own marriage—to "make ourselves vulnerable"—and that this was a vital factor in moving a group of couples toward mutual trust, the sharing of experiences, and commitment to new growth.

Now, more than 20 years later, we have tested out our convictions again and again, and we remain very much persuaded. Today we can identify hundreds of couples across the country, and elsewhere in the world, who through the marriage enrichment experience have enjoyed extensive growth and development in the quality of their interpersonal relationships.

This finally led us, in 1973, to establish the Association of Couples for Marriage Enrichment (ACME)—an organization of couples committed "to work for better marriages, beginning with our own"[1] The organization now has member couples scattered across North America and in about 18 other countries. Its head office is at 459 South Church St., Winston-Salem, NC 27108 (phone 719/724-1526).

We have made little effort to turn ACME into anything like a mass movement. It works quietly, experimenting and learning; but we cannot escape the conviction that we are dealing with something new and important that elucidates for us the preventive aspect of working for better marriages.

THE MARRIAGE ENRICHMENT MOVEMENT

I am not suggesting that ACME is the only group working in this new field of marriage enrichment. Others, of course, have explored the concept again and again. Father Gabriel Calvo, a Catholic priest, held the first Marriage Encounter (ME) weekend in Spain in January 1962; the movement he began has extended throughout the world and is now well known. Many other groups have developed marriage enrichment programs. some years ago my wife and I established the Council for Affiliated Marriage Enrichment Organizations (CAMEO), which brings together every year the representatives of some 25 national groups in North America, to exchange experiences and to learn from one another. All kinds of organizations, and especially the churches, are getting into this field, and marriage enrichment may already begin to look like a new fad that will go out of fashion. However, this does not greatly trouble us, because we are quietly confident that we are on the track of something that will prove to be vitally important, and that has a significant future.

What we see clearly, however, is that marriage enrichment is not likely to develop quickly; its components are too threatening. Let me elaborate.

I have long been aware that there exists in out culture a protective mechanism that I have named the "intermarital taboo." My guess is that it developed in small rural communities where people lived in close proximity

---

1. In this chapter, I emphasize ACME, the enrichment association/program with which I have been most closely associated. More complete information on other enrichment programs is included in the "Types of Enrichment Programs" and "Key Books and Articles" sections.

to each other, and where married couples needed to enjoy privacy and freedom from the curiosity of inquisitive neighbors. Like some taboos, it has continued to operate in a very different kind of cultural setting, in which it no longer serves a useful purpose, but actually puts married couples at a serious disadvantage. Especially in today's world, where expectations of marriage have become so high, spouses need very much the opportunity to find out about each other's experiences and to learn from each other. But the taboo intervenes. Partners can give to, and receive help and guidance from, each other about most of the issues of life that concern them— but *not* about how to interact as a married couple! Consequently, there can be no sharing of intimate marital experience, no learning from each other, no helping and supporting each other.

What we are doing in marriage enrichment is to establish an environment that simply does not exist anywhere else in our society—a group situation in which spouses can, without fear or anxiety, open up their interpersonal relationships and give each other sympathy and support as they struggle to achieve their interpersonal goals. When such an environment does not exist, the widely held assumptions about marriage in today's culture are grossly inaccurate, embodied in unrealistic concepts and expectations that continue unexamined because partners have no opportunity of talking to each other about their real experiences.

The goal of marriage enrichment is therefore to break through these encompassing veils of needless privacy and to bring the real facts about the marriage relationship out into the open. To some extent, this is also what therapy does; however, it does it only with one couple at a time, and not until the spouses are in serious enough trouble to be able to acknowledge their desperate need of help.

SOME KEY CONCEPTS

As our marriage enrichment programs have developed, we have gradually begun to recognize the truth about marriage: that in terms of today's high expectations, the achievement of the kind of relationship most couples are seeking is impossible unless they have the chance to learn, in practical terms, a set of skills. However, these skills are not formally taught and, under the taboo, are not even openly practiced.

As a result of our experience in marriage enrichment programs, we have adopted the view that there are three essentials that couples will need if they are to achieve the type of companionship marriage that is the general objective today. Here they are:

1. *Commitment to growth and change.* The traditional view of marriage is that if the partners are "in love," this will guarantee them lasting hap-

piness. Given this, they "get married," and then "live happily ever after." It would be much more realistic to say that they "get wedded," and then spend the rest of their lives in the process of "getting married." The very different view that marriage is a task in which the spouses work together to adapt continuously to each other in a process of mutual growth, through behavioral change, is seldom considered. Instead, the wedding service calls for a commitment "for better or for worse," as though it was not in the partners' power to shape the relationship to meet their needs, but only to endure meekly whatever happens.

In marriage enrichment we try to widen the horizons of couples, and to get them to see the task before them as one of continuous growth and adjustment to the realities which they encounter. In ACME our practice is to have each couple, after examining their relationship in depth, make a "growth plan" privately together, sign it, and then take a year to carry it out, reporting monthly to the other members of a "support group" in which they meet regularly.

2. *An effective communication system.* As we see it, only the spouses who are in continuing communication with each other have a real chance of growing together. For an ACME couple, this takes the form of a "daily sharing time" in which all issues in their relationship are continuously reported on and heard. Without this, we find that serious misunderstandings can easily build up and lead to progressive alienation.

We have gladly incorporated into what we teach our couples the new insights about communication that have come our way in recent years: the need for daily self-examination and self-disclosure; completing communication cycles in order to avoid misunderstandings; the wise use of communication styles; and mutual affirmation. We have also learned the great value of the couple dialogue as a means of developing trust in the group, and uniting the couples in mutual support. Again and again we have seen the dramatic change in the group atmosphere as the sharing through dialogue becomes more and more open.

3. *Creative use of anger and conflict.* Our experiences with hundreds of couples have helped us realize that the positive management of anger is probably the crucial factor in building a close relationship. All couples need to understand how their differences, in a space-limited relationship, easily become disagreements, and how anger then heats up the situation and produces conflict. We need to teach them how to accept anger as the defense system of the ego; to process the fear or hurt that lies behind it; and so to clear away the obstacles that otherwise block the achievement of warm, loving, intimacy. We also have to teach them that love and anger are not opponents, but actually partners in the building of a flexible relationship that enables the couple to be intimately loving, yet to avoid becoming enmeshed.

We find these three essentials to be interdependent. A commitment to growth and change will not work for long without an effective communication system, and the onset of conflict that cannot be resolved blocks open and honest communication.

In marriage enrichment, these key concepts are not just explained. They are described and demonstrated in couple dialogue, first by the leader couple, then by others. What is needed is for the member couples of the group to *see* these procedures demonstrated, and so to become convinced that by adopting them they can enjoy a happier and more effectively functioning relationship. This releases in them the necessary motivation for behavioral change.

LEADERSHIP OF ENRICHMENT EVENTS

Our Theory and Rationale

Once we had come to understand and to test out the goals we wanted to achieve, our next step was to consider how marriage enrichment events could best be structured. We began with the weekend residential retreat, and found that it proved to be very effective. However, we also found that the experiences the couples went through were so new and strange to them that it took time for them to adapt themselves to the process. Our finding was that while some couples did this quite quickly, others needed more time. We finally decided that, for a full retreat, a minimum of 15 hours was necessary. What took time was bringing couples to the point where spouses could venture to engage in dialogue with each other in the group. This was never an absolute requirement, but we hoped most of them would give it a try. For the benefit of couples who wanted only to be introduced to the *idea* of marriage enrichment, however, we devised what we called a "miniretreat," covering only 9 or 10 hours, in which the open dialogue was demonstrated only by the leader couple, and where the other couples experienced only private dialogue with each other.

It has become clear to us, however, that leading marriage enrichment events requires special sensitivity and skill on the part of the leader couple. Even people who have been trained in group dynamics sometimes experience great difficulty, because the marriage enrichment group as we perceive it is *not* a group of individuals, but a group of social units who enter the experience with a shared past and move out together into a shared future. It has always been our strong conviction that leadership of such a group should be *by a couple* who not only can explain, but also can *demonstrate*, what they are trying to teach. Also, we have consistently found that it is when the leader couple can be honest enough to make themselves vulnerable that trust builds quickly among the other couples in the group. Only those who have experienced this can understand its vital importance.

Early in ACME's history, therefore, we established a system for the selection, training, and certification of leader couples. A brief explanation of this system follows.

Training Leader Couples

A couple considering ACME leadership training must begin by completing an application form. They may then sign up for a Basic Training Workshop. These are held wherever and whenever we find enough prospective trainees to justify arranging them. The workshop is full-time and residential, and lasts $4\frac{1}{2}$ days. It begins with a retreat that meets all ACME standards. Then there is a full day for learning theory and process. Finally, all the couples have an opportunity to lead a small group, with feedback. Also, all couples have an opportunity for an in-depth dialogue in which for an hour they share the experiences of their own marriage with the rest of the group.

The trainer couple or couples then assess the skills and potentials of the trainees and complete the necessary reports, which are later evaluated by a national committee. If no apparent obstacles appear, the couple will be given the status of Provisional Certification and allowed to lead retreats in the name of ACME, which must meet all requirements. They must lead five such retreats, and send in to the ACME office the names and addresses of all the couples who were involved. To each of these a special questionnaire is mailed by the ACME office for evaluation. Only if no serious concerns arise can the leader couple in question proceed further.

The next stage is for the couple to attend an advanced Training Workshop, where a decidedly higher level of knowledge of the field, and level of competence, are expected. If the couple pass this test, they may be fully certified as a qualified ACME leader couple, but their certification must then be renewed every 3 years.

We have operated this system now for some 10 years, and more than 500 couples have met our requirements. We are well satisfied with the results. Our leader couples also are involved in a continuing education process, and any question raised about any couple will be fully investigated.

We are aware, of course, that marriage enrichment events outside ACME vary greatly in character, and are led by people with a wide range of training and experiences—not necessarily even by married couples.

THE NEED FOR FOLLOW-UP

In ACME's early days, we were concerned to find out the effectiveness of marriage enrichment. The retreat experience was almost invariably a meaningful one for the couples concerned. We have made it a practice always to require anonymously written "spontaneous evaluations," and to pay close attention to any complaints or criticisms that occur. But we also wanted to know whether the effects were lasting over time.

We found it difficult to get follow-up reports from couples, either by completed questionnaires or by making phone calls 6 or 12 months later. What we did get, however, indicated rather clearly that at least some couples were not keeping up their good intentions, and that they would welcome some kind of support system. In the light of this discovery, we decided to redefine marriage enrichment to include both a retreat experience (or equivalent) and 1 year in an appropriate support system.

The way in which ACME is organized has made it quite possible to put this into effect. The goal is to establish ACME chapters on a community basis, with all offices filled by couples. Early on, we also developed a system of setting up "support groups"—perhaps five to eight couples who would pledge to give high priority to attending monthly meetings, which are held in each other's homes. At each such meeting the couples report on their marriages, and help and encourage each other to put their growth plans into action.

The general plan has been to draft all interested member couples in the chapter into a support group in September. Meetings are then held monthly until the following June. In that period no new couples may join a group, so that the trust level may be fully sustained. These support groups have proved a vital and valuable part of the ACME program, and we have seen very real growth in the couples concerned. It is usual to reshuffle the groups each year. Some ACME couples have now been in support groups for as long as 8 years, and their circle of friendships with other couples has become a tremendous source of support to them. Needless to say, their interpersonal growth has brought them to a very high level of marital satisfaction.

TESTING THE PRODUCT: RESEARCH

When we say that couples who have been through marriage enrichment have experienced growth and change, what do we mean? Up to now, we have been largely dependent on the couples' own testimony, on the images they project as we meet with them and work with them over the years, and on the confirmation of others who know them well. By those standards, we possess all the evidence we need that marriage enrichment does what it claims to do.

We do, of course, have setbacks. Out of the many hundreds of couples who have moved into positions of leadership in the marriage enrichment movement, a very few have gone into reverse, become alienated, and divorced. This has obviously troubled us greatly. We have even made some efforts to investigate it and to discover what went wrong. But this has proved very difficult.

What research has been undertaken, and what have we learned? ACME has never had the time, money, or personnel to carry out a research program of its own (although ACME welcomes such evaluation by others). Anyway, research done from the outside is far more convincing. In the "Key Books and Articles" section at the end of this chapter, several such reports of research are identified.

One particularly significant study has been done recently in this field by Paul Giblin and his colleagues (Giblin, Sprenkle, & Sheehan, 1985) at Purdue University. In a massive project, the results of no fewer than 85 enrichment events involving 3,836 couples or families were assembled and subjected to a meta-analysis. Giblin and his associates' major finding was that, on the whole, the effects of these events were, beyond any doubt, helpful and positive. On the other hand, suggestions that other forms of enrichment, such as Marriage Encounter, have had negative effects have failed to be supported.

The events reported in the Giblin *et al.* (1985) study were of wide variety. My understanding is that no ACME programs as such were included. One very interesting finding was that the couples who benefited most were those who might be designated as "clinical" rather than "nonclinical" couples—the very ones we would have discouraged as participants in an ACME retreat, and referred instead to a therapist!

WHERE PREVENTION BEGINS

A Step beyond Present Enrichment Programs

The development of marriage enrichment has been largely motivated by the desire to add a preventive component to our present well-developed remedial services. The logic of this is unassailable; yet, in fact, our culture has never given much attention to the obvious logic that it is better to prevent than to cure. Today, however, we are so overwhelmed by the results of bad, foolish, or ignorant misbehavior that we are being driven relentlessly to go back and ask why so many people lack the knowledge, the skill, and the motivation to plan their lives better.

Perhaps, because of the taboos that have surrounded the subject, there is no field where this is more true than that of marriage. If automobiles, airplanes, or banks failed to function effectively at a rate remotely resembling the incidence of marriage breakdown and divorce, a state of crisis would be declared that would summon all our available resources to find a solution. Yet when marriage and parenthood, on which we depend for the production of responsible future citizens, malfunction on an appalling scale, we seem unable to see this as a major crisis that threatens the future of our culture.

One response is that a great deal *is* now being done at the *remedial* level, and that is what the present book is about. I have personally made some contributions at that level. But what I am now concerned about is to match those developments in the area of prevention.

When the therapist begins to work with a family, he/she is confronting human beings who have, more by accident than by design, misbehaved. They have lacked the knowledge and the skill to manage their close relationships in a manner that might have rewarded them in the ways they hoped and expected. Now they are hurt and frustrated, and hope the therapist can get them on the right track so that in the future they will live together more happily. To make this possible, the therapist must understand how, in their journey through life, they took wrong turns, and even how their families of origin failed to provide what they needed. Correcting those errors of the past, and reorganizing their ways of behaving and interacting so that they will enjoy a better future—all this is the task of the therapist, and to that troubled family it is a gift of tremendous significance.

But if we now understand how the events of the past led to distress for those family members, may we not use this knowledge to enable other families, now beginning, to avoid the mistakes that, unless corrected, can lead them to repeat the errors of ignorance? Is it not our duty to do so?

What we are doing in the enrichment movement is to reach couples and families who are on their life's journey together, get their attention, and enable them to adjust their behavior patterns so that they can avoid getting into serious trouble later. This is not easy to do, because the whole subject is generally avoided or ignored until trouble strikes. The people who seek enrichment experiences are enlightened enough to see the importance of planning for the best possible future they can have—what we call achieving their full marriage potential. Our claim is simply that there are already enough of such people to use what we can provide, and that when they do so, we have evidence that in most cases the outcome is successful. But if prevention works at that level, we can surely go a step further.

Programs for Newlyweds

In the field of prevention, our culture has not been inactive. We have family life education in the schools, and marriage preparation for engaged couples is widely offered by pastors. However, I have now become convinced that, while these programs are welcome, the real opportunity for prevention is being totally ignored.

Our culture's present services to marriages and families follow what I call a "before-and-after system." We provide *information* at a time when its possible application at the level of experience is strictly limited. Students in school can learn how families *ought* to behave, but it is their parents at home who largely decide what happens. Engaged couples are at a point in life at which almost all their hopes and expectations are focused on an experience that lies in the future. In the course of time, the students will grow up and marry, and the engaged couples will move into their fully shared life together. The hope is that now they will pull out all the valuable information they received earlier and stowed away for future use. But does this really happen?

For a period of some years, I asked couples who came to me for marriage counseling about what use they had made of that they had learned from educational opportunities. I asked them for specific instances. The results were almost entirely negative. It was a shattering and disillusioning investigation. Only one wife remembered something she had learned earlier that she had specifically applied in her marital crisis. All the rest confessed that they remembered little and used nothing. This led me to ask the question, "Why do we teach these things *before* couples have the experience of marriage, and then cut off all connection with them when they move into the experience?" It seemed rather like teaching children to swim through lectures in a classroom, and then walking away and leaving them when they get into the water!

So I said to myself, "Why not work with couples *during the critical time*— in their first married year together, when they are shaping, for good or for ill, their interaction patterns?" We used to think that the first year of marriage was, naturally and inevitably, a time of serene happiness and continuous delight. Yet an extensive British study of divorced persons found that one-third of them admitted they had been in serious trouble by the time they reached their first wedding anniversary!

Acting on this hunch, I have been able to get ACME chapters in three cities to launch a program called Growth in Marriage for Newlyweds. The first of these programs, in Kansas City, is now in its sixth year. The programs are led by ACME-trained and ACME- certified couples. We still have a lot to learn, but we are now in no doubt that the couples who have gone through the enrichment course have derived great benefit, and they are deeply grateful for being given the help they needed precisely when they needed it most.

I now see an exciting future for this new approach. I am inclined to think that training couples to use their new interpersonal skills, as they go through that critical first year together, could play an important part in reducing today's disturbing divorce rates. My dream for the future is to make possible, for every marrying couple with the good sense to use it, the opportunity to be guided through their first year together, preferably by a suitably trained and qualified couple. I would recommend a regular monthly time together, in which the newlyweds can report on how they are shaping their interaction patterns, and where they need help and guidance in their adjustments to each other. This would not only head them away from making painful and costly mistakes; it would also accustom them to seek help naturally when they need it, so that any future piling up of negative attitudes would be unlikely to occur.

WHAT ABOUT FAMILY ENRICHMENT?

While ACME, as its name applies, has focused its attention on the married couple, this must not be taken to mean that our goal is exclusively limited to the improvement of the marriage. That is our *primary* goal, indeed, because we take the view that the quality of the marriage is the key to the quality of the family. Or, to put it a little differently, it is not easy to improve family life if the relationship between the parents is out of kilter. Even in a single-parent family the situation is usually the result of a marriage that failed, and the most likely sequel is that in a few years the single parent will move into another marriage that he/she hopes will succeed.

A prominent feature of the growth plans of most ACME couples is a commitment to involve their children in the new and better relationships they hope to establish for themselves. We have heard some moving stories about couples returning from a marriage enrichment retreat and gathering their children together to involve them in a "fresh start" in their family relationships.

Beyond this, however, some of our ACME couples have followed up their own new beginning by setting up a "family cluster." The Family Cluster (FC) program, initiated by Margaret Sawin and described in her 1979 book (see "Key Books and Articles" section) is an arrangement in which a number of families decide to form themselves into an "extended family," meeting together and giving each other help and support, for an agreed-upon period of time. Each family must include all its members, acting voluntarily, from the oldest grandparent to the youngest child.

Another program in which ACME is very interested is Minnesota Early Learning Design (MELD), an organization in Minneapolis that brings together expectant parents, beginning with the pregnant mother, and puts them into neighborhood groups under the direction of specially trained leaders with access to a team of specialists. The group continues to meet regularly to support and help each other to become effective parents. This is a program that could very appropriately follow up newlyweds when in due course they are expecting their first child. The program has been developed by Ann Ellwood. The address of MELD is 123 East Grant St., Minneapolis, MN 55403.

PROFESSIONAL ROLES IN ENRICHMENT PROGRAMS

Does the marriage and family enrichment field offer opportunities for participation by family therapists? Can it use their services? The answer is an unhesitating "Yes." But there are two difficulties.

First, as previously stated, in ACME we do almost everything on a *couple* basis. All our officers are couples (President Couple, Secretary Couple, Treasurer Couple, etc.). And all enrichment events are led by couples acting together as a team. Actually, in a fairly large proportion of our certified couples, one or both spouses are professionals. But they have learned to work *together*, and have been through every phase of training together. We know, however, that not all therapists are married, and not all married therapists can easily team up with their partners in a leadership role.

It is also true that the role of leaders of a marriage enrichment event is very different from that of a therapist. All the same, quite a number of therapists, with their spouses, have been through our training and certification process and have found it to be a significant experience. Many of them testify that it has given them vital new insights, which they have applied to their practice as therapists. Participation in a basic training workshop can be a meaningful experience for any couple, even if they go no further.

The second difficulty is that none of the programs I have described are remunerative. We usually make a small charge, beyond room and board, for participation in a marriage enrichment retreat. But what the leader couple can be paid is so little that it is not remotely comparable to professional fees. At the present time, there is no money to be made in the enrichment field, especially in preventive programs!

However, at the time when marriage counseling began, this was equally true. When we developed a network of marriage guidance services in Britain, all the counselors were volunteers, though they had been in training in their spare time for at least a year. In the early days of marriage counseling in this country, it was also hard to earn a living. It has taken most of half a century to bring family therapists up to their present level of earning power. The time may come when newlywed couples or their parents will pay for them to be guided into effectively functioning marriages, and it will be money well spent. But I can assure readers that that time still lies in the distant future.

However, let us look at the other side of the picture—services that therapists *as therapists* can provide in marriage and family enrichment.

We definitely and actively desire the participation of family therapists in this new field. They can give us support, encouragement, and cooperation. When we find a couple in real trouble in our ACME chapter, in a retreat, or in a growth group, we invariably make a referral to a local therapist; all our certified couples accept this obligation. And if there is a therapist available who is known to be sympathetic to our cause, or understands what we are trying to do, or will cooperate with us, so much the better.

Marriage enrichment is now just about where marriage counseling was 40 years ago—little known, viewed with uncertainty, and perhaps regarded with some suspicion. But I am confident that, over time, this is going to change. I believe that prevention is the significant message for the future, and that in time we shall shake off the hindering taboos, recognize the immense importance of healthy and happy families for the future of our culture, and act accordingly.

TYPES OF ENRICHMENT PROGRAMS

Various types of enrichment programs have developed in recent years. Those best known nationally include Marriage Encounter, mentioned earlier (see p. 189); Couple Communication Program (CCP); Relationship Enhancement (RE or CRE); Association of Couples for Marital Enrichment (ACME) which has just been described in detail; and, for families, Family Cluster (FC) (see p. 198) and Understanding Us (UU). The diversity of these programs is highlighted in Table 8-1.

It is possible to use characteristics of each of these programs to develop program typologies. For example, one can utilize the target audience to divide programs into those for (1) married couples (e.g., CCP); (2) premarital couples (e.g., engaged ME), and (3) families (e.g., UU). One can also categorize programs into those that are secular or religious.

Hof and Miller (1981) classify programs as either intensive weekend programs or multiweek programs. Intensive weekend programs vary from highly structured and couple-centered to nonstructured and group-centered. According to this typology, ME (Calvo, 1975) is highly structured, with limited group interaction, and is very couple-centered. The Marriage Communication Lab (Smith & Smith, 1976), is moderately structured and has a mix of couple-oriented and group-oriented experiences. ACME is minimally structured and is highly group-oriented. The intensive weekend programs are similar in that they provide an opportunity to get away from normal routines, commitments, and pressures in order to focus on relationships. The multiweek programs allow spaced learning and continuing reinforcement of ideas or skills learned. They typically tend to be highly structured and behaviorally oriented around the acquisition of specific

Table 8-1

Comparison of Marital and Family Enrichment Programs

Program	Degree of structure[a]	Size	Theory	Teaching modality	Length
CCP	High	Six to eight couples	Humanistic, systems	Experiential, role-play	Four 3-hour meetings
ACME	Low	No limit	Practical	Rational, personal	Weekend retreats
ME	High	Up to 18–20 couples	Religious, mystical	Didactic, experiential, individualistic	Weekend retreats
CRE	High	Three to five couples	Rogerian, social learning	Rehearsal, modeling, role-play	20 hours, various formats
Structured Marital Enrichment Program	High	One couple	Eclectic	Role-play, variety of techniques	6 weeks, 1-hour meetings
FC	Low	Four to five families	Religious, systems	Modeling, experiential, role-play	10 weeks, 2-hour meetings
UU	Medium	Eight to twelve families	Humanistic, systems	Experiential, role-play	4 weeks, 2-hour meetings

Note. From *A Meta-Analysis of Premarital, Marital, and Family Enrichment Research* by P. Giblin, 1982, unpublished doctoral dissertation, Purdue University. Reprinted by permission.

[a]Relative to other programs in this table. The classification system is adapted from L'Abate (1981).

skills. Homework is typically employed, which allows for skill practice and the reinforcement of change. Examples include RE and CCP.

Programs also can be classified in terms of leadership styles. Three basic enrichment leadership styles have been noted elsewhere (Mace, 1982):

1. *Models for self-help.* This is the style employed in ME, where the leaders present their own relationship as a model of both struggle and accomplishment in marriage. Leaders engage in dialogue in front of a group of couples, who, in turn, discuss the same issues privately.
2. *Experiential educators.* This is the leadership style employed in skill-based programs like RE and CCP. Leaders not only model and demonstrate skills, but facilitate skill practice by couples and/or families.
3. *Participating facilitators.* This model is employed in ACME, where leaders are not so much models or trainers as fellow sojourners who facilitate and simultaneously participate in group and couple experiences.

TEACHING TOOLS AND TECHNIQUES

Enrichment skills and procedures are best learned through observation and practice. Most of the nationally recognized programs have intensive leadership training opportunities and, in some instances (e.g., ACME), have an active certification process. Several universities, such as Purdue and Iowa State, have academic courses in enrichment; these survey the history, theory, and various forms of enrichment, as well as offering experiential "samples" of the process.

The Purdue course utilizes the following outline:

1. History and basic assumptions of enrichment.
2. Theoretical basis of enrichment in the literature on healthy family functioning.
3. Types of enrichment models. Similarities and differences among programs are highlighted, and students are given a "taste" of each model. Specific attention is given to ME, RE, CCP, ACME, UU, FC, and Hof and Miller's (1981) Marriage Enrichment Model.

Although some lecturing is done, the course (in the spirit of enrichment) focuses mostly on experiential activities. The instructor selects a variety of experiences, consistent with each of the models, for the class to try. Several examples follow:

1. CCP (Miller, Nunnally, & Wackman, 1976). The instructor explains the Awareness Wheel (which focuses on five dimensions of self-awareness), and students are asked, in pairs, to describe recent incidents from their

lives utilizing the dimensions of sensing, thinking, feeling, intending, and acting.

2. ME (Calvo, 1975). A guest speaker models a typical ME talk. The students are asked to do a "10 and 10": They are to write for 10 minutes in their personal notebooks about the theme of the talk and then spend 10 minutes sharing this information with a classmate.

3. Creative Marriage Enrichment Program (Hof & Miller, 1981). Students are given the opportunity to choose from among the scores of enrichment exercises in Chapters 7, 8, and 9 of Hof and Miller's (1981) excellent text. These exercises are oriented around the dimension of inclusion, control, and affection, which Schutz (1977) believes are central in defining all relationships.

The following are some excellent resources for practical enrichment activities that can be used in either classroom or retreat settings: Calvo (1975; Carnes (1981); Clinebell (1975); Demarest, Sexton, and Sexton (1977); Hof and Miller (1981); L'Abate and Associates (1975a, 1975b); Miller, Nunnally, and Wackman (1979); and Sawin (1979).

RESEARCH ISSUES

Although enrichment research is still in its infancy, several studies have been conducted on enrichment programs. Questions and issues regarding enrichment still needing research include the following:

• Does marriage enrichment appear attractive to some personality types and unattractive to others (Mace, 1982)? Are expectations regarding enrichment related to gains?

• How much can enrichment programs really accomplish (L'Abate, 1981)? What are the indications and contraindications for their use? What are the characteristics of those individuals most likely to benefit from enrichment?

• What enrichment programs maintain change over time? More studies should use follow-up tests to determine whether initial changes continue (Gurman & Kniskern, 1977).

• Current follow-up studies generally indicate a significant drop in results between posttest and follow-up, but not a return to baseline (Giblin et al., 1985). Can "booster sessions," support groups, or some other intervention be used to maintain initial changes over an extended period of time?

• Are the gains made in marital enrichment programs generalizable to parent-child interactions (Gurman & Kniskern, 1977) or social relationships (Avery, Ridley, Leslie, & Milholland, 1980)?

• Most research on enrichment programs has dealt with middle-class couples and/or those affiliated with religious organizations. More studies need to evaluate how enrichment affects members of other socioeconomic and religious groups (Gurman & Kniskern, 1977; L'Abate, 1981; Wampler, 1982).

• We need to know more about optimal enrichment group size and makeup. For example, what size group maximizes group sharing and trust? Do similarities and differences in group makeup (e.g., race, education, age, religion, or socioeconomic status) make a difference in outcome? Do participants with certain ethnic, social, or religious characteristics improve more in certain enrichment programs than in others (Mace, 1982)?

• Can enrichment programs be effective with nontraditional marital and family constellations (e.g., cohabiting couples, single-parent families, and homosexual couples) (L'Abate, 1981)?

• Are enrichment programs and techniques effective with more severely distressed couples and families (Brock & Joanning, 1983; Giblin et al., 1985; Wampler, 1982)?

• At what point in the family life cycle do enrichment programs have the most profound and lasting effects (Gurman & Kniskern, 1977)?

• Assumptions of certain enrichment programs also need to be tested. For example, is the trust level established in an enrichment group the decisive factor in the effectiveness of the experience (Mace, 1982)? Moreover, should enrichment leaders avoid confrontation "because it inhibits the growth of trust" (Mace, 1982, p. 213)? If these are valid assumptions, research should then logically examine the most effective procedures for maximizing trust and minimizing confrontation.

• Dismantling studies would be particularly useful in studying enrichment programs. Such studies should attempt to determine the specific components of various enrichment programs (in operational terms) and how effective each is in eliciting various kinds of change (Gurman & Kniskern, 1977; Wampler, 1982).

• We still need more research regarding the optimal structure (Giblin et al., 1985; Gurman & Kniskern, 1977) and time frame (Davis, Hovestadt, Piercy, & Cochran, 1982; Gurman & Kniskern, 1977) of various enrichment programs.

• Group leadership is also a fertile area of inquiry. For example, are couples enrichment groups best led by couples, or are individual leaders equally effective? Are the results different when the coleaders are themselves married (Mace, 1982)? And are certain characteristics of leaders more important than others?

• Since most enrichment programs proport to work with healthy families and couples, change may be difficult to measure because of ceiling effects. New, more sensitive instruments should be developed, and existing instruments should be examined regarding their sensitivity to small levels of change (Giblin *et al.*, 1985).

- Self-report instruments are frequently used in enrichment research. More objective, nonreactive measures (e.g., divorce rate) need to incorporated in assessing program outcomes (Gurman & Kniskern, 1977; Milholland & Avery, 1982).

- Giblin *et al.* (1985) have noted that greater effect sizes are achieved with objective measures than with self-report measures. Why? Is the researcher "stacking the deck" for a positive outcome when he/she measures the specific skills taught in the enrichment program (as one might give Spanish exams before and after a Spanish class)?

- Research clearly needs to be conducted on the *type* of change brought abut through enrichment, and how various types of change may relate to one another. To what extent, for example, are skill change and marital satisfaction correlated? Are some skills more closely correlated with marital satisfaction than others?

KEY BOOKS AND ARTICLES

Anderson, D. A. (1976). The family growth group: Guidelines for an emerging means of strengthening families. In H. A. Otto (Ed.), *Marriage and family enrichment: New perspectives and programs*. Nashville: Parthenon Press.

This chapter provides an overview of several family enrichment programs. The author takes the salient points from these programs to create a unifying set of guidelines for program goals, methods, and evaluations.

Bosco, A. (1972). *Marriage encounters: The rediscovery of love*. Meinrad, IN: Abbey Press.

This small book presents the ME movement from both a firsthand and an outside perspective. The encounter weekend is presented, and a rationale is provided for its effectiveness. Also discussed are follow-up programs, a history of ME, and a critical evaluation of the problems existing in the movement.

Brock, G. W., & Joanning, H. (1983). A comparison of the Relationship Enhancement program and the Minnesota Couple Communication Program. *Journal of Marital and Family Therapy, 9*, 413–421.

This well-conceived study compared the effectiveness of RE and the Minnesota Couple Communication Program (MCCP) on a sample comprised of couples exhibiting several levels of marital functioning. Result of the posttest and 3-month follow-ups indicated RE to be superior to MCCP on measures of marital communication and satisfaction. RE also fared better with more problematic married couples.

Calvo, G. (1975). *Marriage Encounter*. St. Paul, MN: Marriage Encounter.

This often-cited manual by the founder of ME presents a day-by-day description of the encounter weekend. The author provides several activities, as well as pertinent parables and scriptures.

Clinebell, H. J., Jr., & Clinebell, C. H. (1970). *The intimate marriage*. New York: Harper & Row.

This book, written for the general public by early pioneers in the marriage enrichment field, does a fine job of discussing the importance of intimacy in marriage. The authors point out that marriage and marital issues change over time and that the couple needs to make appropriate changes in their relationship. Also discussed are issues regarding intimacy in communication, sexual relations, and spirituality.

Davis, E. C., Hovestadt, A. J., Piercy, F. P., & Cochran, S. W. (1982). Effects of weekend and weekly marriage enrichment program formats. *Family Relations, 31,* 85–90.

This study compared a 5-week marriage enrichment program to the same program conducted over one weekend. Results reveal that participants in the 5-week group showed more indications of improved marital adjustment than those in the weekend group. Regardless of group, wives demonstrated more positive changes than husbands.

Demarest, O., Sexton, M., & Sexton, J. (1977). *Marriage Encounter: A guide to sharing*. St. Paul, MN: Carillon.

This book presents a firsthand experience of an ME weekend. This is probably the best account of the early development and the basic principles of the ME movement. Many exercises used in an ME weekend are presented, as well as descriptions of offshoot groups such as family encounter, engaged ME, and Jewish ME.

Denton, W. (1986). *Marriage and family enrichment*. New York: Haworth Press.

This is an up-to-date practical reference, with articles by some of the pioneers in the enrichment field. It is also an excellent source of further information on enrichment. (This book was originally published as Volume 2, Number 1 of the *Journal of Psychotherapy and the Family*.)

Denton, W, & Denton, J. H. (19820. *Creative couples: The growth factor in marriage*. Philadelphia: Westminster Press.

This delightful, straightforward book for the general public speaks to the need for couples to deal with the problems of marriage and family life in a positive, creative way. Individuals, according to the authors, make up a marriage, so there can be no marital growth without individual growth. The chapter on family rituals is particularly good.

Doherty, W. J., McCabe, P., & Ryder, R. G. (1978). Marriage Encounter: A critical appraisal. *Journal of Marriage and Family Counseling, 4*(4), 99–107.

This article gives a critical review of the ME movement. The authors cite lack of empirical research and express concerns about potentially destructive and illusory effects of the ME program.

Genovese, R. J. (1975). Marriage Encounter. *Small Group Behavior, 6*, 45–56.

This article presents a brief introduction to the ME movement. The author discusses the history of the movement within the Catholic Church, emphasizing the theoretical weaving of religion and couple communication (dialogue). An overview of the program and its strengths and limitations are presented.

Giblin, P., Sprenkle, D., & Sheehan, R. (1985). Enrichment outcome research: A meta-analysis of premarital, marital, and family findings. *Journal of Marital and Family Therapy, 11*, 257–272.

This article is the most comprehensive review of the enrichment research to date. Through the use of meta-analysis, the authors found that enrichment is effective in enhancing interpersonal relationships (effect size = .44). Breakdowns are provided by programs and specific populations, and research issues pertaining to measurement tools and design quality are discussed.

Gottman, J., Notarius, C., Donso, J., & Markman, H. (1976). *A couple's guide to communication*. Champaign, IL: Research Press.

This book is an excellent guide for couples who wish to improve their communication. The first part is based on the author's research on how distressed and nondistressed couples differ when solving problems. Presented are several useful exercises and examples for improving couples communication. The second part deals with more general issues of sexual problems, crisis resolution, increasing intimacy, and getting out of a bad marriage.

Guerney, B. G., Jr. (1977). *Relationship Enhancement*. San Francisco: Jossey-Bass.

This is the most complete work on RE to date. Guerney gives a spirited rationale for the use of an educational model. He also summarizes research studies supporting relationship enhancement. Several instruments used in previous RE research are presented and discussed. This is an excellent source of information on RE.

Gurman, A. S., & Kniskern, D. P. (1977). Enriching research on marital enrichment programs. *Journal of Marriage and Family Counseling, 3*(2), 3–11.

This important article critically reviews the empirical literature on the outcomes of marital and premarital enrichment programs. The authors point out specific methodological flaws common to those studies and suggest a cautious optimism regarding the efficacy of enrichment programs. Recommendations are provided for future research.

Hof, L., & Miller, W. R. (1981). *Marriage enrichment: Philosophy, process, and program*. Bowie, MD: Robert J. Brady.

This small but important book is divided into two parts. The first section provides a thorough overview of the field of marriage enrichment and its fundamental issues. The second section gives a "nuts-and-bolts" presentation of the authors' Creative Marriage Enrichment Program.

Joanning, H. (1982). The long-term effects of the Couple Communication Program. *Journal of Marital and Family Therapy, 8,* 463–468.

This study reports on short- and long-term results of the CCP. Immediate postprogram evaluations indicated positive gains on several measures, while long-term results indicated a return to pretest levels in some areas. Joanning offers suggestions for improvement of this program.

Kligfeld, B. (1976). The Jewish Marriage Encounter. In H. A. Otto (Ed.), *Marriage and family enrichment: New perspectives and programs.* Nashville: Parthenon Press.

This chapter presents an introduction to Jewish ME. The author discusses its origins in Catholic ME and its present-day development. An overview of the encounter weekend is presented with a rationale based on Jewish theology and thought.

L'Abate, L. (1977). *Enrichment: Structured interventions with couples, families, and groups.* Washington, DC: University Press of America.

This book does a fine job of presenting a theoretical rationale for marriage and family enrichment. Enrichment is described as a separate entity from therapy and as an adjunct to treatment. The author presents several empirical studies and core reports indicating the positive results and problems inherent in the enrichment methods discussed.

L'Abate, L. (1981). Skill training programs for couples and families. In A. S. Gurman & D. P. Kniskern (Eds.), *Handbook of family therapy.* New York: Brunner/ Mazel.

This chapter provides an excellent overview of the educational movement for couples and families. Discussed are the historical antecedents, theoretical rationale, and empirical support for this educational orientation. L'Abate provides brief sections on the major, as well as several of the lesser-known, programs in premarital, marital, parental, and family skills training.

Lester, M. E., & Doherty, W. (1983). Couples long term evaluation of their Marriage Encounter weekend. *Journal of Marital and Family Therapy, 9,* 183–188.

In a study of the long-term effects of the ME program, the authors found that about 80% of the couples reported a completely positive experience, while nearly 10% cited at least three negative effects of the program on their relationship. The authors see ME as a predominantly helpful program, but caution against negative effects in a minority of couples.

Mace, D. R. (1975). We call it ACME. *Small Group Behavior, 6,* 31–44.

This article gives a brief introduction to ACME. Discussed are the need for marriage enrichment programs and the societal hindrances to their development.

Mace, D. R. (1982). *Close companions: The marriage enrichment handbook.* New York: Continuum.

This excellent book presents the ACME philosophy on the makeup and achievement of the companionship model of marriage. The role of marital enrichment is examined as an important aid in the process of teaching couples to achieve a well-working marriage.

Mace, D. R. (Ed.). (1983). *Prevention in family services.* Beverly Hills, CA: Sage.

More than 20 pioneers describe their innovative preventive programs directed toward "family wellness."

Mace, D. R., & Mace, V. (1973). *We can have better marriages if we really want them.* Nashville: Abingdon Press.

This book emphasizes that marriage is still a viable institution. The need for continuous work if marriages are to grow is stressed. Chapters are provided on the need for better communications and marital enrichment.

Mace, D. R., & Mace, V. (1976). Marriage enrichment—a preventive group approach for couples. In D. H. L. Olson (Ed.), *Treating relationships.* Lake Mills, IA: Graphic.

This chapter provides a compelling rationale for the need for marriage enrichment programs. The preventive model of treatment is contrasted to the reparative one of therapy. Societal myths of naturalism and privatism are examined in terms of their inhibiting effects on marital couples reaching out for help.

Mace, D. R., & Mace, V. (1977). *How to have a happy marriage.* Nashville: Abingdon Press.

This book describes a 6-week at-home program for a couple unable to participate in a marriage enrichment retreat. It seeks to cover every aspect of the process in very practical terms.

Milholland, G., & Avery, A. (1982). The effects of Marriage Encounter on self-disclosure, trust, and marital satisfaction. *Journal of Marital and Family Therapy,* *8*(2), 84–89.

This study describes positive effects of ME on trust, marital satisfaction, and self-disclosure. A 5-week follow-up showed these findings to persist.

Miller, S. (Ed.). (1975). *Marriage and families: Enrichment through communication.* Beverly Hills, CA: Sage.

This edited book, which originally appeared as a special issue of *Small Group Behavior* (Volume 6, Number 1, February 1975), provides many good chapters on both marital and family enrichment. The chapters range from theoretical discussions of the enrichment movement to descriptions of specific enrichment programs.

Miller, S., Nunnally, E. W., & Wackman, D. B. (1975). *Alive and aware: How to improve your relationships through better communication.* Minneapolis: Interpersonal Communication Programs.

This book presents the essence of the MCCP as a learning tool for the general public. The specific program skills are presented in an engaging and in-depth manner for the general public and interested professionals.

Miller, S., Nunnally, E. W., & Wackman, D. B. (1976). Minnesota Couples Communication Program (MCCP): Premarital and marital groups. In D. H. L. Olson (Ed.), *Treating relationships.* Lake Mills, IA: Graphic.

This chapter provides a good introduction to the MCCP. Discussed are the underlying dimensions of the model, the program structure, an outcome research study on the MCCP, and advantages and limitations regarding the use of the program.

Otto, H. A. (Ed.). (1976). *Marriage and family enrichment: New perspectives and programs.* Nashville: Abingdon Press.

This edited book is an excellent, often-cited resource. It is divided into sections on family-centered programs, marriage-centered programs, and national and regional programs. In this book, Otto has brought together contributions from most of the pioneers in the enrichment field.

Piercy, F., & Schultz K. (1978). Values clarification strategies for couples enrichment. *Family Coordinator, 27,* 175–178.

This paper presents experiential values clarification strategies for use in couples enrichment groups. This is a useful article for those looking for enrichment ideas.

Rappaport, A. F. (1976). Conjugal Relationship Enhancement program. In D. H. L. Olson (Ed.), *Treating relationships.* Lake Mills, IA: Graphic.

This study on the effectiveness of a short-term delivery format of the CRE program showed significant changes in the participant couples' communication, marital adjustment, intimacy, marital satisfaction, and problem-solving skills. A brief introduction to this program is provided.

Regula, R. R. (1975). Marriage Encounter: What makes it work? *Family Coordinator, 24,* 153–159.

This article provides a look at the theoretical underpinnings of ME. Discussed are specific dynamics and areas of impact of the encounter experience.

Sawin, M. M. (1979). *Family enrichment with family clusters.* Valley Forge, PA: Judson Press.

This book presents the well-known FC model of family enrichment. This family growth model is based on experiential education and Christian beliefs. A rationale is provided for the promotion of family growth; also discussed are issues related to leadership and organization in the creation of an FC group.

Sawin, M. M. (Ed.). (1982). *Hope for families: Stories of family clusters in diverse settings.* New York: Sadlier.

The FC model of enrichment combines aspects of family systems, group dynamics, education, and religion, with the aim of strengthening family life. This edited book presents several case studies of FC groups in diverse settings. The editor provides a good overview of the FC movement.

Smith, R. M., Shoffner, S. M., & Scott, J. P. (1979). Marriage and family enrichment: A new professional area. *Family Coordinator, 28,* 87–93.

The authors discuss the growth of marriage and family enrichment as a professional area separate from marriage and family therapy and family life education. An overview of the field is provided, as are recommendations for its development.

Stephen, S. S., & Saunders, B. C. (1982). The systems marriage enrichment program: An alternative model based on systems theory. *Family Relations, 31,* 53–60.

This article presents a 10-session marital enrichment program based on systems theory. The leaders facilitate interactional change in the marriage through the use of marital sculpture.

Travis, R. R., & Travis, P. Y. (1975). The Pairing Enrichment program: Actualizing the marriage. *Family Coordinator, 24*, 161–165.

This article describes the Pairing Enrichment program, an interpersonal communication program based on Maslow's concept of self-actualization. Presented are the basic philosophy, procedures, and evaluation of the program.

Wampler, K. S., & Sprenkle, D. H. (1980). The Minnesota Couple Communication Program: A follow up study. *Journal of Marriage and the Family, 42*, 557–584.

This article presents the results of a study on the immediate and long-term effects of the MCCP. Short-term results indicated a positive increase in the couples' use of an open-style communication and on the perceived quality of the couples' relationships. However, follow-up testing showed that only the perceived quality of the couples' relationship persisted. Suggestions are provided for the improvement of the program.

Wampler, K. S. (1982). The effectiveness of the Minnesota Couple Communication Program: A review of research. *Journal of Marital and Family Therapy, 8*, 345–356.

This article presents a thorough review of the research done on the MCCP. The results suggest an immediate positive change in communication behavior at posttest, with some support for an improvement in relationship satisfaction. Follow-up reports indicated some decline in effects, but none below those recorded at pretest. The author provides several recommendations for future research.

ACKNOWLEDGMENT

Joseph L. Wetchler provided invaluable aid in researching the enrichment literature and in writing many of the "Key Books and Articles" citations.

REFERENCES

Avery, A., Ridley, C., Leslie, L., & Milholland, T. (1980). Relationship Enhancement with premarital dyads: A six-month followup. *American Journal of Family Therapy, 8*(3), 23–80.

Brock, G. W., & Joanning, H. (1983). A comparison of the Relationship Enhancement program and the Minnesota Couple Communication Program. *Journal of Marital and Family Therapy, 9*, 413–421.

Calvo, G. (1975). *Marriage Encounter*. St. Paul, MN: Marriage Encounter.

Carnes, P. (1981). *Understanding Us*. Minneapolis: Interpersonal Communications Program.

Clinebell, H. J., Jr. (1975). *Growth counseling for marriage enrichment.* Philadelphia: Fortress Press.

Davis, C., Hovestadt, A., Piercy, F., & Cochran, S. (1982). Effects of weekend and weekly marriage enrichment program formats. *Family Relations, 31,* 85–90.

Demarest, D., Sexton, M., & Sexton, J. (1977). *Marriage Encounter: A guide to sharing.* St. Paul, MN: Carillon.

Giblin, P. (1982). *A meta-analysis of premarital, marital, and family enrichment research.* Unpublished doctoral dissertation, Purdue University.

Giblin, P., Sprenkle, D., & Sheehan, R. (1985). Enrichment outcome research: A meta-analysis of premarital, marital, and family findings. *Journal of Marital and Family Therapy, 11,* 257–272.

Gurman, A. S., & Kniskern, D. P. (1977). Enriching research on marital enrichment programs. *Journal of Marriage and Family Counseling, 3*(2), 3–11.

Hof, L., & Miller, W. R. (1981). *Marriage enrichment: Philosophy, process, and program.* Bowie, MD: Robert J. Brady.

L'Abate, L. (1981). Skill training programs for couples and families. In A. S. Gurman & D. P. Kniskern (Eds.), *Handbook of family therapy.* New York: Brunner/Mazel.

L'Abate, L., & Associates. (1975a). *Manual: Enrichment programs for family life cycles.* Atlanta: Georgia State University.

L'Abate, L., & Associates. (1975b). *Manual: Family enrichment programs.* Atlanta: Georgia State University.

Mace, D. R. (1982). *Close companions: The marriage enrichment handbook.* New York: Continuum.

Miller, S., Nunnally, E. W., & Wackman, D. B. (1976). Minnesota Couple Communication Program (MCCP): Premarital and marital groups. In D. H. L. Olson (Ed.), *Treating relationships.* Lake Mills, IA: Graphic.

Miller, S., Nunnally, E., & Wackman, D. (1979). *Talking together.* Minneapolis: Interpersonal Communications Programs.

Milholland, T., & Avery, A. (1982). The effects of Marriage Encounter on self-disclosure, trust, and marital satisfaction. *Journal of Marital and Family Therapy, 82*(2), 84–89.

Sawin, M. (1979). *Family enrichment with family clusters.* Valley Forge, PA: Judson Press.

Schutz, W. C. (1977). *FIRO-B.* Palo Alto, CA: Consulting Psychologists Press.

Smith, L., & Smith, A. (1976). Developing a national marriage communication lab training program. In H. A. Otto (Ed.), *Marriage and family enrichment: New perspectives and programs.* Nashville: Abingdon Press.

Wampler, K. S. (1982). The effectiveness of the Minnesota Couple Communication Program: A review of research. *Journal of Marital and Family Therapy, 8,* 345–356.

9

FEMINIST ISSUES IN FAMILY THERAPY*

JUDITH MYERS AVIS

Six years ago this chapter could not have been written: There *was* no feminist literature in family therapy, with the exception of two or three pioneering efforts, and the women's movement had had no visible impact on the field. In the ensuing years, however, a growing feminist voice has been heard in family therapy, expressed in more than 30 articles and books. This critique has grown out of and been grounded in the massive research and literature on women produced in other disciplines during the late 1960s and 1970s. The basic themes running through the feminist critique of family therapy are presented below.

THE FEMINIST CRITIQUE OF FAMILY THERAPY

Isolation from Contemporary Theory and Research Concerning Women

A recurring theme in the feminist critique of family therapy is the isolation of the field from contemporary theory and research concerning women developed in other disciplines (Avis, 1985a; Caust, Libow, & Raskin, 1981; Goldner, 1985a; James & McIntyre, 1983; Lerner, in press). Various reasons have been suggested for family therapy's failure to respond to or incorporate the literature on women, including the dominance of family therapy by male leaders, the awkward questions that the feminist critique raises regarding the viability of the family and of family therapy itself, and the possibility that family therapists believe they are already practicing in a nonsexist, nonblaming way that incorporates the major concerns of the

*Portions of this chapter have been presented in different form in Avis, J. M. (1986) Deepening awareness: A private study guide to feminism and family therapy. In L. Braverman (Ed.), *Women, feminism, and family therapy*. New York: Haworth.

213

women's movement (James & McIntyre, 1983). However, the fundamental factor that most authors cite as being primarily responsible for the field's isolation is family therapy's commitment to and reliance upon systems theory as the single organizing framework for conceptualizing and intervening in family relationships. This is a central theme in the feminist critique of family therapy.

The Inadequacy of Systemic Formulations of Family Dysfunction

In spite of its early promise for providing a powerful and apparently non-blaming means of intervening in family problems, family systems theory has come under severe attack by feminist writers who argue that viewing families through a systems-theory lens has critical consequences for how family therapists see women and their problems. Couched in the abstract, neutral language of cybernetics, family systems theory likens the family to a machine and reduces family functioning to what James and McIntyre (1983) call "a special case of a system" (p. 122), which functions according to specific systemic rules and is divorced from its historical, social, economic, and political contexts. By viewing the family out of context, family therapists tend to locate family dysfunction within interpersonal relationships in the family, ignore broader patterns of dysfunction occurring across families, and fail to notice the relationship between social context and family dysfunction (James & McIntyre, 1983; Lerner, in press). By taking the family out of its historical context, systems theory also blinds the therapist to the historical roots of the family, including the impact of the industrial revolution on contemporary family structure and the gendered division of labor. In addition, systems theory prevents the therapist from raising questions concerning the causality of family dysfunction, since it is a theory of problem maintenance, not of etiology (James & McIntyre, 1983; Taggart, 1985).

Feminists also find problematic the systemic concepts of circularity, neutrality, and complementary. Notions of circularity imply that members engage in a never-ending, repetitive pattern of mutually reinforcing behaviors, and are regarded by feminists as looking "suspiciously like a hypersophisticated version of blaming the victim and rationalizing the status quo" (Goldner, 1985a, p. 33). When applied to problems such as battering, rape, and incest, the concept of circular causality subtly removes responsibility from the man while implying that the woman is coresponsible, in some way playing into the interactional pattern that results in violence and abuse (Bograd, 1984).

Similarly, systemic notions of neutrality emphasize that all parts of the system contribute *equally* to the production and maintenance of problems/dysfunction, and render totally invisible differences in power and influence between different family members. Within a systemic framework, questions of individual rights and responsibilities tend to disappear (Taggart, 1985). Further, concepts of sex roles and complementarity "obscure aspects of power and domination by appealing to the prettier, democratic construct of 'separate but equal' " (Goldner, 1985a, p. 37).

A number of feminist family therapists have written of the struggles and dilemmas of integrating feminist and family systems perspectives. Some suggest that such an integration is possible and that, by challenging the systems perspective to include broader social contexts, feminist theory may actually enable family systems theory to become more truly systemic (Lerner, in press; Taggart, 1985).

Goldner (1985b), however, sees feminism as "dangerous" to family therapy in that any genuine encounter between the two will involve a rethinking of many basic family therapy axioms and assumptions, as well as the introduction of new categories of analysis such as gender, individual functioning, and "the material and social bases of interpersonal power . . . money, power, access to power, fairness, the ability to leave, and so on" (p. 23).

Gender as a Fundamental Category

An emerging theme in the feminist critique of family therapy is an emphasis on gender as a fundamental and "irreducible category of clinical observation and theorizing" (Goldner, 1985b, p. 22), similar in character to the basic categories of race and class. Reducing this elemental category to constructs such as "gender issues" and "gender roles" is seen as both trivializing gender and obscuring the reality of patriarchy as expressed in the power differences between genders (Goldner, 1985b; James, 1984; Thorne, 1982, 1985). For example, the construct of sex roles implies that, similar to work or social roles, one can choose to "play" them or not, and that men and women are equally disadvantaged by this "common enemy" (Goldner, 1985b). Several feminist writers argue strongly for the necessity of understanding the whole of human experience as being gendered, including such aspects as society, the family, and individual identity. These writers hold as equally necessary an understanding of the symbolic dimensions by which patriarchy is embedded in language, culture, and experience and is thus subtly communicated and internalized from the moment of birth (Goldner, 1985b; James, 1984; Taggart, 1985).

The Tendency to Blame Mothers and Idealize Fathers

Feminists have expressed deep concern over subtle biases in family therapy theory that result in holding women responsible for causing family problems as well as for changing them (Bograd, 1984; Layton, 1984; Wheeler, 1985). This concern may surprise many, since most family therapists have prided themselves on employing a nonblaming notion of systemic interaction that involves neither victims nor villains. However, by its very nonblaming stance, family systems theory removes individual responsibility by simultaneously implying that men are not ultimately responsible for their actions and that women play into the violence enacted against them. Subtle assumptions of women's primary responsibility for child rearing underlie much of family therapy practice, resulting in a tendency to view children's problems as predominantly caused by their mothers. Although emphasis is placed upon involving fathers in family therapy, it is often with a view to helping mothers out, giving them a holiday, or teaching them more effective parenting skills.

Mother blaming has been found to be prevalent in major clinical journals of several disciplines, most strongly so in *Family Process* and various psychoanalytic journals (Caplan & Hall-McCorquodale, 1985). Caplan and Hall-McCorquodale found that two thirds of the authors in nine major clinical journals, across 3 target years (1972, 1976, & 1982) attributed responsibility to mothers for a total of 72 different types of psychopathology in their children. They also documented a parallel tendency in clinical journals to idealize fathers, to describe them in only positive terms, and to not view their behavior (or nonbehavior) as contributing to their children's difficulties.

Reinforcing Traditional Roles and Values

A recurrent theme regarding family therapy practice relates to what Hare-Mustin (1978) calls the "unquestioned reinforcement of stereotyped sex roles [that] takes place in much of family therapy" (p. 181). Feminists argue that family therapists often have stereotypical expectations of men and women, accept traditional relationship arrangements as the ideal (or at least as the most functional) of possible arrangements and fail to appreciate the consequences of traditional socialization for both women and the development of family dysfunction. As a result of these assumptions, feminists suggest that family therapists often respond differently to men and women and behave in ways that reinforce stereotyped roles and behaviors, whether or not they do so intentionally (Avis, 1985a,1985b; Gurman & Klein,1984; Hare-Mustin, 1978, 1979, 1980; Jacobson, 1983; Lerner, in press; Margolin, Fernandez, Talovic, & Onorato, 1983).

These traditional expectations and assumptions derive in part from the male-based, male-focused theories of development, behavior, and relationships that have been central to American professional education during the past 40 years. Weiner and Boss (1985) point out that as a result of this theoretical bias, most therapists view their clients through the distorted lens of male-defined reality and through theories that frequently blame women and view their socialized behaviors as signs of inherent weakness, passivity, or masochism.

Four major sources of sexist bias or sex-role stereotyping have been identified by the American Psychological Association Task Force on Sex Bias and Sex Role Stereotyping in Psychotherapeutic Practice (1975) as prevalent in clinical practice in general: (1) fostering traditional sex roles; (2) a bias in expectations for women and the devaluation of women; (3) sexist use of psychoanalytic concepts; and (4) responding to women as sex objects.

In addition, the Task Force finds the following biases particularly prevalent among family therapists: (1) assuming that remaining in a marriage would result in better adjustment for women; (2) demonstrating less interest in and sensitivity to a woman's career than a man's; (3) perpetuating the belief that a child's problems and child rearing are primarily women's responsibilities; (4) exhibiting a double standard regarding a wife's versus a husband's extramarital affair; and (5) deferring to a husband's needs over a wife's. Concern regarding these and similar biases echoes throughout the feminist family therapy literature.

Ignoring the Political Dimensions of Family Therapy

Another feminist concern relates to the tendency of family therapists to ignore or deny the political aspects of what they do. Many therapists attempt to take a neutral stance regarding gender arrangements in the families they work with, believing that such a stance shows maximum respect for a family's values. Feminist writers however, assert that power is inherent in the therapeutic relationship, that therapists cannot *not* express values, and that therapeutic neutrality is an impossible and dangerous myth (Avis, 1985a; Jacobson, 1983). Therapists who adhere to this myth inadvertently adopt political positions, and, by what they choose to focus on, respond to, challenge, or ignore, they may reinforce traditional values oppressive to women. Such reinforcement occurs primarily by default; The therapist's failure to challenge traditional arrangements is frequently perceived by clients as tacit approval. It is thus essential that therapists be aware of their own values and beliefs, as well as of what values they are, indeed, reinforcing (Avis, 1985a, 1985b, Gurman & Klein, 1984; Jacobson, 1983).

GENDER ISSUES IN FAMILY THERAPY TRAINING

Feminists emphasize the central importance of gender and sex-role issues in both the content and process of family therapy training (Avis, 1986;

Caust *et al.*, 1981; Libow, 1986; Okun, 1983; Wheeler, Avis, Miller, & Chaney, 1985). Major issues include (1) the failure to incorporate content related to gender, power, or current research and theory on women into family therapy training programs; (2) the teaching of theories and interventions that disadvantage women; (3) difficulties in training both men and women in behaviors that are contrary to their gender socialization (i.e., directive, task-oriented skills for women and affective, expressive skills for men); and (4) gender issues that arise in the training process itself, in interactions between supervisor and trainee, between trainees, or between trainee and family. Family therapy's inattention to gender in both the content and process of training appears to be reflected in the failure of the Commission on Accreditation of the American Association for Marriage and Family Therapy (AAMFT, 1981) to require course content on gender or women. It is also borne out by a study of graduate-level curricula for marriage and family therapy education (Winkle, Piercy, & Hovestadt, 1981). Winkle *et al.*'s (1981) national panel of 25 training directors of graduate-level marriage and family therapy programs and 20 AAMFT Approved Supervisors mention gender in only one of the 63 clinically related course content areas they consider important. Further, 47 of the 63 areas are rated as more important than that of gender.

Feminist recommendations regarding training include (1) required readings and course content dealing with feminist theory and gender issues; (2) analysis of videotapes to identify sex-role and power behaviors of both therapist and family members; (3) use of group supervision to explore trainees' feelings and values concerning gender roles and issues; (4) Bowenian family of origin work focusing on the therapist's own sex-role issues; (5) training experiences such as assertiveness training and behavior rehearsal that help trainees develop nonstereotypical behaviors; and (6) ensuring that all trainees experience both male and female supervisors. (*See* Avis, 1986; Caust *et al.*, 1981; Libow, 1986; Okun, 1983; Wheeler *et al.*, 1985). These and other training ideas will be discussed further under the heading "Teaching Tools and Techniques."

FEMINIST ALTERNATIVES TO THEORY AND PRACTICE

Theoretical Alternatives

Weiner and Boss (1985) note that the call for "conceptual affirmative action—a rethinking of gender-role issues based on research and theory development about women over the life cycle" (p. 15) has begun to be reflected in the family therapy literature.

Perhaps most notable of these new theoretical perspectives has been the work on mothering, particularly that of Chodorow (1978) and Dinnerstein (1976). Chodorow's theory of the social construction of the psychological processes of mothering has been drawn on repeatedly by feminist family therapists for its help in expanding an understanding of the inextricable relationship between family functioning and the socioeconomic context, as well as an understanding of the development and maintenance ("reproduction") of different roles and relational capacities in men and women (Goldner, 1985a, 1985b; James, 1984; James & McIntyre, 1983; Layton, 1984; Luepnitz, 1982; Okun, 1983; Weiner & Boss, 1985). Chodorow links the sexual division of labor to the economic dictates of Western capitalism, resulting in women working primarily in the home and men primarily outside. She argues that the resulting allocation to women of primary responsibility for child care results in psychological processes through which girls identify with their mothers, develop female relational capacities, and grow up to be mothers themselves. Boys, on the other hand, identify themselves as different from their mothers, separate psychologically from them, and grow up to be as absent as their own fathers, involved in the world outside the home. Chodorow concludes that this division of labor, roles, and relationship capacities will continue to be reproduced in families as long as women continue to be the primary caretakers of children.

Dinnerstein's (1976) work is also cited extensively by feminist family therapists as helpful in understanding the relationship between conventional parenting arrangements and the distinctly different ways in which male and female power is experienced (Goldner, 1985a; Layton, 1984; Luepnitz, 1982; Weiner & Boss, 1985). Dinnerstein (1976) hypothesizes that the domination of infant care by women results in exaggerated images and deep-seated fears of women's power, in a view of women's power as irrational and engulfing, and in a tendency to displace rage at adult powerlessness onto women.

A number of other feminist theorists have provided conceptual frameworks that challenge traditional assumptions regarding women's behavior and psychosocial development. Most notable among these is Jean Baker Miller (1976) whose *Toward a New Psychology of Women* provides a model of adulthood based not on the male model of separation, but on a female-influenced model of connectedness, that is, of valuing, enlarging, and deepening human relationships. Miller's model values and validates women's traditional capacities for nurturing and for cultivating relationships and suggests that as capacities essential to the human community they must be valued and shared by men as well as women.

Carol Gilligan's (1982) research on women's moral development has been revolutionary in its impact on the understanding not only of women's development, but of sexist bias in social science. Her research challenges Kohlberg's model of moral development, which was developed on males but was claimed to be equally applicable to women. Gilligan's work not only distinguishes women's moral development as different from men's; it also demonstrates the vulnerability of social science to invisible bias, the tendency to judge women by male norms, and the fallacy of assuming that theory and research developed on men apply equally to women.

Caplan (1985) has examined and challenged the traditional myth of women's masochism that has been consistently used in the mental health field to explain why women stay in abusive marriages and unhappy relationships, or sacrifice themselves for their children. Caplan analyzes women's stereotypical behavior in terms of its social context and finds that what has often been mislabled as masochistic is actually an ability to behave in altruistic, caring ways, or an attempt to avoid punishment or guilt.

Within the field of family therapy, conceptual affirmative action has taken place in a variety of ways. In addition to major efforts to extend and expand systems theory to consider the family within its broader social contexts (Goldner, 1985a; James & McIntyre, 1983; Lerner, in press; Taggart, 1985), innovative work has been done to integrate an understanding of gender-linked power dynamics into our thinking about the functioning and treatment of family systems (Bepko, 1985, 1986; Bograd, 1984, 1986; Goldner, 1985a, 1985b; Jacobson, 1983; James, 1984). In addition, several feminist family therapists have developed new theoretical perspectives on particular problems (such as anger, wife abuse, alcoholism) through an integration of feminist and systemic thinking (Bepko, 1986; Bograd, 1984, 1986; Lerner, 1985b).

Clinical Alternatives

Beginning with Hare-Mustin's (1978) suggestions for a feminist approach to family therapy, feminists in the field have written about their attempt to integrate feminist theory and values into their clinical work. Some have suggested specific techniques and interventions, while others, such as Goldner (1985a, 1985b) have simply raised provocative questions and cautioned against facile or simplistic solutions to complex and fundamental issues. Recent attempts at integration have moved beyond the tentative suggestion stage; feminist family therapists are writing about their clinical dilemmas and thinking processes and of their varying degrees of success in applying feminist principles to their practice. Specific alternatives include (1) talking about gender issues during therapy (money, power, child care, housework, the division of labor, etc.); being direct about the therapist's own beliefs; (2) relabeling deviance and redefining normality so as to highlight women's strengths; (3) using Bowenian family systems theory to aid women in defining themselves independently of what others expect them to be; (4) focusing on the needs of women as individuals as well as on the needs of the relationship; (5) avoiding conjoint therapy in cases of wife abuse; and (6) empowering women in a wide variety of ways both inside and outside the therapy room (Avis, 1985a; Bepko, 1985, 1986; Bograd, 1984, 1986; Braverman, 1986; Goldner, 1985a, 1985b; Goodrich, Rampage, Ellman, & Halstead, 1985; Guttman, 1986; Hare-Mustin, 1978, 1980; Imber-Black, 1986; Jacobson, 1983; Lerner, 1985a, in press; Margolin et al., 1983; Pinderhughes, 1986; Roth & Murphy, 1986; Weiner & Boss, 1985; Wheeler, 1985; Wheeler et al., 1985). These alternatives will be further elaborated under the heading "Key Clinical Skills."

KEY CONCEPTS

Feminism. The *Penguin English Dictionary* (1965) defines feminism as "a social movement claiming political and economic equality of women with men." Historian Linda Gordon (1979, p. 107) defines it as "an analysis of women's subordination for the purpose of figuring out how to change it," while Eisenstein (1983, p. xiv) suggests that it "encompasses a concept of social transformation that, as part of the eventual liberation of women, will change all human relationships for the better." Feminism, then, includes a recognition of women's subordination and inferior social position, an analysis of the forces that maintain it, a commitment to changing it, and a vision of future equality between men and women.

Feminist approach to family therapy. An approach that includes all of the above aspects of feminism, plus an awareness of and attempts to counteract the ways in which family therapy may reinforce women's subordinate position.

Feminist frameworks. Within the feminist movement there can be distinguished several different feminist frameworks, each based on a somewhat different conceptual analysis of the nature and causes of women's oppression and each suggesting different foci and solutions for change (Jaggar & Rothenberg, 1984). Three major feminist frameworks identified by Jaggar and Rothenberg (1984) liberal, socialist, and radical feminisms. (See the definitions of each in this secton.)

Gender. A person's learned or cultural status as feminine or masculine, as distinguished from her/his biological status as female or male. Gender is culturally assigned to a person on the basis of sex (Greenglass, 1982). Many feminists emphasize the fundamental nature of gender as a basic category of social organization and discrimination, similar in nature to the categories of race and class (Goldner, 1985b, James, 1984; Thorne, 1985).

Gender role. The culturally prescribed and learned behaviors, attitudes, and characteristics associated with being masculine or feminine (Greenglass, 1982; Thorne, 1985). This concept has been criticized by feminists for depicting gender differences in sociopsychological rather than structural terms. Critics suggest that the concept of gender roles obscures the differences in power between the genders by implying both that one can choose whether or not to play one's gender role, and that men and women are equally disadvantaged by them (Goldner, 1985b; James, 1984; Thorne, 1985).

Gender-sensitive. An awareness of the impact of gender-role socialization on an individual's psychological, emotional, and interpersonal functioning, as well as on her/his power, status, position, and privilege in social/cultural systems (familial, political, economic).

Liberal feminism. A feminist framework that emphasizes equality in terms of equal rights and equal opportunity for women. Liberal feminists conceptualize women's oppression as resulting from legal constraints and social policies that discriminate against women and that result in unequal civil rights and unequal educational and occupational opportunities. Liberal feminism does not attempt a historical analysis of the causes of this discrimination, but focuses effort on removing economic and legal barriers to women's equality. The key to women's liberation is seen as being the removal of sexist discrimination (Jaggar & Rothenberg, 1984). Thus, liberal feminists tend to distinguish between women's personal and public lives, and to focus attention on removing barriers to women's equal participation in the public sphere (e.g. elimination of sex discrimination in employment, and the provision of equal education and job training).

Nonsexist. Any policy, approach, attitude, and so on that does not discriminate on the basis of sex (i.e., that treats men and women equally) is defined as nonsexist. This is to be distinuished from a *feminist* approach, which is based on an understanding of the differential in power and privilege that exists between men and women in society, and which actively attempts to redress this imbalance. This difference is important. Jacobson (1983), for example, points out that a nonsexist approach to behavioral marital therapy may result in the perpetuation of preexisting inequities, while a feminist approach may require giving greater weight to a woman's requests for change than to a man's, in order to correct the power imbalance between them.

Patriarchy. The social structure through which men of different races, classes, and cultures join together in their domination over women. Patriarchy is "a social structure in which women are systematically dominated, eploited, and oppressed" (Hartman, 1984, p. 175).

"The personal is political." A concept that emphasizes that what happens in the private sphere, in women's personal lives, is an expression of their oppression in the wider public sphere. The personal sphere is seen as extending beyond the personal and individual by virtue of its being the area in which women's subordinate position is enacted and reproduced (Gilbert, 1980). As Lerner (1985a) states, "There is a circular connection

between the patterns of our intimate relationships and the degree to which women are represented, valued, and empowered in every aspect of society and culture. The patterns that keep us stuck in our close relationships derive their shape and form from the patterns of a stuck society" (p. 223).

Radical feminism. A feminist framework that is relatively new, still evolving, and takes a number of different forms (Jaggar & Rothenberg, 1984). All forms of radical feminism, however, are based on the assumption that the oppression of women is a fundamental oppression. It has operated across time, across culture, across class, is embedded in every aspect of life, and is therefore the hardest form of oppression to eradicate. Radical feminism emphasizes the personal as political and patriarchy as a social structure through which men of all classes and cultures dominate and exploit women. Women's problems and unhappiness are seen as a response to their oppression by the patriarchal system.

Socialist feminism. A feminist framework that draws on Marxist traditions in its analysis of women's oppression. Like traditional Marxists, socialist feminists believe that human nature is created by the type of society and form of social organization in which people live. They also agree that it is impossible to have equal opportunity while living in a class society. They do not, however, view women's oppression as simply a result of the class oppression embodied in capitalism, but believe that in order to understand the oppression of women across classes, Marxist theory must be expanded from an analysis simply of the means of production to an analysis of the social organization and distribution of the means of *reproduction*, including sexuality, nurturing, and raising children (Jaggar & Rothenberg, 1984). Socialist feminists argue that such an expansion is necessary in order to analyze why women in every class are subordinate to men, both within and outside the family. Some socialist feminists view patriarchy and capitalism as reciprocal and mutually reinforcing systems that allow men to control women's labor, and that must both be abolished if women are to be liberated (Hartman, 1984).

KEY CLINICAL SKILLS

Skills relevant to a feminist approach to family therapy have been delineated by several authors (e.g., Chaney, 1986; Hare-Mustin, 1978; Wheeler, 1985; Wheeler et al., 1985). In addition, numerous others have discussed specific interventions or the application of feminist thinking and skills to specific situations (Avis, 1985a; Bepko, 1985, 1986; Bograd, 1984, 1986; Braverman, 1986; Goldner, 1985b; Goodrich et al., 1985; Gurman & Klein, 1984; Guttman, 1986; Jacobson, 1983; Layton, 1985; Lerner, 1985a; Margolin et al., 1983; Pinderhughes, 1986; Roth & Murphy, 1986; Weiner & Boss,

1985). The reader is referred to these sources for more extensive description and discussion of a wide range of interventions. Wheeler *et al.* (1985) have developed the most extensive list of both cognitive and intervention skills, while Chaney (1986) does a particularly thorough job of describing and giving examples of specific interventions.

Below are listed some representative skills that are endorsed by a number of writers and are considered basic to a feminist approach. The findings of both the Wheeler (1985) and Avis (1986) studies emphasized the importance of therapists developing a feminist understanding as a prerequisite to making feminist interventions. In keeping with this emphasis, clinical skills will be discussed under both conceptual and intervention categories.

Conceptual Skills

A POSITIVE ATTITUDE TOWARDS WOMEN

Many interventions that have been called feminist or feminist-informed are based on the therapist's positive attitude towards women and the verbal and nonverbal communication of this attitude. The following aspects of this attitude are of particular importance: respect for and a positive evaluation of women; taking women's concerns, perceptions, and ideas seriously; seeing women as experts on themselves; understanding and validating women's experience as different from men's; and not blaming women or seeing them as primarily responsible for problems and change in their families.

SOCIAL ANALYSIS

Russell (1986) defines social analysis as the "assessment of sex-related social and cultural restraints impinging internally and externally on women's behavior." At the perceptual/conceptual level, this skill involves an understanding of how the discrepancy in power and privilege between men and women is implicated in the development and maintenance of both women's difficulties and family problems, an understanding of how traditional socialization and the gendered division of labor serves to perpetuate this power discrepancy, and an understanding of the social, economic, and political structures that maintain women's subordinate position and men's dominant one, both within and outside of the family. It also involves the ability to conceptualize and analyze family problems in terms of power and gender, as well as the ability to recognize the exercise of power and stereotypical behaviors and attitudes as they are expressed in the therapy room.

Intervention Skills

A number of the skills discussed here are not unique to a feminist approach. The uniqueness lies in the use of this particular *configuration* of skills, as well as in their intended purpose. The therapist has an underlying understanding of the imbalance in power and privilege between men and women and the role of this imbalance in family problems, plus a commitment to redressing this imbalance as it is played out in all aspects of women's lives, including their family relationships. Although different feminist therapists emphasize different interventions, the skills cited below are endorsed by most authors and appear to form the core of a feminist approach.

EMPOWERING WOMEN

Most family therapy attempts to empower and strengthen all family members. A feminist approach is singular for its emphasis on empowering women in particular. This is a corrective measure to counteract women's usual paradoxical position of having primary responsibility for the family while having reduced power for carrying out that responsibility. Therapists need to help women feel powerful enough both to meet their own needs and to influence their spouses and children. This issue is complicated by the traditional gender socialization that has taught most women not to assert their own needs or to use their personal power.

Feminist family therapists use a wide range of interventions to empower women specifically. These include (1) encouraging women to value and assert their own feelings, needs, wants, and ideas with both their partners and their children; (2) affirming and validating women's ideas, experiences, and perceptions; (3) encouraging and underscoring women's competence; (4) building women's self-esteem by highlighting their important contributions to the family; (5) supporting and strengthening single mothers' parenting skills; (6) relabeling deviance and redefining normality in order to emphasize women's strengths; (7) encouraging and helping women to develop their own social support networks; (8) helping women to anticipate and deal with "change back" reactions from their families and others following change; (9) encouraging assertive behavior; and (10) affirming women's rights to their own space, time, needs, work, and income, and their importance as individuals separate from their roles as spouse/partner and parent (Wheeler, 1985; Wheeler et al., 1985).

MAKING GENDER ISSUES EXPLICIT

This intervention is perhaps the most characteristic of a feminist approach, and the one that distinguishes it most clearly from other approaches. Feminists raise issues of gender in a variety of ways, whether or not clients introduce these issues themselves. These include (1) defining the problem in such a way as to include the dimensions of power and gender; (2) introducing and discussing in therapy gender issues such as money, power, equity, flexibility, options, housekeeping and childcare; (3) making connections for the family between gender issues in the family and those in the wider social system; (4) challenging sterotypical behaviors, attitudes, and expectations; (5) discussing the differing impact of divorce on women and on men; and (6) raising gender issues in relation to family of origin. Other interventions in this category involve educating families regarding the costs of traditional sex roles and the research data on the relationships among sex, marital status, and depression; being direct about one's own beliefs and values regarding gender; and making explicit the fact that there are differences between women's and men's experiences of family.

SHIFTING THE POWER BALANCE BETWEEN MEN AND WOMEN IN THE FAMILY

This intervention is based on an understanding that women usually have less access than men to the sources of direct power (i.e., money, status, education, position, control over resources) and that their usual primary responsibility for the devalued, unpaid work of parenting and homemaking is a reflection of their reduced power. Feminists attempt to shift the imbalance in power between male and female clients in a variety of ways. The following are representative: (1) placing the same demands for change on men as on women; (2) sometimes giving greater weight to women's change requests than to men's; (3) challenging traditional arrangements of childrearing and housekeeping tasks and negotiating a more balanced distribution of these tasks; (4) defining parenting and homemaking as important concerns for men as well as for women; (5) focusing on the needs of women as individuals as well as on the needs of the relationship; (6) challenging patterns of male dominance and female subordination or accommodation; (7) challenging gender-specific rules; (8) supporting freedom from a gendered task assignment among children; (9) valuing women's work in the family; (10) valuing and validating emotional expression and nurturing in both men and women; and (11) requesting changes that alter roles rather than merely the quality of role performance.

Skill Training

Chaney (1986) outlines a number of specific skills that can be taught as part of a feminist approach. These include (1) teaching women how to express anger assertively and effectively; (2) using role play to help clients practice new sex-role behaviors; (3) teaching women to assess and meet their own needs; (4) teaching men to recognize and express their feelings; and (5) instructing men in how to respond effectively to their families' emotional and nurturing needs.

Use of Self

Most works on feminist family therapy suggest that in a feminist approach, the therapist uses herself/himself in a somewhat different way than in traditional family therapy. This includes such dimensions as the selective use of self-disclosure to emphasize the commonality of gender-related problems, the modeling of an integration of both instrumental and affective behaviors and of the exercize of personal power, and the direct communication of the therapist's own beliefs and values regarding power. It may also include taking a collaborative problem-solving role with the family, using a therapeutic contract, and avoiding taking the positions of "expert" or final authority on the family.

TEACHING TOOLS AND TECHNIQUES

Most of the teaching ideas discussed below are drawn from the author's recent research on training and supervision in feminist-informed family therapy (Avis, 1986). This study polled the thinking of 26 highly experienced family therapy educators who had been integrating feminist thinking into their therapy and training for several years. Most authors who have published regarding gender issues in family therapy participated in the study, and the following teaching suggestions reflect their collective experience and/or thinking.

Feminist Course Content

One of the most powerful ways to promote shifts in trainees' thinking regarding gender is to include gender issues and feminist theory content in family therapy and related courses. This includes theoretical and empirical work from other disciplines on the relationship between gender, marital status, sex roles, and mental health; on women's psychology and development; on sex role socialization, sex differences, and female stereotypes; and on the politics of therapy and gender issues in family therapy.

In addition to the integration of feminist content into existing courses, requiring trainees to take a separate course focused specifically on gender issues or women's studies is highly recommended.

Addressing Gender Issues Directly

In training in a feminist approach, educators and supervisors address gender issues directly and openly rather than regarding students' attitudes and assumptions as a matter of personal choice. This includes teaching feminist issues overtly and nonapologetically, as well as being open about the trainer's own beliefs about power in family systems. It also includes incorporating gender-linked theory and research data into teaching, teaching about the biases and limitations of traditional theory, and directly challenging trainees' sexist assumptions and beliefs.

Prescribed Readings

Students may be asked to read articles, research reports, autobiographies, and books that sensitize them to feminist issues in general, and to the feminist critique of family therapy in particular. The writings of feminist family therapists are recommended, as well as background reading on women's psychology and development, women and mental health, and feminist analyses of mothering, the family, and gender relations. See the "Key Books and Articles" section at the end of this chapter for suggestions.

Making Gender Issues Explicit

This intervention in training parallels the intervention in therapy discussed earlier. Trainers and supervisors can make gender issues explicit during training in a wide variety of ways. Some of these include (1) questioning trainees' assumptions about "normal" families; (2) asking questions that force trainees to think about issues of power and gender, and about how these issues might be handled; (3) commenting on women-blaming, father-ignoring, gender-biased coalitions, and sexist language whenever such biases occur in therapy or in training; and (4) pointing out abuses of women in traditional therapies.

Including Gender in Therapy

It is important to encourage trainees to apply their awareness of gender issues to their work with particular families. To this end, it is helpful to have therapists do the following: (1) always include the dimensions of power and gender in any conceptualization of a case; (2) discuss cultural forces and their impact upon the presenting problems; (3) set treatment goals that are gender-fair; and (4) design interventions that include power and gender issues.

Examining Therapists' Own Values and Socializations

Having trainees analyze their values, their own sex-role socializations, and the rules and expectations regarding gender in their families of origin is an important aspect of training in a feminist perspective. A number of specific techniques may be used to facilitate this process, such as asking trainees to write papers on their own gender values or on those of their families of origin, construct and examine their own genograms, or participate in therapist's own family groups. Trainees may also be asked to compare gender and power in their client families to that in their families of origin.

Case analysis

The application of feminist principles to particular cases is an essential part of helping trainees translate them into practice. This may be done in a number of ways; the following are two possibilities: Trainees may be presented with a standard case history (e.g., enmeshed mother/daughter, peripheral father), and then asked to develop various analyses of the case and discuss how some of these analyses may be subtly biased against women. As an alternative, trainees may be asked to present cases they are curently seeing during group supervision. The group may then be asked to analyze and discuss the gender issues involved in the family and the presenting problem. Relaxed, open, nonconfrontational discussion seems most helpful.

Video Analysis and Role Play

Video analysis may be a particularly helpful tool for heightening trainees' awareness of gender issues in therapy. One method is to have therapists view tapes of themselves, watching for subtle signs in their own behavior that suggest that they respond differently to men than to women (e.g., being protective of the father, or talking to the mother about childcare and to the father about finances). Role plays or video tapes of therapy may be used to analyze traditional assumptions or approaches to treatment, as well as to develop feminist hypotheses and interventions. Tapes of traditional therapy may also be viewed in order to analyze political and gender issues in therapy. Also, exaggerated "how *not* to do therapy" role plays and videotapes may provide useful, memorable learning experiences.

The Structure and Use of the Training Group

Training or supervisory groups may be deliberately structured in order to maximize learning regarding gender and diversity. Groups that are coed and that represent a range of life experiences, ethnicities, and life-styles elicit different world views and help to challenge and expand trainees' perceptions of "normality." When a less hierarchical model is desired, collaborative teams may be used to move the supervisor from a hierarchical to a collaborative position and to empower trainees.

Modeling

In a feminist approach to training, the supervisor/trainer attempts to model for students the integration of expert and nurturant roles as well as the various skills of a feminist approach. Because of the importance of modeling in the learning process, it is considered vital that all trainees have the opportunity to experience both male and female trainers and supervisors.

RESEARCH ISSUES

A feminist approach to family therapy has implications at both general and specific levels. At a general level, just as an awareness of the fundamental importance of gender is essential to a nonandrocentric approach to family therapy, this awareness is likewise essential to a nonandrocentric approach to research. This implies making a conscious effort to counteract the dominant cultural conception of marriage and family relationships reflected in family therapy research. Gurman and Klein (1980) state that in the research on marital conflict, "traditional views of marriage have been apparent in the questions researchers have asked and in their definitions of variables chosen for measurement" (p. 168). This androcentric bias in research is expressed, for example, by definitions of marital stability and happiness based on "the wife's conformity to the husband's values and needs, and . . . a division of labor, with task specialization along sex-role lines" (Gurman & Klein, 1980, p. 169), and by the use of normative behavior as the criteria for change in outcome studies of marital therapy. As Gurman and Klein point out, correcting this bias will require careful gender-conscious scrutiny of the assumptions underlying research criteria for assessing marital and family change, as well as for the types of treatment goals against which change is measured. It will be important, for example, to use outcome criteria that recognize as positive change the increased conflict resulting from a wife's growing assertiveness, and that allow family therapists and researchers to discriminate between positive and negative divorce outcomes as well as positive and negative marital continuation outcomes.

A second implication of a feminist approach to family therapy research is a recognition that gender and science are both socially constructed categories, and that science expresses the divisions in society between feminine and masculine, subjective and objective, and love and power (Keller, 1985). Counteracting these divisions involves recognizing research as a "deeply personal as well as a social activity" (Keller, 1985, p. 7), influenced and directed by the researcher's own values and world view. This suggests that researchers in family therapy must recognize their work as highly political, examine and openly state their own underlying assumptions and values concerning men, women, children, and the relations between them, and abandon any claims to scientific "neutrality."

More specific research issues and questions also arise from a feminist approach. Although a great deal has now been written critiquing traditional family therapy from a feminist perspective and suggesting a variety of feminist-informed alternatives, the actual impact of these alternatives on trainees and families has yet to be determined empirically. The first necessary step is to articulate more clearly various strategies for counteracting traditional gender socialization, for empowering women, and for involving men more centrally in their marriages and families. The Wheeler (1985) and Chaney (1986) studies represent an initial step in this direction, but further elaboration is necessary. A second step will be to test empirically the effectiveness and impact on families of various gender-sensitive strategies.

A third step will involve the development of training methods that promote feminist awareness in family therapy trainees. The present author's research (Avis, 1986) has begun the process of articulating such training methods. It will be necessary eventually to test empirically these methods in order to determine their actual impact on therapists and families, as well as to deterine which methods or combination of methods are most effective for helping trainees to conceptualize and intervene differently.

Other research questions that could be addressed include an examination of the impact on families and on trainees of more and less hierarchical relationships and a study of the actual level of gender-related content currently being taught by family therapy training programs. There is also a need to develop model curricula, bibliographies, and source materials to support the integration of gender content into family therapy training.

KEY BOOKS AND ARTICLES

Ault-Riché, M. (Ed.). (1986). *Women and family therapy.* Rockville, MD: Aspen Systems.

As the first book that focuses specifically on issues related to women and family therapy, this edited volume is an important addition to the field. Its ten chapters, written by many well-known feminist family therapists, cover a wide range of therapeutic topics related to both the larger context of patriarchal society and to smaller contexts of particular concern to women. These topics include training; larger systems; wife abuse; minority women; alcoholism; feminist systems therapy with lesbian clients; with depressed women; and with anorectic women; and nuclear issues.

Avis, J. M. (1985). The politics of functional family therapy: A feminist critique. *Journal of Marital and Family Therapy, 11*, 127–138.

This paper examines the political processes and gender biases inherent in functional family therapy. It argues that this model of family therapy subtly reinforces traditional gender roles in both family and therapist and examines the implicatons of this bias. In the article that follows (in the journal), James Alexander and his colleagues provide a spirited defense of what they maintain is the nonsexist nature of functional family therapy.

Avis, J. M. (1986). *Training and supervision in feminist-informed family therapy: A Delphi study.* Unpublished doctoral dissertation, Purdue University, West Lafayette, IN.

This study followed Wheeler's (1985) study. It polled the thinking of a panel of feminist family therapists on training and supervision issues relevant to a feminist approach. It provides a profile of major teaching methods, supervisory processes, content areas, and reading resources useful in training family therapists to be sensitive to issues of gender.

Bograd, M. (1984). Family systems approaches to wife battering: A feminist critique. *American Journal of Orthopsychiatry, 54*, 558–568.

This incisive analysis demonstrates how subtle biases implicit in systems formulations are translated into practice, rendering systems theory an inadequate conceptual framework for intervening in situations of violence and abuse.

Brodsky, A. M., & Hare-Mustin, R. (Eds.). (1980). *Women and psychotherapy.* New York: Guilford Press.

This excellent book provides a comprehensive examination of major issues concerning women and therapy, including research on gender differences in therapy, high-frequency disorders among women, critiques of traditional approaches, and alternative interventions.

Broverman, I., Broverman, D., Clarkson, F., Rosenkrantz, P., & Vogel, S. (1970). Sex role stereotypes and clinical judgments of mental health. *Journal of Consulting and Clinical Psychology, 34*, 1–7.

This often-cited study examines clinicians' differential perceptions of and criteria for mental health in men and women. Findings revealed that while clinicians judged stereotypically masculine behavior as adult, they judged stereotypically feminine behavior as nonadult, leaving women with a choice of being regarded as adult but unfeminine, or as being feminine but nonadult.

Caplan, P. J. (1985). *The myth of women's masochism.* New York: Dutton.

This fascinating book debunks the traditional psychoanalytic myth of women's masochism. Caplan studies the origin and persistence of the myth, its expression in distorted societal and psychiatric beliefs about women, and its impact on women's lives and perceptions of themselves.

Caplan, P. J., & Hall-McCorquodale, I. (1985). Mother-blaming in major clinical journals. *American Journal of Orthopsychiatry, 55*, 345–353.

This eye-opening study reports vivid examples of mother-blaming and father-idealizing in clinical journals. It is a great consciousness-raiser regarding subtle biases in the literature.

Caust, B. L., Libow, J. A., & Raskin, P. A. (1981). Challenge and promises of training women as family systems therapists. *Family Process, 20*, 439–447.

The authors discuss challenges that may arise in training women as family therapists, such as difficulties in expressing authority and power, countertransference, the sexual politics of supervision, the lack of female role models, difficulties in maintaining boundaries, and traditional expectations of the female role. They suggest that a feminist orientation is helpful in empowering trainees and promoting nonstereotypical behavior.

Chesler, P. (1972). *Women and madness*. New York: Doubleday.

This classic provides a piercing analysis and indictment of how women have been viewed and treated by psychiatric systems, as well as a call for a new psychology of women.

Chodorow, N. (1978). *The reproduction of mothering: Psychoanalysis and the sociology of gender*. Berkeley: University of California Press.

This important book provides a ground-breaking analysis of the social and psychological consequences of women's mothering. Chodorow suggests that it is women's primary responsibility for mothering that reproduces and maintains emotional and psychological differences between men and women, and makes a strong argument for the need for both men and women to parent equally. This is important reading.

Dinnerstein, D. (1976). *The mermaid and the minotaur: Sexual arrangements and human malaise*. New York: Harper & Row.

This book provides an eloquent and powerful analysis of the effects of female-dominated child care on adult perceptions of women and female power.

Ehrenreich, B. (1983). *The hearts of men: American dreams and the flight from commitment*. New York: Anchor Books.

This is an original and intriguing analysis of the changing bonds between men and women over the past 30 years.

Ehrenreich, B., & English, D. (1978). *For her own good: 150 years of the experts' advice to women*. Garden City, NY: Anchor Books.

This fascinating book recounts a history of women's experience at the hands of professional "experts", especially doctors, from the witch hunts to the contemporary single woman. It is well-researched, witty, and highly illuminating.

Eisenstein, H. (1983). *Contemporary feminist thought*. Boston: Hall.

This is an excellent introduction and guide to contemporary feminist thought in America. Written for readers unfamiliar with feminism, it traces the evolution of feminist thought since 1970 and helps make sense of changing ideas. It is highly recommended.

Feldman, L. (1982). Sex roles and family dynamics. In F. Walsh (Ed.), *Normal family processes*. New York: Guilford Press.

This chapter combines research findings with family theory in a thought-provoking discussion of the negative effects of traditional gender roles on all family members as well as on family structure and functioning. Implications for family therapists are discussed.

Fishman, P. (1978). Interaction: The work women do. *Social Problems, 25*, 397–406.

This dramatic study demonstrates how gender hierarchy is established and maintained in everyday verbal interaction. The author analyzed tapes of daily conversations of male–female couples and found that women did most of the interactional work (asking questions, listening, responding), while men controlled the direction and content of the conversations.

Gilligan, C. (1982). *In a different voice: Psychological theory and women's development*. Cambridge, MA: Harvard University Press.

This extremely important book reports Gilligan's influential research on women's moral development. Her work not only distinguishes women's moral development as different from men's, but also demonstrates the hidden fallacy of assuming that theory and research developed on men applies equally to women.

Goldner, V. (1985a). Feminism and family therapy. *Family Process, 24*, 31–47.

This is an eloquent and scholarly feminist analysis of family therapy ideology and the complexities and dilemmas of sexual politics in family therapy practice. If you have time to read only one article, this it it.

Goldner, V. (1985b). Warning: Family therapy may be dangerous to your health. *The Family Therapy Networker, 9*, 19–23.

This thought-provoking paper proposes the universality of gender as a basic category of human organization and domination. Goldner also discusses the necessity of rethinking core family therapy assumptions in order to account for gender and power differences. This is important reading.

Gurman, A. S., & Klein, M. H. (1980). Marital and family conflicts. In A. M. Brodsky & R. Hare-Mustin (Eds.), *Women and psychotherapy*. New York: Guilford Press.

The authors examine the impact of marital conflict on women, the need for integration among structural, cultural, and interactional theories of marital and family conflicts, the implications of different clinical models for women, and sources of gender bias in marital and family therapy outcome research. The article is particularly useful for its suggestions regarding research on therapy outcome.

Gurman, A. S., & Klein, M. H. (1984). Marriage and the family: An unconscious male bias in behavioral treatment? In E. A. Blechman (Ed.), *Behavior modification with women*. New York: Guilford Press.

This chapter critiques the unconscious gender bias inherent in the philosophy and practice of behavioral marital and family therapy. The authors argue persuasively that the clarification and acknowledgment of the therapist's own personal and professional values are essential to avoid this bias in practice.

Hare-Mustin, R. T. (1978). A feminist approach to family therapy. *Family Process, 17*, 181–194.

The first to raise feminist concerns in family therapy, this pioneering article examines the unquestioned reinforcement of traditional gender roles in practice, and the application of feminist principles to family therapy practice.

Hare-Mustin, R. T. (1979). Family therapy and sex role stereotypes. *The Counseling Psychologist, 8*, 31–32.

This is primarily a summary of her 1978 article. Hare-Mustin critiques techniques of family therapy and suggests knowledge, skills, and attitudes necessary for family therapists to confront sex-role stereotypes in their own lives and those of their clients.

Hare-Mustin, R. T. (1980). Family therapy may be dangerous to your health. *Professional Psychology, 11*, 935–938.

Hare-Mustin points out the dangers involved when therapists give priority to the good of the family, thereby ignoring what may be the best interests of individual family members (most often those of women). She also suggests that many family therapists accept the traditional model of the family and make this model their goal. As a result, they often foster stereotyped roles and other behaviors that impinge upon the well-being of women.

Henley, N. (1977). *Body politics: Power, sex, and nonverbal communication.* Englewood Cliffs, NJ: Prentice-Hall.

This book presents a fascinating analysis of research on male–female differences in nonverbal communication, and on how these differences express and maintain gender hierarchy. It is important and entertaining reading.

Jacobson, N. S. (1983). Beyond empiricism: The politics of marital therapy. *American Journal of Family Therapy, 11*, 11–24.

Jacobson's article provides an excellent discussion of the political (i.e., power) issues inherent in therapy in general and behavioral marital therapy (BMT) in particular. Jacobson identifies the processes through which traditional values and roles oppressive to women are inadvertently reinforced in BMT and makes specific recommendations for changing them.

Jaggar, A. M., & Rothenberg, P. S. (Eds.). (1984). *Feminist frameworks: Alternative theoretical accounts of the relations between women and men* (2nd ed.). New York: McGraw-Hill.

This edited volume offers an extremely helpful organization of major feminist theories. Excellent selections of lively and instructive readings are provided.

James, K. (1984). Breaking the chains of gender. *Australian Journal of Family Therapy, 5*, 241–248.

James provides a thought-provoking discussion of the symbolic dimensions of patriarchy that exists in all aspects of culture. A challenge is issued to break the "chains of gender" in families and in family therapy.

236 Feminist Issues in Family Therapy

James, K., & McIntyre, D. (1983). The reproduction of families: The social role of family therapy? *Journal of Marital and Family Therapy, 9*, 119–129.

The authors challenge family therapy's failure to respond to recent critical analyses of the family, as well as its failure to consider the socioeconomic and political contexts of family functioning. They examine the limitations and consequences of systems theory as employed by family therapists, problems inherent in the institution of motherhood, and the social role of the family therapist. This scholarly analysis is highly recommended.

Keller, E. F. (1985). *Reflections on gender and science*. New Haven: Yale University Press.

Keller has produced a highly readable, thought-provoking analysis of the relationship between gender and science. She writes from the perspective of a respected mathematician and starts from the assumption that both gender and science are socially constructed categories. This is very important reading for everyone, but in particular for those engaged in research.

Layton, M. (1984). Tipping the therapeutic balance: Masculine, feminine or neuter? *The Family Therapy Networker, 8*, 21–27.

This short, well-written article touches on many gender issues that arise in family therapy, and in particular on the tendency to blame mothers and hold them responsible for change. The author includes her own very helpful annotated guide to the literature.

Lerner, H. G. (1985). *The dance of anger: A women's guide to changing the patterns of intimate relationships*. New York: Harper & Row.

In this wise and well-written book, Lerner brings together her systemic understanding of family relationships and her feminist understanding of women's experience to create a most helpful guide for women in dealing with anger in important relationships. She discusses the patterns and dynamics of anger in both family and work relationships, the central place of anger in women's lives, and the particular problems women experience in dealing with their anger constructively. Filled with strategies and options for using anger productively to change and develop relationships as well as to define the self, this book is a valuable resource for clients and therapists alike. Highly recommended.

Lerner, H. G. (in press). Is family systems theory really systemic? A feminist communication. *Journal of Psychotherapy and the Family*.

This fine article examines the inadequacies and clinical implications of family systems theory. The author suggests that systems theory can become more contextual by examining the reciprocal relationship between patriarchal society and family dysfunction.

Libow, J. A., Raskin, P. A., & Caust, B. L. (1982). Feminist and family systems therapy: Are they irreconcilable? *American Journal of Family Therapy, 10*, 3–12.

This article identifies the differences and similarities between feminist and family therapy, both in theory and technique. Differences include views of causality, locus of change, the role of insight, and the use of power. The two frameworks share techniques of modeling and reframing, contextual concepts of pathology, and an emphasis on behavioral change. Further integration of the two frameworks is encouraged.

Mainardi, P. (1970). The politics of housework. In R. Morgan (Ed.), *Sisterhood is powerful.* New York: Vintage.

This delightfully funny piece is painful in its accuracy.

Margolin, G., Fernandez, V., Talovic, S., & Onorato, R. (1983). Sex role considerations and behavioral marital therapy: Equal does not mean identical. *Journal of Marital and Family Therapy, 9,* 131–145.

This worthwhile paper examines the advantages and disadvantages of behavioral marital therapy (BMT) in terms of its treatment of men and women. The authors identify a variety of ways in which BMT gives contradictory messages regarding sex role issues. Recommendations are provided for how BMT can become more sensitive to these issues as well as more flexible in handling them.

Miller, J. B. (1976). *Toward a new psychology of women.* Boston: Beacon Press.

This wonderful little book provides a model of adulthood based not on the male model of separation, but on a female-influenced model of connectedness. Miller's model validates women's traditional capacities for nurturing and for building relationships and suggests that these capacities are essential for men as well as for women.

Okun, B. F. (1983). Gender issues of family systems therapists. In B. F. Okun & S. T. Gladding (Eds.), *Issues in training marriage and family therapists.* Ann Arbor, MI: ERIC/CAPS.

This well-written chapter provides a good introduction to gender issues in both the training of family therapists and the practice of family therapy. It raises a number of key issues relevant to all family therapists regardless of theoretical orientation, such as the impact of gender differences and socialization on the supervisory relationship, on therapists' attitudes and behavior, and on the training process.

Rich, A. (1976). *Of woman born: Motherhood as experience and institution.* New York: Norton.

Rich draws on her own experience as well as on research and literature to explore the power and powerlessness of motherhood in a patriarchal society. This book is personal, intense, and scholarly—a classic.

Simon, R. (Ed.). (1984). From ideology to practice: The Women's Project in Family Therapy. *Family Therapy Networker, 8*(3), 28–32, 38–40.

Richard Simon interviews the four organizers of The Woman's Project in Family Therapy: Betty Carter, Olga Silverstein, Peggy Papp, and Marianne Walters. These leaders candidly discuss their own experiences with sexism, the development of the Woman's Project, and ways in which they implement their feminist ideology in family therapy.

Simon, R. (Ed.). (1985). Feminism: Shedding new light on the family, *Family Therapy Networker* (Special Issue), *9*(6).

Provocative and well-written articles by Virginia Goidner and Dorothy Wheeler explore the role and impact of feminism on family therapy. In addition, five case studies by experienced feminist family therapists (Bepko, Goodrich *et al.*, Layton, Lerner, & Silverstein) demonstrate the application of feminist principles in family therapy, while thought-provoking commentaries on the case studies are offered by Michael Nichols and Betty Carter. This special issue should be read from cover to cover.

Taggart, M. (1985). The feminist critique in epistemological perspective: Questions of context in family therapy. *Journal of Marital and Family Therapy, 11*, 113–126.

This article provides a highly theoretical discussion of the feminist critique of systemic epistemology. Taggart suggests that feminist thought may serve to enrich and expand systems theory by challenging it to include broader contexts and thus to become more truly systemic.

Tavris, D., & Wade, C. (Eds.). (1984). *The longest war: Sex differences in perspective.* New York: Harcourt, Brace & Jovanovich.

Research on sex differences is presented from the perspective of several different disciplines. This book is valuable not only for its summary of research findings, but for the light it sheds on the differing perspectives from which various disciplines approach the study of sex differences.

Thorne, B., & Yalom, M. (Eds.). (1982). *Rethinking the family: Some feminist questions.* New York: Longman.

This outstanding edited volume presents feminist analyses and revisioning of the family from the perspectives of varied disciplines. The introductory chapter by Thorne is particularly helpful in its overview of themes and assumptions central to feminist critiques of the family. This book is highly recommended.

Weiner, J. P., & Boss, P. (1985). Exploring gender bias against women: Ethics for marriage and family therapy. *Counseling and Values, 30*, 9–23.

These authors cast gender issues in family therapy in ethical terms and call for affirmative action in both theory and training. Most valuable are their ethical guidelines for reducing gender bias in family therapy.

Wheeler, D. (1985). *The theory and practice of feminist-informed family therapy: A Delphi study.* Unpublished doctoral dissertation, Purdue University, West Lafayette, IN.

This study is the first to poll the thinking of feminists in the family therapy field. It provides a profile of assumptions, interventions, and goals considered basic to a feminist approach, feminist criticisms of a family systems approach, and a comparison of the similarities and differences between feminist and traditional approaches to family therapy.

Wheeler, D., Avis, J. M., Miller, L., & Chaney, S. (1985). Rethinking family therapy education and supervision: A feminist model. *Journal of Psychotherapy and the Family, 1*(4), 53–71.

The authors delineate perceptual, conceptual, and executive skills relevant to feminist-informed family therapy, as well as methods for teaching them. This article may be particularly useful for trainers interested in integrating feminist ideas and skills into their family therapy training programs. Please note that a major portion of Table 3 is missing from the original article, but may be obtained from the following issue of the *Journal of Psychotherapy and the Family, 2*(1).

ACKNOWLEDGMENTS

The author would like to acknowledge Sita Chaney's contribution in writing several of the annotated citations, which also appeared in Wheeler, Avis, Miller, and Chaney (1985).

REFERENCES

American Association for Marriage and Family Therapy. (1981). *Manual on accreditation.* Washington, DC: AAMFT.

American Psychological Association Task Force (1975). Report of the task force on sex bias and sex-role stereotyping in psychotherapeutic practice. *American Psychologist, 30,* 1169–1175.

Avis, J. M. (1985a). The politics of functional family therapy: A feminist critique. *Journal of Marital and Family Therapy, 11,* 127–138.

Avis, J. M. (1985b). Through a different lens: A reply to Alexander, Warburton, Waldron and Mas. *Journal of Marital and Family Therapy, 11,* 145–148.

Avis, J. M. (1986). *Training and supervision in feminist-informed family therapy: A Delphi study.* Unpublished doctoral dissertation, Purdue University, West Lafayette, IN.

Bepko, C. (1985). Mary and John: Power, power, who's got the power? *The Family Therapy Networker, 9,* 47–49.

Bepko, C. S. (1986). Alcoholism as oppression: The dilemma of the woman in the alcoholic system. In M. Ault-Riché (Ed.), *Women and family therapy.* Rockville, MD: Aspen Systems.

Bograd, M. (1984). Family systems approaches to wife battering: A feminist critique. *American Journal of Orthopsychiatry, 54,* 558–568.

Bograd, M. (1986). A feminist examination of family systems models of violence against women in the family. In M. Ault-Riché (Ed.), *Women and family therapy.* Rockville, MD: Aspen Systems.

Braverman, L. (1986). The depressed woman in context: A feminist family therapist's analysis. In M. Ault-Riché (Ed.), *Women and family therapy.* Rockville, MD: Aspen Systems.

Caplan, P. J. (1985). *The myth of women's masochism.* New York: Dutton.

Caplan, P. J., & Hall-McCorquodale, I. (1985). Mother-blaming in major clinical journals. *American Journal of Orthopsychiatry, 55,* 345–353.

Caust, B. L., Libow, J. A., & Raskin, P. A. (1981). Challenges and promises of training women as family systems therapists. *Family Process, 20,* 439–447.

Chaney, S. (1986). *The development of a feminist family therapy rating scale*. Unpublished doctoral dissertation, Purdue University, West Lafayette, IN.

Chesler, P. (1972). *Women and madness*. New York: Doubleday.

Chodorow, N. (1978). *The reproduction of mothering: Psychoanalysis and the sociology of gender*. Berkeley: University of California Press.

Dinnerstein, D. (1976). *The mermaid and the minotaur: Sexual arrangements and human malaise*. New York: Harper & Row.

Eisenstein, H. (1983). *Contemporary feminist thought*. Boston: Hall.

Gilbert, L. A. (1980). Feminist therapy. In A. E. Brodsky & R. T. Hare-Mustin (Eds.), *Women in psychotherapy: An assessment of research and practice*. New York: Guilford Press.

Gilligan, C. (1982). *In a different voice: Psychological theory and women's development*. Cambridge: Harvard University Press.

Goldner, V. (1985a). Feminism and family therapy. *Family Process, 24*, 31–47.

Goldner, V. (1985b). Warning: Family therapy may be dangerous to your health. *The Family Therapy Networker, 9*, 19–23.

Goodrich, T. J., Rampage, C., Ellman, B., & Halstead, K. (1985). Angie and Hank. *The Family Therapy Networker, 9*, 50–52.

Gordon, L. (1979). The struggle for reproductive freedom: Three stages of feminism. In Z. R. Eisenstein (Ed.), *Capitalist patriarchy and the case for socialist feminism*. New York: Monthly Review Press.

Greenglass, E. R. (1982). *A world of difference: Gender roles in perspective*. New York: Wiley.

Gurman, A. S., & Klein, M. H. (1980). Marital and family conflicts. In A. M. Brodsky & R. Hare-Mustin (Eds.), *Women and psychotherapy*. New York: Guilford Press.

Gurman, A. S., & Klein, M. H. (1984). Marriage and the family: An unconscious male bias in behavioral treatment? In E. A. Blechman (Ed.), *Behavior modification with women*. New York: Guilford Press.

Guttman, H. A. (1986). Family therapy of anorexia nervosa and bulimia: A feminist perspective. In M. Ault-Riché, (Ed.), *Women and family therapy*. Rockville, MD: Aspen Systems.

Hare-Mustin, R. T. (1978). A feminist approach to family therapy. *Family Process, 17*, 181–194.

Hare-Mustin, R. T. (1979). Family therapy and sex role stereotypes. *The Counseling Psychologist, 8*, 31–32.

Hare-Mustin, R. T. (1980). Family therapy may be dangerous for your health. *Professional Psychology, 11*, 935–938.

Hartman, H. (1984). The unhappy marriage of Marxism and feminism: Towards a more progressive union. In A. M. Jaggar & P. S. Rothenberg (Eds.), *Feminist frameworks: Alternative theoretical accounts of the relations between women and men* (2nd ed.). New York: McGraw-Hill.

Imber-Black, E. (1986). Women, families, and larger systems. In M. Ault-Riché (Ed.), *Women and family therapy*. Rockville, MD: Aspen Systems.

Jacobson, N. S. (1983). Beyond empiricism: The politics of marital therapy. *American Journal of Family Therapy, 11*, 11–24.

Jaggar, A. M., & Rothenberg, P. S. (Eds.). (1984). *Feminist frameworks: Alternative theoretical accounts of the relations between women and men* (2nd ed.). New York: McGraw-Hill.

James, K. (1984). Breaking the chains of gender. *Australian Journal of Family Therapy*, *5*, 241–248.

James, K., & McIntyre, D. (1983). The reproduction of families: The social role of family therapy? *Journal of Marital and Family Therapy*, *9*, 119–129.

Keller, E. F. (1985). *Reflections on gender and science*. New Haven: Yale University Press.

Layton, M. (1984). Tipping the therapeutic balance: Masculine, feminine or neuter? *The Family Therapy Networker*, *8*, 21–27.

Layton, M. (1985). Paula and Don: A marriage in search of a nag. *The Family Therapy Networker*, *9*(6), 40–41, 44–46.

Lerner, H. (1985a). Dianna and Lillie: Can a feminist still like Murray Bowen? *The Family Therapy Networker*, *9*(6), 36–39.

Lerner, H. G. (1985b). *The dance of anger: A woman's guide to changing the patterns of intimate relationships*. New York: Harper & Row.

Lerner, H. G. (1986). Is family systems theory really systemic? A feminist communication. *Journal of Psychotherapy and the Family*, *3*, (4).

Libow, J. A. (1986). Training family therapists as feminists. In M. Ault-Riché (Ed.), *Women and family therapy*. Rockville, MD: Aspen Systems.

Libow, J. A., Raskin, P. A., & Caust, B. L. (1982). Feminist and family systems therapy: Are they irreconcilable? *American Journal of Family Therapy*, *10*, 3–12.

Luepnitz, D. (1982). *Child custody: A study of families after divorce*. Lexington, MA: Lexington Books.

Margolin, G., Fernandez, V., Talovic, S., & Onorato, R. (1983). Sex role considerations and behavioral marital therapy: Equal does not mean identical. *Journal of Marital and Family Therapy*, *9*, 131–145.

Miller, J. B. (1976). *Toward a new psychology of women*. Boston: Beacon Press.

Okun, B. F. (1983). Gender issues of family systems therapists. In B. F. Okun & S. T. Gladding (Eds.), *Issues in training marriage and family therapists*. Ann Arbor, MI: ERIC/CAPS.

Pinderhughes, E. B. (1986). Minority women: A nodal position in the functioning of the social system. In M. Ault-Riché (Ed.), *Women and family therapy*. Rockville, MD: Aspen Systems.

Roth, S., & Murphy, B. C. (1986). Therapeutic work with lesbian clients: A systemic therapy view: In M. Ault-Riché (Ed.), *Women and family therapy*. Rockville, MD: Aspen Systems.

Russell, M. (1986). Teaching feminist counseling skills: An evaluation. *Counselor Education and Supervision*, *25* (4), 320–331.

Taggart, M. (1985). The feminist critique in epistemological perspective: Questions of context in family therapy. *Journal of Marital and Family Therapy*, *11*, 113–126.

Thorne, B. (1982). Feminist rethinking of the family: An overview. In B. Thorne and M. Yalom (Eds.), *Rethinking the family: Some feminist questions*. New York: Longman.

Thorne, B. (1985). *Feminist rethinking of the family: Some feminist questions*. Presentation to the Annual Conference of the National Council on Family Relations.

Weiner, J. P., & Boss, P. (1985). Exploring gender bias against women: Ethics for marriage and family therapy. *Counseling and Values*, *30*, 9–23.

Wheeler, D. (1985). *The theory and practice of feminist-informed family therapy: A Delphi study*. Unpublished doctoral dissertation, Purdue University, West Lafayette, IN.

Wheeler, D., Avis, J. M., Miller, L. A., & Chaney, S. (1985). Rethinking family therapy education and supervision: A feminist model. *Journal of Psychotherapy and the Family, 1*(4), 53–71.

Winkle, W. C., Piercy, F. P., & Hovestadt, A. J. (1981). A curriculum for graduate-level marriage and family therapy education. *Journal of Marital and Family Therapy, 7*, 201–210.

10

OTHER FAMILY THERAPIES

Each chapter in this book deals with a different family therapy theory or domain. The rich diversity of the family therapy field is reflected in the fact that a variety of other family therapies also have had and continue to have a significant impact on the field's development. This chapter is intended to provide both an introduction to and key resources on five of these important approaches to family therapy. Specifically, this chapter includes sections on (1) multiple family group therapy; (2) multiple-impact therapy; (3) marital group therapy; (4) network therapy; and (5) Gerald Zuk's triadic therapy.

MULTIPLE-FAMILY GROUP THERAPY

Introduction to the Therapy

Multiple-family group therapy (MFT) involves the treatment of several families together within regularly scheduled therapy sessions. Cotherapists typically act as active facilitators to promote improved communication, to encourage insight into problematic interactions, and to restructure family relationship patterns. The MFT format has been employed on both an inpatient and an outpatient basis by theoretically diverse therapists working with families with a wide range of symptomatic behaviors. The person most closely associated with MFT, however, is Laqueur (1966, 1972a, 1972b, 1976).

Generally, MFT appears to combine many of the advantages of both family and group therapy. It provides for indirect learning from other families through analogy, indirect interpretation, and modeling (Laqueur, 1976). Also, a supportive context is created for trying new behaviors and developing more flexible roles (Gritzer & Okun, 1983). The families themselves sometimes serve as "cotherapists," in that they often can confront members of other families more effectively and powerfully than the therapist. Confrontation from other families minimizes potential denial or panic and is typically "heard" (McFarlane, 1982).

The annotated citations below reflect the theoretical underpinnings and creative applications of MFT.

Key Books and Articles

Benningfield, A. B. (1978). Multiple family therapy systems. *Journal of Marriage and Family Counseling, 4,* 25–34.

A table is provided that organizes over 40 reports on MFT in terms of population, setting, and conclusions or outcomes of the report. The role of the therapist and implications for research are discussed, as well as other topics that are covered more thoroughly in the Strelnick (1977) review.

Gritzer, P. H., & Okun, H. S. (1983). Multiple family group therapy: A model for all families. In B. B. Wolman & G. Stricker (Eds.), *Handbook of family and marital therapy.* New York: Plenum Press.

This well-written chapter includes a comprehensive description of MFT as applied to outpatient settings. This article would provide a useful preparation for conducting an MFT group when read in conjunction with the Leichter and Schulman (1972, 1974) articles and the McFarlane (1982) chapter.

Laqueur, H. P. (1966). General systems theory and multiple family therapy. In J. H. Masserman (Ed.) *Handbook of psychiatric therapies.* New York: Grune & Stratton.

This brief and pithy chapter is devoted to each of the MFT theories and their interface. Such a discussion is not available in such detail in the other Laqueur writings.

Laqueur, H. P. (1972a). Mechanisms of change in multiple family therapy. In C. J. Sager & H. S. Kaplan (Eds.), *Progress in group and family therapy.* New York: Brunner/Mazel.

Unique to this chapter are excellent clinical illustrations of the 11 mechanisms of change in MFT as conceptualized by Laqueur.

Laqueur, H. P. (1972b). Multiple family therapy. In A. Ferber, M. Mendelsohn, & A. Napier (Eds.), *The book of family therapy.* Boston: Houghton Mifflin.

This chapter provides a straightforward description of how families are introduced, how a group is led, and how to respond to absenteeism. Also, examples of interaction in an MFT group and a comparison of successful and unsuccessful cotherapy operations are provided.

Laqueur, H. P. (1976). Multiple family therapy. In P. J. Guerin (Ed.), *Family therapy: Theory and practice.* New York: Gardner Press.

This is one of Laqueur's latest writings. It is an important piece of work, in that it clearly articulates his chief concepts. Topics covered include the history and description of MFT; its theoretical framework; the process and mechanisms of change; and goals and results. Particularly interesting is Laqueur's summary of the structure of disturbed and healthy families. Of considerable help is the lucid description of several MFT interventions.

Laqueur, H. P., & LaBurt, H. A. (1973). Multiple family therapy: Questions and answers. In D. Block (Ed.), *Techniques of family psychotherapy: A primer*. New York: Grune & Stratton.

This chapter offers much of the same information contained in the Laqueur (1976) chapter. However, its question-and-answer format and the section on the typical problems in the conduct of a group are unique.

Laqueur, H. P., LaBurt, H. A., & Morong, E. (1964). Multiple family therapy. In J. H. Masserman (Ed.), *Current psychiatric therapies* (Vol. 4). New York: Grune & Stratton.

This is a very early and widely cited Laqueur writing, but offers nothing that cannot be found in Laqueur's (1976) chapter in a more lucid form.

Laqueur, H. P., Wells, C. F., & Agresti, M. (1969). Multiple family therapy in a state hospital. *Hospital and Community Psychiatry, 20*, 13–19.

This article offers the most comprehensive description of Laquer's actual work at a state hospital. However, it does not include a description of his research study.

Leichter, E., & Schulman, G. L. (1972). Interplay of group and family treatment techniques in multi-family group therapy. *International Journal of Group Psychotherapy, 22*, 167–176.

After working several years as cotherapists in outpatient MFT, the authors articulate their own thinking about process and goals. They have found one of the greatest values of MFT to be the interaction between members across family boundaries. For example, an adolescent can practice differentiation first with adults who are not his/her parents. The authors provide numerous examples of their concepts from their own clinical practice.

Leichter, E., & Schulman, G. L. (1974). Multi-family group therapy: Multidimensional approach. *Family Process, 13*(1), 95–110.

Case examples are used to illustrate the dynamics and process of outpatient MFT. This is an excellent article, and would be useful for anyone about to initiate outpatient MFT.

McFarlane, W. R. (1982). Multiple-family therapy in the psychiatric hospital. In H. T. Harbin (Ed.), *The psychiatric hospital and the family*. New York: Spectrum.

This lucid chapter is by an author who practices MFT in an inpatient setting. McFarlane believes that groups made up of nonpsychotic clients need to be run differently from those made up of psychotic clients. Guidelines for managing both are provided. Also discussed are nine mechanisms for change "unique" to MFT. The author also outlines five problems that result from the institutionalization of the psychotic client and reviews how MFT can ameliorate or solve them.

Paul, N. L., Bloom, J. D., & Paul, B. B. (1981). Out-patient multiple family group therapy—why not? In L. R. Wolterg & M. L. Aronson (Eds.), *Group and family therapy*. New York: Brunner/Mazel.

The participating families are well described. Transcripts of sessions are included to demonstrate the impact on others in the group when hidden critical historical material is revealed. Norman Paul is the therapist of the group. A worthwhile chapter.

Strelnick, A. H. (1977). Multiple family group therapy: A review of the literature. *Family Process*, *16*, 307–325.

This review is neatly organized into subsections which include origins, methods, development of the group, goals, themes, and mechanisms of change. Also provided are comparisons of MFT with group and individual family therapy, as well as an evaluation of outcome.

MULTIPLE IMPACT THERAPY

Introduction to the Therapy

Robert MacGregor and his colleagues (MacGregor, *et al.*, 1964) developed multiple impact therapy (MIT) as a means of having a maximum impact on families with a disturbed adolescent in crisis. These highly motivated families would come long distances to the University of Texas Medical Branch in Galveston, Texas, and spend several days in intense therapy with a large team of professionals. The team typically included psychologists, psychiatric residents, social workers, and trainees, who would meet with family members individually and in various combinations in order to assess and treat problematic aspects of a family's functioning. On the second afternoon of these sessions, a team–family conference was held where findings were reviewed, recommendations made, and follow-up sessions scheduled for several months later.

During the 2 days of sessions, the team would attempt to examine and strengthen the parents' marital relationship, and would focus intensely on parent–adolescent communication patterns. Beyond helping families develop insight into their problems and restructure their relationship patterns, the MIT process took family members through a powerful emotional experience that jolted them toward more open system functioning. The experience often resulted in better communication, greater acceptance of differences, clearer hierarchies and boundaries, and a resolve to look toward the future for more creative, growth-producing ways of functioning (MacGregor, 1972; Richie, 1971).

MIT is not practiced extensively today, perhaps because of the considerable time, expense, and number of professional staff members needed to implement it, as well as its lack of empirical support. Another barrier may be conceptual. Many therapists believe that families need time between sessions to assimilate learning and to facilitate a transfer of gains to real-life situations. Nonetheless, the historical significance of MIT to the field of family therapy is considerable, and many of the assumptions and procedures implemented in MIT are still applicable to other forms of family therapy.

Key Books and Articles

Garrison, C., & Weber, J. (1981). Family crises intervention using multiple impact therapy. *Social Casework, 62*(10), 585–593.

In this study, MIT was employed to (1) reduce the time lag between family crisis onset and professional intervention; (2) minimize removal of children from the family; (3) provide quicker, more intensive treatment than traditional methods; and (4) encourage more effective cooperation among agencies involved with a particular family. Representatives from each caregiving agency formed a team that met with the family for a day and then divided responsibilities so as to be allied with different family members for the following month. The reported results of this cooperation are encouraging.

MacGregor, R. (1967). Progress in multiple impact theory. In N. W. Ackerman, F. L. Beatman, & S. N. Sherman (Eds.), *Expanding theory and practice in family therapy.* New York: Family Service Association.

In this chapter, MacGregor defines MIT as a freeing up of natural processes in the family, as opposed to an insight-oriented therapy. A historical perspective is given on this treatment modality, as well as a look at the underlying theory and techniques used to change a "closed" family system into an "open" one.

MacGregor, R. (1972). Multiple impact psychotherapy with families. In G. D. Erickson & T. P. Hogan (Eds.), *Family therapy: An introduction to theory and technique.* Monterey, CA: Brooks/Cole.

This is perhaps the most complete explication of MIT offered by MacGregor. He expands his earlier works by discussing how to incorporate the contributions of relevant community personnel into the treatment team's impact. The results of a 2-year study suggest that disturbed adolescents and their families may be better thought of as developmentally arrested then as requiring a particular diagnostic category for the acting-out child.

MacGregor, R., Richie, A. M., Serrano, A. C., Schuster, F. P., McDonald, E. C., & Goolishian, H. A. (1964). *Multiple impact therapy with families.* New York: McGraw-Hill.

This volume represents the authors' initial, formal evaluation of their MIT experiences with 62 adolescents and their families over a 3-year period. The treatment team was designed to spend 2–3 days with a family for 6–8 hours per day. The study confirmed hypotheses that extreme behavior in an adolescent was related to extreme behavior on the part of at least one parent, and found that the approach increased flexibility of roles in 49 of the 62 families examined. Today's researchers would consider this study to be "descriptive" at best.

Richie, A. (1971). Multiple impact therapy: An experiment. In J. Haley (Ed.), *Changing families: A family therapy reader.* New York: Grune & Stratton.

This reprint of Richie's 1960 article gives an overall description of how MIT was done at the Youth Development Project of the University of Texas Medical Branch at Galveston, Texas. This article lacks a discussion of theoretical underpinning, but reflects much of the excitement over what was, at the time, a new treatment procedure.

MARITAL GROUP THERAPY

Introduction to the Approach

While a variety of authors have written about marital group therapy, their rationales vary considerably. Proponents have identified such advantages as (1) facilitation of communications; (2) relief of guilt, shame, and embarrassment through observing other couples with similar problems; (3) cost; (4) reality testing aided by group feedback; (5) identification by group members of inappropriate behaviors and expectations; (6) development of insight and skills through observation of other couples; (7) group support that encourages ventilation and change, and reduces fear of reprisal; (8) differentiation from marital symbiosis; and (9) identification and interruption of counterproductive "games" (Alger, 1976; Framo, 1973; Linden, Goodwin, & Resnik, 1968). In essence, the marital group becomes a "third family" that gives each couple an opportunity for growth (Leichter, 1973).

Marital group formats and procedures also vary widely. Alger (1976), for example, discusses his own creative uses of role playing, family choreography, and videotape feedback. Framo (1973) has at least one session with each group member and his/her family of origin. In contrast, Liberman, Wheeler, and Sanders (1976) advocate behavioral communication skills training in their couples groups.

Various psychoanalytic therapists have identified potential disadvantages of the marital group format (see Boas, 1962; Gottlieb & Pattison, 1966; Linde *et al.*, 1968). For example, complications in the development of the essential transference neurosis within the marital group format have been thought to lead to a dilution of transference reactions (Boas, 1962). Additional fears include the potential for acting out within the group and the strengthening of marital defenses. However, these psychoanalytic criticisms do not appear to have a substantive basis, either empirically or in therapeutic practice (Gurman, 1971).

Framo (1973) has summed up the enthusiasm of many marital group therapy proponents in stating that marital group therapy is "probably the treatment of choice for dealing with marital problems" (p. 96). As with other marital and family therapies, however, more empirical support clearly is needed to substantiate such a claim. Moreover, the dearth of important articles on marital group therapy over the past decade may reflect a general waning of interest in this therapy format.

Key Books and Articles

Alger, I. (1976). Multiple couple therapy. In P. J. Guerin (Ed.), *Family therapy: Theory and practice*. New York: Gardner Press.

This chapter does a good job of covering many of the important issues in couples group therapy from an eclectic framework. Topics include the indications for use of couples group therapy, stages of evolution in the group, the therapist's role, size and structure of the group, and specialized techniques.

Arieli, A. (1981). Multicouple group therapy of alcoholics. *International Journal of the Addictions, 16*, 773–782.

This article presents the author's experience in the treatment of alcoholics in a group marital format. The author cites the interactional nature of alcoholism and speaks of how these issues are highlighted in the group format.

Blinder, M. G., & Kirschenbaum, M. (1967). The technique of married couple group therapy. *Archives of General Psychiatry, 17*, 44–52.

This article presents a theoretical and practical approach to their "married couple group therapy," based on treating the interpersonal marital relationship. The authors believe that mate selection is based on the fulfillment of neurotic needs. They discuss the curative aspects of the group, as well as positive therapeutic interventions.

Boas, C. V. E. (1962). Intensive group psychotherapy with married couples. *International Journal of Group Psychotherapy, 12*, 142–153.

This article presents the author's early experiences with a marital couples group. Boas discusses the positive effects of breaking away from psychoanalytic "taboos" regarding seeing married couples together in a group. This is an excellent historical article in its reflection of the excitement that existed when marital group therapy was first initiated.

Burton, G. (1962). Group counseling with alcoholic husbands and their nonalcoholic wives. *Marriage and Family Living, 24*, 56–61.

This early article discusses the profit gained in working with alcoholics in a group marital format. Emphasis is placed on the need to analyze the interpersonal relationship of these couples, and to make these interactions the focus of change in treatment.

Flint, A. A. Jr., & MacLennan, B. W. (1962). Some dynamic factors in marital group psychotherapy. *International Journal of Group Psychotherapy, 12*, 355–361.

This articlce presents common characteristics observed in six marital therapy groups. The authors present the group process in terms of five specific stages, and describe such pertinent aspects of treatment dynamics as (1) the marital partner in the therapeutic role, (2) the relationship of the couple to the group, and (3) the relationship of the couple to the therapist.

Framo, J. L. (1973). Marriage therapy in a couples group. In D. A. Block (Ed.), *Techniques of family therapy: A primer*. New York: Grune & Stratton.

This excellent overview of Framo's approach to couples group therapy is must reading. Many important issues, such as therapeutic rationale, selection of couples, session structure, and group process, are presented. In keeping with Framo's orientation toward family-of-origin theory, attention is paid to helping couples recognize patterns in their marriages that stem from their respective families of origin.

Gottlieb, A., & Pattison, E. M. (1966). Married couples group psychotherapy. *Archives of General Psychiatry, 14,* 143–152.

This article maintains that many of the early psychoanalytic fears of seeing couples together in a group are unfounded. Specific attention is shown to the positive aspects of the group in facilitating the couples' growth. Also discussed is the breaking up of symbiosis in disturbed marital relationships.

Gurman, A. S. (1971). Group marital therapy: Clinical and empirical implications for outcome research. *International Journal of Group Psychotherapy, 21,* 174–189.

This article provides an excellent review of the literature on couples group therapy through 1970. The section on theoretical and clinical implications discusses the early psychoanalytic controversy over whether or not to include spouses in group therapy. Gurman also raises the question of whether group marital goals should stress individual or interactional change. The assessment section critically examines the research to date and make recommendations for future research.

Leichter, E. (1962). Group psychotherapy with married couples: Some characteristic treatment dynamics. *International Journal of Group Psychotherapy, 12,* 154–163.

This article highlights several interactional dynamics that couples enact in marital group therapy. Particularly interesting topics include the use of the spouse as an alter ego to facilitate treatment; negative reactions spouses may have to changes in their mates; and how marital group therapy helps diminish symbiotic marital ties.

Leichter, E. (1973). Treatment of married couples groups. *Family Coordinator, 22,* 31–42.

Discussed are the differences between couples group therapy and treatment groups in which participants are not related. Special emphasis is placed on the need to have homogeneous groups based on marital stages, due to the unique problems that exist at each stage. This article demonstrates how the group serves a curative function for problematic marriages in each of these stages.

Liberman, R. P., Wheeler, E., & Sanders, W. (1976). Behavioral therapy for marital disharmony: An educational approach. *Journal of Marriage and Family Counseling, 2,* 383–395.

This article presents a good example of the behavioral approach to marital group therapy. This brief treatment model employs 8–10 highly structured sessions focused on (1) improvement of communication skills; (2) enhancement of the recognition, initiation, and acknowledgment of pleasing interactions; and (3) introduction of contingency-contracting skills.

Linden, M. E., Goodwin H. M., & Resnik, H. (1968). Group psychotherapy of couples in marriage counseling. *International Journal of Group Psychotherapy, 18,* 313–324.

This important article is one of the first by group marital therapists to state that in most instances of marital discord, the problem is relational. The authors state that their goal is improvement in interpersonal relationships rather than individual character change. Further discussion is given to selection of clients, therapist qualities, and other important therapeutic issues.

McCarrich, A. K., Manderscheid, R. W., Silbergeld, S., & McIntyre, J. J. (1982). Control patterns in dyadic systems: Marital group psychotherapy as change agent. *American Journal of Family Therapy, 10*(2), 3–14.

This study used log-linear analysis to assess change in rigid marital interaction patterns after brief marital group psychotherapy. The results indicate that subjects exhibited more flexible interaction patterns following a group therapy experience. While this article suggests an interesting assessment procedure for marital group therapy, the results should be accepted tentatively because of the uncontrolled nature of the study.

Neubeck, G. (1954). Factors affecting group psychotherapy with married couples. *Marriage and Family Living, 16,* 216–220.

This classic study examined whether treating married couples in a group would have a positive or a negative effect on the therapy. Several factors were found that both enhanced and inhibited the therapeutic process. In analyzing those factors, the author concludes that the advantages of group therapy outweigh the disadvantages.

Occhetti, A. E., & Occhetti, D. R. (1981). Group therapy with married couples. *Social Casework, 62,* 74–79.

The authors present an existentialist approach to marital group therapy, succinctly discussing such issues as group impact on a couple, types of couples appropriate for marital group therapy, and specific techniques. Particularly useful is the presentation regarding the roles of the cotherapy team and the importance of the pregroup interview.

Ohlsen, M. M. (1979). *Marriage counseling in groups.* Champaign, IL: Research Press.

This basic text, written for marriage counselors and prospective clients, presents an introduction to counseling couples in groups. The author provides sections on selecting couples, starting up the group, couples' exercises, and termination.

Papp, P. (1976). Brief therapy with couples groups. In P. Guerin (Ed.), *Family therapy: Theory and practice.* New York: Gardner Press.

This chapter presents an excellent example of a brief strategic approach to couples group therapy. Papp uses choreography in the group, with follow-up tasks designed to alter repetitive cycles of marital interaction. Case studies are provided, with informative commentary on the use and rationale of these techniques.

Papp, P. (1980). The use of fantasy in a couples' group. In M. Andolfi & I. Zwerling (Eds.), *Dimensions of family therapy*. New York: Guilford Press.

This chapter presents a structured format for a couples group based on an interactional theory of marriage. Family choreography is used to discover each couple's reciprocal sequences of behaviors and to intervene accordingly.

Papp, P. (1982). Staging reciprocal metaphors in a couples group. *Family Process, 21*, 453–467.

In this interesting article, Papp presents an approach to couples therapy in which the technique of couples choreography is used to help married couples define and act out their patterns of behavior in metaphorical terms.

Perelman, J. (1960). Group treatment of married couples: A symposium. *International Journal of Group Psychotherapy, 10*, 136–142.

This classic article deals with the author's first attempts at including marital couples in a group therapy format. Although spending much time on the pitfalls he experienced, Perelman points out several important lessons to be learned—most notably that, despite psychoanalytic doubts, couples can be seen together effectively in a group.

NETWORK THERAPY

Introduction to the Therapy

Network therapy is a procedure for intervening in families in crisis and is associated with the work of Ross Speck, Carolyn Attneave, and Uri Rueveni. In network therapy, a therapeutic team (usually two or three individuals) assembles no fewer than 40 members of the social network of the family in crisis, in order to use the therapeutic force of this network in a systematic way. The networking process is aimed at breaking up destructive patterns of family relationships and providing support for alternative options (Rueveni, 1979; Speck & Attneave, 1971).

A therapeutic team typically meets with a network for about six 3- to 4-hour sessions (Speck & Attneave, 1971). The leader's role is that of a director and facilitator who can be both charismatic and self-effacing, and can mobilize the resources of the group. The members of the therapeutic team are often from different generations, and support the networking process in a variety of ways (Speck & Attneave, 1971).

The leader typically uses a series of encounter/sensitivity techniques to shake up the system and encourage change to occur. Change basically occurs through setting in motion the forces of healing within the network. The leader encourages the network's members to support one another by strengthening bonds, opening channels of communication, and generally enabling the social network to nurture and sustain the individual in crisis. This approach implies a basic faith in the ability of human beings to support one another in handling crises (Speck & Attneave, 1971, 1973).

Speck and Attneave (1973) have identified the six phases of the networking process as retribalization, polarization, mobilization, depression, breakthrough, and exhaustion–elation, and have outlined the therapist's role and the dynamics of the group associated with each of these phases. The basic agent of change in network therapy, however, is not so easy to categorize and objectify. Speck and Attneave (1971, 1973) have termed it the "network effect"—a euphoric connectedness to others that they liken to the emotions created by religious revival meetings, tribal healing ceremonies, peace marches, and contemporary rock concerts. They maintain that the group atmosphere generated within a social network, as well as the resources of the network members, can help bring about change better than a professional therapist alone. Rueveni (1979), however, warns that family network intervention should be reserved for times of difficult family crises and should not be considered a substitute for other forms of therapy.

Key Books and Articles

Attneave, C. (1969). Therapy in tribal settings and urban network intervention. *Family Process, 8*, 192–210.

By providing a case example of an naturally evolved Indian clan, Attneave shows the effect of network therapy and the subsequent changes brought about by it. She then compares, contrasts, and evaluates the use of network therapy with naturally evolved groups and with therapist-created groups in an urban setting. Also discussed is the network therapist's role as facilitator (as opposed to leader).

Attneave, C. (1976). Social networks as the unit of intervention. In P. J. Guerin (Ed.), *Family therapy: Theory and practice.* New York: Gardner Press.

In this well-written chapter, Attneave deals with many of the important issues related to network therapy. Discussed are practical issues such as how to map a family network, who to include in therapy, and the use of network therapy as a preventative mental health tool.

Bishop, S. M. (1984). Perspectives on individual–family–social network interrelations. *International Journal of Family Therapy, 6*, 124–133.

Bishop urges family therapists to expand their focus of assessment and intervention to the larger social network of the family. In his rationale, Bishop attempts to bridge network theory with mainstream family therapy theory. The author also presents different ways in which networking approaches may be used.

Bott, E. (1957). *Family and social networks: Roles, norms, and external relationships in ordinary urban families.* London: Tavistock.

This book has been very influential in the early writings of the network therapists. It is an early study of the interactional patterns of 20 English families. Emphasis is placed on marital roles and social network interaction.

Erickson, G. D. (1975). The concept of personal network and clinical practice. *Family Process, 14,* 487–498.

Erickson brings together the emerging strands of network practice and attempts to form a conceptual framework for network analysis. Topics discussed include the characteristics that make up a network; a rationale for clinicians to think in terms of a client's personal network; and the characteristics of a client's network that appear to be indicators that network therapy is the treatment of choice.

Erickson, G. D. (1984). A framework and themes for social network interventions. *Family Process, 23,* 187–198.

In this article, Erickson presents his hypothesis that the networks of psychiatric clients tends to be truncated in comparison to those of normal individuals. He further states that assessment of a client's network is important in identifying the nature of the truncation and in deciding what type of network therapy is required. A framework of network types and treatment modalities is presented.

Garrison, J. (1974). Network techniques: Studies in the screening–linking–planning conference method. *Family Process, 13,* 337–353.

This often-cited article is a good example of network therapy used in a brief, problem-solving manner. Stressed are the use of positive connotation and the avoidance of pathology. In-depth case studies are provided to exemplify the use of this method with crisis and chronic hospitalized cases.

Hemly van der Velden, E. M., Halevy-Martini, J., Rulf, L. L., & Schoenfeld, P. (1984). Conceptual issues in network therapy. *International Journal of Family Therapy, 6,* 68–81.

This interesting article presents three concepts developed by the authors while engaged in a project to study and conduct network therapy. The concepts discussed are (1) the achievement of a balanced network to create change; (2) the technique of polarizing the network against the team; and (3) the development of a "multiconductor" model of team leadership.

Rueveni, U. (1977). Family network intervention: Mobilizing support for families in crisis. *International Journal of Family Counseling, 5,* 77–83.

This article provides a brief overview of network therapy; its process, phases, goals, and strategies are discussed. Short summaries of cases are also presented to demonstrate the variety of crisis situations treated and subsequent outcomes produced. In all, this is a good introduction to network therapy.

Rueveni, U., (1979). *Networking families in crisis.* New York: Human Sciences Press.

This straightforward and readable book is a "cookbook" for the family therapist who wants to know more about networking. The author does a good job of presenting detailed case studies. He also gives ample space to a review of network research, the process of network intervention, and the therapist's role, as well as network techniques. This book provides a good, in-depth description of network therapy.

Rueveni, U. (Ed.). (1984). Application of networking in family and community (special issue). *International Journal of Family Therapy, 6*(2).

This special issue of the *International Journal of Family Therapy* is an excellent source of recent innovations in network therapy, as well as information on its application to specific client populations.

Rueveni, U., & Winer, M. (1976). Network intervention of disturbed families: The key role of the network activists. *Psychotherapy: Theory, Research and Practice, 13,* 173–176.

This brief article demonstrates, by way of case presentation, the importance of network activists— the volunteers who actively help create and implement the solutions generated by the assembled network. This article also emphasizes that nonfamily members of the network may play as important a role in network therapy as the family members themselves.

Speck, R. V. (1967). Psychotherapy of the social network of a schizophrenic family. *Family Process, 6,* 208–214.

In this often-quoted article, Speck discusses the important role that nonmembers of the nuclear family play in the maintenance of a schizophrenic pattern and in its resistance to change. Also, an initial report is presented regarding the use of network therapy to induce change in a schizophrenic family and its network. This is an interesting article.

Speck, R. V., & Attneave, C. A. (1971). Social network intervention. In J. Haley (Ed.), *Changing families: A family therapy reader.* New York: Grune & Stratton.

This excellent chapter presents an interesting look at many important issues in network therapy. Included are important pragmatic issues, such as (1) makeup of a network team, (2) goals of the network team, and (3) initiating the network process, as well as a theoretical discussion on the effects of social networks on individuals. Although the chapter is very informative, no citations of other works are given.

Speck, R. V., & Attneave, C. A. (1973). *Family networks.* New York: Pantheon.

This book is without references and is somewhat dated in its style of presentation. However, it provides the reader with a good sense of network therapy in the early 1970s. Its often-cited section on network phases is extremely important to understanding the network therapy process.

Speck, R. V., & Rueveni, U. (1969). Network therapy—a developing concept. *Family Process, 8,* 182–191.

This article presents network therapy as a developing mode of treatment. The reader is able to feel much of the authors' excitement and energy as they struggle with this emerging treatment modality. The focus of the article is on the techniques used as the authors treat schizophrenics' family networks. An important concept discussed is that of creating a new curative synthesis in the family network by creating polarities.

GERALD ZUK'S TRIADIC FAMILY THERAPY

Introduction to the Therapy

A focus on the role of values in systems underlies all of Gerlad Zuk's work, including his discussions of triadic family therapy. He defines two basic types of values and views all interactive processes in terms of these dichotomous male–female value sets. He calls the values most characteristic of males in our society "discontinuous" (e.g., adherence to structure, instrumentality, law and order, and rational process) and those more characteristic of females "continuous" (e.g., nurturance, empathy, aesthetics).

Zuk (1975, 1979) says that much of pathogenic family relating results from imbalances or conflicts between these sets of values. These conflicts can also occur in the interfaces between marriage partners, between parents and children, and between family members and the outer society.

One of Zuk's (1975, 1979) overriding impressions is that much pathogenic relating results from the overemphasis on continuous values and underemphasis on discontinuous values that results from what he sees as the overinvolvement of mothers with their children and the isolation and alienation of fathers from child rearing and family life in modern society. Children reaching adolescence have not sufficiently learned the values of discontinuity and therefore are ill prepared to assume adult roles and responsibility in society.

In his later writings, Zuk (1975, 1978, 1979) addresses the need for societiy-wide changes involving sex roles and ethnic groups to enhance functioning at all systemic levels.

The "go-between" process, for which Zuk is primarily recognized, outlines the methods by which therapists get families to enact pathogenic patterns and then strategically intervene by acting as either go-between (negotiator), side taker (shifter of the balance of relating), or celebrant (empowered representative for the family) to disrupt their dysfunctional relating (Zuk, 1966, 1967, 1968, 1971, 1975, 1981). Zuk (1966) sees all pathogenic family behavior as occurring in triads, with two parties drawing in a third in an attempt to resolve conflict or stress. Zuk (1967, 1968) asserts that there is no way for the therapist to stay outside this process, as the family system will automatically move to incorporate him/her. Therefore, the therapist must respond according to a rational scheme. The therapist will act as side taker or go-between, representing continuous or discontinuous values, depending upon which side he/she takes (Zuk, 1979).

Change in triadic family therapy is directed at the process by which the family relates. The focus of therapy is not on the content of family issues, although content will be used as a lever if deemed useful. Outcome is achieved when the pathogenic process is eliminated or reduced to the point where the symptom is relieved (Zuk, 1971, 1975, 1981).

Triadic family therapy, then, is therapy that utilizes the concepts of group process for assessment and intervention in disturbed families (Zuk, 1966). The focus is on coalitions, alliances, and cliques, and the process is one of mediation and side taking. The go-between process occurs when the therapist initiates the enactment of conflict between two principals; intensifies that conflict and begins movement of a third party into the role of go-between; engages in a process of negotiation of roles and positions; and finally induces a change in positions and roles that the therapist determines is more functional. This results in reduction or elimination of symptoms (Zuk, 1966, 1967, 1968, 1971, 1975, 1981).

Key Books and Articles

Garrigan, J. J., & Bambrick, A. F. (1975). Short term family therapy with emotionally disturbed children. *Journal of Marriage and Family Counseling, 1*, 379–384.

This study reports on the effect of short-term family therapy, using Zuk's go-between process, on families of emotionally disturbed children. This treatment effected significant improvement in the interpersonal functioning of the families, as perceived by the identified patients.

Garrigan, J. J., & Bambrick, A. F. (1977). Family therapy for disturbed children: Some experimental results in special education. *Journal of Marriage and Family Counseling, 3*, 83–93.

This article reports the results of a study employing Zuk's go-between process with families of emotionally disturbed children. Specific results included a reduction of the identified patients' symptoms in the classroom and home, and the enhancement of mutually experienced empathic understanding and congruence in the marital dyads.

Garrigan, J. J., & Bambrick, A. F. (1979). New findings in research on go-between process. *International Journal of Family Therapy, 1*, 76–85.

This article reports on a follow-up study of emotionally disturbed children treated in family therapy using Zuk's go-between process. Positive gains were found to have persisted over 2 years after therapy, with a concomitant reduction in symptoms and improvement in functioning. This study also found that single-parent, mothers-only families were less responsive to treatment than intact families.

Zuk, G. H. (1964). A further study of laughter in family therapy. *Family Process, 3*, 77–89.

Zuk discusses how laughter is frequently used as an important nonverbal mechanism to qualify meaning for the purpose of disguising or silencing. Laughter may also be used as a disqualifier of certain statements. This article shows how behavior process is as important to assessing families in treatment as their verbal reports.

Zuk, G. H. (1965). On the pathology of silencing strategies. *Family Process, 4,* 32–49.

This article examines a form of pathogenic relating in which various members of a family are silenced by either verbal or nonverbal cues. These strategies, when used often, may induce psychoses in certain family members. Silencing strategies may also be employed by family members and patients to keep the therapist from discovering key family issues.

Zuk, G. H. (1966). The go-between process in family therapy. *Family Process, 5,* 162–178.

In this classic article, Zuk discusses the rationale for the use of the go-between process in family therapy. A theoretical rationale is given, and detailed examples are provided. This is an extremely important article in understanding Zuk's therapeutic techniques.

Zuk, G. H. (1967). The side taking function in family therapy. *American Journal of Orthopsychiatry, 38,* 553–559.

Zuk focuses specifically on the use of side taking as a therapeutic maneuver to disrupt pathogenic relating on the part of the family in treatment. He discusses the inevitability of the therapist's taking sides in family therapy, as well as the difference between side taking that alters pathogenic relating and side taking that reinforces it.

Zuk, G. H. (1968). When the family therapist takes sides: A case report. *Psychotherapy: Theory, Research and Practice, 5,* 24–28.

This transcribed family interview provides an excellent illustration of therapeutic side taking. Zuk, engaging in the go-between process, breaks up the pathogenic relating in a triad by siding with one member against the others.

Zuk, G. H. (1971). Family therapy. In J. Haley (Ed.), *Changing families: A family therapy reader.* New York: Grune & Stratton.

This chapter represents a comprehensive overview of Zuk's methods and theory. Zuk gives many details of the methods and techniques for engaging in the go-between process with families, and shows how this process fits his theoretical framework.

Zuk, G. H. (1975). *Process and practice in family therapy.* Haverford, PA: Psychiatry and Behavior Science Books.

This book presents Zuk's theory of family therapy and family process. Zuk makes ample use of transcripts of family interviews and speaking engagements. A clear presentation is included regarding his ideas on continuity and discontinuity values in families.

Zuk, G. H. (1976). Family therapy: Clinical hodgepodge or clinical science. *Journal of Marriage and Family Counseling, 2,* 299–303.

Zuk sets forth a summary of his perspective on family therapy for the purpose of examination, evaluation, and research. It is a concise recounting of his basic principles, which he regards as a theory of family therapy. In so presenting them, he invites others to test his ideas through research.

Zuk, G. H. (1978). A therapist's perspective on Jewish family values. *Journal of Marriage and Family Counseling, 4*, 103–110.

Zuk discusses the need for more attention to racial, religious, and ethnic values in assessing and treating families. In this article, he attempts to isolate the values peculiar to Jewish families that are salient not only in the development of problems, but also as indicators of therapeutic success.

Zuk, G. H. (1979). Value systems and psychopathology in family therapy. *International Journal of Family Therapy, 1*, 133–151.

Zuk elaborates on the two value types into which he sees most values in families falling: continuity and discontinuity. These two conflictual value types polarize in relationships comprising males versus females, older versus younger generations, and the nuclear family versus society. Zuk discusses the inevitability of encountering these value differences and the importance of being aware of them in therapy.

Zuk, G. H. (1981). *Family therapy: A triadic based approach* (rev. ed.). New York: Human Sciences Press.

This book includes several of Zuk's key articles. It provides an in-depth look at Zuk's conceptualization of family process, family pathology, and the use of the go-between process as a treatment technique. This book is extremely useful in that it captures the development of Zuk's theoretical ideas over time.

ACKNOWLEDGMENTS

We would like to acknowledge the considerable aid Joseph L. Wetchler provided in researching potential books and articles to include in this chapter and in writing annotated citations for the "Key Books and Articles" sections. Also, the following individuals contributed to the writing of annotated citations: Nicholas Aradi, Judith Myers Avis, Marcia Brown-Standridge, Sita Chaney, Linda Stone Fish, Martha Rezelman, Paul Sherman, Cleveland Shields, Cricket Steinweg, and Katrina Shovlin.

REFERENCES

Alger, I. (1976). Multiple couple therapy. In P. J. Guerin (Ed.), *Family therapy: Theory and practice.* New York: Gardner Press.

Boas, C. V. E. (1962). Intensive group psychotherapy with married couples. *International Journal of Group Psychotherapy, 12*, 142–153.

Framo, J. L. (1973). Marriage therapy in a couples group. In D. A. Block (Ed.), *Techniques of family therapy: A primer.* New York: Grune & Stratton.

Gottlieb, A., & Pattison, E. M. (1966). Married couples group psychotherapy. *Archives of General Psychiatry, 14*, 143–152.

Gritzer, P. H., & Okun, H. S. (1983). Multiple family group therapy: A model for all families. In B. B. Wolman & G. Stricker (Eds.), *Handbook of family and marital therapy*. New York: Plenum Press.

Gurman, A. S. (1971). Group marital therapy: Clinical and empirical implications for outcome research. *International Journal of Group Psychotherapy, 21*, 174–189.

Laqueur, H. P. (1966). General systems theory and multiple family therapy. In J. H. Masserman (Ed.), *Handbook of psychiatric therapies*. New York: Grune & Stratton.

Laqueur, H. P. (1972a). Mechanisms of change in multiple family therapy. In C. J. Sager & H. S. Kaplan (Eds), *Progress in group and family therapy*. New York: Brunner/Mazel.

Laqueur, H. P. (1972b). Multiple family therapy. In A. Ferber, M. Mendelsohn, & A. Napier (Eds.), *The book of family therapy*. Boston: Houghton Mifflin.

Laqueur, H. P. (1976). Multiple family therapy. In P. J. Guerin (Ed.), *Family therapy: Theory and practice*. New York: Gardner Press.

Leichter, E. (1973). Treatment of married couples groups. *Family Coordinator, 22*, 31–42.

Liberman, R. P., Wheeler, E., & Sanders, W. (1976). Behavioral therapy for marital disharmony: An educational approach. *Journal of Marriage and Family Counseling, 2*, 383–395.

Linden, M. E., Goodwin, H. M., & Resnik, H. (1968). Group psychotherapy of couples in marriage counseling. *International Journal of Group Psychotherapy, 18*, 313–324.

MacGregor, R. (1972). Multiple impact psychotherapy with families. In G. D. Erickson & T. P. Hogan (Eds.), *Family therapy: An introduction to theory and technique*. Monterey, CA: Brooks/Cole.

MacGregor, R., Richie, A. M., Serrano, A. C., Schuster, F. P., McDonald, E. C., & Goolishian, H. A. (1964). *Multiple impact therapy with families*. New York: McGraw-Hill.

McFarlane, W. R. (1982). Multiple-family therapy in the psychiatric hospital. In H. T. Harbin (Ed.), *The psychiatric hospital and the family*. New York: Spectrum.

Richie, A. (1971). Multiple impact therapy: An experiment. In J. Haley (Ed.), *Changing families: A family therapy reader*. New York: Grune & Stratton.

Ruevini, U. (1979). *Networking families in crisis*. New York: Human Sciences Press.

Speck, R. V., & Attneave, C. A. (1971). Social network intervention. In J. Haley (Ed.), *Changing families: A family therapy reader*. New York: Grune & Stratton.

Speck, R. V., & Attneave, C. A. (1973). *Family networks*. New York: Pantheon.

Zuk, G. H. (1966). The go-between process in family therapy. *Family Process, 5*, 162–178.

Zuk, G. H. (1967). The side taking function in family therapy. *American Journal of Orthopsychiatry, 38*, 553–559.

Zuk, G. H. (1968). When the family therapist takes sides: A case report. *Psychotherapy: Theory, Research and Practice, 5*, 24–28.

Zuk, G. H. (1971). Family therapy. In J. Haley (Ed.), *Changing families: A family therapy reader*. New York: Grune & Stratton.

Zuk, G. H. (1975). *Process and practice in family therapy*. Haverford, PA: Psychiatry and Behavior Science Books.

Zuk, G. H. (1978). A therapist's perspective on Jewish family values. *Journal of Marriage and Family Counseling, 4*, 103–110.

Zuk, G. H. (1979). Value systems and psychopathology in family therapy. *International Journal of Family Therapy, 1*, 133–151.

Zuk, G. H. (1981). *Family therapy: A triadic based approach* (rev. ed.). New York: Human Sciences Press.

11

CYBERNETIC FOUNDATIONS OF FAMILY THERAPY

BRADFORD P. KEENEY
FRANK N. THOMAS

Historically, the science of cybernetics was born during the famous Macy meetings in New York City during the 1940s (see Keeney, 1983). The participants included Norbert Wiener (who coined the term "cybernetics"), Heinz von Foerster, John Von Neumann, Warren McCulloch, Gregory Bateson, and Margaret Mead. It was Gregory Bateson, more than anyone else, who then took cybernetic ideas and propagated them throughout the social sciences. In particular, his cybernetic ideas greatly influenced the field of family therapy and provided it with its intellectual foundation.

In the field of family therapy, a number of therapeutic approaches have drawn upon cybernetic ideas. In particular, the following have direct roots to cybernetic ideas: the communicational approach of Virginia Satir; the brief therapy work of the Mental Research Institute, developed by Watzlawick, Weakland, and their colleagues; the strategic approach of Jay Haley, the team work of Selvini-Palazzoli, Cecchin, Prata, and Boscolo; the so-called "neurolinguistic programming" of Bandler and Grinder; and the systemic approach of Olga Silverstein.

Anyone exploring the connection of cybernetic ideas to the social sciences, particularly family therapy, must necessarily build upon the work of Gregory Bateson. A major contribution in this regard was the book by Watzlawick, Beavin, and Jackson, entitled *Pragmatics of Human Communiation* (1967). Although the book was dedicated to Gregory Bateson, its publication was curiously marked by controversy between Bateson and the first author. The book, largely written by Watzlawick, is for the most part a summary and rearticulation of many of Bateson's early cybernetic and communicational ideas. Bateson, who had originally planned to write such a book himself, received *Pragmatics* with mixed reactions. After reading an early draft of the book, he protested that it contained numerous errors.

This chapter is partly based on excerpts from *Aesthetics of Change* by Bradford P. Keeney, 1983, New York: Guilford Press.

Although Watzlawick has claimed that he subsequently corrected most of these points, Bateson repeatedly complained that the published book was laden with problems.

We will probably never know the full story about the Bateson–Watzlawick controversy, but a few facts are clear. Some of the disagreement concerned specific technical details, such as Bateson's insistence on emphasizing that credit should be clearly given to Warren McCulloch for the idea that messages can be seen as structured in terms of "report" and "command." The more general and serious disagreement concerned Watzlawick's emphasis on the term "pragmatics." Throughout the later years of Bateson's career, he bitterly renounced anyone who emphasized a solely pragmatic view of human interaction and communication, unchecked by what he preferred to call an "aesthetic view."

In videotapes, audiotapes, public lectures, and his own writings, Bateson argued that an aesthetic view must contextualize pragmatic action. He used the term "aesthetic" to mean a pervasive responsiveness to patterns that connect. Any proposal of a rigorous either–or dichotomy, such as the difference between so-called "monadic" and "interactional" views, is overly simplistic and obscures more encompassing patterns that connect both sides of the distinction. Bateson's criticism of pragmatic approaches that were untempered by a respect for aesthetics extended beyond the clinical work of his former students and colleagues. He was concerned that an arrogant pragmatic view, whether in education, psychotherapy, medicine, science, or art, led to moral bankruptcy and ecological ruin.

The book *Aesthetics of Change* (Keeney, 1983) is an attempt to present a cybernetic approach to the aesthetics of family therapy. The aesthetic view set forth is not depicted as an alternative to pragmatics, but as a contextual frame of reference that organizes one's pragmatic strategies.

In the discussion that follows in this chapter, the most basic cybernetic ideas underlying family therapy are presented. Cybernetics is primarily concerned with understanding and managing the organization of systems— whether machines, individuals, families, industries, or whole ecosystems. First, the most basic idea of cybernetics, "feedback," is discussed and is demonstrated as a way in which systems maintain stability through processes of change. Subsequently, the distinction between two levels of feedback organization—negative and positive feedback—is presented, along with a definition of "mind" as a cybernetic system.

With this background of basic cybernetic ideas, a cybernetic analysis of therapeutic change is delineated that begins with a cybernetic specification of unconscious mental process. The structure of calibration in therapy and the contribution of symptomatic behavior to therapeutic change are discussed. Finally, a description of the cybernetic organization of therapy in terms of "sociofeedback" and a discussion of the therapist's participation in therapy are presented.

FEEDBACK

The basic idea of cybernetics is that of "feedback," which Wiener (1954/ 1967) defines as follows:

> Feedback is a method of controlling a system by reinserting into it the results of its past performance. If these results are merely used as numerical data for the criticism of the system and its regulation, we have the simple feedback of the control engineers. If, however, the information which proceeds backward from the performance is able to change the general method and pattern of performance, we have a process which may be called learning. (p. 84)

Stated differently, all simple and complex regulation, as well as learning, involves feedback. Contexts of learning and change are therefore principally concerned with altering or establishing feedback. Successful therapy requires the creation of alternative forms of feedback, which will provide an avenue for appropriate change.

The classic example of feedback is the thermostatically controlled heating system. When fluctuating temperature exceeds the boundaries of a calibrated thermostat, the furnace will be triggered to turn on or off, bringing the temperature back within the desired range. The system therefore monitors its own performance and is self-corrective. This maintenance of a range of fluctuation represents a process where "feedback opposes the direction of the initial change that produced the feedback" (Parsegian, 1973, p. 67). This process, called "negative feedback," is simply "a circular chain of causal events, with somewhere a link in the chain such that the more of something, the less of the next thing in the circuit" (G. Bateson, 1972, p. 429). For example, the more one's traveling speed in an automobile exceeds the speed limit, particularly in the presence of a police officer, the less likely it is that one's foot will press against the gas pedal.

In a family, an argument between two members may escalate, like the temperature of a house, until an unbearable threshold is reached. That threshold is sometimes regulated or defined, like a thermostat, by another member's presenting behavior that stops the argument. For instance, a brother and sister may quarrel until the family dog begins growling. The dog's behavior diverts the siblings to approach the dog and begin playing.

Sometimes feedback works to correct deviation in the other direction. A husband and wife may be "getting along" harmoniously until a call from their grown daughter provokes them into quarreling about some relatively ridiculous issue. In this case, the escalating complementarity of the couple may have reached a threshold that triggers their reaction to their daughter's call, which "rescues" them from getting "too stuck together."

All families embody feedback processes that provide stability for the whole family organization. By controlling escalating bits of behavior, interactional themes, and complex patterns of choreography, the family is able to stay together. An enduring family system is said to be "self-corrective."

Rosenblueth, Wiener, and Bigelow (1943) originally suggested, however, that feedback control may lead to clumsy behavior if the feedback is inadequately structured. For example, when an individual with ataxia is offered a cigarette, he/she will swing a hand past it in an effort to pick it up. The person will then swing past it again and again until the motion becomes a violent oscillation. Similarly, a poorly designed thermostat system may send the temperature of a house into wild oscillations. In the case of an automobile's steering system, too much "lag" or slowness of response will result in the car's weaving in and out of the lane. Since it takes too long for the wheels to move when the driver turns the steering wheel, he/she responds by turning it even more. By the time the effects of the steering change the direction of the car, the driver will have steered it too far in one direction. This will consequently result in a similar sequence of oversteering in the other direction. In this feedback loop, the corrective behaviors of the system appear to overshoot and result in escalating oscillations.

When a social system is caught in a feedback loop in which the corrective behaviors overshoot, its action will also appear to oscillate wildly. A classic paper by Fry (1962), entitled "The Marital Context of an Anxiety Syndrome," demonstrates that clinical anxiety sometimes oscillates between both spouses. For example, a wife may experience an anxiety attack in response to an invitation to a party. Although the husband responds by complaining that he isn't able to see their friends because of her "condition," one implication is that her system serves to protect him from being "too social," something he is secretly (or unconsciously) nervous about. When his nervousness (or anxiety) about being with others calms down, his wife may begin to approach social events. This then results in the husband having an anxiety episode, and the entire dramatic enactment becomes reversed. The husband now "protects" his wife, who is possibly fearful of her husband's establishing outside relationships. Each spouse provides overcorrective behavior, which leaves both experiencing oscillating anxiety.

CONNECTIONS OF CHANGE AND STABILITY

It is important to realize that cybernetic process never elects a static, steady state. As G. Bateson (1972) has noted, "Corrective action is brought about by difference" (p. 381). The system is technically "error-activated" in that "the difference between some present state and some 'preferred' state activates the corrective response" (p. 381). Cybernetics therefore suggests that "all change can be understood as the effort to maintain some constancy and all constancy as maintained through change" (G. Bateson, cited in M. C. Bateson, 1972, p. 17).

For example, the term "homeostasis" is used in discussing how processes of change lead to stability. Unfortunately, the term may be a misnomer, in that it is often taken to indicate some sort of "steady state." Perhaps, as Brand (1976) has suggested, it should be renamed "homeodynamics" (p 53). "Homeo" and "dynamics," when considered together, provide a double description of the cybernetic connection of stability and change.[1]

These ideas concerning cybernetic process presuppose that all variables in a system rarely, if ever at all, can be held to an exact value. No behavior, interaction, or system of choreography is ever consistently the same. Families, for example, are perpetual climates of change: Each individual varies his/her behavior in a whirlwind of interactional permutations.

Technically speaking, a variable will "hunt," or vary, around a "control" value. Either a variable in a feedback circuit will vary within a controlled range, or the range of deviation itself will be amplified. Someone may, week after week, smoke 8–10 cigarettes a day, maintaining a controlled range. Another smoker, however, may escalate the range of cigarettes smoked from 8–10 per day for one week to 20–30 per day in later weeks. In this case, the range of deviation has amplified its limits. Such an increase indicates a runaway in one direction.

On the other hand, the smoker could have gradually changed from 8–10 cigarettes per day to 2–30 cigarettes a day. In this case, the range of deviation has amplified its limits in two directions. This increase suggests an escalating oscillation in the range of deviation.

Thus, we see that there are different patterns of amplified deviation. A cybernetic system may be amplifying deviation in one direction or amplifying deviation in an ever-widening range of oscillations. Runaways in one direction, such as the escalating wealth of an oil baron, are usually triggered by efforts to maximize or minimize one variable. Wild range oscillations, such as the behavior of the patient with ataxia, are usually the result of uncoordinated feedback.

The difference between seeing a range of deviation as controlled or amplified is sometimes discussed in terms of two different kinds of feedback or cybernetic systems. Maruyama (1968), for example, suggests that there are deviation-counteracting and deviation-amplifying systems that incorporate so-called "negative" and "positive" feedback, respectively.

The potential problem with this view is that it too easily depicts change

---

1. The problem with "dynamics," however, is that it is too often regarded as pertaining to physical forces or energy. Perhaps we should restrict ourselves to the term "negative feedback" when indicating the cybernetic relation of change and stability.

and stability as a dualism of polar opposites. Families are described as either change-oriented, homeostatic, or a balanced combination of these distinct processes. This division is simply not a cybernetic view. One cannot, in cybernetics, separate stability from change; both are complementary sides of a systemic coin. Cybernetics proposes that change cannot be found without a roof of stabiity over its head. Similarly, stability will always be rooted to underlying processes of change.

Thus, the French proverb, "The more things change, the more they remain the same," can be stood on its head: "The more things remain the same, the more they are changing." The tightrope walker must continously sway in order to remain in balance. Similarly, the way to remain balanced while standing in a canoe is to make it rock. Applying this perspective to social systems, Bateson (cited in Bateson & Brown, 1975) proposes, "You can't have a marriage and not quarrel with your wife" (p. 47).

Whether it be the acrobatics of tightrope walking or marriage, what remains "stable" or "balanced" is a self-correcting cybernetic system. What change are the behaviors within a cybernetic system: The interlinked parts change to keep the whole a whole. However, a whole system itself is part of a higher-order cybernetic system, and so on, *ad infinitum*. To account for the stability of higher-order systems, we must point to higher orders of change.

Wiener originally proposed that there are different orders of feedback control accounting for stability and change. In other words, "Feedback can refer to the success or failure of a simple act or it may occur at a higher level when information of a whole policy of conduct or pattern of behavior is fed back, enabling the organism to change its strategic planning of further action" (Rosenblueth, cited in Wiener, 1954/1967, p. 276). Wiener (1954/1967) acknowledged that this latter form of feedback "differs from more elementary feedbacks in what Bertrand Russell would call its 'logical type' " (p. 82). Such higher-order feedback often provides a way of maintaining and changing a particular social organization.

As Haley's (1973) work masterfully demonstrates, an adolescent diagnosed as "psychotic" often signals that a family is having trouble in the developmental stage of weaning their child. The emergence of adolescent "psychotic" behavior that appears to escalate toward being unmanageable by the parents will eventually trigger a higher order of control. The parents may, for example, seek a therapist who institutionalizes the adolescent. By locking the youth up in a room the parents pay for, the family remains unaltered. In other words, feedback involving the therapist and the institution now helps maintain the family organization in a way that continues to block the adolescent's successful venture into the adult world. Effective therapy for such a complicated system would therefore necessitate establishing an alternative order of feedback process, which would change the pattern recursively connecting family, therapist, and institution.

Feedback that is not subject to higher-order control—that is, a situation lacking feedback of feedback—will inevitably lead to unchecked escalation and schismogenesis. Ultimately uncontrolled escalation destroys a system. However, change in the direction of learning, adaptation, and evolution arises from the control of control, rather than being unchecked changes per se. In general, for the survival and coevolution of any ecology of systems, feedback processes must be embodied by a recursive hierarchy of control circuits. Bateson (1979) provides the example of a driver of an automobile:

> A driver of an automobile travels at 70 miles per hour and thereby alerts the sense organ (radar, perhaps) of a traffic policeman. The bias or threshold of the policeman dictates that he shall respond to any difference greater than 10 miles per hour above or below the speed limit.
>
> The policeman's bias was set by the local chief of police, who acted self-correctively with his eye on orders (i.e., calibration) received from the state capital.
>
> The state capital acted self-correctively with the legislators' eyes on their voters. The voters, in turn, set a calibration within the legislature in favor of Democratic or Republican policy. (pp. 198–199)

Cybernetics studies how processes of change determine various orders of stability or control. From this perspective, a therapist must be able to distinguish not only simple feedback that maintains the client's presenting problem, but also higher-order feedback that maintains these lower-order processes. The therapist's goal is to activate the order of feedback process that will enable a disturbed ecology to correct itself.

AN APPROPRIATE FICTION FOR FAMILY THERAPY

Von Neumann and Morgenstern (1944) once commented that someone needs to provide a fiction for the behavioral sciences that would work like the elegant fiction upon which physics was built—its Newtonian particle. Without an appropriate fiction or hypothesis,[2] no behavioral science could be built.

The idea of a recursive network with feedback structure provides a useful fiction for behavioral science and family therapy. In their classic book *Plans and the Structure of Behavior*, Miller, Galanter, and Pribram (1960)

---

2. In one of his metalogues, G. Bateson (1972) defines "hypotheses" as made-up notions that serve as "a sort of conventional agreement between scientists to stop trying to explain things at a certain point" (p. 39).

similarly propose that "the unit we should use as the element of behavior" is "the feedback loop itself" (p. 27).

Simple feedback should be taken as a beginning conceptual building block or hypothesis. Using this, we can construct the broader perspective of recursive orders of feedback process, which enables us to characterize mental and living process. Complex systems involve a hierarchical arrangement of feedback. It is important to remember that such a hierarchy is a recursive network rather than a layered pyramid. When we speak of feedback process, we are referring to this recursive network.

Furthermore, we prefer to think in terms of hierarchically arranged (in the recursive sense) negative feedback. With this perspective, we avoid the dualism that otherwise arises between "positive" and "negative" feedback. What sometimes appears as so-called "positive feedback"—for example, the escalating building of armaments—is actually a part of higher-order negative feedback. In the case of an armaments race, a nuclear war may be the corrective action in a negative-feedback process. Humankind's present hope, however, rests upon the assumption that fear of such an order of self-correction (i.e., war) will itself lead to a recalibration of the arms race.

Thus, cybernetic exaplanation, as G. Bateson (1972) argued, is always "negative" (p. 399). What is sometimes called "positive feedback" or "amplified deviation" is therefore a partial arc or sequence of a more encompassing negative-feedback process. The appearance of escalating runaways in systems is a consequence of the frame of reference an observer has punctuated. Enlarging one's frame of reference enables the "runaway" to be seen as a variation subject to higher orders of control.[3]

"MIND" AS A CYBERNETIC SYSTEM

One of Bateson's most important contributions has been his definition of "mind" as a cybernetic system. From this perspective, mind is an aggregate of interactive parts with feedback structure.[4] The complexity of such systems ranges from simple feedback to what Bateson called an "ecology of mind." Seen this way, the issue of limiting mind to within the boundaries of a skull becomes nonsense. Instead, wherever there is feedback, mental characteristics will be evident. The mind of a blind person crossing a street

---

3. We can always choose to keep the term "positive feedback" to use as an approximation for higher orders of negative feedback.

4. Varela (1979) credits Bateson as the first to identify mind with the cybernetic system rather than what is inside the skull. Mind is therefore immanent not only in simple living systems "but also [in] ecological aggregates, social units of various sorts, brains, conversations, and many others, however spatially distributed or shortlived" (Varela, 1979, pp. 270–271).

necessarily includes his/her walking cane. The cane, after all, is an active part of the feedback process that guides the person. Similarly, a musician's instrument and a carpenter's tool become parts of mental systems during the process of performance and construction. M. C. Bateson (1972) proposes that the substitution of the word "mind" for the word "system" enables one to see that "mind becomes a property not just of single organisms, but of relations between them, including systems consisting of man and man, or a man and a horse, a man and a garden or a beetle and a plant" (p. 253). Such a view leads to Holt's metaphoric understanding, "The rock sculpts the sculptor, as much as the sculptor sculpts the rock" (cited in M. C. Bateson, 1972, p. 249).

The cybernetic view makes it clear that the unit of therapy is not individuals, couples, families, neighborhoods, or societies. Instead, cybernetics focuses on mental process. Mind in therapy may be immanent within and across a wide variety of social units, including individuals, family subsystems, and whole families. The cybernetician's eye is focused on seeing these underlying patterns of feedback process (see Keeney & Ross, 1985).

UNCONSCIOUS PROCESS

Higher orders of learning and change can be described in terms of unconscious mental process. To orient ourselves to this perspective, we need to begin by acknowledging that the more "fundamental" a premise, the less accessible it will be to consciousness. As Samuel Butler proposed, the more one "knows" something, the less aware one becomes of that knowledge. In addition, it is economical that premises controlling vital habits of action, such as breathing and perceptual process, are wired in at less accessible orders of mental process.

Premises that are deeply habitual and consciously inaccessible specify unconscious orders of mind. The major characteristic of unconscious orders of mind is that they embody the premises of relationship. For example, unconscious process cannot directly specify the "it" that must change. It cannot explicitly indicate that a past action, interaction, or system of choreography needs to be changed, nor can it propose that it could change.

THE STRUCTURE OF CALIBRATION

Since premises of unconscious mind are concerned only with relationship, they embody the more encompassing patterns of cybernetic epistemology. The distortion of these whole patterns of recursion and relationship by conscious orders of mind is potentially pathological. For example, the whole recursive organization of human-being-and-environment may become broken into either—or dualisms of human being versus environment by the conscious mind. Correcting such a distortion requires reconnecting it to the more encompassing unconscious premises of the whole relationship.

This idea has been implicitly understood by therapists such as Milton Erickson, who describe unconscious mind as a healing agent. Because it is recursively organized, unconscious process is a self-correcting system. When therapists and clients abandon their conscious, purposeful strategies of action and attend to the "doing of nondoing" or the *we-wei* of the Taoist, they attend to unconscious orders of mind. Jung (1939) advised, "Wait for what the unconscious has to say about the situation" (pp. 31–32). A fundamental premise of ecology that seems beyond the understanding of a great portion of Occidental culture is that an ecosystem will heal itself if left alone. An ecosystem is self-corrective because, as we have noted, it embodies a recursive organization of feedback processes. Letting an ecology heal itself does not mean being lazy or unresponsive. Rather, the doing of nondoing is a call for a higher order of action. Therapy thus becomes a context wherein a system finds its own adjustments.

One way in which a system begins to adjust itself is by generating symptomatic behavior. Such behavior is comparable to an itch, a beacon of light, or a bugle call, in that it attracts the attention of quite a few people. Family, friends, neighbors, and therapists, for example, may attempt to be "helpful." Their attempts will organize the problem either as part of a process of self-correction or as runaway and oscillation.

The latter consequence is dramatically exemplified by an alcoholic who swings back and forth between sobriety and drunkenness. With each full swing, the problem intensifies, and, if unchecked, the extent of drunkenness will eventually be fatal. Embedded within this oscillatory pattern are runaway sequences of behavior. Each drinking binge is itself a runaway phenomenon where one drink always proposes another drink. This escalating pattern is eventually calibrated by higher-order feedback. For example, the alcoholic may eventually pass out or will not be given another drink. Calibration helps lead the victim back to sobriety. The process underlying sobriety, however, may also be depicted as an escalating runaway. This runaway pattern, which often includes the "helping behavior" of others, is eventually calibrated when the temptation to take a drink becomes too overwhelming, thus initiating another runaway drinking bout.

Each episode of drinking and sobriety is itself organized within a larger oscillatory pattern that swings between episodes of sobriety and drunkenness. The range of this oscillation will also increase (i.e., run away) until it, too, is checked by higher orders of feedback process. The cybernetic organization of such an ecosystem may therefore include escalating patterns of drinking and sobriety, as well as escalation of the intensity of these escalations.

We can generally propose that any cybernetic system entering therapy has been problematic in the sense that it has wildly oscillated or has gone into runaway. The challenge for a therapist is to join that system in a way that will promote appropriate self-correction. Unfortunately, family therapists have often referred to negative feedback (or self-correction) as a way in which families maintain symptomatic behavior, while positive feedback is regarded as the process of therapeutic change. The more encompassing perspective is that symptomatic behavior is always subject to some form of higher-order control.[5] The avenue to therapeutic change is initiating an alternative form of higher-order self-corrective feedback. This alternative self-corrective change attempts to generate a more adaptive way of maintaining the whole organization of a system.

It is important to note that the cybernetic system that emerges when a therapist joins a family will also be self-corrective, oscillating or going toward runaway. There is simply no way a therapist can avoid being part of a cybernetic system recursively connecting his/her behavior with that of other members of the treatment ecology. The goal of therapy, then, is to activate this cybernetic system to provide an alternative higher-order feedback correction of the lower-order process involving symptomatic escalation.

PATTERNS THAT CONNECT AND CORRECT

Bateson's (1971) analysis of alcoholism provides a cybernetic way of thinking about how people aid in either maintaining or correcting problematic behavior. His theory claims that what is fundamentally wrong with an alcoholic is a dissociated epistemological premise, usually some variation of self versus environment or body versus mind. (These disconnections refer to what we have earlier called distortions of unconscious premises of relationship by conscious orders of mind.) Bateson depicts an alcoholic as engaged in a battle arising from a false separation between mind and body, which is sometimes expressed as "My 'will' can resist my body's 'hunger' to drink." "Will" represents a part of conscious mind that attempts to control the body's "hunger" for alcohol. In this contextual structure, body and mind do not represent a cybernetic system with corrective feedback, but a symmetrical battle.

For an alcoholic, the battle is first expressed as "I can control my drinking." The symmetrical relation between mind and body helps construct another erroneous epistemological premise called "self-control," the idea that one part of a system can have unilateral control over other parts. Although an alcoholic's challenge of self-control provides the motivation

5. Recall the argument that any punctuation of positive feedback or runaway can be seen as part of more encompassing negative-feedback processes.

to attain sobriety, achievement of sobriety destroys the very challenge that generated his/her sobriety. In other words, the more the alcoholic tries to stay sober, the more likely he/she is to get drunk, and vice versa.

When psychotherapeutic, family, and social network interventions reassure and console an alcoholic with an emphasis on "You'll do better next time," the premise of self-control, with its underlying disconnection of self and body, is reinforced. What the alcoholic hears is "You'll conquer your hunger for booze next time." This helps trigger the vicious oscillatory pattern again. Unfortunately, with each oscillation between sobriety and drunkenness, the intensity steps up. Attempts to control drinking then change to trying to stay sober, and, finally, to trying to stay alive.

Other forms of symptomatic behavior also involve this type of escalating process. In general, the more a client tries to control a symptom, the more the erroneous epistemological premise of "will" versus "symptom" is reinforced. The client will subsequently be caught in an escalating runaway until a "bottom," or threshold, is hit. The intensity of an "anxiety episode," for example, builds as the victim attempts to stop it. The battle against panic causes it to escalate until the patient gives up and declares a kind of helplessness, at which time the anxiety may be relieved.

Another function of symptoms in a self-correcting system is to provide communication to the social context surrounding them. Watzlawick *et al.* (1967), for example, propose that a symptom is a way of communicating "It is not I who does not (or does) want to do this, it is something outside my control, e.g., my nerves, my illness, my anxiety, my bad eyes, alcohol, my upbringing, the Communists, or my wife" (p. 80). Epistemologically, part of the message of a symptom is quite accurate: It is a message that "self-control" is an illusion, and that one is always part of a more encompassing self-corrective system. Seen in this light, symptoms represent communication regarding a higher-order cybernetic process.

Along these lines, G. Bateson (1972) sees the alcoholic's battle to prove control, sobriety, or survival as a "determined effort to test 'self-control' " with the "unstated purpose of proving that 'self-control' is ineffectual and absurd" (p. 327). In general, we can view symptomatic behavior as striving toward higher orders of self-correction. Symptomatic behavior starts this process by attempting to negate the distorted premises organizing a problematic sequence of experience and interaction. In this way, an ecosystem can begin healing itself. Therapeutic change is only possible when an ecosystem becomes appropriately responsive to symptomatic behavior: It is not enough for a symptom to be spoken; it must be heard by the entire system.

Unconscious process can never literally say "Something is wrong" or "Change the frame, premise, or punctuation." At unconscious orders of mind, negation is communicated by acting out the proposition to be negated. For an alcoholic, "hitting bottom" represents a behavioral *reductio ad absurdum* of the premise of self-control. Moments of "hitting bottom" typically occur when a person realizes that he/she doesn't have control over a situation. The experience is a "panic of discovering it (the system . . .) is bigger than he is" (G. Bateson, 1972, p. 330). Through an experience of hitting bottom, a symptom leads its victim to self-correction, epistemologically speaking, in that the dissociated dualism between self and symptom is reconnected.[6]

Unfortunately, at the moment of correction (or immediately thereafter), an individual's social context often tends to reinforce the old mind–body dualism by suggesting that he/she try again. Even if a patient continues to recover, relapses may occur if he/she is congratulated for "improvement," "will power," or "self-discipline." In this manner, dismembered epistemological premises of dualism may be reinforced, helping to maintain the problematic context.

Successful intervention must therefore block these reinforcements and allow a system to heal itself. One responsibility of a therapist is therefore to encourage clients to avoid doing battle with their symptoms. This does not mean that a therapist should be unresponsive to a client's dilemma, if that were even possible. On the contrary, a therapist must help structure a context of learning where both therapist and client can successfully respond to the self-corrective communication of symptomatic behavior.

The success of therapeutic maneuvers that encourage symptomatic behavior have long been known in family therapy and hypnotism. These so-called "paradoxical interventions" are explained by Watzlawick *et al.* (1967) as follows:

> If someone is asked to engage in a specific type of behavior which is seen as spontaneous, then he cannot be spontaneous anymore, because the demand makes spontaneity impossible. By the same token, if a therapist instructs a patient to perform his symptom, he is demanding spontaneous behavior and by this paradoxical injunction imposes on his patient a behavioral change. (p. 237)

This explanation can be further elaborated by noting that the message of prescribing a symptom is actually congruent with the message a symptom proposes. That is, the premise of self-control is negated. By being instructed to spontaneously generate a symptom, a patient finds that self-control is not possible. One cannot purposefully "will" a symptom to occur any more than one can "will" it away. By experiencing this demonstration, a system

---

6. More precisely, a symptom leads to a "correction" of the dismembered epistemological premise by reconnecting mind and body as a complementary rather than a symmetrical relationship.

can learn that efforts of self-control with regard to symptomatic behavior are absurd.

Whitaker's "psychotherapy of the absurd" has also recognized the relation between prescribing a symptom and "reducing to absurdity the escalating process of the family struggle" (Whitaker, 1975, p. 11). He describes this *reductio ad absurdum* in the following metaphoric language (Whitaker, 1975):

> It's as though an individual patient comes with a leaning tower of Pisa and the therapist, instead of trying to straighten the tower, builds it higher and higher and higher until, when it falls, the entire building falls rather than just the construct that the therapist has helped with. (p. 12)

A family therapist once developed a reputation for treating members of the clergy who claimed to have "lost God." Such individuals, after failing to resolve their problem through self-effort and numerous encounters with other therapists, would come to this therapist's office and relate a sad story of how "God has left my life." Obviously, this was not a very useful frame within which to practice their livelihood. The therapist would prescribe that these clients take an architectural tour of all the churches in the town where they lived. If they were not successful in "locating God" in this town, they were to plan trips to other towns in order to explore other churches.

The bewildered clients would then be dismissed to immediately begin their "search for God." In the process of going from church to church, the clients would eventually encounter a wall of absurdity, a sort of hitting bottom. In that moment, the dismembered epistemological premise separating "humanity from God," or, in more general terms, "self from others," would evaporate in the experience of a *reductio ad absurdum*. Consequently, the clients could no longer take their "problem" seriously.

Perhaps the greatest master of staging a *reductio ad absurdum* was Milton H. Erickson. Erickson's view was that he "accepted" whatever a client brought to him as an indication of what to do. Haley (1973) reports Erickson's explanation as follows:

> The analogy Erickson uses is that of a person who wants to change the course of a river. If he opposes the river by trying to block it, the river will merely go over and around him. But if he accepts the force of the river and diverts it in a new direction, the force of the river will cut a new channel. (p. 24)

Symptoms therefore provide a road map for a therapist and signal where therapy should begin. In sum, symptomatic behavior enables a cybernetic system to communicate that a particular epistemological premise is distorted, erroneous, or ineffective. Correction, arising from unconscious process, takes form through an enactment of *reductio ad absurdum*. This enactment provides a platform for changing the distorted epistemological premise.

SOCIOFEEDBACK

The goals of therapy are twofold: (1) enabling a symptomatic enactment to unfold and thereby to produce a *reductio ad absurdum*, and (2) helping a system to evolve toward an alternative structure for maintaining its organization. In terms of cybernetics, the first goal involves establishing appropriate self-corrective feedback. This occurs when symptomatic behavior can be expressed in a way that allows an individual, couple, or family to encounter the absurdity of the premises underlying their behavior, interaction, or choreography. The second goal of change concerns the alternative structures a system will generate following correction of its erroneous premises. We will soon see that the new patterns and structures a system evolves are usually a surprise to both therapist and client.

As we have suggested, any therapist who blocks a symptomatic enactment will probably reinforce an erroneous epistemological premise of mind–body dualism and risk escalating a system to a higher order of pathology. Cybernetics prescribes that techniques of therapy must allow symptomatic behavior to create a dramatic scenario for the problematic system; by cooperating with symptomatic communication, clients may go through the ritual of *reductio ad absurdum*. These "cooperative" therapeutic techniques may include prescribing the symptom, positively connoting the symptom, and deliberately escalating the absurdity of the symptom.

By facilitating a *reductio ad absurdum*, a family therapist becomes the director of a play: A symptom generates the script, while a family becomes the cast. Like a director, the therapist can only set the stage and help facilitate the unfolding scenario. Similarly, Watts (1961) has summarized the "teacher of liberation" as one who structures a situation where the false premises of a "student" are amplified to demonstrate their absurdity:

> The "guru" or teacher of liberation must therefore use all his skill to persuade the student to act upon his own delusions, for the latter will always resist any undermining of the props of his security. He teaches, not by explanation, but by pointing out new ways of acting upon the student's false assumption until the student convinces himself that they are false. (p. 68)

The therapist, too, must carefully promote the unfolding of symptomatic behavior to create a theatre of the absurd.

A therapist's participation in therapy thereby helps create "sociofeedback"; that is, the hybrid system merging family and therapist is analogous to a social form of biofeedback. In biofeedback, a person learns to bring about a particular physiological change, such as voluntarily producing an "alpha wave" of bioelectrical activity. To do so requires that the individual's brain be coupled to a machine capable of feeding back to that person the results of his/her cortical behavior. A therapist and family, at a higher order of process, represent a similar form of cybernetic system. When a family therapist "recognizes" a family's relevant activity, he/she can signal that back to them. Following this metaphor, the therapist must lock in on symptomatic communication and mirror or feed it back to the family. In this way, the family encounters its own "absurdity."

A therapist must therefore be able to create "transforms" of a system's symptomatic communication. A therapist perceives pattern in therapy by constructing different models. In other words, the use of the term "model" indicates how a therapist comes to know the system he/she treats. The term "transform" refers more to how a therapist shapes his/her response to that system. In other words, models and transforms are complementary sides of the systemic pattern involving description and prescription, respectively. Seen this way, sociofeedback in therapy suggests that diagnosis (knowing) is inseparable from intervention (action).

The process of creating transforms is demonstrated when a therapist extends the propositions of clients. If a wife complains that she can't tolerate her husband, a therapist, following Whitaker (1975), can create a transform of this communication by commenting, "Why haven't you divorced him?" or "Why don't you have an affair?" or "Why don't you have him eliminated?" When the client claims that such a statement is ridiculous, nonsensical, or absurd, the therapist can insist that he/she is being "therapeutically logical," "professional," "trying to help," and so on. When this process is followed, a *reductio ad absurdum* is created within the therapeutic system. When this absurdity is fully encountered, an erroneous premise can be negated and corrected. Consequently, a family may then generate an alternative structure for maintaining its organization.

Like all processes of stochastic learning and evolution, alternative structures are partially drawn from the so-called random. The leap toward a structural change necessarily requires that there be something "new" from which to create an alternative structure. As Bateson (1979) states, "Ross Ashby long ago pointed out that no system (neither computer nor organism) can produce anything new unless the system contains some source of the random" (p. 174).

Therefore, a necessary ingredient of effective sociofeedback in therapy involves the introduction of random "noise." Some noise, of course, is introduced by any effort to create a transform of symptomatic behavior.

The process of therapeutic change, however, usually requires a bit more precision. The cybernetic system of therapy must therefore provide sufficient noise from which an alternative structure can be constructed.

The task of introducing noise in therapy can be likened to that of presenting a "Rorschach" to the client. Not just any Rorschach will do; the client must assume that there is meaning or order in it. His/her search for meaning will then generate new structure and pattern. A part of therapy must always be presenting meaningful Rorschachs[7] that clients (and sometimes, therapists) believe to contain "answers" and "solutions." These Rorschachs may be constructed from family history, cultural myth, psychobabble, religious metaphor, stories about other clients (fictional or not), and so forth. The explanations clients propose or request usually provide a clue for what form of Rorschach will be useful. A student of Eastern thought might be given a reading from the *I Ching*, whereas a deacon of a Baptist church may require some obscure Biblical reference. A client who happens to be a family therapist, however, may have to be given a theoretical mythology, such as Bowenese, Whitakerese, or Weaklandese.

Thus, a cybernetic orientation to therapy centers around the construction of transforms that model symptomatic communication. These transforms must be "packaged" to provide an adequate source of random noise as a basis for structural change. The packaging can be regarded as a Rorschach or crystal ball that helps a troubled system create a new pattern and structure. The particularities of the presenting problem, as well as the way it is presented, direct how a therapist should construct and package a transform.

The recursive cycling of transforms in sociofeedback constitutes the context of therapeutic change. When a therapist constructs a transform of symptomatic communication with a little noise sprinkled in, the client then constructs a transform of that transform. The therapist subsequently transforms it, and so on, around and around. The cybernetic system becomes a recursive flow of different transforms.

A recursive cycle occurs whenever a transform of symptomatic communication is constructed. With every recycling of interaction, a different order of recursion is generated. A therapist must be able to utilize the difference between these orders of recursion as a guide for creating his/her next transform. This is, of course, another way of saying that a therapist must use the effect of his/her intervention to shape subsequent intervention. Such a feedback process reminds us that clients help shape their therapists' interventions and that therapists help shape their clients' behavior. Both are interlocked in feedback.

7. In a more recent work (Keeney & Ross, 1985), the term "meaningful noise" is used.

THE CYBERNETIC THERAPIST

A therapist who attempts to avoid mistakes or errors might be disastrous to clients. The very basis for cybernetic self-correction arises from the generation of error or difference, which enables future behavior to be altered. Oscar Peterson (cited in Lyons, 1978), widely acclaimed as the jazz pianist's jazz pianist, was once asked how he feels when he hits an occasional wrong note. He responded as follows:

> My classical teacher used to tell me, "If you make a mistake, don't stop. Make it a part of what you're playing as much as possible . . . " One thing I try to convey to my students when I'm teaching is the relativity of notes. From a melodic standpoint, there are no wrong notes because every note can be related to a chord. Every note can be made part of your line depending on how fast you can integrate it into your schematic arrangement. (Lyons, 1978, p. 31)

Peterson's point applies to the world of therapy. A therapist can view every action, including those called "intervention," as part of a creative unfolding. In this sense, there are no mistakes per se, but only action that is connected to a structured sequence of action. This perspective suggests that looking for the "right" intervention or the "correct" behavior simply misses the larger point. The therapist should focus on discovering the broader structure that always encompasses any particular bit of behavior.

These considerations suggest that a therapist needs several basic skills: an ability to vary his/her behavior, and an ability to discern and use the effects of that behavior to direct his/her subsequent behavior. These therapeutic skills correspond to the ways a therapist operates as an "effector" and a "sensor." The task of creating difference concerns one's "effectors," whereas discerning difference is the job of one's "sensors." When the relationship between effector and sensor, or intervention and diagnosis, is recursively organized, we may speak of a cybernetic system.

In general, any problematic system requires three ingredients for correction: first, a sufficient range of sensors to detect difference; second, a sufficient range of varied behavior to facilitate the creation of difference; and finally, and most importantly, the ability to recursively link sensors and effectors so as to provide self-correction. The therapist's task is to enter a system and participate in a way that connects the sensors and effectors as recursive parts of self-corrective feedback. This process represents socio-feedback in therapy.

A cybernetic therapist is always a practitioner, theorist, and researcher. To be effective, a therapist must be able to construct models, package them as interventions, and discern what happens. Cybernetics reconnects these arbitrarily punctuated facets of therapeutic process as parts of a more encompassing process called sociofeedback.

KEY CONCEPTS

Aesthetics. Although traditionally a term formally associated with the philosophical study of art and beauty, it is used by Bateson (1979, p. 9) in a more specific way to indicate a systemic responsivity to patterns that connect. An aesthetics of family therapy therefore refers to a systemic responsivity to patterns that organize therapeutic contexts. (Since these patterns *include* the practical techniques and strategies of clients and therapists, the term "aesthetics" is not to be taken as the antonym of "pragmatics.")

Autonomy. In relation to a system, the condition of being organizationally closed and self-referential. The term provides a precise way of specifying the wholeness of a system—whether that system be a cell, an individual organism, or a family. (The view of autonomy is always observer-dependent: An autonomous system may be viewed, from another level of observation, as a complementary part of a larger system.)

Calibration. The control of feedback. For example, the setting of a thermostat refers to the specification of limits, both maximal and minimal, to which temperature will be allowed to deviate before activating self-correction (the furnace will turn on or off). In this case, the thermostat with its specific setting provides a way of calibrating the house temperature feedback circuit. Family therapy attempts to provide an alternative form of calibration for problematic sequences of social interaction.

Cybernetics. The science of discerning and managing patterns of organization. In particular, cybernetics is the study of recursive complementarities concerned with the interrelation of stability and change. Two rules should be noted in the discernment of a cybernetic system: (1) recursive organization must be perceived, and (2) a system must have feedback structure (i.e., the recursive process must involve self-correction at some level).

Cybernetics of cybernetics. A term first used by Margaret Mead to refer to the cybernetician's inclusion and participation in the system he/she is observing and working with. (The term helps reminds cyberneticians that cybernetics itself may be seen cybernetically.)

Epistemology. The "study of how particular organisms . . . know, think, and decide" (Bateson, 1979, p. 250), thus involving the basic premises underlying action and cognition. Clinical epistemology primarily concerns the formal study of how therapeutic realities become constructed, maintained, and changed.

Feedback. The control of a system by utilizing the results of the system's performance to organize its subsequent performance: Output is returned as input that, on some level, directs self-correcting action.

Several points are of primary importance when discussing feedback:

1. Cybernetic systems are comprised of feedback structures that self-correct.
2. Higher-order feedback recalibrates lower-order feedback process. The highest order of feedback in a system indicates the system's own autonomy.
3. "Positive feedback" is always a partial arc pattern that is corrected by a more encompassing pattern of negative feedback (systemic self-correction). For instance, the escalating nuclear arms race may be corrected by nuclear holocaust (albeit not humanely!).

In therapy, the goal of the therapist is to activate the order of feedback process that will enable a disturbed ecology to more adaptively correct itself.

Homeostasis. The process of maintaining stability through the management of change, and/or the process of achieving change through the management of stability. (See the beginning of this chapter for examples.)

Logical typing. A way of keeping track of the levels of one's descriptions, intentions, perception, action, and knowing. For instance, formal theoretical understanding and practical clinical strategy are of different logical types, just as a dream state and a waking state are of different logical types. (Note that the idea of logical typing may be used as a rule prohibiting confoundment of different logical levels, as Whitehead and Russell originally proposed, or simply as a descriptive tool, as Bateson proposed.)

Meaningful noise. In "stochastic process" (see below), adaptive change is achieved through two ingredients: a source of randomness (noise), and some process of selection that may operate on the random (an observer constructing meaning). In therapy, stories, psychological jargon, or religious metaphors may prove sources of meaningful noise for clients, while theories of therapeutic change may provide sources of meaningful noise for therapists.

Mechanistic. Focusing on patterns of organization rather than on the ingredients or materials that make up a system. In this sense, cybernetics is mechanistic. (Note that this broad definition of "mechanistic" does not necessarily imply reductionism or the use of machine analogies. For instance, a machine may be seen in terms of its parts, a reductionistic view, or in terms of the whole patterns that organize it, a mechanistic view.)

Mind. The definition of "mind" as a cybernetic system was first proposed by Bateson. The view of "mind in therapy" involves discerning how cybernetic patterns construct, organize, maintain, and change therapeutic realities.

Pragmatics. In therapy, a view most often associated with the mechanics of practical strategies and problem solving.

Recursion. The recycling of a process. For example, a recursive view of therapy follows: "The client directs the therapist how to direct the client, who in turn redirects the therapist how to subsequently direct the client. . . ."

Stochastic process. As Bateson defines this (1979), "if a sequence of events combines a random component with a selective process so that only certain outcomes of the random are allowed to endure, that sequence is said to be *stochastic* (p. 253). Stochastic process in therapy may be thought of as "meaningful noise" (Keeney & Ross, 1985) to indicate a source of randomness (noise) and a selective process (an observer constructing meaning).

TEACHING TOOLS AND TECHNIQUES

An Exercise for Distinguishing and Relating Theory and Practice

We have found it useful to distinguish between two contexts in therapy: "formal understanding" and "practical strategy." In the first, the primary purpose is to achieve formal theoretical understanding, whereas in the second, the primary purpose revolves around practical means for organizing one's action in conducting therapy. Confusion may easily arise in a conversation where the intention of one person is to formally understand through theoretical abstractions while the other is focusing on concrete descriptions of practical strategy.

As a learning exercise, clinical students may carry different-colored flash cards. One color, say red, indicates to a student's colleagues (as well as to the student himself/herself) that he/she is presenting in the context of formal understanding. Another color, perhaps purple, indicates a shift to emphasizing practical strategy. A third color, green, signals those times when he/she struggles with the *relation* between formal ideas and practical action. By practicing keeping track of their thinking for any given moment, clinical students may learn how to avoid constructing a great deal of misunderstanding and impractical advice.

Monologues, Dialogues, and Metalogues

Writing conversations between an epistemologist and a therapist helps illuminate the relation between theory and practice. As a learning exercise, clinical students are given several theoretical notions such as "feedback," "stochastic process," and "logical typing," and then asked to construct an imaginary conversation between an epistemologist and a therapist about these ideas. The conversation may be monological, in that the clinician simply asks the epistemologist for definitions and clarifications. The conversation can then be rewritten in the form of a dialogue; here, it is apparent that the epistemologist is learning as much from the therapist as the therapist is learning from the epistemologist. And finally, the conversation can be written as a metalogue, where the very pattern of the conversation is an example of what is being discussed in the conversation.

Teaching Cybernetic Systems Epistemology

Henry and Storm (1984) have written an article that presents a variety of suggestions for how systems epistemology can be taught in family therapy training programs. On the basis of interviews with family therapy writers who embrace a systems epistemology, these authors discuss the goals and problems of introducing systemic ideas to clinical students, and also provide examples of strategies for helping clinicians learn to think "systemically."

RESEARCH ISSUES

One example of family therapy research based on cybernetic epistemology is our development of cybernetic ethnographies of communication in the context of systemic family therapy. Dell Hymes (1974), one of the pioneers in developing ethnographic studies of communication, discusses their applicability in directly investigating the use of language in particular contexts. Hymes (1974) states that little work has been done in developing a cybernetic approach to ethnographic studies, although he acknowledges that two distinguished social scientists have made pioneering contributions to developing such an approach—Claude Lévi-Strauss and Gregory Bateson.

We have developed ethnographic methods for analyzing systemic family therapy that enable a researcher to identify and articulate the most basic cybernetic patterns organizing clinical work. Outcomes of this research include the book, *Mind in Therapy: Constructing Systemic Family Therapies* (Keeney & Ross, 1985), which sets forth the basic patterns organizing the work of such systemic therapists as Haley, Weakland, Fishman, Silverstein, Boscolo, and Cecchin. Another book, *The Therapeutic Voice of Olga Silverstein* (Keeney & Silverstein, 1986), is a more detailed ethnographic study of a full case conducted by Olga Silverstein. This work arises out of a project for the ethnographic study of communication in systemic therapy at Texas Tech University, the purpose of which is to connect state-of-the-art ethnographic research methods with the finest examples of clinical work in the field.

KEY BOOKS

Ashby, W. R. (1956). *An introduction to cybernetics.* London: Chapman & Hall.
　　Not difficult if you work at it—Ashby worked hard to really teach cybernetics.

Bateson, G. (1979). *Mind and Nature: A necessary unity.* New York: E. P. Dutton.
　　Bateson's ideas are simply expressed; no background is required. The major contribution of the book is the recursive dialectical ladder between form and process.

Bateson, G. (1972). *Steps to an ecology of mind.* New York: Ballantine Books.
　　A collection of Bateson's seminal papers. His best piece of work: "The Cybernetics of 'Self': A Theory of Alcoholism." His personal favorite ("because it wrote itself"): "Form, Substance, and Difference." Stewart Brand correctly describes Bateson's ideas as "mental baklava."

Bateson, M. C. (1972). *Our own metaphor: A personal account of a conference on the effects of conscious purpose on human adaptation.* New York: Knopf.
　　The story of a living conference in which cybernetic ideas are applied to understanding almost everything.

Beer, S. (1959). *Cybernetics and management.* New York: Wiley.
　　This book tells the story of cybernetics through the view of management science.

Beer, S. (1975). *Platform for change.* New York: Wiley.
　　This one must be seen to be believed: different-colored pages that recursively connect.

Courant, R. (1981). *Mechanisms of intelligence: Ross Ashby's writings on cybernetics.* Seaside, CA: Intersystems.
　　The best papers of Ashby, who with Wiener and McCulloch deserves to share the title of founder of cybernetics. A special treat: The appendix has some of his zany class handouts (e.g., a decision tree for entering his office).

Haley, J. (1973). *Uncommon therapy: The psychiatric techniques of Milton H. Erickson.* New York: Norton.
　　Milton H. Erickson was cybernetic! Haley does a fine job of capturing his artistry in print.

Keeney, B. P. (1983). *Aesthetics of change.* New York: Guilford Press.
　　Cybernetic ideas for therapists.

Keeney, B. P. & Ross, J. M. (1985). *Mind in therapy: Constructing systemic family therapies.* New York: Basic Books.
　　A cybernetic cookbook for clinicians: The major approaches to systemic family therapy are unpacked.

Keeney, B. P., & Silverstein, O. (1986). *The therapeutic voice of Olga Silverstein.* New York: Guilford Press.
　　A detailed study of a complete family therapy case conducted by the master

clinician, Olga Silverstein. Emphasis is on the "nuts and bolts" of constructing a systemic therapeutic reality.

Lipset, D. (1980). *Gregory Bateson: The legacy of a scientist*. Englewood Cliffs, NJ: Prentice-Hall.
An entertaining biography of cybernetics' famous missionary to the biological and social sciences.

McCulloch, W. (1965). *Embodiments of mind*. Cambridge, MA: MIT Press.
Here the poet of cybernetics sets forth a potpourri of papers that only Mc-Culloch could have created.

Powers, W. (1973). *Behavior: The control of perception*. Chicago: Aldine.
This book, largely overlooked by family therapists, is a classic that has made a difference in the behavioral sciences.

Varela, F. (1979). *Principles of biological autonomy*. New York: Elsevier/North-Holland.
The best entry to the work of Varela *and* Maturana.

Von Foerster, H. (1981). *Observing systems*. Seaside, CA: Intersystems.
Heinz von Foerster, the magician of cybernetics, has the ability to put the most difficult ideas in a hat and then pull out a *koan* of unbelievable clarity. (Favorite von Foerster quote: "If you want to see, learn to act.")

Watzlawick, P., Beavin, J., & Jackson, D. (1967). *Pragmatics of human communication*. New York: Norton.
This is the book that made Bateson's ideas more approachable for many therapists.

Watzlawick, P., Weakland, J., & Fisch, R. (1974). *Change: Principles of problem formation and problem resolution*. New York: Norton.
The most parsimonious view of problem solving.

Wiener, N. (1967). *The human use of human beings: Cybernetics and society*. (2nd ed.). New York: Avon. (2nd ed. originally published, 1954).
Wiener could write for the general reader as well as for a scientific audience. Some of Bateson's favorite metaphors came out of this book.

Wiener, N. (1975). *Cybernetics: Or the control and communication in the animal and the machine* (2nd ed.). Cambridge, MA: MIT Press. (2nd ed. originally published, 1954).
The beginning. Reading is difficult and sometimes stimulating. Stafford Beer describes it this way: "Think of it like this—the great man (he really was) holds forth to his friends after dinner, ruins the tablecloth by scribbling mathematics all over it, sings a little song in German, and changes your life. It is tough going: You have to stay the night."

Wilson, K. (Ed.). (1976). *The collected works of the Biological Computer Laboratory*. Peoria, IL: Illinois Blueprint Corporation.

The book is what it claims to be: Practically all the cybernetic pioneers are in it—Ashby, Varela, Maturana, and von Foerster. There's also a bonus prize: a journal called *Cybernetics of Cybernetics*.

REFERENCES

Bateson, G. (1971). The cybernetics of "self": A theory of alcoholism. *Psychiatry, 34*, 1–18.

Bateson, G. (1972). *Steps to an ecology of mind*. New York: Ballantine Books.

Bateson, G. (1979). *Mind and nature: A necessary unity*. New York: E. P. Dutton.

Bateson, G., & Brown, J. (1975). Caring and clarity. *CoEvolution Quarterly, 1*, 32–47.

Bateson, M. C. (1972). *Our own metaphor: A personal account of a conference on the effects of conscious purpose or human adaptation*. New York: Knopf.

Beer, S. (1976). Definition of cybernetics. In K. Wilson (Ed.), *The collected works of the Biological Computer Laboratory*. Peoria, IL: Illinois Blueprint Corporation.

Brand, S. (1976). Homeostasis. In K. Wilson (Ed.), *The collected works of the Biological Computer Laboratory*. Peoria, IL: Illinois Blueprint Corporation.

Fry, W. (1962). The marital context of an anxiety syndrome. *Family Process, 1*, 245–252.

Haley, J. (1973). *Uncommon therapy: The psychiatric techniques of Milton H. Erickson*. New York: Norton.

Henry, P., & Storm, C. (1984). The training metamorphosis: Teaching systemic thinking in family therapy programs. *Journal of Strategic and Systemic Therapies, 3*(2), 41–49.

Hymes, D. (1974). *Foundations in sociolinguistics: An ethnographic approach*. Philadelphia: University of Pennsylvania Press.

Jung, C. (1939). *The integration of personality*. New York: Rinehart.

Keeney, B. P. (1983). *Aesthetics of change*. New York: Guilford Press.

Keeney, B. P., & Ross, J. (1985). *Mind in therapy: Constructing systemic family therapies*. New York: Basic Books.

Keeney, B. P., & Silverstein, O. (1986). *The therapeutic voice of Olga Silverstein*. New York: Guilford Press.

Lyons, L. (1978, March). Interview with Oscar Peterson. *Contemporary Keyboard*, pp. 30–33.

Maruyama, M. (1968). The second cybernetics: Deviation-amplifying mutual causal processes. In W. Buckley (Ed.), *Modern systems research for the behavioral scientist*. Chicago: Aldine.

Miller, G. A., Galanter, E., & Pribram, K. H. (1960). *Plans and the structure of behavior*. New York: Holt.

Parsegian, V. (1973). *The cybernetic world of men, machines and earth systems*. New York: Anchor Books.

Rosenblueth, A., Wiener, N., & Bigelow, J. (1943). Behavior, purpose, and teleology. *Philosophy of Science, 10*, 18–24.

Varela, F. (1979). *Principles of biological autonomy*. New York: Elsevier/North Holland.

Von Neumann, J., & Morgenstern, O. (1944). *Theory of games and economic behavior*. Princeton, NJ: Princeton University Press.

Watts, A. (1961). *Psychotherapy East and West.* New York: Ballantine Books.

Watzlawick, P., Beavin, J., & Jackson, D. (1967). *Pragmatics of human communication.* New York: Norton.

Whitaker, C. (1975). Psychotherapy of the absurd. *Family Process, 14,* 1–16.

Wiener, N. (1967). *The human use of human beings: Cybernetics and society* (2nd ed.). New York: Avon. (2nd ed. originally published, 1954).

12

SUPERVISION AND TRAINING

If marriage and family therapy is a young field, the subspecialty of supervision and training is in its infancy. Only a small number of books on the topic have been written or are in progress (Liddle, Breunlin, & Schwartz, in press; Liddle & Saba, in press; Piercy, 1985; Whiffen & Byng-Hall, 1982). The field is also empirically underdeveloped, as is attested in the research reviews by Kniskern and Gurman (1979) and Avis and Sprenkle (1986). While a rather large number of articles have been written about supervision and training (Brown, Hirschmann, Lasley, & Steinweg, 1985), much of this literature is impressionistic, atheoretical, and inconsistent in quality.

BASIC TERMS

Although the terms "therapy," "training," "supervision," and "consultation" are widely used in the literature, they are seldom defined and differentiated clearly.

Family "therapy" is the treatment of dysfunctional interpersonal systems. In most cases, the aim of therapy is to solve a problem, although the focus may be on engendering healthy functioning or psychological growth. The basic relationship of therapist to client is complementary, with the therapist assuming a hierarchically higher position because of his/her presumed expert knowledge. Clients expect the therapist to support, guide, direct, or provoke them out of their difficulties. The therapist bears the major responsibility for both the in-session process and the final outcome, although, as with many experts, the degree of explicitness concerning goals is left to the judgment of the therapist. He/she may even choose to appear as "one of the family" or as "one down," but such maneuvers are typically tactics rather than attempts to abolish social and emotional distance. Indeed, some distance from the family is typically thought to be necessary in a professional therapeutic relationship.

"Training," in contrast to therapy, relates to the domain of education.

While families can be trained (e.g., in marriage and family enrichment programs), the term is typically applied in marriage and family therapy to education for professionals. It refers to the broad, comprehensive teaching of family therapy theories and techniques (such as in seminars, workshops, courses, and programs) that either precedes or occurs alongside the development of a trainee's clinical skills through supervised clinical practice (Saba & Liddle, 1986). Trainers are concerned with a more general transmission of conceptual and clinical knowledge. Like the therapist–client relationship, the trainer–trainee relationship (a form of teacher–student relationship) is also complementary. However, it requires somewhat less social–emotional distance and is typically less personally intense. Also, sometimes the trainer's hierarchical superiority to the trainee may be determined more by institutional position than by expert knowledge. A professor, for example, may be "one up" on his/her students even if the professors knows less than they do. Typically, however, the trainer does know more, and as training progresses the relationship of the trainer with his/her trainees becomes less complementary and more symmetrical (i.e., equal).

"Supervision" refers to a continuous relationship, in a real-world work setting, which focuses on the specific development of a therapist's skills as he/she gains practical experience in treating client families (Saba & Liddle, 1986). Focused attention on specific cases, therefore, is the hallmark of supervision. The relationship often involves considerable complementarity, since the settings in which supervisors operate (e.g., universities, social service agencies) confer authority on them in a variety of ways. For example, a supervisor, unlike a consultant (see below), has direct responsibility for the quality of work performed by the therapist being supervised. In actual practice, there is considerable variation in the supervisor–supervisee relationship, depending upon such factors as the skill level of the supervisee. At one extreme might be the supervision of beginners, involving close oversight and frequent directives; at the other extreme would be the supervision of experienced therapists for the purpose of fostering creativity and autonomy. Therefore, the relationship can range from one that is mostly complementary to one that is primarily symmetrical (Magee, 1985).

"Consultation" differs from supervision in that it is a short-term, symmetrical, peer-like relationship between a therapist and an invited expert. The consultant's power is derived from his/her expertise and skill. There is no formal stake in evaluating the therapist's progress in learning or job performance (Nielsen & Kaslow, 1980). Even highly experienced family therapists may request the input of consultants for the purposes of overcoming therapeutic impasses, verifying diagnostic impressions, confirming intervention strategies, and stimulating professional and personal development. Consultations can take place in a variety of forms, including discussion, observation through a one-way mirror, tape reviews, and cotherapy.

HISTORY AND OVERVIEW OF THE STATE OF THE FIELD

Numbers and Types of Programs

Supervision and training takes place in two major settings: (1) academic degree-granting programs, and (2) free-standing institutes. Programs may also be divided into (1) those that are accredited by the American Association for Marriage and Family Therapy (AAMFT) and (2) those that are not so accredited. The largest number of programs are free-standing and nonaccredited. Bloch and Weiss (1981) reported on the existence of over 175 training programs, only about 55 of which were degree-granting. As of the summer of 1986, AAMFT-accredited programs included 19 masters, 8 doctral, and 10 post-degree level programs.

Brief History of Training Programs

It is difficult to say much with certainty about the content or history of most nonaccredited programs. Some, despite impressive brochures, are little more than a few courses offered by overextended, if well-meaning, faculty members. Others, however, are world-renowned centers such as the Philadelphia Child Guidance Clinic. The quality of these programs varies, since they neither have been designed to meet a set of objective standards nor have subjected themselves to outside review by the AAMFT Commission on Accreditation for Marriage and Family Therapy Education, which has been recognized by the U.S. Department of Education as the official accrediting body for training programs in marriage and family therapy. This group periodically publishes rigorous requirements in terms of organizational guidelines, curriculum, faculty, physical facilities, and clinical training.

A history of the accredited programs is found in Nichols (1979), Smith and Nichols (1979), and Burman and Dixon-Murphy (1979). Briefly, although AAMFT (originally the American Association of Marriage Counselors, or AAMC) was founded in 1942, it did not publish standards on training centers in postgraduate professional marriage counseling until 1958. Standards for degree-granting programs were published in 1959. In its early years, AAMC was more concerned with establishing standards for marriage counselors (in 1949) and with centers for marriage counseling (in 1953) than it was with training. It also assumed that marriage counseling was a professional activity that people entered after having earned a graduate degree in another discipline. Marriage counseling was typically learned through postgraduate internships (Nichols, 1979). This seemed reasonable, in that early practitioners considered marriage counseling supplemental to their primary occupations as psychologists, psychiatrists, social workers, ministers, and so forth (Broderick & Schrader, 1981).

By the time of the 1959 standards on graduate education in marriage counseling, certain universities had begun to develop graduate programs, which implied that marrige counseling was a separate area of graduate education and a professional field in its own right (Nichols, 1979). The early standards called for a 4-year minimum doctoral program with internship. As the field developed, it was assumed that training would cease to be done primarily at the postdoctoral level and would shift to doctoral programs in marriage counseling itself. During the 1950s, somewhat loosely defined doctoral programs could be found at Columbia University Teachers College, the University of Southern California, Florida State University, and Purdue University (Nichols, 1979).

The growth that subsequently occurred in graduate programs during the 1960s, 1970s, and 1980s has been primarily at the master's level. By 1971, AAMFT's standards concerning training centers in marriage and family counseling clearly designated the master's degree as the entry-level credential. By 1974, standards for degree programs were applicable to both master's and doctoral programs. Currently, the Commission on Accreditation for Marriage and Family Therapy Education is developing more stringent requirements for doctoral programs, as well as revising its 1981 standards.

Two of the oldest accredited free-standing programs are the Marriage Council of Philadelphia, which has offered training since 1947, and the Blanton–Peale Graduate Institute, which has offered training since 1956 (Burman & Dixon-Murphy, 1979). The free-standing programs have special appeal to those who already have advanced degrees and seek intensive training in marriage and family therapy free of the constraints of a degree program. The programs are almost always available to the part-time student.

Who Are the Supervisors?

There have been three studies of approved supervisors in AAMFT (Everett, 1980; McKenzie, Atkinson, & Quinn, in press; Saba & Liddle, 1986). The last also included responses from half of the membership of the American Family Therapy Association (AFTA). According to these investigations, about two-thirds of supervisors are men, and the average age is middle to late 40s. The overwhelming majority are Caucasian, and over 50% have earned doctorates. McKenzie *et al.* (in press) report a slight increase in master's-level supervisors over Everett's (1980; data gathered in 1976) figures. McKenzie *et al.* (in press) also report a significantly larger percentage who have less than 5 years of supervisory experience. The largest group of supervisors, 42% in the McKenzie *et al.* (in press) study, supervise within their private practice. McKenzie *et al.* also report a significantly smaller percentage (15.4%) of supervisors currently working within an educational setting than that reported in the earlier Everett study (26.3%). Saba and Liddle (1986), however, report that AFTA subjects listed academic departments as their primary training–supervising site.

It is significant that in none of these studies did the respondents list "marriage and family therapist" as their primary professional identification. This may well continue to be the case until the majority of the supervisors receive their basic graduate education in marriage and family therapy. Nonetheless, the vast majority of respondents in 22 family therapy programs studied by Henry (1983) considered family therapy to be a unique clinical profession, as opposed to simply a technique used within established professions.

Methods Employed

Data on the actual use of the various supervisory modalities (see "Key Clinical Concepts" section below, for definitions) are found in studies by Saba and Liddle (1986), McKenzie *et al.* (in press), Henry (1983), and Sprenkle (in press). The Saba and Liddle (1983) and McKenzie *et al.* (in press) studies (of AAMFT-approved supervisors and AFTA members) suggest that even though supervisors believe that live supervision and videotape supervision are the most effective modalities, these are in fact, used less frequently than such procedures as reviewing audiotapes and case notes. The fact that audiotapes and case notes are used most frequently probably reflects the aforementioned finding that the largest number of supervisors work in private practice settings. Studies of supervision in more formal training centers (Henry, 1983; Sprenkle, in press) have found that video and live supervision procedures predominate.

Theoretical Orientations

The various studies that have examined the theoretical orientations of supervisors/trainers indicate that the modal professional is not a "purist." The majority espouse an eclectic view. Nonetheless, the McKenzie *et al.* (in press), Sprenkle (in press), and Henry (1983) studies all found that the structural and strategic models are taught most frequently. Other relatively popular approaches include communicational/humanistic (Satir), intergenerational (Bowen, Framo), and experiential (Whitaker).

KEY CLINICAL CONCEPTS

Supervisory Modalities

LIVE SUPERVISION

Live supervision entails the supervisor's observing the therapy as it actually occurs. Eight different forms of live supervision (see Figure 12-1) can be delineated by using (1) temporal, (2) spatial, and (3) personnel dimensions. With regard to timing, live supervision can be "immediate" or "delayed." With regard to space, it can occur from within the therapy room or outside it. With regard to personnel, it can include one supervisor or a team of two or more persons.

The Temporal Dimension. Regarding timing, delayed feedback (given after the session is completed) is less popular than immediate feedback, since it offers no opportunity to engender during-therapy change. One advantage of delayed feedback is that it gives the therapist the opportunity to work "solo" (perhaps to increase his/her confidence). It also may serve as a "bridging modality" for therapists who will be moving on to settings where live supervision is not feasible.

	Individual supervision		Team supervision	
	Within room	Outside room	Within room	Outside room
Immediate				
Delayed				

Figure 12-1
Supervisory modalities for live supervision.

Immediate feedback can occur through a variety of mechanisms. Two of the most popular are the telephone and the "bug in the ear." The latter entails the supervisor's speaking to the therapist through a hearing-aid-type device, which may be either wireless or connected to the trainee by wire. Essentially, it is a one-way form of communication that, from the family's point of view, is unobstrusive. Earphone interventions are typically brief and direct, and, if done skillfully, can be carried out as though the therapist originated them. Disadvantages include the inability to clarify messages and the potential for the therapist to become dependent on the supervisor (Byng-Hall, 1982).

A characteristic of the telephone that may be seen as either an advantage or a disadvantage is the fact that it interrupts the interaction of the session. As such, it serves as an intervention in and of itself, apart from the message being sent. This may be useful, for example, if the supervisor wants to stop an inappropriate or destructive family interaction. Also, there is the opportunity to clarify and/or amplify interventions, and communication is potentially two-way. On the other hand, the telephone lacks the immediacy and unobstrusiveness of the earphone. Many creative ways in which to use the telephone in live supervision are described by Coppersmith (1980).

Other ways in which a supervisor may intervene immediately include coming into the room and giving directives either to the supervisor or directly to the family (a procedure used often by Salvador Minuchin). Or the supervisor may request that the therapist come out for a midsession conference. This request can be made by telephone, by earphone, or through knocking on the door. Of course, the therapist may come out on his/her own initiative. Finally, the supervisor (or team) may send the therapist written messages. Examples of the framing of such messages and their impact are described in Breunlin and Cade (1981).

The Spatial Dimension.   Concerning the spatial dimension of live supervision, supervisory input is much more likely to come from outside the room than from within it. Since one-way mirrors are not always available, however, the supervisor (or team) may stay in the same room as the therapist and family. One article has called this "direct open supervision" (Olson & Pegg, 1979). We also know of several centers where behind-the-glass observation is possible, but where direct open supervision is often the method of choice (Landau & Stanton, 1983). One potential advantage of the "open" method is that the family may benefit from hearing what the supervisor says. Another advantage is that the supervisor can better detect the emotional climate of the family from within the room. Disadvantages include loss of a different perspective that may come from spatial distance; the loss of leverage made possible by feedback outside of the family's awareness (including a markedly reduced potential for indirect interventions); and a reduced ability to use technical language. The supervisor may also be overly protective of the therapist, may avoid conflict (and/or disagreement, or may usurp the therapist's authority (Carter, 1982).

The Personnel Dimension. Concerning the personnel dimension, the field has witnessed an explosion in the use of team supervision approaches, probably due to the enormous influence of the Milan and Ackerman groups. While there are no data on the matter, team supervision may be the norm rather than the exception in training settings where live supervision is practiced. Teams differ in a variety of ways, including the extent to which they are composed of peers (as opposed to formed around a senior supervisor and the extent to which they participate in the formulation of interventions. Team supervision has the advantages of facilitating brainstorming (and hence of enhancing creativity), of developing camaraderie among team members, and of enhancing learning among team members as well as therapists (Heath, 1983). Indeed, Roberts (1983) considers the team an important "third tier" (alongside the therapist and supervisor), which needs to be nurtured every bit as much as the therapist. Roberts (1983) offers guidelines for the development of effective collaborative therapy teams.

Coppersmith (1980), DeShazer and Molnar (1984), Landau and Stanton (1983), and Papp (1980) offer rich illustrations of ways in which teams can be used in highly creative ways to affect the therapy process. For example, the team can be used as "Greek chorus" to support, confront, provoke, confuse, or challenge the family. The therapist can side with or oppose the chorus. In the latter case, this "split" highlights the family's ambivalence about change and gives the therapist leverage to capitalize on resistance (e.g., "The team is convinced you can't make this change, but I believe you've got the stuff to do it.").

Whatever the form of live supervision, it is clear that the basic modality has advantages. Any other method is *ex post facto*, in that there is no opportunity to influence therapeutic interventions (live supervision with delayed feedback is also *ex post facto*). Like videotape review (see below), live supervision provides reliable information about the therapist's nonverbal as well as verbal skills, but, unlike video review, it gives the supervisor some sense of the emotional climate of the session. If this immediacy is buffered by a one-way mirror, the method also provides a metaperspective on the therapy which is quite advantageous (Aradi, 1985). The supervisor is freer to concentrate upon patterns and to detect ways a therapist might be participating in dysfunctional transactions (Berger & Dammann, 1982). Moreover, family members generally like live supervision procedures (Piercy, Sprenke, & Constantine, in press). The most obvious disadvantages of live supervision are the physical and mechanical requirements. In addition, as Beroza (1983) notes, the modality has the potential for undermining therapist confidence. The ethical objections to live supervision noted in earlier writings (Liddle & Halpin, 1978) seem to be of less concern today.

EX POST FACTO METHODS OF SUPERVISION

The Case Presentation. The case presentation entails the therapist's giving a verbal report of a session or case to the supervisor or supervisory group. As noted above, the method is used quite frequently and is often a supplement to other more expensive forms such as live supervision or video review. In addition to low cost and convenience, the method has the advantage of disciplining the therapist to integrate data and present it as a coherent whole. Morever, the emotional distance from the actual therapy experience may allow a more relaxed learning and planning environment. In addition, this is also a good method for reviewing one's metagoals and progress as opposed to focusing on a single case. Finally, in a group context, the method lends itself well to role playing and other forms of behavior rehearsal.

Other than its *ex post facto* nature, the obvious other major disadvantage is the supervisor's inability to determine what actually occurred in sessions, and hence his/her inability to truly assess and monitor therapist performance (Aradi, 1985).

The Review of Case Notes. The review of case notes entails rereading the supervisee's written accounts of the therapy session, most typically, but not necessarily, in the absence of the supervisee (Aradi, 1985). The primary advantage of this method is that it encourages the therapist to describe behaviors, hypotheses, interventions, goals, and so on in an organized manner, especially if a structured form for case notes is utilized. The report can also serve as a stimulus for discussion during supervision. As with the case presentation, a disadvantage is that this modality may provide highly unreliable information (Aradi, 1985). An example of a useful form for case notes is found in Fisher and Sprenkle (1980).

Audiotape Review. Audiotape review entails the supervisor's listening to all or part of the audiotape of a session (either with or in the absence of the therapist). The advantage of this over the case presentation and review of case notes is that the supervisor does have reliable information concerning at least the auditory dimensions of the therapist–family interaction. Even though important nonverbal information is lost, the supervisor is better able to assess the therapist's progress and give useful feedback. The audiotape review method is also cheaper and more convenient than video or live supervision.

Disadvantage of the audiotape review method include its *ex post facto* nature, the loss of nonverbal information, and the fact that the process is often considered boring. For best results, the supervisor should encourage the therapist to edit his/her audiotape into short sequences that highlight crucial incidents or areas in which the therapist is "stuck."

The advantages of each of the *ex post facto* methods may be maximized by using several such methods in concert. For example, a therapist–supervisor audiotape review may precede or be used in conjunction with a case presentation, where interventions and family dynamics heard on the tape are discussed in more depth.

Videotape Review. The visual component makes videotape review the most advantageous of the *ex post facto* methods. Most importantly, the supervisor has the opportunity to observe and evaluate the supervisee's perceptual, conceptual, and executive skills, rather than having to rely on the trainee's reports. In addition, as Whiffen (1982) notes, videotape provides three unique opportunities: (1) It freezes time so that a crucial sequence can be studied; (2) the therapist sees himself/herself subjectively as one of the contributors to the system; and (3) the effect of the intervention can be observed and assessed. The videotape review even has certain advantages over live supervison. It can be done at a convenient time and at a leisurely pace. Subtle gestures and mannerisms are often crucial to the therapeutic impact, and therapist and client microbehaviors are often lost in live supervision. The fact that key segments can be played and replayed can be of enormous pedagogical significance. The fact that the therapist can directly observe his/her own appearance, style, mannerisms, and intervention cannot be underestimated. In our opinion, even when live supervision is readily available, it should be supplemented with videotape review. It is probably the most powerful self-teaching tool in the therapist's armamentarium.

Videotape review has most of the same disadvantages as the other *ex post facto* methods. One potential unique disadvantage is that it is a rather cool medium. Poignant moments often appear to be toned down on video, and they seem less powerful or may even go unnoticed (Aradi, 1985).

COTHERAPY

Cotherapy, while typically a therapeutic modality, is sometimes utilized as a form of supervision. This is the method of choice in the experiential school (Whitaker & Keith, 1981). It typically combines elements of both live and *ex post facto* supervision. The supervisor is with the trainee in the room and can intervene as the case progresses. However, the bulk of the feedback to the trainee (cotherapist) is typically given outside the therapy hour. The therapeutic advantages of cotherapy have been described elsewhere (Whitaker & Keith, 1981). As a supervisory modality, it allows the trainee to observe his/her mentor, enables the trainee to balance the interacting with the family with watching for patterns, and often reduces the trainee's anxiety over being solely responsible for the session. Potential disadvantages include trainee dependency on the supervisor, the trainee's lack of awareness of the supervisor's goals or intentions, lack of clarity with regard to responsibility for the case, and competition or conflicting strategies.

Other Clinical Concepts

CONCEPTUAL, PERCEPTUAL, AND EXECUTIVE SKILLS

Three types of skills have been described in an influential article by Cleg-horn and Levin (1973), and this description has influenced others who have delineated and categorized therapeutic skills (e.g. Tomm & Wright, 1979; Falicov, Constantine, & Breunlin, 1981). "Conceptual skills" are those relating to the trainee's ability to look at the raw data of the session through the lens of family theory. "Perceptual skills" are those required to see and describe accurately the behavioral data of a therapy session. "Executive skills" include all therapeutic interventions as well as activities necessary to prepare for therapy (e.g., effective telephone contacts) and case management (e.g., making referrals).

ISOMORPHISM

The isomorphism of therapy and supervision has been strongly emphasized in writings by Howard Liddle (Liddle, 1982b; Liddle & Saba, 1984; Liddle & Schwartz, 1983). Basically, Liddle argues that, although therapy and training/supervision are different, they are nonetheless parallel processes. What one does in supervision/training is guided by what one believes are the central tasks of therapy. For example, for the structural–strategic professional, both therapy and supervision/training include the processes of joining and restructuring.

PRESESSION, MIDSESSION, AND POSTSESSION MEETINGS

"Presession," "midsession," and "postsession" are terms used widely in the literature on live supervision to describe interactions at different points between supervisor and trainee. In the presession meeting, the supervisor and trainee review goals and strategies for the session. Midsession meetings typically occur behind the mirror, in the hallway, or in places other than the therapy room. They serve as midcourse corrections for what is occurring in the session, as an opportunity to plan interventions or homework, and as a "breather" from the intensity of the therapy. In a postsession meeting, the therapist and supervisor debrief. Typically, the performance of the trainee is assessed, and plans for the subsequent session are discussed.

STRUCTURING AND RELATIONSHIP SKILLS

Described by Alexander and his colleagues (e.g., Alexander, Barton, Schiavo, & Parsons, 1976), structuring and relationship skills are generic family therapy skills that cut across theoretical orientations. "Structuring skills" are the abilities necessary to structure a session, such as being direct, being clear, and modeling good communication. "Relationship skills" are those necessary to create an interpersonal climate where change can take place. They include humor, warmth, and the ability to connect feelings with behaviors. Alexander *et al.* (1976), in their influential study, found that these two sets of skills accounted for 60% of the variance in treatment outcome. Relationship skills alone accounted for 45% of the outcome variance.

MAJOR ISSUES IN THE FIELD

In an important review article, Liddle (1982a) identified five generic training issues that form the outline for this section.

Who Should Teach and Be Taught Family Therapy?

It remains unclear today which are the most relevant and salient variables for the selection of both family therapy trainees and trainers. It is not known whether previous psychotherapy experience, significant life experience, or other factors help to determine the effectiveness of a family therapist. To what extent are family therapists "made" or "born"? AAMFT's Commission on Supervision is the first group to grapple seriously with qualifications for supervisors, although the majority of persons supervising family therapy in this country are not credentialed by this organization.

What Should Be Taught?

The issue of the content of supervision is controversial because of the aforementioned isomorphism between therapy and supervision. Since there are a variety of schools of therapy, it is not surprising that there are a variety of schools of training/supervision. McDaniel, Weber, and McKeever (1983) show how structural, strategic, family-of-origin, and experiential therapies have been translated into supervisory modalities consistent with these theories of change. Other examples of models of supervision based on therapy theories are found in Connell (1984) and Keller and Protinsky (1984).

Another issue related to the content of training is whether trainees should be schooled in one pure approach and whether eclectic training models lead to confusion or contradiction (Liddle, 1982b). The extent to which a trainee's personal life should be examined in training is also controversial.

Finally, trainers are being challenged to identify and differentiate specific clusters of skills that are associated with the various approaches to supervision. The most recent attempt to specify supervisory skills (for the structural–strategic approach) is offered by Liddle and Schwartz (1983).

How Should the Content and Skills Be Taught?

Another problem is that many family therapies rely heavily on right-brain activities, such as metaphor, pattern recognition, humor, and the like. Frequently, however, trainers try to teach such right-hemispheric operations through left-hemispheric methods such as reading and writing. There is little consensus as to how one should teach such nondigitial processes. Also, certain theoretical models, such as Whitaker's experiential therapy, do not lend themselves well to goal-specific objectives. Liddle's (1982c) article on using mental imagery to create therapeutic and supervisory realities, and Prosky's (1982) chapter on the use of analogic and digital communication in training, are among the first publications in the literature to address this issue.

Another promising method, adapted from individual therapy training, is microtraining. Its application to family therapy is described in Street and Treacher (1980). Specific family therapy skills are described and demonstrated to students with video examples. Students are then challenged to demonstrate the skills while being taped. They observe their own work and receive feedback.

How Does the Setting Influence Training, and How Does Training Influence the Setting?

As anyone who has tried to teach family therapy in a non-family-therapy setting knows, the discipline has considerable political ramifications (Framo, 1976; Haley, 1975; Liddle, 1978). Many systems resist family therapy and are powerfully influenced by it. For this reason, Liddle (1982a) believes that we need the ability to make interactional/structural assessments of the training systems and the ecosystem in which it functions, and to prepare students and organizations for the personal and political consequences of adopting a systemic view.

How Should Training Be Assessed?

The issue of research on training/supervision is explored in more detail below. Suffice it to say here that this is a grossly neglected area, ready for exploration. If the "bottom line" of training is to produce effective therapists, it is a sad commentary that there is not a single training/supervision study in which the therapeutic outcome is the dependent variable.

TEACHING TOOLS AND TECHNIQUES

As noted at the outset of this chapter, "training is a generic term that encompasses all of the aspects of family therapy education. As such, the topic is too broad to be covered here. In fact, this entire book can be seen only as a partial answer to the question, "What is training?" Beyond the model curriculum of the Commission on Accreditation for Marriage and Family Therapy Education (1981), and the revision now in process, readers are referred to several useful resources. For example, Liddle and Saba (1982) have described an introductory family therapy course that demonstrates the isomorphic relationship between teaching and therapy. Nichols (1979) has written a general article on doctoral programs in family therapy, and Everett (1979) has written a similar article about master's programs. There are also several articles describing the curricula of particular programs (e.g., Garfield, 1979; L'Abate, Berger, Wright, & O'Shea, 1979). More recently, we have published papers describing the content and teaching methods for courses in ethical, legal, and professional issues in family therapy (Piercy & Sprenkle, 1983) and family therapy outcome research (Sprenkle & Piercy, 1984). We have also prepared a general article on the process of family therapy classroom education, which delineates basic educational assumptions and the variety of techniques applicable to many courses (Piercy & Sprenkle, 1984). Finally, we have written a chapter on the process of helping students develop their own integrative theories of family intervention (Piercy & Sprenkle, 1985).

The remainder of this section offers suggestions for a course specifically on family therapy supervision. Such a course might entail both a content track and a clinical track. The content track is fulfilled through a seminar that meets for several hours each week. Activities (from Sprenkle, in press) include the following:

1. Students are asked to prepare outlines and critiques of the major readings on supervision published in the past 5 years.

2. They write brief papers in response to a series of questions about supervision; this helps them to articulate their personal theory of supervision. Here are some sample questions:

a. What is the relationship between your theory of therapy and your theory of supervision?

b. What are the implications of operating from a specific framework versus an eclectic approach?

c. What are the relative advantages and disadvantages of live supervision, case conferences, audiotaping, videotaping, and the other modes of supervision?

d. Develop a plan for the assessment of your supervision. This should include methods for assessing your supervisory strengths as well as errors.

3. Students are asked to observe the faculty supervisors for several weeks. Then they are required to make an oral presentation on the theory and practice of the supervision of these faculty members.

4. They present their own goals as supervisors, using the Goal Attainment Scaling format. These goals, developed early in the course, are used to evaluate progress at the end of the term.

5. Class members prepare a worksheet that a supervisor could use to help a therapist increase his/her supervisory skills. One published model is by Schwartz (1981). For example, a student might develop a worksheet to facilitate learning circular diagramming. Another might prepare one to teach positive connotation (Constantine, Stone Fish, & Piercy, 1984). Alternatively, students may develop forms for supervisory note taking, such as the one published by Heath (1983).

The clinical track focuses on supervision of supervision, a process described in articles by Constantine, Piercy, and Sprenkle (1984) and by Liddle, Breunlin, Schwartz, and Constantine (1984). At Purdue University, for example, several supervisors in training are assigned to a supervisor of supervisors (a faculty member). The supervisors in training are assigned to one of the practica in the on-campus Marriage and Family Therapy Clinic, which typically meets from 2:00 to 9:00 P.M. The supervisors in training and the supervisor of supervisors meet at the beginning and end of this time to discuss progress of therapists, specific issues that have arisen during the process of supervision, and the group process (Constantine, Piercy, & Sprenkle, 1984). During the balance of the time, the supervisors in training conduct presession meetings with the therapists, do live supervision of cases, and conduct posttherapy feedback sessions. In addition, they typically meet with the therapists before supervision begins, in order to establish a relationship, to discuss the therapists' overall goals for supervision, and to ascertain how the supervisors in training can be helpful. The supervisor of supervisors keeps his/her contact with the therapists to a minimum and works through the supervisors in training. The supervisor of supervisors is not in the therapy room during the presession or postsession meetings, but remains in the observation booth to monitor the work of the supervisors in training. A supervisor of supervisors, may, however, call in to make suggestions and/or provide support for the supervisors in training. The supervisors in training answer all such calls to assure that there is little direct contact between therapists and the supervisor of supervisors (Constantine, Piercy, & Sprenkle, 1984; Sprenkle, in press).

RESEARCH ISSUES

In a recent empirical evaluation of the training program of the Family Institute of Chicago, Tucker and Pinsof (1984) assert that most positive reports of training outcome

> have been based primarily on clinical impressions . . .or training self-reports post training. . . . Unfortunately, these positive conclusions rest on the tacit and untested assumption that a self-reported, positive training experience is associated with change in actual practice or outcome with patients. In fact, no research evidence exists to show that training in marital and family therapy increases clinical effectiveness. Consequently, family therapy training has been planned and conducted without the benefit of a scientific foundation. (p. 437).

Unfortunately, this quotation accurately reflects the state of research in the field. As noted earlier in this chapter, there is not a single study that directly connects training and family therapy client outcome.

Fortunately, however, in recent years there have been some studies that indirectly (inferentially) assess the degree to which a particular program teaches its trainees those skills believed to be associated with positive therapy outcome (Avis & Sprenkle, 1986). In the first major review on research in training in marriage and family therapy, Kniskern and Gurman (1979) note that training can be evaluated by several other criteria: (1) Does the training increase the trainee's conceptual knowledge about family functions? (2) Does the training have an impact on the trainee's personal life? While valid issues for educators, these last criteria are too indirect to be used to assess the impact training has on the treatment of families.

Description of Recent Studies

Ten studies on family therapy training have been located that are not discussed in the Kniskern and Gurman (1979) review. They fall into two major categories: Four have described the development of instruments for measuring the outcome of training/supervision, and six have actually evaluated training programs. The latter have assessed the impact of a variety of training–learning experiences on the trainees' skills and behavior (Avis & Sprenkle, 1986).

EVALUATION INSTRUMENTS

The Allred Interaction Analysis for Counselors (Allred & Kersey, 1977) was developed to provide family therapy trainees with "a method for acquiring meaningful, objective feedback about counseling behaviors" (p. 17).

It has seven categories for therapist behaviors and three categories for client behaviors. Pinsof (1979) developed the Family Therapist Behavioral Scale to specify clinically relevant verbal behaviors of family therapists. It is comprised of 19 mutually exclusive code categories, based theoretically on the executive skills identified by Cleghorn and Levin (1973). Pinsof (1981) has used this system to devise his more complex Family Therapist Coding System, which was designed to be totally "reconstructive" (i.e., the therapist can reconstruct which happened in the session by examining the codes). Piercy, Laird, and Mohammed (1983) developed the Family Therapist Rating Scale as a measure of in-therapy skills. It consists of 10 items within each of five skill categories (Structuring, Relationship, Historical, Structural/Process, and Experiential). It is the first coding system to describe nonverbal behaviors and is more global than Allred and Pinsof's scale. Breunlin, Schwartz, Krause, and Selby (1983) developed a training evaluation instrument that consists of a 30-minute videotape of a simulated family therapy session, followed by a series of multiple-choice questions about the session. It has been designed to be easily quantifiable and does not require the laborious task of coding or rating actual therapy sessions or tapes.

EVALUATION OF FAMILY THERAPY TRAINING

The six studies that have actually evaluated training programs are described in greater detail below in the "Key Books and Articles" section. Tomm and Leahey (1980) compared three methods of teaching basic family therapy assessment to beginning medical students. Churven and McKinnon (1982) investigated the impact of a 3-day intensive workshop in basic therapy on the cognitive and intervention skills of 24 trainees. Byles, Bishop, and Horn (1983) investigated the results of a training program designed to teach family therapy skills to 24 master's-level social workers who were employed at a family service agency. Kolevzon and Green (1983) examined the differential effect of three types of family therapy training on therapists' therapeutic assumptions and in-therapy behavior. Mohammed and Piercy (1983) examined the differential effect of two training methods on the acquisition of structuring and relationship skills. Finally, Tucker and Pinsof (1984) completed a comprehensive evaluation of 19 family therapy trainees who had completed the first year of a training program at the Family Institute of Chicago.

Conclusions and Recommendations

On the basis of these 10 studies, Avis and Sprenkle (1986) have reached the following conclusions:

1. There are now several instruments with some degree of reliability and validity that appear able to distinguish beginning and advanced therapists, to measure the acquisition of conceptual and/or intervention skills, and to offer feedback to therapists on their in-therapy behavior.

2. There is evidence that various types of family therapy training produce an increase in trainees' cognitive and intervention skills.

3. In-service family therapy training programs for agency staff members may be an effective way to increase agency services.

4. Beginning assessment skills may be as effectively taught by using traditional classroom methods as by using more expensive experiential methods.

5. Sequencing of training activities may be a significant variable in the acquisition of family therapy skills.

6. Cognitive and intervention skills may develop independently of each other.

Avis and Sprenkle (1986) have also made the following recommendations:

1. There is a need for controlled research on both training and supervision. Only four of the studies noted above used some type of comparison group, and only one (Tomm & Leahey, 1980) used random assignment and had an adequate sample size.

2. There is a need for replications of existing studies in order to confirm or disconfirm what have to be considered tentative findings. Such replications will require much more specification of teaching/supervisory methods used, context of training, and conditions under which training occurs.

3. There is an urgent need for more valid and reliable instruments to measure change in trainee skills. The instruments developed thus far, while promising, either have problems with reliability and validity or are so complex that they use overwhelming amounts of information and are too cumbersome and time-consuming for the average person to administer.

4. There remains a need for research that directly assesses the impact of training upon therapeutic outcome.

5. Various design improvements are necessary to make research in this area methodologically adequate. These include specifying and controlling trainer/supervisor-in-training variables, including more follow-ups to determine the stability of training effects, using more adequate samples, and assuring trainer–investigator nonequivalence.

6. Comparative studies will be increasingly necessary to answer the specificity question–that is, what training is effective, when, for whom, under what conditions, and for what type of clinical situation?

KEY BOOKS AND ARTICLES[1]

Overviews

Liddle, H. A. (1982). Family therapy training: Current issues, future trends. *International Journal of Family Therapy, 4,* 31–47.

This article extrapolates five realms of focus from previous literature on family therapy training: (1) personnel, (2) content, (3) methodology, (4) context, and (5) evaluation. Corresponding to each domain, the following questions are raised: (1) Who should teach or be taught family therapy? (2) What should be taught? (3) How should the content be taught? (4) How do the training system and training methods influence each other? and (5) How should training be assessed? The article thoroughly examines controversial issues in training that have yet to be resolved. While the author shows some bias for learning from a particular theory as opposed to eclecticism, he otherwise attempts to present both sides of the issues.

Liddle, H. A. (1982). On the problems of eclecticism: A call for epistemologic clarification and human-scale theories. *Family Process, 21,* 243–250.

This paper examines several theoretical issues facing family therapists: (1) competitive struggles among schools of therapy for followers; (2) limits to what one can know with any theory; (3) problems with eclecticism, including its role and scope; and (4) a proposed method for aiding therapists in the process of clarifying and refining their basic beliefs. The author challenges clinicians to avoid loose usage of the word "eclectic" and spurs them on to elucidate issues related to their theory and practice.

Liddle, H. A., & Halpin, R. J. (1978). Family therapy training and supervision literature: A comparative review. *Journal of Marriage and Family Counseling, 4,* 77–98.

This overview compares and categorizes the prevailing family therapy training and supervision literature by focusing upon six areas: (1) goals of training/supervision and supervisor skills, (2) supervisory techniques, (3) the supervisor–supervisee relationship, (4) personal therapy for trainees, (5) politics of family therapy training, and (6) evaluation. Gaps in the literature, both conceptual and empirical, are identified. Over 100 references are categorized within a comprehensive table, making this article a handy resource.

Okun, B., & Gladding, S. (Eds.). (1983). *Issues in training marriage and family therapists.* Ann Arbor, MI: ERIC/CAPS.

This monograph of the Association of Counselor Education and Supervision

---

1. This is an expanded version of "Annotated Bibliography of Key Resources in Training and Supervision" by M. Brown-Standridge, M. J. Hirschmann, J. H. Lasley, and C. Steinweg, 1985, in F. P. Piercy (Ed.), *Family Therapy Education and Supervision.* New York. Haworth Press. Used by permission. Additional annotations were contributed by Judy Myers Avis, Nicholas Aradi, Rozelyn Cantrell, and Sita Chaney.

(ACES) focuses on relevant family therapy training issues for counselor educators. There are several good articles on training and supervision. One article suggests a creative alternative to the either–or issue of family therapy as a profession or a professional specialty, and another identifies some important gender issues relevant to training family therapists.

Piercy, F. P. (Ed.). (1985). *Family therapy education and supervision*. New York: Haworth Press. (Also published as Volume 1, Number 4 of the *Journal of Psychotherapy and the Family*.)

This volume includes some excellent articles on topics such as family therapy theory building, feminist training, training implications of family therapy as a profession or a professional specialty, and an introduction and consumer's guide to family therapy supervision. Many of the contributors are leaders in the area of family therapy training, and many of the articles provide a firsthand view of training approaches that the reader may use as either a trainer or a participant.

Simon, R., & Brewster, F. (1983). What is training? *Family Therapy Networker, 7*(2), 25–29, 66.

The authors of this article take a "human interest" approach to the topic of training. They identify five phases a student in any training program might encounter, emphasizing the feelings that such a process may arouse. This article is peppered with interesting quotes from leaders in the field that reveal their dilemmas with family therapy and supervision. The article is not intended to be a rigorous discourse on training, but rather an evocative experience with the subject matter, putting the reader in touch with the emotional issues involved from either side of the one-way mirror.

Whiffen, R., & Byng-Hall, J. (Eds.). (1982). *Family therapy supervision: Recent developments in practice*. New York: Grune & Stratton.

This is the first published book exclusively on family therapy supervision. This edited volume includes contributions by luminaries in Great Britain, the United States, Canada, Italy, and elsewhere. Most chapters describe the supervision model of the authors, although a few focus on specific techniques (e.g., earphone, videotape) and theoretical issues. Although the volume is not overly narrow in scope, the predominant emphases are on live supervision, team approaches, and strategic orientations.

Live Supervision

Berger, M., & Dammann, C. (1982). Live supervision as context, treatment, and training. *Family Process, 21*, 337–344.

The uniqueness of this contribution lies in the willingness of the authors to examine not only the advantages of live supervision, but also the potential pitfalls. The article addresses the inevitable struggle between the perceptions of therapist and supervisor that originate from opposite sides of the one-way screen. In addition, the value of varying perspectives is lauded, and the synthesis of multiple views is recommended for enhanced treatment and training.

Beroza, R. (1983). The shoemaker's children. *Family Therapy Networker, 7*(2), 31–33.

This essay takes the stand that live supervision has sufficiently come of age to be no longer just the political symbol for directive versus traditional therapy, but to be also justly deserving of constructive criticism. The main caution offered is that a therapist may not always emerge confident from a session with live supervision. The author's tack is likely to be highly useful to supervisors struggling to define their roles with therapists in training.

Byng-Hall, J. (1982). The use of the earphone in supervision. In R. Whiffen & J. Byng-Hall (Eds.), *Family therapy supervision: Recent developments in practice.* New York: Grune & Stratton.

The author describes the main uses of the "bug in the ear," its advantages and disadvantages, and ways to utilize the modality most effectively. The importance of the supervisor being sensitive to the trainee's position is stressed, as the method is potentially intimidating as well as helpful.

Coppersmith, E. I. (1980). Expanding uses of the telephone in family therapy. *Family Process, 19*, 411–417.

Creative uses of the telephone in family therapy are described. The author gives examples of calls to the therapist, calls from the team to specific family members, and calls between family members. These case examples demonstrate the impact of the format on recalcitrant families. The author additionally shows how she simultaneously capitalizes on use of the team for both therapeutic and training purposes.

Olson, U., & Pegg, P. F. (1979). Direct open supervision: A team approach. *Family Process, 18*, 463–469.

This article describes the model utilized by the Family Therapy Training Institute of London. Here, "direct" refers to supervisory interventions that are made directly and immediately to the therapists during a family session. "Open" means that the supervisor and other team members are present in the same room as the family during sessions. The functions of the team in this model include combining expertise and support, serving as actors or models for behaviors for the family, and providing feedback about the session to both the therapist and the family. Four forms of direct supervision are discussed: authoritarian, supportive, explorative, and collaborative. The problems as well as the benefits of such a supervisory approach are discussed.

Papp, P. (1980). The Greek chorus and other techniques of paradoxical therapy. *Family Process, 19*, 45–57.

This important article describes the process of paradoxical family therapy, including the indications, principles, and limitations of such techniques as reframing, prescription, and reversals. The "Greek chorus" (the supervisory team) is highlighted as useful to several paradoxical interventions appropriate for a family resistant to change. This article is rich in examples and is a prime source for family therapists interested in live supervision and/or paradoxical intervention strategies.

Supervisory Skills and Techniques

Breunlin, D. C., & Cade, B. (1981). Intervening in family systems with observer messages. *Journal of Marital and Family Therapy, 7,* 453–460.

The authors describe an approach to family therapy in which observers become part of the therapeutic team by sending messages in to the session. Five components of observer messages are discussed: function, target, timing, content, and delivery. Guidelines for effective team functioning and implications for training are also considered. In addition to presenting practical suggestions for implementing this mode of therapy, the article includes a thoughtful discussion of the evolution of the role of observers from passive to active participants in the therapeutic process.

Constantine, J. A., Stone Fish, L. S., & Piercy, F. P. (1984). A systematic procedure for teaching positive connotation. *Journal of Marital and Family Therapy, 10*(3), 313–316.

A unique step-by-step approach is proposed for teaching trainees the strategic technique of circumventing family resistance via positive connotation of noxious behavior. The training procedure is group-oriented and systematically moves from brainstorming, to contributions behind a one-way mirror, to generalization in therapy. The brief nature of the article makes for easy introductory reading.

Garrigan, J. J., & Bambrick, A. F. (1977). Introducing novice therapists to "go-between" techniques of family therapy. *Family Process, 16*(2), 237–246.

This paper identifies the competencies, objectives, and evaluation criteria used in a program to train therapists in Zuk's "go-between" method of family therapy (see Chapter 9). This was one of the first family training programs to carefully identify operationalizable objectives. The authors' method of graphically articulating competencies with corresponding perceptual/conceptual and therapeutic skills, as well as criteria for evaluating these skills, is a useful paradigm for family therapy trainers to consider.

Heath, A. W., & Storm, C. L. (1983). Answering the call: A manual for beginning supervisors. *Family Therapy Networker, 7*(2), 36–37, 66.

This highly readable article contains a set of guidelines for the family therapist who is assuming supervisory responsibility for the first time. The authors urge the development of a conceptual framework of supervision based, in part, on the similarities of therapy and supervision. This "manual" to supervision also offers a supplemental list of readings to compensate for its brevity.

Heath, T. (1983). The live supervision form: Structure and theory for assessment in live supervision. In J. C. Hansen & B. P. Keeney (Eds.), *Diagnosis and assessment in family therapy.* Rockville, MD: Aspen Systems Corpoation.

The author uses a live supervision instrument as a vehicle to present his theory and practice of supervision. The instrument is isomorphic to the activity for which it is designed. It is structured, goal-specific, and theory-based. The purpose of the instrument (supervision) is described, followed by a clear and thorough analysis of its components.

Liddle, H. A. (1982). Using mental imagery to create therapeutic and supervisory realities. *American Journal of Family Therapy, 10*, 68–72.

This is a short but potent article that reminds supervisors to create experiential bridges for their supervisees through the use of visual and auditory imagery. The thoughts presented are innovative and provocative and set the mind spinning in new directions. This is an unusually analogic style for the author, and the content will probably be a refreshing addition to a supervisor's repertoire.

Liddle, H. A., & Schwartz, R. C. (1983). Live supervision/consultation: Conceptual and pragmatic guidelines for family therapy trainers. *Family Process, 22*, 477–490.

In this article, the authors provide a rather thorough list of live supervision skills. These skills could be useful to supervisors in developing learning objectives and/or evaluation tools for live supervision.

Nielsen, E., & Kaslow, F. (1980). Consultation in family therapy. *American Journal of Family Therapy, 8*, 35–42.

The authors advocate the regular use of consultants (either peers or visiting experts) by experienced family therapists for the purposes of overcoming therapeutic impasses, verifying diagnostic impressions, confirming intervention strategies, and stimulating professional and personal development. Consultations can take place in several forms, including discussion, tape reviews, observation through a one-way mirror, and participation in a session as cotherapist. Concrete recommendations are made for the careful preparation for and carrying out of consultant-conducted interviews, with special emphasis on the way that such interviews can best be integrated into the continuing process of therapy.

Roberts, J. (1983). The third tier: The overlooked dimension in family therapy training. *Family Therapy Networker, 7*(2), 30–31, 60–61.

The case is made that the field of family therapy should begin to "appreciate the importance of the larger therapeutic–educational system that includes the supervisor, therapist, family, and the group of trainees behind the mirror" (p. 30). The author identifies supervisory responsibilities in developing a "collaborative team" that will expand the potential of the training group. Some of the training techniques suggested are likely to be controversial, in that team trainees may be left unsupervised to rise to the occasion on their own.

Whiffen, R. (1982). The use of videotape in supervision. In R. Whiffen & J. Byng-Hall (Eds.), *Family therapy supervision: Recent developments in practice.* New York: Grune & Stratton.

This excellent brief chapter discusses the various uses of videotape in the process of family therapy supervision. Addressed are its contributions to teaching circular functioning in systems, increasing the therapist's awareness of his/her own contribution to the system, encouraging skill development, and offering useful feedback to the family, along with helpful examples of each. A format is suggested for using videotapes within supervisory sessions in such a way as to maximize learning and minimize boredom. Finally, administrative considerations and issues related to the actual process of filming and using the camera are discussed.

Family Therapy Education and Training

Cade, B. W., & Seligman, P. M. (1982). Teaching a strategic approach. In R. Whiffen & J. Byng-Hall (Eds.), *Family therapy supervision: Recent developments in practice.* New York: Grune & Stratton.

General interactional and systemic principles underlie strategic therapy and live supervision. Family and trainee behavioral changes are enhanced through the extension of interactional skills, especially through the use of humor. A set of examples demonstrates the versatility of this style of supervision and provides introductory ideas to the novice family therapy trainer.

Keller, J. F., & Protinsky, H. (1984). A self-management model for supervision. *Journal of Marital and Family Therapy, 10,* 281–288.

This article presents the model of supervision currently used in the family therapy program at Virginia Polytechnic Institute and State University. It is based on the assumption that as supervisees develop an understanding of their own family-of-origin issues and patterns, they will be better able to interrupt those patterns as they are reenacted in the therapeutic context. Self-understanding is emphasized as an essential ingredient in the therapist's management of self in the clinical setting. The article's main value lies in its elaboration of how psychodynamic and family-of-origin concepts may be applied to the process of supervision, and it will undoubtedly be of greatest interest to those working from these orientations.

Kolevzon, M. S., & Green, R. G. (1983). Practice and training in family therapy: A known group study. *Family Process, 22,* 179–190.

This article reports the findings of a survey comparing the therapeutic assumptions and styles of family therapists trained intensively in one of three major models: Bowenian, communications, or strategic. Greater divergence than convergence on therapists' assumptions and style was found among the three models. In addition, intervention styles reported within each model were found to be highly consistent with the belief system (assumptions) of that model. The authors suggest that these findings indicate that attempts to integrate divergent models into a generic or unified theory run the risk of internal inconsistency and therapeutic failure. A major problem with this study is its reliance on therapists' self-reports to determine their therapeutic behavior.

Liddle, H. A., & Saba, G. W. (1982). Teaching family therapy at the introductory level: A conceptual model emphasizing a pattern which connects training and therapy. *Journal of Marital and Family Therapy, 8,* 63–72.

An introductory family therapy course that has evolved over 6 years is thoroughly outlined. The parallel nature of the processes of teaching and therapy are emphasized. Three stages of this course—joining, restructuring, and consolidation—focus upon the issue of working from a systemic point of view with trainees. Fundamental issues for trainers in family therapy are raised for consideration, and a suggested final examination is included for those planning similar courses.

McDaniel, S. H., Weber, T., & McKeever, J. (1983). Multiple theoretical approaches to supervision: Choices in family therapy training. *Family Process, 22,* 491–500.

This paper chooses several family therapy orientations to illustrate how supervision may be used to further the training of a family therapist in ways consistent with the orientations' respective theories of human behavior and change. Structural, strategic, experiential, and family-of-origin approaches to supervision are described, along with an exploration of the similarities and differences in these particular approaches. The article includes a discussion of the relative merits of multiple versus single theoretical orientations in family therapy training programs. Recommendations are offered with regard to training and supervision as it relates to the developmental level of the trainee.

Piercy, F. P., & Sprenkle, D. H. (1983). Ethical, legal, and professional issues in family therapy: A graduate level course. *Journal of Marital and Family Therapy, 9*(4), 393–401.

This presentation of a 16-week academic course in ethical, legal, and professional issues facing family therapists may be used as a model for training clinicians in real-life dilemmas typically not described in texts. In addition, students are offered assignments and experiential activities geared to promote their own professional development. While it is conceded that the topics covered are not comprehensive, the course is global enough in focus that the sources introduced provide a solid foundation and launching pad for exploring related considerations.

Piercy, F. P., & Sprenkle, D. H. (1984). The process of family therapy education. *Journal of Marital and Family Therapy, 10*(4), 399–407.

Suggestions for the process of graduate family therapy education are prefaced with theoretical assumptions promoting student involvement and critical evaluation of key works in the field. Examples of course assignments intended to synergize theory, research, and practice are included, along with multiple assessment methods for capitalizing upon student strengths. This is a prime source for family therapy trainers seeking to expand their existing modes of instruction.

Prosky, P. (1982). The use of analogic and digital communication in training systems perception and intervention. In R. Whiffen & J. Byng-Hall (Eds.), *Family therapy supervision: Recent developments in practice.* New York: Grune & Stratton.

Prosky suggests that incongruencies of analogic and digital communication serve as indicators of systemic dysfunction. Trainers are encouraged to help trainees to maintain consistency between verbal and nonverbal behaviors and to extend their analogic range by using metaphoric messages and sculpting techniques. The chapter's most important contribution is the call to investigate the interface between the communicative behaviors of therapist and family in treatment.

Sprenkle, D. H., & Piercy, F. P. (1984). Research in family therapy: A graduate level course. *Journal of Marital and Family Therapy, 10*(3), 225–240.

This guide to developing a thorough graduate course in family therapy research is rich in examples from a teaching repertoire that are designed to ease students' anxiety about the subject, to provide exposure to existing studies and assessment tools, and to foster interest in the prevailing issues. Traditional methods of teaching are juxtaposed with more discovery-oriented modalities. Of particular significance is a section developed to acquaint budding researchers with the dilemmas of how to measure systemic change as opposed to change in individual family members.

Tomm, K. M., & Wright, L. M. (1982). Multilevel training and supervision in an outpatient service program. In R. Whiffen & J. Byng-Hall (Eds.), *Family therapy supervision: Recent developments in practice.* New York: Grune & Stratton.

This chapter articulates many of the policies and procedures adopted at the family therapy program at the University of Calgary. Training facilities, content of training, levels of training, methods of training, and evaluation methods are covered. The hallmark of this piece is the author's discussion of circular pattern diagramming as a teaching tool.

Winkle, C. W., Piercy, F. P., & Hovestadt, A. J. (1981). A curriculum for graduate-level marriage and family therapy education. *Journal of Marital and Family Therapy,* 7(2), 201–210.

This study, employing the Delphi technique to approach consensus among AAMFT-approved supervisors and training directors, compared subjects' choices of topics to be covered in a graduate-level family therapy training program with those recommended by AAMFT guidelines. Areas of overlap and points of disagreement are noted, with the expressed purpose of providing feedback to educators and practitioners in the field. This is a quality source for those planning or re-evaluating training programs and for those wanting to identify areas for independent study to fill in gaps in their own educational background.

Supervision of Supervision

Constantine, J. A., Piercy, F. P., & Sprenkle, D. H. (1984). Live supervision of supervision in family therapy. *Journal of Marital and Family Therapy, 10,* 95–97.

This brief report concentrates on the live supervision of the supervisor in training. A multitiered supervisory process is described, and the issues involved as one moves up the hierarchy are delineated. Of special interest is the authors' analysis of their past mistakes that interfered with clear differentiation of roles among therapist, supervisor, and metasupervisor.

Heath, A. W., & Storm, C. L. (1985). From the institute to the Ivory Tower: The live supervision stage approach for teaching supervision in academic settings. *American Journal of Family Therapy, 13*(3), 27–36.

This article describes the components of Purdue's course in family therapy supervision, which combines a supervision seminar and practicum and culminates in students' live supervision of live supervision. This is a good resource for anyone planning such a course.

Liddle, H. A., Breunlin, D. C., Schwartz, R. C., & Constantine, J. A. (1984). Training family therapy supervisors: Issues of content, form, and context. *Journal of Marital and Family Therapy, 10*(2), 139–150.

This paper elaborates on the form, structure, and process of a program to train family therapy supervisors in the live supervision of structural–strategic therapy. The program includes a small-group supervision seminar, individual supervision-of-supervision meetings, and a supervision group which involves the direct observation/supervision of a supervisor in training's work. This article would be quite useful for anyone involved in supervision of supervision.

Family Therapy Skills

Cleghorn, J. M., & Levin, S. (1973). Training family therapists by setting learning objectives. *American Journal of Orthopsychiatry, 43*, 439–446.

The authors of this article exhibit considerable clarity in distinguishing behavioral objectives for basic-level, advanced, and experienced family therapists. Distinctions among the proposed categories of perceptual, conceptual, and executive skills are less clear, although the classification is cited widely in the family therapy training literature. Therapists who are making the transition from individual therapy to systemic modalities will find this source particularly valuable, as will their trainers.

Falicov, C. J., Constantine, J. A., & Breunlin, D. C. (1981). Teaching family therapy: A program based on training objectives. *Journal of Marital and Family Therapy, 7*, 497–505.

This paper represents an initial step in identifying family therapy training objectives toward the goal of training evaluation. Observational, conceptual, and therapeutic skills are delineated for a direct, problem-solving family therapy approach. The authors concede that the curriculum components in their training program probably overlap and should be integrated in practice more than their list of objectives would suggest.

Tomm, K. M., & Wright, L. M. (1979). Training in family therapy: Perceptual, conceptual, and executive skills. *Family Process, 18*(3), 227–250.

A rather thorough link-up between perceptual/conceptual skills and corresponding executive skills is presented with numerous examples for family therapists' use in sessions. The model delineates therapist functions, competencies, and skills to be displayed over the course of therapy, and provides a handy reference for trainers who wish to underscore the strengths of their trainees as well as areas needing improvement. The bulk of the article is in outline form and may be difficult to absorb in one sitting.

Evaluation

Barton, C., & Alexander, J. F. (1977). Therapists' skills as determinants of effective systems–behavioral family therapy. *International Journal of Family Counseling, 5,* 11–19.

   This article discusses therapy skills that the authors suggest are likely to be related to treatment success. Structuring and relationship skills, in particular, were found to account for 60% of the variance in treatment outcome in a previous study. This article provides a useful format for clinicians or supervisors in training who are looking for a conceptual framework to evaluate therapist skills rather than just techniques.

Breunlin, D. C., Schwartz, R C., Krause, M. S., & Selby, L. M. (1983). Evaluating family therapy training: The development of an instrument. *Journal of Marital and Family Therapy, 9,* 37–47.

   An instrument for assessing trainees' degree of systemic thinking evolved out of a series of studies to establish content and predictive validity. Family therapy trainees are given questions to answer in response to a studio-produced videotape based upon an actual initial family therapy session. The authors openly discuss the challenges of creating an effective questionnaire that distinguishes beginning (linear-thinking) therapists from advanced (circular-thinking) practitioners of family therapy.

Byles, J., Bishop, D., & Horn, D. (1983). Evaluation of a family therapy training program. *Journal of Marital and Family Therapy, 9,* 299–304.

   This article describes a 14-month training program based on the McMaster model of family functioning. Trainees were 24 social workers employed by a metropolitan family service agency that was interested in increasing the use of family therapy as a treatment method. The program consisted of 6 months of training in conceptual and perceptual skills, and 8 months of training in executive skills through peer-group review of audio-taped therapy sessions. Outcome measures of skill acquisition were inconclusive. The most significant result was greatly increased use of family therapy by agency staff. The article is important as a case study in program innovation within an agency setting.

Churven, P., & McKinnon, T. (1982). Family therapy training: An evaluation of a workshop. *Family Process, 21,* 345–352.

   This article reports the results of an outcome study of the effectiveness of a 3-day training workshop designed to teach basic family therapy skills. A pretest–posttest design was used to compare trainees' performance before and after the workshop on both cognitive and intervention skills. Three measures were used to evaluate trainees' learning: written case analyses, videotaped interviews with simulated families, and self-ratings. Significant improvements were found on all three measures, although no significant differences were found between different professional groups participating. Changes in cognitive and intervention skills were found to be relatively independent.

Kniskern, D. P., & Gurman, A. S. (1979). Research on training in marriage and family therapy: Status, issues, and directions. *Journal of Marital and Family Therapy*, 5, 83–92.

This overview of the evaluative literature for family therapy training raises many important research questions. The article exposes the "empirical ignorance" associated with gaps in the profession's knowledge base regarding training, and is thorough in raising issues for clinicians, supervisors, and researchers alike. The authors pinpoint a variety of uncharted areas ripe for investigation.

Mohammed, Z., & Piercy, F. P. (1983). The effects of two methods of training and sequencing on structuring and relationship skills of family therapists. *American Journal of Family Therapy*, 11, 64–71.

This study compares the effectiveness of observation–feedback (OF) (use of supervisor-led group discussion of therapists' videotapes) and skill-based (SB) (use of skills training videotapes in group supervision) training methods, as well as the sequence (OF-SB vs. SB-OF) of training, on structuring and relationship skills. Relationship skills of family therapists improved with the OF-SB sequence. Overall, neither of the methods or sequences was more effective in direct comparisons. Both the directionality of nonsignificant changes and therapist self-reports were generally positive for both methods. Implications for training family therapists are discussed.

Piercy, F. P., Laird, R. A., & Mohammed, Z. (1983). A family therapist rating scale. *Journal of Marital and Family Therapy*, 9, 49–59.

The development and validation of a scale for evaluating family therapist skills is presented. The scale includes five skill categories: Structuring, Relationship, Historical, Structural/Process, and Experiential, each with 10 items. An initial validation study found that the scale discriminated significantly between experienced and inexperienced family therapists. Additional psychometric data are presented, and possible uses of the scale are discussed.

Tomm, K. M., & Leahey, M. (1980). Training in family assessment: A comparison of three teaching methods. *Journal of Marital and Family Therapy*, 6, 453–457.

This article reports the results of a study at the University of Calgary on the relative effectiveness of differing methods used to teach basic family assessment to first-year medical students. Three teaching methods were compared: (1) lecture with videotaped demonstration; (2) small-group discussion with the same videotaped demonstration; and (3) learning groups that included the experiential component of interviewing and assessing a family and presenting a videotape of the interview to the group for discussion. Results showed that posttest achievement was significantly higher than pretest for all methods. However, no method was shown to be superior to the others, leading to a conclusion that the lecture–demonstration approach is the method of choice for teaching family assessment to beginning medical students, on the basis of cost-effectiveness.

Tucker, S. J., & Pinsof, W. M. (1984). The empirical evaluation of family therapy training. *Family Process, 23*, 437–456.

This article reports the results of an empirical evaluation of a family therapy training program. Nineteen trainees (all practicing psychotherapists from various disciplines) in a 2-year training program were evaluated before and after their first year of training, using a single-group pretest–posttest design. Significant changes were found on some dimensions of trainees' clinical conceptualizations and in-therapy verbal behaviors. However, many predicted changes did *not* occur (or were not discriminated by the instruments used), including increases in trainees' personal skills, increases in 21 of 25 verbal behaviors, and increases in two out of three scales on the Family Concept Assessment instrument. The results of this study are thus far from conclusive. However, the article is worthwhile for its detailed description of an outcome evaluation of an entire training program, and it is notable as the first such comprehensive study reported in the literature.

REFERENCES

Alexander, J., Barton, C., Schiavo, R., & Parsons, B. (1976). Systems–behavioral intervention with families of delinquents: therapist characteristics, family behavior, and outcome. *Journal of Consulting and Clinical Psychology, 44*, 656–664.

Allred, G., & Kersey, F. (1977). The AIAC, a design for systematically analyzing marriage and family counseling: A progress report. *Journal of Marriage and Family Counseling, 3*, 17–26.

Aradi, N. (1985). *Advantages and disdvantages of the major forms of family therapy supervision.* Unpublished manuscript prepared for a seminar on supervision, Purdue University.

Avis, J., & Sprenkle, D. H. (1986). *A review of outcome research on family therapy training.* Unpublished manuscript, Purdue University.

Berger, M., & Dammann, C. (1982). Live supervision as context, treatment, and training. *Family Process, 21*, 337–344.

Beroza, R. (1983). The shoemaker's children. *Family Therapy Networker, 7*(2), 31–33.

Bloch, D., & Weiss, H. (1981). Training facilities in marital and family therapy. *Family Process, 20*, 133–146.

Breunlin, D. C., & Cade, B. (1981). Intervening in family systems with observer messages. *Journal of Marital and Family Therapy, 7*, 453–460.

Breunlin, D. C., Schwartz, R. C., Krause, M. S., & Selby, L. M. (1983). Evaluating family therapy training: The development of an instrument. *Journal of Marital and Family Therapy, 9*(1), 37–47.

Broderick, C. B., & Schrader, S. S. (1981). The history of professional marriage and family therapy. In A. S. Gurman & D. P. Kniskern (Eds.), *Handbook of family therapy.* New York: Brunner/Mazel.

Brown, M., Hirschmann, M. J., Lasley, J. H., & Steinweg, C. (1985). Annotated bibliography of key resources in training and supervision. In F. P. Piercy (Ed.), *Family therapy education and supervision.* New York: Haworth Press.

Burman, E., & Dixon-Murphy, T. (1979). Training in marital and family therapy at free standing institutes. *Journal of Marital and Family Therapy, 5,* 29–42.

Byles, J., Bishop, D., & Horn, D. (1983). Evaluation of a family therapy training program. *Journal of Marital and Family Therapy, 9,* 299–304.

Byng-Hall, J. (1982). The use of the earphone in supervision. In R. Whiffen & J. Byng-Hall (Eds.), *Family therapy supervision: Recent developments in practice.* New York: Grune & Stratton.

Carter, E. (1982). Supervisory discussion in the presence of the family. In R. Whitten & J. Byng-Hall (Eds.), *Family therapy supervision.* New York: Grune & Stratton.

Churven, P., & McKinnon, T. (1982). Family therapy training: An evaluation of a workshop. *Family Process, 21,* 345–352.

Cleghorn, J. M., & Levin, S. (1973). Training family therapists by setting instructional objectives. *American Journal of Orthopsychiatry, 43,* 439–446.

Commission on Accreditation for Marriage and Family Therapy Education (1981). *Manual on accreditation.* Upland, CA: American Association for Marriage and Family Therapy.

Connell, G. M. (1984). An approach to supervision of symbolic–experiential psychotherapy. *Journal of Marital and Family Therapy, 10,* 273–280.

Constantine, J. A., Piercy, F. P., & Sprenkle, D. H. (1984). Live supervision of supervision in family therapy. *Journal of Marital and Family Therapy, 10,* 95–97.

Constantine, J. A., Stone Fish, L. S., & Piercy, F. P. (1984). A systematic procedure for teaching positive connotation. *Journal of Marital and Family Therapy, 10*(3), 313 –316.

Coppersmith, E. I. (1980). Expanding uses of the telephone in family therapy. *Family Process, 19,* 411–417.

DeShazer, S., & Molnar, A. (1984). Changing teams/changing families. *Family Process, 22,* 481–486.

Everett, C. (1979). The masters degree in marriage and family therapy. *Journal of Marital and Family Therapy, 5,* 7–13.

Everett, C. (1980). An analysis of AAMFT supervisors: their identities, roles, and resources. *Journal of Marital and Family Therapy, 6,* 215–226.

Falicov, C. J., Constantine, J. A., & Breunlin, D. C. (1981). Teaching family therapy: A program based on training objectives. *Journal of Marital and Family Therapy, 7,* 497–505.

Fisher, B. L., & Sprenkle, D. H. (1980). Family therapy conceptualization and use of "case notes." *Family Therapy, 2,* 177–184.

Framo, J. (1976). Chronicle of a struggle to establish a family unit within a community mental health center. In P. J. Guerin (Ed.), *Family therapy: Theory and practice.* New York: Gardner Press.

Garfield, R. (1979). An integrative training model for family therapists: The Hahnemann Master of Family Therapy program. *Journal of Marital and Family Therapy, 5,* 15–22.

Haley, J. (1975). Why a mental health clinic should avoid family therapy. *Journal of Marriage and Family Counseling, 1,* 3–14.

Heath, T. (1983). The live supervision form: Structure and theory for assessment in live supervision. In J. C. Hansen & B. P. Keeney (Eds.), *Diagnosis and assessment in family therapy.* Rockville, MD: Aspen Systems Corporation.

Henry, P. W. (1983). *The family therapy profession: University and institute perspectives.* Unpublished doctoral dissertation, Purdue University.

Keller, J. F., & Protinsky, H. (1984). A self-management model for supervision. *Journal of Marital and Family Therapy, 10,* 281–288.

Kolevzon, M. S., & Green, R. G. (1983). Practice and training in family therapy: A known group study. *Family Process, 22,* 179–190.

Kniskern, D. P., & Gurman, A. S. (1979). Research on training in marriage and family: Status, issues and directions. *Journal of Marital and Family Therapy, 5,* 83–92.

L'Abate, L., Berger, M., Wright, L., & O'Shea, M. (1979). Training family psychologists: The far .ly studies program at Georgia State University. *Professional Psychology, 10,* 58–65.

Landau, J., & Stanton, M.D. (1983). Aspects of supervision with the "Pick-A-Dali Circus" model. *Journal of Strategic and Systemic Therapies, 2*(2), 31–39.

Liddle, H. A. (1978). The emotional and political hazards of teaching and learning family therapy. *Family Therapy, 5,* 1–12.

Liddle, H. A. (1982a). Family therapy training: Current issues, future trends. *International Journal of Family Therapy, 4,* 31–47.

Liddle, H. A. (1982b). On the problems of eclecticism: A call for epistemologic clarification and human scale theories. *Family Process, 21,* 243–250.

Liddle, H. A. (1982c). Using mental imagery to creat therapeutic and supervisory realities. *American Journal of Family Therapy, 10,* 68–72.

Liddle, H. A., Breunlin, D. C., & Schwartz, R. C. (Eds.). (in press). *Handbook of family therapy training and supervision.* New York: Guilford Press.

Liddle, H. A., Breunlin, D. C., Schwartz, R. C., & Constantine, J. A. (1984). Training family therapy supervisors: Issues of content, form, and context. *Journal of Marital and Family Therapy, 10*(2), 139–150.

Liddle, H. A., & Halpin, R. J. (1978). Family therapy training and supervision literature: A comparative review. *Journal of Marriage and Family Counseling, 4,* 77–98.

Liddle, H. A., & Saba, G. W. (1982). Teaching family therapy at the introductory level: A conceptual model emphasizing a pattern which connects training and therapy. *Journal of Marital and Family Therapy, 8,* 63–72.

Liddle, H. A., & Saba, G. (1984). The isomorphic nature of training and therapy: Epistemological foundation for a structural–strategic training program. In J. Schwartzman (Ed.), *Families and other systems: The macrosystemic context of family therapy.* New York: Guilford Press.

Liddle, H. A., & Saba, G. W. (in press). *Family therapy training and supervision: Creating a context of competence.* New York: Grune & Stratton.

Liddle, H. A., & Schwartz, R. C. (1983). Live supervision/consultation: Conceptual and pragmatic guidelines for family therapy trainers. *Family Process, 22,* 477–490.

Magee, R. (1985). Advantages and disadvantages of various forms of family therapy supervision. Unpublished manuscript prepared for a seminar on supervision, Purdue University.

McDaniel, S. H., Weber, T., & McKeever, J. (1983). Multiple theoretical approaches to supervision: Choices in family therapy training. *Family Process, 22,* 491–500.

McKenzie, P. N., Atkinson, B. J., & Quinn, W. H. (in press) Training and supervision in marriage and family therapy: A national survey. *The American Journal of Family Therapy.*

Mohammed, Z., & Piercy, F. P. (1983). The effects of two methods of training and sequencing on structuring and relationship skills of family therapists. *American Journal of Family Therapy, 4,* 64–71.

Nichols, W. C. (1979). Doctoral programs in marital and family therapy. *Journal of Marital and Family Therapy, 5,* 23–28.

Nielsen, E., & Kaslow, F. (1980). Consultation in family therapy. *American Journal of Family Therapy, 8,* 35–42.

Olson, U., & Pegg, P. F. (1979). Direct open supervision: A team approach. *Family Process, 18,* 463–469.

Papp, P. (1980). The Greek chorus and other techniques of paradoxical therapy. *Family Process, 19,* 45–57.

Piercy, F. P. (Ed.). (1985). *Family therapy education and supervision.* New York: Haworth Press. (Also published as Volume 1, Number 4 of the *Journal of Psychotherapy and the Family.*)

Piercy, F. P. Laird, R. A. & Mohammed, Z. (1983). A family therapist rating scale. *Journal of Marital and Family Therapy, 9,* 49–60.

Piercy, F. P., & Sprenkle, D. H. (1983). Ethical, legal, and professional issues in family therapy: A graduate level course. *Journal of Marital and Family Therapy, 9*(4), 393–401.

Piercy, F. P., & Sprenkle, D. H. (1984). The process of family therapy education. *Journal of Marital and Family Therapy, 10*(4), 399–407.

Piercy, F. P., & Sprenkle, D. H. (1985). Family therapy theory development: An integrated training approach. In F. P. Piercy (Ed.), *Family therapy education and supervision.* New York: Haworth Press.

Piercy, F. P., Sprenkle, D. H., & Constantine, J. A. (in press). Family members' perceptions of live observation/supervision: An exploratory study. *Contemporay Family Therapy: An International Journal.*

Pinsof, W. M. (1979). The Family Therapist Behavior Scale (FTBS): Development and evaluation of a coding system. *Family Process, 18,* 451–461.

Pinsof, W. M. (1981). Family therapy process research. In A. S. Gurman & D. P. Kniskern (Eds.), *Handbook of family therapy.* New York: Brunner/Mazel.

Prosky, P. (1982). The use of analogic and digital communication in training systems perception and intervention. In R. Whiffen & J. Byng-Hall (Eds.), *Family therapy supervision: Recent developments in practice.* New York: Grune & Stratton.

Quinn, W., & Davidson, B. (1985). *Training and supervision in marriage and family therapy.* Unpublished manuscript, Texas Tech University.

Roberts, J. (1983). The third tier: The overlooked dimension in family therapy training. *Family Therapy Networker, 72*(2), 30–31, 60–61.

Saba, G. W., & Liddle, H. A. (1986). Perceptions of professional needs, practice patterns and initial issues facing family therapy trainers and supervisors. *American Journal of Family Therapy, 14,* 109–122.

Schwartz, R. (1981). The conceptual development of family therapy trainees. *American Journal of Family Therapy, 9,* 89–90.

Smith, V. G., & Nichols, W. C. (1979). Accreditation in marital and family therapy. *Journal of Marital and Family Therapy, 5,* 95–100.

Sprenkle, D. H. (in press). Training and supervision in degree granting graduate programs in family therapy. In H. Liddle, D. Breunlin, & R. Schwartz (Eds.), *Handbook of family therapy training and superivison.* New York: Guilford Press.

Sprenkle, D. H., & Piercy, F. P. (1984). Research in family therapy: A graduate level course. *Journal of Marital and Family Therapy, 10*(3), 225–240.

Street, E., & Treacher, A. (1980). Microtraining and family therapy skills. *Journal of Family Therapy, 2,* 243–257.

Tomm, K. M., & Leahey, M. (1980). Training in family assessment: A comparison of three teaching methods. *Journal of Marital and Family Therapy, 6,* 453–457.

Tomm, K. M., & Wright, L. M. (1979). Training in family therapy: Perceptual, conceptual, and executive skills. *Family Process, 18,* 227–250.

Tucker, S. J., & Pinsof, W. M. (1984). The empirical evaluation of family therapy training. *Family Process, 23,* 437–456.

Whiffen, R. (1982). The use of videotape in supervision. In R. Whiffen & J. Byng-Hall (Eds.), *Family therapy supervision: Recent developments in practice.* New York: Grune & Stratton.

Whiffen, R., & Byng-Hall, J. (Eds.). (1982). *Family therapy supervision: Recent developments in practice.* New York: Grune & Stratton.

Whitaker, C. A., & Keith, D. V. (1981). Symbolic–experiential family therapy. In A. S. Gurman & D. P. Kniskern (Eds.), *Handbook of family therapy.* New York: Brunner/Mazel.

13

RESEARCH IN FAMILY THERAPY

For family therapy to mature as a discipline and become respectable in the mental health field, it must be able to authenticate its efficacy through high-quality research (Olson, Russell, & Sprenkle, 1980). Moreover, there should be a synergistic interplay among research, theory, and practice (Olson, 1976; Sprenkle, 1976). It is certainly no secret that theory (often "armchair" theory) has far outstripped the field's ability to authenticate it. Our practice, sad to say, is too often a grab bag of techniques, few of which have been proven superior to others in any reasonably controlled investigation. This is ironic, since, as Wynne (1983) states, our field began with a strong bond between research and practice. It is too often true that clinicians and re-searchers tend to be two different types of people who do not understand each other's language and concerns and seldom talk to each other (Olson, 1981; Schwartz & Breunlin, 1983). Our field remains too often dominated by charismatic clinician/teachers whose ideas have rarely been empirically tested with anything approaching scientific rigor.

NEED FOR SPECIFIC TRAINING IN FAMILY THERAPY RESEARCH

Since family therapy is a unique discipline, training in family therapy re-search cannot be adequately completed by simply taking traditional re-search methods courses. Most courses, and books on research, are devel-oped by people with little understanding of family therapy. Sociologists tend to emphasize large-scale survey research and design, and sampling and analysis techniques that are of marginal relevance to family therapy researchers. Traditional psychologists often emphasize experimental de-signs that cannot be easily replicated in family therapy settings. Research

Portions of this chapter are adapted from "Research in Family Therapy: A Graduate Level Course" by D. H. Sprenkle and F. P. Piercy, 1984, *Journal of Marital and Family Therapy*, *10*(3), 225–240. Used by permission.

examples infrequently focus on intervention, and if they do, they often are not sensitive to the special problems of measuring family interaction and change. Other issues of interest to family therapy researchers (e.g., the cost-effectiveness of interventions; attention to process as well as outcome variables) are seldom understood by most methodologists.

This chapter opens with a glossary of basic terms related to family therapy research. Then a number of basic content areas, and relevant resources and teaching strategies, are described. The chapter concludes with an annotated bibliography of key resources on family therapy research.

KEY CONCEPTS

Comparative studies of outcome. In the marriage and family therapy field, studies that compare different types of marital and family therapy with each other and with other therapies (Gurman & Kniskern, 1978). An example of the former would be Cookerly's (1976) investigation of various marital treatment modalities. An example of the latter would be Stanton and Todd's (1979) comparison of family versus individual treatment of heroin addiction. Jacobson (1985) questions the value of comparative studies of the various schools of marriage and family therapy, since the results are typically inconclusive.

Controlled studies of outcome. Studies that include random assignment by the investigator to at least one experimental treatment group and one control group. The latter could be a no-treatment and/or an alternative treatment group. Most controlled studies in marriage and family therapy have been published in the last decade. Jacobson (1985) and Kniskern (1985) disagree on the necessity of studies in this field being controlled; Kniskern is more amenable to noncontrolled exploratory research.

Core battery. Marital and family therapists, like individual therapists, have argued the relative merits of a core or common battery of assessment instruments. The clear advantage would be comparability across studies. It appears, however, that there is not sufficient consensus in the field concerning what dependent variables should be utilized to reach agreement on a core battery (Gurman & Kniskern, 1981). Todd and Stanton (1983) offer specific suggestions concerning a core battery.

Cost-effectiveness analysis (CEA) and cost–benefit analysis (CBA). Two sets of procedures that can help decision makers to determine the value of psychotherapy. In CEA, the investigator determines what the costs of therapy (personnel, facilities and equipment, patients' time, etc.) are in dollar terms. The effects can be in any unit (e.g., increase in marital satisfaction scores). A CEA study in marriage and family therapy might examine the relative cost of conjoint versus conjoint group treatment in reducing marital distress. CBA is more difficult, because it requires that the effects or outcomes must also be in dollar terms (e.g., money saved from reduced worker absenteeism due to marital therapy for chemically dependent couples). CBA leads to a ratio whereby total benefits are divided by total costs. This ratio must be greater than 1 if the intervention is to be deemed worthwhile (Parloff, 1980).

Design criteria. In their classic review article on research in marriage and family therapy, Gurman & Kniskern (1978, pp. 820–821) gave the field an influential list of 14 criteria by which the adequacy of outcome studies may be evaluated. Points are assigned for each criterion (e.g., "controlled assignment of treatment condition," 5 points). Point totals enable one to classify the design of a study on a continuum from "poor" to "very good."

Deterioration effects. Researchers in marriage and family therapy have not given enough attention to the fact that some clients get worse or are harmed by intervention. Gurman and Kniskern (1978) estimate that 5–10% of clients or relationships get worse in marriage and family therapy. Using a large number of uncontrolled studies of nonbehavioral therapy, they estimate that the three relationship methods (conjoint, conjoint group, and collaborative concurrent) have a deterioration rate of 5.6%, as opposed to 11.6% for individual marital therapy.

Discovery versus verification. Uncontrolled or descriptive studies may be argued to be of value if they are viewed to be operating in the context of discovery (discovering or exploring new relationships, generating hypotheses, etc.). Experimentally controlled studies are done in a context of verifying theoretically or empirically derived hypotheses. Gurman and Kniskern (1981, p. 753) believe that the marriage and family therapy field is not sufficiently advanced to apply all its empirical efforts toward verification.

Effect size. The most typical dependent variable in "meta-analysis" (see below). In its most common expression, it is the difference between two means divided by a standard deviation. In most cases, researchers employing meta-analyses subtract the mean of the control group from the mean of the experimental group and divide by the standard deviation of the control group (Wampler, 1982).

Exhaustiveness (of a coding system). The degree to which the instrument codes every possible therapist and/or client behavior. Pinsof's (1981) Family Therapy Coding System is an example of an exhaustive coding system.

Experimental research. A study in which an investigator manipulates (has control over) at least one independent variable (see also "*ex post facto* research"). In marriage and family therapy research, this independent variable is typically the treatment. Experimental research in this field typically involves the random assignment of subjects to groups and the random assignment of treatment to groups. Some authors (e.g., Todd & Stanton, 1983) do not believe that random assignment of therapists to treatment is advisable, since this means that a therapist must try to utilize a method to which he/she may not be committed. Good experimental designs are reviewed in Kerlinger (1973, Chapter 17).

Ex post facto *research.* Literally, research "from what is done afterward." There can be no random assignment of subjects or treatments, because the independent variables have already occurred. The investigator begins with observations of dependent variables and retrospectively studies the independent variables (Kerlinger, 1973). Beck and Jones's (1973) study of the effectiveness of family service agency therapy is a good example of *ex post facto* research.

History. One of the major threats to validity in poorly controlled research. Specifically, it refers to extraneous variables that occur during a study that might affect outcome and could inadvertently be attributed to the intervention under study (Kerlinger, 1973). For example, if subjects in a Couples Communication Program (CCP) outcome study attended a Marriage Encounter (ME) weekend, the latter might contribute to the observed change during this time period. (See also "Maturation.")

Maturation. Another threat to validity in uncontrolled research. It is similar to history except that extraneous variables are not specific. It refers more to general change or growth as a result of passage of time or daily living (Kerlinger, 1973). The fact that most untreated people recover from divorce with the passage of time might threaten an uncontrolled (no "no-treatment" control group) study of the effectiveness of a divorce recovery intervention program.

Mediating versus ultimate goals. When measuring outcome in marriage and family therapy, researchers need to distinguish between goals that represent enabling or intermediate (mediating) conditions and those that represent the final or broader (ultimate) goals of therapy. For example, if getting Sally to attend school is an ultimate goal, a mediating goal might be to increase the parents' authority with their children. Gurman and Kniskern (1981, p. 463) argue that in family therapy outcome research this distinction should be kept in clear focus, and that outcome studies should include measures of both types of goals.

Meta-analysis, narrative report, and box score. Terms that relate to procedures for reviewing and summarizing research results. In its most generic sense, meta-analysis is any literature review that uses a quantitative approach to summarize results across studies. A common metric is identified and then used to standardize studies in order to combine results (Wampler,

1982). The most common metric is the "effect size" (see above), which typically transforms results into standard deviation units. The more typical qualitative literature review is the narrative report, in which the researcher makes his/her own subjective integration of the data. The box score approach to reviewing the literature typically tallies studies on the basis of statistically significant results. For example, "nonbehavioral family therapy has yielded results superior to those of no treatment in 8 out of 13 comparisons, with five finding no differences" (Gurman & Kniskern, 1978, p. 845). Meta-analysts assert that relying on statistical significance ignores subtle but meaningful change and does not often measure the magnitude of change.

Process research. Research that focuses on the attempt to operationally and/or reliably describe the actual events of the therapy process (Pinsof, 1981, p. 700). Process researchers believe their endeavors are essential to answer the specificity question of what treatment (intervention) by what therapist works best for what clients under what circumstances (Paul, 1967). Process research is in its infancy, and Gurman, Kniskern, and Pinsof (1986) offer the field research strategies that we may hope will elucidate the relationship between process and outcome variables.

Reactive measures. The act of measuring subjects often changes them. A measurement is reactive when the subject is directly involved in the study and he/she reacts to the measurement process itself. A nonreactive measure is an unobtrusive or passive measure and does not itself change the subject's behavior (Isaac & Michael, 1971, pp. 61–62). In family therapy research, measures of weight gain following anorexia or recidivism following family therapy for delinquency are considered nonreactive measures.

Reconstructivity (of a coding system). The ability of a coding system to permit clinically meaningful reconstruction of the specific behaviors or experiences denoted by the codes. Pinsof's (1981) Family Therapy Coding System is high on reconstructivity.

Regression effects. Another threat to validity. This term refers to the fact that very high and low scores on a test are often due to chance factors; upon a second testing they are likely to regress toward the mean (i.e., high pretest scores for some individuals will yield lower posttest scores and vice versa). These changes will often occur independently of treatment.

Reliability. Essentially, the stability and consistency of measurement by an instrument. Like "validity" (see below), reliability cannot be dealt with comprehensively here.

"Test-retest reliability" is ascertained by having subjects take an instrument on several occasions and then correlating these scores. Developers of coding systems for behavioral measures report measures of "interrater reliability," which is the degree to which two or more raters agree when coding the same data. "Intrarater reliability," on the other hand, is the degree to which a single rater agrees with himself/herself when coding the same data at two different time periods. Adequate intrarater reliability shows that a coding system can be learned and applied consistently, whereas interrater reliability shows that raters have the same understanding and are consistent among themselves. Researchers in marriage and family therapy are also concerned with the "internal consistency reliability" of their instruments. Items within a subscale, for example, are analyzed to make sure that they correlate positively with other subscale items (or a hypothesized universe of such items, as in Cronbach's alpha).

Single-case designs. In marriage and family therapy research, designs that measure a single couple, family, or individual. Typically, a baseline is established by repeated measures of a dependent variable in the absence of intervention. Then an independent (usually treatment) variable is introduced, with the effect noted in the dependent variable. Finally, the process of withdrawing and introducing treatment is repeated several times. The results may then be replicated across different subjects, behaviors, or settings (Crane, 1985, p. 69). Although the method has been touted as promising for research in the field (Rabin, 1981), several important issues related to single-case designs have not been adequately addressed (Crane, 1985).

Stimulus heterogeneity. When researching the effect of different therapeutic behaviors, the researcher must control for the fact that families (and hence the degree of difficulty of cases) differ. Stimulus heterogeneity across treatment groups may be maximized through (1) random assignment of families and therapists, or (2) standardization of the in-therapy behavior of the family members through the use of actors or a simulated therapy situation in which the therapist responds to a family or videotape (Pinsof, 1981).

Triple threat. A term coined by David Olson (1976) to refer to the ideal synergistic interplay among theory, research, and practice in the family field. A therapist will be a better clinician, for example, if his/her practice is guided by theory and is tested empirically. Each of the three domains enriches the other two.

Treatment on demand (TOD). A method devised as an alternative to no-treatment control groups, due to ethical concerns about not treating clients. Each control family has access to a therapist "on demand" (if necessary), but such visits are severely limited in number (Gurman & Kniskern, 1981). Todd and Stanton (1983) criticize the TOD design because there is self-selection among those clients who do not use TOD sessions, those who do but do not exceed the limits, and those who exceed the cutoff number of sessions.

Validity. A complex topic that can only be dealt with in broad strokes here. In marriage and family therapy research, "internal validity" would ask the question of whether the treatment being studied really made a significant difference. The major threats to internal validity are such aforementioned issues as history, maturation, regression, and reactive measurement effects (see Isaac & Michaels, 1971). "External validity" would ask to what other subject populations, settings, and conditions this treatment effect could be generalized.

Researchers in marriage and family therapy are also frequently interested in several other types of validity, as follows:

The "content validity" of an instrument reflects the extent to which it samples the universe of content about the particular construct being measured. Most typically, instrument developers utilize a panel of experts to help determine whether the instrument sufficiently represents the content of what it proports to represent. For example, the content related to intergenerational family process should be included in the items of a family differentiation scale (Bray, Williamson, & Malone, 1984).

"Discriminant validity" represents the ability of an instrument to distinguish between individuals or groups who are assumed to differ on the variable being measured (e.g., beginning and experienced therapists have been shown to differ on the Family Therapist Rating Scale; see Piercy, Laird, & Mohammed, 1983).

"Predictive validity" refers to the ability of an instrument to predict future behaviors or outcomes on another variable. Alexander, Barton, Schiavo, and Parsons's (1976) measure of structuring and relationship skills has been shown, for example, to predict therapy outcome.

"Construct validity" is concerned with the degree to which the instrument, in fact, measures the theoretical construct it was designed to measure. Allred's research with the Allred Interaction Analysis for Counselors (Allred & Kersey, 1977) represents one of the few attempts within family therapy research to formally test the construct validity of an instrument (Pinsof, 1981, p. 736).

FOUNDATIONS FOR FAMILY THERAPY RESEARCH: CONTENT AREAS AND LEARNING ACTIVITIES

Review of Basic Designs

COMMENTS ON THE AREA

Although most family therapists have had some training in methodology and statistics, an excellent review of research design can be found in Kerlinger (1973, Chapters 16 & 17). These chapters review the typical faculty designs and explain carefully the components of good design. They deal well with such threats to validity as history, maturation, reactivity, and regression effects, and they discuss major forms of reliability and validity.

LEARNING ACTIVITY

Students are given a hypothetical situation and then asked, in small groups, to develop a study utilizing the various designs. Here is one example: "You are a family therapist who has devised what you consider to be an effective program of mediating child custody disputes. Your local court system has given you funding to test your model. Describe your study utilizing a matched-subjects experimental design. Also, make a list of the strengths and limitations of this design." Different small groups are assigned different designs.

Lessons from Psychotherapy Research

COMMENTS ON THE AREA

It is instructive to review the history of psychotherapy research, beginning with Eysenck's (1952) challenge that nonbehavioral psychotherapy is ineffective. There are many lessons to be learned from this rich history, and psychotherapy research forms an excellent foundation for the study of family therapy research. Parloff (1980) is an excellent single resource. His monograph describes the basic research designs used in psychotherapy research, delineates the difficulties in conducting research, and critically evaluates the various methods of integrating findings such as box score analysis and meta-analysis. Parloff also devotes several chapters to a topic that has never been adequately discussed in the family therapy research literature—namely, methods for conducting CEA and CBA in regard to therapy.

LEARNING ACTIVITY 1

Students (individually or in teams) are assigned to play the roles of the various protagonists in a debate on the effectiveness of psychotherapy. For example, one student, playing the role of "Eysenck," throws down the gauntlet to the psychotherapy profession and offers a rationale for his challenge. Another student, playing the role of "Bergin," disputes Eysenck's findings by telling how he recomputed Eysenck's treatment remission rates using different assumptions and procedures. Depending on time and the number of students, the debate can continue through the most recent challenge to psychotherapy by Zilbergeld (1983).

LEARNING ACTIVITY 2

The most comprehensive sourcebook about psychotherapy research is Garfield and Bergin (1986). One can pursue the ideas noted above in more depth by assigning key chapters in this handbook.

LEARNING ACTIVITY 3

In small groups, students are asked to design a CEA or CBA of some aspect of family therapy.

Key Review Articles

COMMENTS ON THE AREA

The review articles on family therapy research constitute the "forest" in which are set the "trees" of the individual investigations mentioned below. There have been many review articles, and these are catalogued by Gurman and Kniskern (1981, p. 745). In our judgment, although there is some value in all these articles, the most comprehensive and indispensable reviews are those by Gurman and Kniskern (1978, 1981), Pinsof (1981), Todd and Stanton (1983), and Gurman *et al.* (1986). The Gurman and Kniskern reviews, probably best known to readers of this chapter, offer "state-of-the-art" information that addresses such important topics as these:

- How effective are the family therapies?
- Which family therapies are the most effective?
- What therapist factors, client factors, and treatment factors influence the effectiveness of family therapies?
- What are the major measurement problems in family therapy outcome research?
- What are the key directions for future research?

The Gurman *et al.* (1986) review is organized around topical or content areas of outcome research, including the following: child and adolescent disorders; such adult disorders as schizophrenia, substance abuse, affective disorders, and anxiety disorders; and marital conflict, divorce therapy, and preventive interventions. A major section is devoted to a summary analysis of the effectiveness of the major schools of marital and family therapy. The authors reach the conclusion that "proponents of most of the major methods of family and marital therapy have thus far produced little or no empirical evidence of the effectiveness of their treatments, and the proponents of most of the remaining major methods as a group have provided only slightly more. Reassuringly, however, when family therapy methods have been rigorously tested, they have been found to be effective without exception" (p. 58).

Pinsof's (1981) review focuses on process research, which deals with the behavior/experience of the therapist or family member during a family therapy interview. The strength of this chapter relies on its emphasis on interactional coding systems in family therapy research. The last third of the chapter includes a particularly valuable treatise on methodological issues in process research. Pinsof covers important issues related to variable selection, evaluating coding systems, reliability and validity, the training of coders, and data analysis. An update on process research can be found in Gurman et al. (1986).

The Todd and Stanton (1983) review is perhaps less well known. It offers a concise summary of the effectiveness of marital and family therapy. It also demonstrates how one's epistemology affects even the reviewers of family therapy research. Consequently, these authors take a balanced stance between the behavioral researchers and reviewers and their nonbehavioral counterparts. In addition, the authors show how an intervention package is modified by a research project, and vice versa. The authors are quite candid about the limitations of research and present a balanced picture of the tradeoffs real-life researchers must make. Also, they make suggestions regarding a core battery of instruments for the field.

LEARNING ACTIVITIES

The review articles refer to a series of debates that students can pursue further using original source materials. For example, several authors (Jacobson, 1978; Wells & Dezen, 1978a, 1978b) have challenged Gurman and Kniskern's use of uncontrolled or otherwise weak studies in accumulating knowledge about the effectiveness of marital and family therapy. Another potential debate concerns the relative merits of various approaches to control groups. Jacobson (1978) considers the no-treatment control group to be the essential ingredient in adequate design. Gurman and Kniskern (1981) note considerable difficulties with the design and offer the TOD approach as an alternative. Todd and Stanton (1983), in turn, criticize the TOD approach and offer several varieties of parallel treatment groups as more productive alternatives.

Students are asked to play the role of the various protagonists in these debates, which can become quite heated.

Instrumentation

COMMENTS ON THE AREA

There are many important issues in the assessment of change in marital and family therapy. A few important principles discussed in the literature include the following:

1. The measurement of family therapy outcome requires multiple perspectives. We agree wholeheartedly with Todd and Stanton (1983) that variance in outcome is greatly affected by who is asked (client, therapist, friend) and how the data are collected (coded task, behavioral checklist, structured interview, etc.). A helpful table (Gurman & Kniskern, 1981, p. 770) illustrates a variety of perspectives and shows how they vary in the degree of inference involved in making an evaluative judgement about a family. For example, a therapist's rating of a family as "enmeshed" is a high-inference judgment, relative to a researcher's examining hospital records to determine whether rehospitalization occurred following therapy. Cromwell, Olson, and Fournier (1976) offer a somewhat different but nonetheless useful typology of measurement perspectives.

2. An instrument package should include both standardized forms and measures tailor-made to specific cases. Standardized instruments allow for increased confidence concerning reliability and validity, as well as for comparisons across studies. Conversely, ideographic measures enable the researcher to address the presenting problem as well as the therapist's unique goals for the case. We agree with Todd and Stanton (1983) that measures of the family's primary complaints should be the *sine qua non* of outcome research. Training in the Goal Attainment Scaling format (Kiresuk & Sherman, 1968) and in single-case experimental designs (Crane, 1985; Rabin, 1981) offers methods of operationalizing and measuring client complaints and therapist goals.

3. There should be attention to both ultimate and mediating goals. Gurman and Kniskern (1981) and Todd and Stanton (1983) stress the importance of distinguishing between goals that represent the end toward which one hopes to move a family and the means or subgoals one employs to achieve this end.

4. The units to be assessed, at a minimum, include the identified patient, the marriage, and the total system.

LEARNING ACTIVITY 1: AN EXERCISE IN MULTIPLE
RESEARCH PERSPECTIVES

Students are presented with a case vignette of a family whose principal complaint is the poor school performance and truancy of a teenage son. The parents also make reference to communication difficulties in the marital dyad and the wife's lack of sexual desire. Students are divided into small groups and are challenged to formulate as many research perspectives as possible. In keeping with Gurman and Kniskern (1981), p. 770), each perspective must include a statement of the type of information sought (e.g., performance on clinically relevant, nonfamilial objective criteria); an illustration of this type of information (e.g., school grades); and an opinion about the best judge or source of this information (e.g., school records). Students are also asked to note several disadvantages of using this criterion as the sole measure of outcome in family therapy.

LEARNING ACTIVITY 2: ASSESSMENT WORKUP

Students perform a comprehensive family assessment on a volunteer family. The literature offers several suggestions for comprehensive family assessment (Cromwell & Keeney, 1979; Cromwell & Peterson, 1983). Students are encouraged to use tools and techniques that tap the individual, couple, and family units, and to employ several of the research perspectives discussed above.

Key Studies

COMMENTS ON THE AREA

Deciding what studies constitute the key ones in the field is a subjective evaluation, and some readers will undoubtedly believe we are guilty of sins of omission and commission. We are omitting here the body of research that focuses on family interaction or healthy versus dysfunctional patterns, where therapeutic outcome is not an immediate concern. Therefore, the excellent research done by such scholars as Wynne, Gottman, Reiss, Beavers, and Olson is not directly addressed.

The primary focus of this section is on the major programmatic research efforts in family therapy and on certain highly significant single studies. The major programmatic efforts are those that (1) are designed to test a particular theoretical orientation to therapy; (2) entail multiple studies that build upon previous results; (3) utilize a variety of investigations, even though they may be built around the work of a single prominent researcher; and (4) span at least a decade of effort. The key single studies generally do not meet the last three of these criteria, but are judged to have made major methodological or substantive contributions to the field. The four major programmatic efforts are as follows:

1. Relationship Enhancement (RE) research, centered on the work of Guerney and associates (Avery, Ridley, Leslie, & Milholland, 1980; Guerney, 1977, Guerney, Coufal, & Vogelsong, 1981; Jessee & Guerney, 1981).

2. The Oregon family behavioral research program on aggressive children, led by Patterson (Fleischman, 1981; Patterson, 1976, 1982; Patterson, Reid, Jones, & Conger, 1975; Reid, 1978).

3. The Oregon behavioral marital research conducted by Weiss, his associates, and his students (Birchler & Spinks, 1980; Jacobson, 1979, 1981; Jacobson & Margolin, 1979; Margolin, 1980; Weiss, 1978; Weiss & Cerreto, 1980).

4. Alexander's behavioral—systems (now called "functional family therapy") research with families with "soft" delinquents (Alexander & Barton, 1976, 1980; Alexander & Parsons, 1982; Barton & Alexander, 1977, 1981).

The accretive nature of this research is interesting to follow. In each case, one investigation led to research questions that were addressed in subsequent studies.

Some key individual studies include the following:

1. The Philadelphia investigation of structural family therapy with the families of heroin addicts (Stanton & Todd, 1979, 1980; Stanton, Steier & Todd, 1982; Stanton *et al.*, 1980). In our judgment, this is the finest example of the integration of theory, research, and practice in the family therapy research literature.

2. The McMaster family therapy outcome study (Santa-Barbara *et al.* 1979). This is an excellent example of a research program that led to the development of a more clearly articulated approach to therapy—namely, "problem-centered systems therapy" (Epstein, Baldwin, & Bishop, 1983; Epstein & Bishop, 1981).

3. Beck and Jones's (1973) investigation of the effectiveness of the work of the Family Service Association of America. This study is notable for its huge sample (3,596 cases), and subsequently for the authors' ability to control for many important therapist, client, and treatment variables. In our judgment, this is the best example in the literature of survey research related to family therapy outcome. The authors also offer a companion volume, *How to Conduct a Client Follow-up Study* (Beck & Jones, 1976), which offers a step-by-step blueprint for program evaluation research. It discusses questionnaire construction, the relative value of mail versus telephone follow-ups, the computation of change scores, and other issues.

4. Cookerly's (1976, 1980) work on the effectiveness of six basic forms of marital therapy is also significant. While he completed a series of cumulative studies, his work does not meet the other criteria of a major programmatic effort. Nonetheless, Cookerly has contributed significant data concerning the relative effectiveness of conjoint versus individual versus group approaches. Also, the fact that this research was completed by a single individual in a private practice setting should serve as an inspiration to all aspiring clincian/researchers.

We are also following significant work in progress, such as Pinsof's (1982) comprehensive study of integrative family therapy at the Family Institute of Chicago.

The following are key resources on certain content themes:

1. Sprenkle and Storm (1983) offer a detailed substantive and methodological review of research in the area of divorce therapy.

2. While there are no current methodological reviews of the entire field of sex therapy research, readers are referred to Heiman, LoPiccolo, and LoPiccolo (1981) for an overview of research issues. Mills and Kilmann (1982) offer a thorough analysis of the research literature on group treatment, and Kilmann (1978) scrutinizes the outcome research on primary and secondary orgasmic dysfunction. Zilbergeld and Evans's (1980) strident criticism of Masters and Johnson's research is responded to by Kolodny (1981).

3. Bagarozzi and Ravens (1981) offer the most recent substantive and methodological review of research on premarital counseling.

4. Kniskern and Gurman (1980) and Avis and Sprenkle (1986) review the small amount of empirical research on supervision and offer directions for needed research. Readers are also referred to the specific studies by Allred and Kersey (1977), Barton and Alexander (1977), Breunlin, Schwartz, Krause, and Selby (1983), Churven and McKinnon (1982), Garrigan and Bambrick (1977), Mohammed and Piercy (1983), and Pinsof (1979).

5. Enrichment is the most heavily researched of these thematic areas. Giblin (1982) has recently completed a meta-analysis of most of the empirical enrichment literature. His subject pool represents 85 studies and 8,365 individuals. This study offers fascinating data on the relative effectiveness of the various programs and the contribution of key variables to outcome variance (see also Giblin, Sprenkle, & Sheehan, 1985). Wampler (1982) has also employed meta-analysis to analyze the research that has been done on the CCP. This paper also compares the results of narrative, box score, and meta-analysis reviews of the same body of literature. Gurman and Kniskern's (1977) earlier general review offers guidelines for future research that have, in fact, been implemented by subsequent researchers. While it is impossible to list all significant single studies here, readers are referred to Brock and Joanning's (1983) comparison of the RE program and the Minnesota Couple Communication Program (MCCP) as an outstanding model of research design and execution.

LEARNING ACTIVITY

Students are asked to prepare a major term paper and class presentation based on a critical analysis of one of the programmatic research projects or key studies. The outline for the paper is as follows:

1. Describe the theoretical basis of the research program/project. Describe the tenets of the theory and the extent to which the theory has, in fact, guided the research program/project.
2. Describe the research program/project itself and do a methodological critique of the study/studies, utilizing the criteria for the evaluation of designs found in Gurman and Kniskern (1978, p. 820).

3. What are the substantive findings or conclusions that we can make on the basis of this research?
4. What are the implications of this research for practice?
5. Critically evaluate the work as a whole, noting its limitations and strengths. What are the major issues for future research?

For the class presentation of this material, students are asked to prepare handouts to facilitate note taking and to make overhead transparency charts to illustrate key concepts and findings. Before each presentation, other class members are required to read the most representative example of the principal investigator's work.

Implications of the New Epistemologies for Family Therapy Research

COMMENTS ON THE AREA

Assigning Colapinto (1979) as a reading sensitizes the students to the fact that research paradigms are not neutral or value-free, but rather reflect one's epistemology. He shows how different epistemologies lead to significant differences in such key concepts as "problems" and "solutions." Therefore, what may be deemed "therapeutic success" in one framework may become "therapeutic failure" in another. Fisher (1982) discusses the frequent discrepancy between transactional theories and individual assessment methods. Many of our assessment methods focus exclusively on the individual, assume that one can know a family perspective by summing the total of individual viewpoints, and reflect linear causality. Russell, Olson, Sprenkle, and Atilano (1983) stress that there is often no clear correspondence between presenting individual symptoms (e.g., alcoholism) and type of family system. Keeney (1983) writes persuasively that any attempt to describe a phenomenon (e.g., a family) is itself an intervention and alters the thing described, just as statements about the stock market ("it is going up") create the very phenomenon being "described." Tomm (1983) also attacks the myth of objective observation and asserts that we need to give more attention to the process of investigation itself. In addition, he discusses how the traditional scientific method of dividing phenomena into smaller segments more amenable to objectification frequently kills the beast in an attempt to understand it. Holistic patterns are reduced to contrived causal explanations that do not fit clinical realities. These so-called "new wavers" (Gurman, 1983b) also call for a greater appreciation of the roles of intuition and creativity in research. Since the context of discovery is deemed as important as the context of verification, descriptive research should be accorded more prestige, and hypothesis testing should no longer be considered the only royal road to the researcher's kingdom.

In a spirited defense of traditional research methodology, "old hatters" Gurman (1983a, 1983b) and Kniskern (1983) point out that it is the only current ethical and responsible way to address the kinds of questions about efficacy of our treatments that are being raised by consumers, government agencies, and third-party payers, as well as by therapists. While the total context of family interaction is circular, important therapeutic subprocesses are linear. Families pay therapists on the premise that therapy (cause) produces change (effects). These writers also catalogue the impressive gains already made by family therapy research and caution us not to throw out the baby with the bathwater until and unless some better way is found. Indeed, they assert, responsible traditional researchers have always been aware of the subjectivity of their underlying assumptions and the fallacy of truly objective and value-free inquiry. Careful traditional researchers are also very much aware of contextual variables and frequently employ statistical techniques (e.g., correlational analysis) that are consistent with circular causality.

LEARNING ACTIVITY

The class is divided into two groups ("old hatters" vs. "new wavers"). Each designates a spokesperson to begin debate, and the protagonists are seated in opposing chairs in the front of the room. At any time, other members of either group can stand behind the spokesperson and act as an "alter ego" for him/her in the debate. The initial stimulus question is this: "Resolved, that traditional research methods are the only ethically responsible means presently available by which we can assess the efficacy of our work and study the facts influencing therapeutic outcomes" (Gurman, 1983a, p. 229).

KEY BOOKS AND ARTICLES

Many annotated citations of important research studies are given in the other topical chapters of this volume and hence are not included here. The works summarized here are either of a general nature or not pertinent for the other chapters.

Beck, D. F., & Jones, M. A. (1973). *Progress on family problems: A nationwide study of clients and counselors' views on family agency services.* New York: Family Service Association of America.

   This publication reports on a large-sample study of 3,956 cases seen at Family Service Association agencies throughout America. Among the hundreds of findings was the fact that the strongest predictors of outcome were the relationship between the client and therapist and the agreement on the agenda for therapy. The study is significant because of the unique method of statistical control, made possible by the huge sample. This nonexperimental study is one of the few sources of information about such variables as the race of the therapist and the effect of client fees.

Beck, D. F., & Jones, M. A. (1976). *How to conduct a client follow-up study.* New York: Family Service Association of America.

This is a primer for agencies who wish to carry out an evaluation of therapy services along the lines of the Beck and Jones (1973) Family Service Association study. Almost every detail from questionnaires to computation procedures to record keeping is discussed.

Bergin, A. E., & Lambert, M. F. (1978). The evaluation of therapeutic outcomes. In S. L. Garfield & A. E.. Bergin (Eds.), *Handbook of psychotherapy and behavior change* (2nd ed.). New York: Wiley.

This important review extends and broadens Bergin's coverage of the therapeutic outcome literature in the first edition of this volume (1971). The authors give detailed summaries of major comparative studies conducted between 1969 and 1977, and consider therapeutic modalities (e.g., group, marital, and family) not included in the earlier review. Psychotherapists should be encouraged by the authors' reading of the evidence for the positive effects of psychotherapy, but perhaps should be humbled by their conclusion that client characteristics and therapist personal factors contribute more to outcome variance than therapeutic technique. While not a chapter in family therapy research, this is an excellent resource on psychotherapy outcome research.

Bray, J. H., Williamson, D. S., & Malone, P. E. (1984). Personal authority in the family system: Development of a questionnaire to measure personal authority in intergenerational family processes. *Journal of Marital and Family Therapy, 10,* 167–178.

This article reports on the development and psychometric properties of the Personal Authority in the Family System (PAFS) questionnaire for transgenerational family theory. Eight scales that reflect three-generational family issues are designed to measure family process.

Cookerly, J. R. (1976). Evaluating different approaches to marriage counseling. In D. H. Olson (Ed.), *Treating relationships.* Lake Mills, IA: Graphic.

This chapter reviews four studies (completed in a private practice setting) designed to test the relative effectiveness of six types of marriage counseling: individual, individual group, concurrent, concurrent group, conjoint, and conjoint group. Overall, the conjoint approach produced the best results except for those couples who went on to divorce. The conjoint group modality was almost as good and was decidedly better for those who went on to divorce.

Cookerly, J. R. (1980). Does marital therapy do any lasting good? *Journal of Marital and Family Therapy, 10,* 393–396.

This is the report of a 5-year longitudinal investigation comparing couples in a private practice who received conjoint as opposed to nonconjoint treatment. Conjoint couples were more likely to remain married and to have much higher "good" outcomes, higher "moderate" outcomes, and lower "poor" outcomes than nonconjoint couples. The results also suggest that conjoint therapy may facilitate somewhat earlier and healthier divorces.

Crane, D. R. (1985). Single-case experimental designs in family therapy research. *Family Process, 24,* 69–78.

The enthusiasm for the use of single-case designs in family therapy research, as reflected in the article by Rabin (1981), needs to be moderated. There are insufficient dependent measures available to meet the requirements of these designs. Other limitations, such as the fact that for ethical reasons family treatments cannot be reversed, contribute to weak designs leading to weak conclusions. The author recommends implementing these studies in more controlled laboratory conditions before commencing more naturalistic, long-term therapy outcome studies.

Cromwell, R. E., & Peterson, G. W. (1983). Multisystem–multimethod family assessment in clinical contexts. *Family Process, 22,* 147–163.

The authors propose a comprehensive evaluation of client families, based on the administration of appropriate tests, to each level of the family system (i.e., individual, marital dyad, family unit). The diagnostic tasks would be to assess the subsystem components and also to integrate the data into a hierarchically coherent interpretation of the whole family. The interested reader should consult the critique of this proposal by David Reiss and the rejoinder by the authors, both of which appear in the same issue of *Family Process.*

Cromwell, R. E., Olson, D. H., & Fournier, D. G. (1976). Tools and techniques for diagnosis and evaluation in marital and family therapy. *Family Process, 16,* 1–49.

This article is a review of the science of measurement of human systems and a listing of many instruments available at the time of writing. The authors present a theoretical framework for understanding levels of measurement in terms of subjective or objective data and insider or outsider perspectives. They discuss the unit of assessment (the individual, the marital dyad, and partial or whole families) and the method of assessment (self-report or observation), and they organize the listing of instruments in these terms.

Epstein, N. B., & Bishop, D. S. (1981). Problem-centered systems therapy of the family. In A. S. Gurman & D. P. Kniskern (Eds.), *Handbook of family therapy.* New York: Brunner/Mazel.

This is an excellent single resource on the therapy that evolved along with the McMaster family therapy outcome study. It also describes later work including the development of the Family Assessment Device (FAD), which measures family functioning in accordance with the problem-centered model.

Fisher, L. (1982). Transactional theories but individual assessment: A frequent discrepancy in family research. *Family Process, 21,* 313–320.

The author contends that while most family therapy theories are transactional, the assessment tools most often used in outcome studies assesses, at best, relational-level variables. Fisher offers a number of suggestions regarding how to use many of the present assessment tools, and also calls for the development of new research tools to assess marriage and family change on a more comprehensive transactional level.

Fisher, S. R. (1984). Time-limited brief therapy with families: A one-year follow-up study. *Family Process, 23,* 101–106.

This article is a 1-year follow-up of an earlier study by Fisher. It is an attempt to see how brief therapy (6 and 12 sessions in duration) with families compares with time-unlimited therapy and no therapy (waiting list). The original study found no differences among the three treatment groups (6, 12, and unlimited sessions). However, the families in treatment had significantly better outcome than the waiting-list families. In the 1-year follow-up, none of the treatment groups exhibited deterioration. The waiting-list control group (now treated) was not significantly different from the three treatment groups. Fisher concludes that treatment effectiveness is not affected by treatment duration or by having been waiting-listed.

Giblin, P., Sprenkle, D., & Sheehan, R. (1985). Enrichment outcome research: A meta-analysis of premarital, marital and family findings. *Journal of Marital and Family Therapy, 11,* 257–272.

This article presents the findings of a meta-analysis of 85 studies of premarital, marital, and family enrichment. Findings are presented in terms of overall effectiveness as well as relevant program, subject, design, measurement, and analysis characteristics. An average overall effect size of .44 was found, indicating that the average person who participates in an enrichment program is better off than 67% of those who do not. Measurement variables (rather than those related to program content, leadership, or participants) proved to be the most powerful predictors of outcome. This article provides an interesting overview of what is known and unknown in enrichment research, as well as a useful discussion of the process of doing a meta-analysis.

Goldstein, M. J., & Doanne, J. A. (1982). Family factors in the onset, course, and treatment of schizophrenic spectrum disorders: An update on current research. *Journal of Nervous and Mental Disease, 170*(11), 692–700.

This is a useful review of current research on the relationship of family factors to schizophrenia. Recent studies of communication deviance and expressed emotion are considered with respect to their implications regarding the onset, course, and treatment of schizophrenia. Detailed summaries are given of four controlled outcome studies in which family interventions combined with maintenance medication successfully reduced patient relapse rates.

Gottman, J. M. (1982). Temporal form: Toward a new language for describing relationship. *Journal of Marriage and the Family, 44,* 943–962.

Gottman posits that temporal form is a new way of conceptualizing relationships. Most important is Gottman's discussion of how one might empirically study temporal form. This includes a brief introduction to probabilistic models (i.e., stochastic models) and how they can ultimately serve to test previously untested theoretical assumptions. Because of its largely nontechnical nature, this article can serve to whet the appetite of researchers who are dissatisfied with traditional ways of conceptualizing relationships and/or of empirically testing their theories.

Gurman, A. S. (1983). Family therapy research and the "new epistemology." *Journal of Marital and Family Therapy, 9*, 227–234.

This article provides a convincing counter argument to the position of the "new epistemology" family therapists who challenge the value of traditional research designs and methods. The author argues that conventional research methodology presents the only ethically responsible and practical approach for evaluating the effectiveness of marriage and family therapy. Several issues are presented that strongly support the compatibility of traditional research strategies with a systemic theoretical perspective. The author proposes that research questions should be posed in a way that acknowledges the multidimensionality of the therapeutic process.

Gurman, A. S., & Kniskern, D. P. (1978). Research on marital and family therapy: Progress, perspective and prospect. In S. L. Garfield & A. E. Bergin (Eds.), *Handbook of psychotherapy and behavior change* (2nd ed.). New York: Wiley.

This is the first of Gurman and Kniskern's classic reviews of outcome research, Although the chapter has historical significance, the information is available in more up-to-date form in Gurman and Kniskern (1981) and Gurman, Kniskern, and Pinsof (1986). The authors' influential design criteria (see the "Key Concepts" section) are included in this paper.

Gurman, A. S., & Kniskern, D. P. (1981). Family therapy outcome research: Knowns and unknowns. In A. S. Gurman & D. P. Kniskern (Eds.), *Handbook of family therapy*. New York: Brunner/Mazel.

This key chapter summarizes the state of outcome research in the field of family therapy at the time of the book's publication. The authors present an overview of what is known and not known regarding the relative effectiveness of different marriage and family therapies for specific clinical populations and problems, as well as factors that contribute to therapeutic effectiveness regardless of method (treatment factors, patient/family factors, and therapist factors). The authors also address a number of crucial issues in doing outcome research in family therapy. The chapter is comprehensive, in that it includes an excellent discussion of both the current state of knowledge and important questions and directions for the future. It is essential reading for clinicians and researchers alike.

Gurman, A. S., Kniskern, D. P., & Pinsof, W. (1986). Research on the process and outcome of marital and family therapy. In S. L. Garfield & A. E. Bergin (Eds.), *Handbook of psychotherapy and behavior change* (3rd ed.). New York: Wiley.

The authors diverge from their previous reviews (Gurman & Kniskern, 1978, 1981) in that there are few tables; the material is organized primarily around research relative to specific clinical disorders and clinical populations (child and adolescent disorders, psychosomatic disorders, divorce therapy, etc.). The chapter also includes an enlightening history of research in the field and a discussion of the new epistemological challenge to traditional research. William Pinsof has undoubtedly had a major influence on the large section of the chapter devoted to process research. A variety of recommendations about design and measurement issues are also included.

Hertel, R. K. (1972). Application of stochastic process analyses to the study of psychotherapeutic processes. *Psychological Bulletin, 77,* 421–430.

This is the first article to suggest the use of stochastic process analysis in psychotherapy process research. Hertel reviews the basic designs that have been used in process research: (1) pretherapy and posttherapy tests; (2) counting frequencies of behaviors; and (3) obtaining contingencies between various categories of behaviors. The nature of stochastic processes and Markov chains is discussed. Finally, Hertel compares stochastic processes with therapy process theory, suggesting that stochastic processes may represent a suitable mathematical model of psychotherapy process.

Jacobson, N. S. (1985). Family therapy outcome research: Potential pitfalls and prospects. *Journal of Marital and Family Therapy, 11,* 149–158.

The author proposes a series of design recommendations for family therapy outcome research: (1) the proportion of clients who improve should become a standard descriptive statistic; (2) between-model outcome studies should de-emphasize statistically significant differences between treatments and should focus more on clinical significance, relative effect size, and demonstrable replicability; (3) the use of random assignment and a control group should be compromised only under specified conditions; (4) there is a need to compare results in research-structured and clinically flexible conditions; (5) more research is needed on the optimal level of therapist experience and the extent to which therapists should be treated as an independent variable in the overall design; and (6) the primary outcome measure should be the most direct possible research of the presenting problem. A response to this article by Kniskern, and a brief rejoinder by Jacobson, follow in the same issue of the journal.

Joanning, H., Brewster, J., & Koval, J. (1984). The communication rapid assessment scale: Development of a behavioral index of communication quality. *Journal of Marital and Family Therapy, 10,* 409–417.

This article outlines the development and psychometric properties of the Communication Rapid Assessment Scale (CRAS) and the studies undertaken to determine its validity, reliability, and usefulness as an outcome measure. The instrument has both verbal and nonverbal forms. Both forms use a 5-point scale ranging from −2 (highly destructive) to +2 (highly conducive) for rating the global quality of dyadic interaction. Its many advantages include being simple to use, inexpensive, widely applicable, and sensitive to change.

Kniskern, D. P. (1983). The new wave is all wet. *Family Therapy Networker, 7*(4), 38, 60–62.

In response to the claims of the new epistemologists that traditional methods of scientific research are inappropriate, Kniskern offers a "plea for caution and conservatism." He points out that the traditional research methods have served the cause of family therapy well by demonstrating its effectiveness in many areas of clinical practice. He suggests that, although the linear and analytic approaches of typical outcome studies may be epistemologically limited, they nevertheless will continue to be of great interest to several consumer groups—namely, prospective clients, third-party payers, and mental health professionals in other fields. So far, says Kniskern, the "new wave" has not produced any serious alternatives to existing research strategies.

Oliveri, M. E., & Reiss, D. (1984). Family concepts and their measurement: Things are seldom what they seem. *Family Process, 23,* 33–48.

This is an important study, in that it clearly shows that care must be taken in our choice and use of testing instruments. The authors compared the Family Environment Scale (FES) and the Card Sort Procedure (CSP) as administered to 30 nonclinic families. Although the two instruments have a number of parallels, *no* associations were found across the various dimensions of the two tests. The results point to the need to consider carefully how dimensions (variables) are being operationalized, and the danger of taking descriptive labels at face value.

Olson, D. H., Russell, C. S., & Sprenkle, D. H. (1980). Marital and family therapy: A decade review. *Journal of Marriage and the Family, 42,* 973–993.

The article provides a thorough review of the impact of the development of the field of marital and family therapy from 1970 to 1980. Theoretical, clinical, and empirical advances are highlighted. The authors identify trends for the future that will further the bridging of research, theory, and practice. The article itself advances the bridging process by presenting the three domains of research, theory, and practice in an integrated manner.

Parloff, M. B. (1980). *The efficacy and cost effectiveness of psychotherapy* (Office of Technical Assessment, Document 052-003-00783-5). Washington, DC. U.S. Government Printing Office.

This report provides a review of four issues centrally related to the evaluation of psychotherapy: (1) the definition and complexity of psychotherapy; (2) the degree to which psychotherapy is amenable to scientific analysis and the availability of appropriate methods for studying psychotherapy; (3) the evidence as to psychotherapy's efficacy, including the results of analyses that synthesize findings across studies; and (4) the appropriateness of CEA and CBA of psychotherapy and the results of their application.

Pinsof, W. (1981). Family therapy process research. In A. S. Gurman & D. P. Kniskern (Eds.), *Handbook of family therapy.* New York: Brunner/Mazel.

This is an essential chapter for methodologists and researchers in the family therapy field. Pinsof explicates the vital function of process research, which is to operationalize and/or reliably describe the in-therapy events that may suggest the effectiveness of a therapy. Furthermore, process research can test clinical theories about the nature and relative effects of different techniques and treatment strategies. The chapter includes a comprehensive literature review of process research, describes the methodological issues involved, and provides a framework for the conduct of process research within the family therapy field.

Rabin, C. (1981). The single-case design in family therapy evaluation research. *Family Process, 20*, 351–365.

This article attempts to bridge the gap between clinicians and researchers through the use of the single-case design. The author shows how it can be used by clinicians to assess better the impact of their interventions with a family. The reader should also see Crane (1985) for a somewhat less optimistic assessment of the single-case design.

Russell, C. S., Atilano, R. B., Anderson, S. A., Jurich, A. P., & Bergen, L. P. (1984). Intervention strategies: Predicting family therapy outcome. *Journal of Marital and Family Therapy, 10*, 241–251.

This is a report of a research project that used stepwise linear regression to predict family therapy outcome. The independent variable was the therapists' perception of the interventions they used during sessions. The dependent variables were the life satisfaction and marital satisfaction of the clients at the conclusion of therapy. Favorable outcome for husbands was associated with active restructuring interventions, while wives responded more favorably to reframing and other similar interventions that did not actively challenge the family structure. One weakness of this study is that there were no observational reliability checks on the therapists' self-reports of their interventions.

Russell, C. S., Olson, D. H., Sprenkle, D. H., & Atilano, R. B. (1983). From family symptom to family system: Review of family therapy research. *American Journal of Family Therapy, 11*, 3–14.

Effective outcomes are linked to the interaction between symptom reduction and healthy family dynamics. The authors demonstrate the fallacy of the assumption that all families presenting with the same symptom (e.g., alcoholism) have similar family system organizations. A research design linking symptom to system is introduced.

Schwartz, R., & Breunlin, D. (1983). Why clinicians should bother with research. *Family Therapy Networker, 7*(4), 22–27.

The authors point out the gap between researchers and clinicians and the steps necessary to bridge it. The authors make three good recommendations for presenting research findings to clinicians: (1) The paper should be readable and understandable; (2) the treatment itself should be described and explained in a precise and thorough manner; and (3) results should be presented in terms of their clinical as well as statistical significance.

Schwartzman, J. (1984). Family therapy and scientific method. *Family Process, 23*, 223–236.

Schwartzman argues that "neutral objectivity" and "analytic reductionism" (the basic philosophical underpinning of traditional research methodology) are incompatible with cybernetic epistemology. He deplores the fact that traditional scientific methods have become self-validating rituals that demand adherence while ignoring context and process. New research methods more appropriate to a cybernetic epistemology are being underutilized, although the author cites recent family interactional research as manifesting a renewed interest in the cybernetic ideas.

Stanton, M. D., & Todd, T. C. (1980). A critique of the Wells and Dezen review of the results of nonbehavioral family therapy. *Family Process, 19,* 169–176.

This critique was written in response to a critical review of nonbehavioral family therapy by Wells and Dezen (1978). Stanton and Todd criticize (1) the inclusion of poorly designed studies; (2) the presentation of studies without sufficient attention to statistical procedures; (3) the unduly harsh treatment of adequately designed studies; and (4) the unfair treatment of their own study. A content analysis indicated that studies of poorer quality tended to receive more complimentary comments, and vice versa. This critique underscores the importance of consistent assessments of studies reviewed in family therapy research.

Stanton, M. D., Todd, T. C., Steier, F., Van Deusen, J. M., Marder, L. Rosoff, R. J., Seaman, S. F., & Skibinski, E. (1980). *Family characteristics and family therapy of heroin addicts: Final report 1974–1978.* (National Institute on Drug Abuse Grant No. R01 DA 01119.) Philadelphia: Philadelphia Child Guidance Clinic.

This excellent report is the most comprehensive resource on the Philadelphia Child Guidance Clinic's research on the family therapy of heroin addicts. This report presents the recruitment of subjects, the complete research design, the differences in interactional patterns between addict and normal families, the breakdown of the different treatment modalities, and the study results. The study showed that paid family therapy and unpaid family therapy were superior to a paid family movie treatment and individual therapy in regard to days free from drug usage. Paid family therapy was also found to be superior to unpaid family therapy in terms of days free of drug usage.

Todd, T. C., & Stanton, M. D. (1983). Research on marital and family therapy: Answers, issues and recommendations for the future. In B. Wolman & G. Stricker (Eds.), *Handbook of family and marital therapy.* New York: Plenum.

This chapter provides an outcome research review with a focus on identifying future needs for specific research based on clinically relevant questions. An excellent summary of the conclusions that can safely be drawn from existing research is presented. A number of critical methodological issues that are currently facing the field are highlighted and recommendations given.

Tomm, K. (1983). The old hat doesn't fit. *Family Therapy Networker, 7*(4), 39–41.

The author contends that the methods of traditional science, based on assumptions of unbiased observation and linear cause and effect relationships, are poor tools for dealing with the phenomena of family therapy, which involve the observer as an active participant in systems of circular interaction. He suggests several possible directions that a new science should take, including more emphasis on process research and increased respect for subjective data. This is a provocative article that, in good systems fashion, gives the reader no final answers or comfortable closure.

Wampler, K. S. (1982). Bringing the review of literature into the age of quantification: Meta-analysis as a strategy for integrating research findings in family study. *Journal of Marriage and the Family*, 1009–1023.

This article serves as an excellent introduction to meta-analysis, a quantitative approach to summarizing research findings in a given area of study. The approach is illustrated by presenting a meta-analysis of research on the effectiveness of the MCCP. The author presents an excellent elucidation of the advantages and disadvantages of meta-analysis. Conclusions reached from the meta-analysis are compared with conclusions reached from both a traditional and a voting method review of the same research literature.

Wells, R. A., & Dezen, A. E. (1978). The results of family therapy revisited: The nonbehavioral methods. *Family Process, 17*, 251–274.

This article reviews outcome research of nonbehavioral family therapies from 1971–1976. The 42 studies were classified according to the methodological adequacy of the research design. The authors reach rather pessimistic conclusions concerning the demonstrated efficacy of family therapy. The article precipitated a rejoinder by Stanton and Todd (1980).

Wynne, L. C. (1983). Family research and family therapy: A reunion? *Journal of Marital and Family Therapy, 9*, 113–117.

In the beginning, family researchers and family therapists were the same people. Wynne is hopeful that the field is returning to the close relationship that family therapy and family research once had. He points to the resurging interest in research in the following areas: (1) studies of therapy outcome; (2) studies of the process of therapy; (3) the use of rating scales and other nonintrusive methods of family assessment; (4) studies of the social networks of families; (5) studies of families at risk through longitudinal and developmental studies; and (6) clinical studies involving detailed scrutiny of observed therapy sessions.

Zweben, A., & Pearlman, S. (1984). Evaluating the effectiveness of conjoint treatment of alcohol-complicated marriages: Clinical and methodological issues. *Journal of Marital and Family Therapy, 9*, 61–72.

This article examines the clinical and methodological strategies employed in an outcome study evaluating effectiveness of a marital therapy approach when one spouse presents with alcohol abuse as the primary problem. The authors raise and attempt to resolve crucial concerns: standardizing the treatment; emphasizing the presenting problems of alcohol abuse; utilizing marital therapy as the primary treatment modality; employing a minimal-care condition to resolve the ethical dilemma of a control group; and developing comprehensive assessment and follow-up procedures. Although the results of this research study are not reported, this article provides an excellent description of a solid research design for a marital treatment of alcoholism.

ACKNOWLEDGMENTS

We wish to acknowledge the contributions of the following persons to an earlier draft of the "Key Books and Articles" section: Judith Myers Avis, Maria Flores, Barbara Frankel, Richard Magee, Paul Sherman, Cleveland Shields, Thomas Shubeck, and Joseph L. Wetchler.

REFERENCES

Alexander, J. F., Barton, C., Schiavo, R. S., & Parsons, B. V. (1976). Behavioral intervention with families of delinquents: Therapist characteristics and outcomes. *Journal of Consulting and Clinical Psychology, 44*(4), 656–664.

Alexander, J. F., & Barton, C. (1976). Behavioral systems therapy for families. In D. H. Olson (Ed.), *Treating relationships*. Lake Mills, IA: Graphic.

Alexander, J. F., & Barton, C. (1980). Intervention with delinquents and their families: Clinical, methodological, and conceptual issues. In J. P. Vincent (Ed.), *Advances in family intervention, assessment and theory*. Greenwich, CT: JAI Press.

Alexander, J. F., & Parsons, B. (1982). *Functional family therapy*. Monterey, CA: Brooks/Cole.

Allred, G., & Kersey, F. (1977). The AIAC, a design for systematically analyzing marriage and family counseling: Progress report. *Journal of Marriage and Family Counseling, 3*, 17–26.

Avery, A. W., Ridley, C. A., Leslie, L. A., & Millholland, T. (1980). Relationship enhancement with premarital dyads: A six month follow-up. *American Journal of Family Therapy, 8*, 23–30.

Avis, J. M., & Sprenkle, D. H. (1986). *A review of outcome research on family therapy training*. Unpublished manuscript, Purdue University.

Bagarozzi, D. A., & Ravens, P. (1981). Premarital counseling: Appraisal and status. *American Journal of Family Therapy, 9*, 13–27.

Barton, C., & Alexander, J. F. (1977). Therapists' skills as determinants of effective systems-behavioral family therapy. *International Journal of Family Counseling, 11*, 1–15.

Barton, C., & Alexander, J. (1981). Functional family therapy. In A. S. Gurman & D. P. Kniskern (Eds.), *Handbook of family therapy*. New York: Brunner/Mazel.

Beck, D. F., & Jones, M. A. (1973). *Progress on family problems: A nationwide study of clients and counselors' views on family agency services*. New York: Family Service Association of America.

Beck, D. F., & Jones, M. A. (1976). *How to conduct a client follow-up study*. New York: Family Service Association of America.

Birchler, G. R., & Spinks, S. H. (1980). Behavioral–systems marital and family therapy—integration and clinical application. *American Journal of Family Therapy, 8*, 6–28.

Bray, J. H., Williamson, D. S., & Malone, P. E. (1984). Personal authority in the family system: Development of a questionnaire to measure personal authority in intergenerational family process. *Journal of Marital and Family Therapy, 10*, 167–178.

Breunlin, D. C., Schwartz, R. C., Krause, M. S., & Selby, L. M. (1983). Evaluating family therapy training: The development of an instrument. *Journal of Marital and Family Therapy, 9,* 37–47.

Brock, G. W., & Joanning, H. (1983). A comparison of the Relationship Enhancement program and the Minnesota Couple Communication Program. *Journal of Marital and Family Therapy, 9,* 413–421.

Churven, P., & McKinnon, T. (1982). Family therapy training: An evaluation of a workshop. *Family Process, 21,* 345–352.

Colapinto, J. (1979). The relative value of empirical evidence. *Family Process, 18,* 427–441.

Cookerly, J. R. (1976) Evaluating different approaches to marriage counseling. In D. H. Olson (Ed.), *Treating relationships.* Lake Mills, IA: Graphic.

Cookerly, J. R. (1980). Does marital therapy do any lasting good? *Journal of Marital and Family Therapy, 6,* 393–397.

Crane, D. R. (1985). Single-case experimental designs in family therapy research: Limitations and considerations. *Family Process, 24,* 69–78.

Cromwell, R. E., & Keeney, B. P. (1979). Diagnosing marital and family systems: A training mode. *Family Coordinator, 28,* 101–108.

Cromwell, R. E., & Peterson, G. W. (1983). Multisystem–multimethod family assessment in clinical contexts. *Family Process, 22,* 147–163.

Cromwell, R. E., Olson, D. H., & Fournier, D. (1976). Diagnosis and evaluation in marital and family counseling. In D. H. Olson (Ed.), *Treating relationships.* Lake Mills, IA: Graphic.

Epstein, N., Baldwin, L., & Bishop, D. (1983). The McMaster family assessment device. *Journal of Marital and Family Therapy, 9,* 171–180.

Epstein, N., & Bishop, D. (1981). Problem-centered systems therapy of the family. In A. S. Gurman & D. P. Kniskern (Eds.), *Handbook of family therapy.* New York: Brunner/Mazel.

Eysenck, H. J. (1952). The effects of psychotherapy: An evaluation. *Journal of Consulting Psychology, 16,* 319–324.

Fisher, L. (1982). Transactional theories but individual assessment: A frequent discrepancy in family research. *Family Process, 21,* 313–320.

Fleischman, M. J. (1981). A replication of Patterson's intervention for boys with conduct problems. *Journal of Consulting and Clinical Psychology, 49,* 342–351.

Garfield, S. L., & Bergin, A. E. (Eds.). (1986). *Handbook of psychotherapy and behavior change* (3rd ed.) New York: Wiley.

Garrigan, J., & Bambrick, A. (1977). Introducing novice therapist to "go between" techniques of family therapy. *Family Process, 16,* 237–246.

Giblin, P. (1982). *A meta-analysis of premarital, marital, and family enrichment research.* Unpublished doctoral dissertation, Purdue University.

Giblin, P., Sprenkle, D. H., & Sheehan, R. (1985). Enrichment outcome research: A meta-analysis of premarital, marital, and family interventions. *Journal of Marital and Family Therapy, 11,* 257–272.

Guerney, B. (1977). *Relationship enhancement.* San Francisco: Jossey-Bass.

Guerney, B., Coufal, J., & Vogelsong, E. (1981). Relationship enhancement versus a traditional approach to therapeutic/preventative/enrichment parent-adolescent programs. *Journal of Consulting and Clinical Psychology, 49,* 927–939.

Gurman, A. S. (1983a). Family therapy research and the "new epistemology." *Journal of Marital and Family Therapy, 9*, 227–234.

Gurman, A. S. (1983b). The old hatters and new wavers. *The Family Therapy Networker, 7*(4), 37.

Gurman, A. S., & Kniskern, D. (1977). Enriching research on marital enrichment. *Journal of Marriage and Family Counseling, 3*, 3–9.

Gurman, A. S., & Kniskern, D. P. (1978). Research on marital and family therapy: Progress, perspective and prospect. In S. L. Garfield & A. E. Bergin (Eds.), *Handbook of psychotherapy and behavior change* (2nd ed.). New York: Wiley.

Gurman, A. S., & Kniskern, D. P. (1981). Family therapy outcome research: Knowns and unknowns. In A. S. Gurman & D. P. Kniskern (Eds.), *Handbook of family therapy*. New York: Brunner/Mazel.

Gurman, A. S., Kniskern, D. P., & Pinsof, W. (1986). Research on the process and outcome of marital and family therapy. In S. L. Garfield & A. E. Bergin (Eds.), *Handbook of psychotherapy and behavior change* (3rd ed.). New York: Wiley.

Heiman, J. R., LoPiccolo, L., & LoPiccolo, J. (1981). The treatment of sexual dysfunction. In A. S. Gurman & D. P. Kniskern (Eds.), *Handbook of family therapy*. New York: Brunner/Mazel.

Isaac, S., & Michael, W. (1971). *Handbook in research and evaluation*. San Diego: Robert Knapp.

Jacobson, N. S. (1978). A review of the research on the effectiveness of marital therapy. In T. J. Paolino & B. S. McCrady (Eds.), *Marriage and marital therapy: Psychoanalytic, behavioral and systems theory perspective*. New York: Brunner/Mazel.

Jacobson, N. S. (1979). Increasing positive behavior in severely distressed marital relationships: The effects of problem-solving training. *Behavior Therapy, 10*, 311–326.

Jacobson, N. S. (1981). Behavioral marital therapy. In A. S. Gurman & D. P. Kniskern (Eds.), *Handbook of family therapy*. New York: Brunner/Mazel.

Jacobson, N. S. (1985). Family therapy outcome research: Potential pitfalls and prospects. *Journal of Marital and Family Therapy, 11*, 149–158.

Jacobson, N. S., & Margolin, G. (1979). *Marital therapy: Strategies based on social learning and behavior exchange principles*. New York: Brunner/Mazel.

Jessee, R., & Guerney, B. (1981). A comparison of Gestalt and relationship enhancement treatments with married couples. *American Journal of Family Therapy, 9*, 31–41.

Keeney, B. P. (1983). *Aesthetics of change*. New York: Guilford Press.

Kerlinger, F. N. (1973). *Foundations of behavioral research*. New York: Holt, Rinehart & Winston.

Kilmann, P. R. (1978). The treatment of primary and secondary orgasmic dysfunction: A methodological review of the literature since 1970. *Journal of Sex and Marital Therapy, 4*, 155–176.

Kiresuk, T. J., & Sherman, R. E. (1968). Goal Attainment Scaling: A general method for evaluating comprehensive community mental health programs. *Community Mental Health Journal, 4*, 443–453.

Kniskern, D. P. (1983). The new wave is all wet. *Family Therapy Networker, 7*(4), 38, 60–62.

Kniskern, D. P. (1985). Climbing out of the pit: Further guidelines for family therapy research. *Journal of Marital and Family Therapy, 11*, 159–162.

Kniskern, D. P. & Gurman, A. S. (1980). Research on training in marriage and family therapy: Status, issues and directions. In M. Andolfi & I. Zwerling (Eds.), *Dimensions of family therapy*. New York: Guilford Press.

Kolodny, R. C. (1981). Evaluating sex therapy: Process and outcome of the Masters and Johnson Institute. *Journal of Sex Research, 17*, 301–318.

Margolin, G. (1980). Contingency contracting in behavioral marriage therapy. *American Journal of Family Therapy, 8*, 71–74.

Mills, K. H., & Kilmann, P. R. (1982). Group treatment of sexual dysfunctions: A methodological review of the outcome literature. *Journal of Sex and Marital Therapy, 8*, 259–280.

Mohammed, Z., & Piercy, F. (1983). The effects of two methods of training and sequencing on the structuring and relationship skills of family therapists. *American Journal of Family Therapy, 11*, 64–71.

Olson, D. H. (1976). Bridging research, theory, and application: The triple threat in science. In D. H. Olson (Ed.), *Treating relationships*. Lake Mills, IA: Graphic.

Olson, D. H. (1981). Family research and family therapy: Bridging two different worlds. In E. E. Filsinger & R. A. Lewis (Eds.), *Assessing marriage: New behavioral approaches*. Beverly Hills, CA: Sage.

Olson, D. H., Russell, C. S., & Sprenkle, D. H. (1980). Marital and family therapy. A decade review. *Journal of Marriage and the Family, 42*, 973–993.

Parloff, M. (1980). *The efficacy and cost effectiveness of psychotherapy* (Office of Technical Assessment, Document 052-003-00783-5) Washington, DC: U.S. Government Printing Office.

Patterson, G. R. (1976). Parents and teachers as change agents: A social learning approach. In D. H. Olson (Ed.), *Treating relationships*. Lake Mills, IA: Graphic.

Patterson, G. R. (1982). *Coercive family process*. Eugene, OR: Castalia.

Patterson, G. R., Reid, J. B., Jones, R. R., & Conger, R. E. (1975). *A social learning approach to family intervention: Vol. 1. Families with aggressive children*. Eugene, OR: Castalia.

Paul, G. (1967). Strategy of outcome research in psychotherapy. *Journal of Consulting Psychology, 31*, 109–118.

Piercy, F., Laird, R., & Mohammed, Z. (1983). A family therapist rating scale. *Journal of Marital and Family Therapy, 9*, 49–59.

Pinsof, W. M. (1979). The Family Therapy Behavior Scale (FTBS): Development and evaluation of a coding system. *Family Process, 18*, 451–461.

Pinsof, W. M. (1981). Family therapy process research. In A. S. Gurman & D. P. Kniskern (Eds.), *Handbook of family therapy*. New York: Brunner/Mazel.

Pinsof, W. M. (1982). *Family clinic study: The predictors of outcome*. Unpublished manuscript, Family Institute of Chicago, Chicago.

Rabin, C. (1981). The potential contribution of single-case design in family therapy evaluation research. *Family Process, 20*, 351–366.

Reid, J. B. (Ed.). (1978). *A social learning approach to family intervention: Vol. 2. Observation in home settings*. Eugene, OR: Castalia.

Russell, C. S., Olson, D. H., Sprenkle, D. H., & Atilano, R. B. (1983). From family symptom to family system: Review of family therapy research. *American Journal of Family Therapy, 11*, 3–14.

Santa-Barbara, J., Woodward, C. A., Levin, S., Goodman, J. T., Streiner, D., & Epstein, N. B. (1979). The McMaster family therapy outcome study: An overview of methods and results. *International Journal of Family Therapy, 1,* 304–323.

Schwartz, R., & Breunlin, D. (1983). Why clinicians should bother with research. *Family Therapy Networker, 7*(4), 22–27.

Sprenkle, D. H. (1976). The need for integration among theory, research and practice in the family field. *Family Coordinator, 24,* 261–263.

Sprenkle, D. H., & Storm, C. L. (1983). Divorce therapy outcome research: A substantive and methodological review. *Journal of Marital and Family Therapy, 9,* 239–258.

Stanton, M. D., Steier, F., & Todd, T. C. (1982). Paying families for attending sessions: Counteracting the dropout problems. *Journal of Marital and Family Therapy, 8,* 371–374.

Stanton, M. D., & Todd, T. C. (1979). Structural family therapy with drug addicts. In E. Kaufman & P. Kaufman (Eds.), *The family therapy of drug and alcohol abuse.* New York: Gardner Press.

Stanton, M. D., & Todd, T. C. (1980). A critique of the Wells and Dezen review of the results of nonbehavioral family therapy. *Family Process, 19,* 169–176.

Stanton, M. D., Todd, T. C., Steier, F., Van Deusen, J. M., Marder, L., Rosoff, R. J., Seaman, S. F., & Skibinkski, E. (1980). *Family characteristics and family therapy of heroin addicts: Final report 1974–1978* (National Institute on Drug Abuse Grant No. RO1 DA 01119). Philadelphia: Philadelphia Child Guidance Clinic.

Todd, T. C., & Stanton, M. D. (1983). Research on marital and family therapy: Answers, issues, and recommedations for the future. In B. Wolman & G. Stricker (Eds.), *Handbook of family and marital therapy.* New York: Plenum.

Tomm, K. (1983). The old hat doesn't fit. *Family Therapy Networker, 7*(4), 39–41.

Wampler, K. S. (1982). Bringing the review of the literature into the age of quantification: Meta-analysis as a strategy for integrating research findings in family studies. *Journal of Marriage and the Family, 44,* 1009–1023.

Weiss, R. L. (1978). The conceptualization of marriage from a behavioral perspective. In T. J Paolino & B. S. McCrady (Eds.), *Marriage and marital therapy: Psychoanalytic, behavioral and systems theory perspectives.* New York: Brunner/Mazel.

Weiss, R. L., & Cerreto, M. C. (1980). Marital Status Inventory—development of a measure of dissolution potential. *American Journal of Family Therapy, 8,* 80–85.

Wells, R. A., & Dezen, A. E. (1978a). The results of family therapy revisited: The nonbehavioral methods. *Family Process, 17,* 251–274.

Wells, R. A., & Dezen, A. E. (1978b). Ideologies, idols (and graven images?): Rejoinder to Gurman and Kniskern. *Family Process, 17,* 283–286.

Wynne, L. (1983). Family research and family therapy: A reunion? *Journal of Marital and Family Therapy, 9,* 113–117.

Zilbergeld, B. (1983). *The shrinking of America.* Boston: Little, Brown.

Zilbergeld, B., & Evans, M. (1980, August). The inadequacy of Masters and Johnson. *Psychology Today,* pp. 29–43.

14

ETHICAL, LEGAL, AND PROFESSIONAL ISSUES

As the family therapy field has moved forward, training procedures have become more explicit, replicable, and assessable. Noticeably lacking in the literature on family therapy education, however, are detailed reports on the content and process of important nontherapy areas of interest intended to supplement the development of well-rounded family therapists.

One such area of interest is that of ethical, legal, and professional issues in family therapy. Margolin (1982) suggests that a general knowledge of a professional ethical code is not adequate preparation for the ethical and legal issues a therapist will face when working with more than one family member. Margolin recommends that "formal training programs in family therapy provide an arena for discussing these specialized ethical concerns" (1982, p. 800).

A Delphi survey of experienced family therapy educators and program directors conducted by Winkle, Piercy, and Hovestadt (1981) resulted in the identification of specific areas of ethics and professional development within a model family therapy curriculum. Similarly, the American Association for Marriage and Family Therapy (AAMFT) specifies studies that include ethical, legal, and professional issues as requirements within its own model curriculum (AAMFT, 1979).

This chapter first defines some key terms, and then identifies some specific ethical, legal, and professional issues in family therapy. Learning activities are suggested for each component. As in other chapters, research issues are also identified, followed by an annotated bibliography of key books and articles.

KEY TERMS

American Association for Marriage and Family Therapy (AAMFT). The

Portions of this chapter are adapted from "Ethical, Legal and Professional Issues in Family Therapy: A Graduate Level Course" by F. P. Piercy and D. H. Sprenkle, 1983, *Journal of Marital and Family Therapy*, 9(4), 393–401. Used by permission.

largest professional association specifically for marriage and family therapists. Founded in 1942, AAMFT represents the interests of family therapists on a variety of issues. For example, AAMFT has an important credentialing function; the designations of "Clinical Member" and "Approved Supervisor" are sought-after symbols of professional stature. AAMFT's Commission on Accreditation is officially recognized by the U.S. government as the accrediting body for graduate education in the field. More information about AAMFT may be secured from its national office at 1717 K St. NW, Suite 407, Washington, DC 20006. The phone number for AAMFT is 202-429-1825. The history of AAMFT is discussed by Mudd (1967).

American Family Therapy Association (AFTA). An association serving an important networking function for senior clinicians and researchers in the field of family therapy. More information about AFTA may be secured from its national office at 1255 23rd St., N.W., Suite 850, Washington, DC 20037. The AFTA phone number is 202-659-7666.

Expert testimony. Subject to the rules of evidence, which vary by jurisdiction, almost anyone who "has knowledge or experience in matters not generally familiar to the public" can serve as an expert witness (Schwitzgebel & Schwitzgebel, 1980, p. 238). Generally, expert witnesses may offer opinions or inferences, whereas lay witnesses may not (Woody & Associates, 1984). (See the discussion of courtroom testimony in the "Key Issues and Teaching Techniques" section for key citations.)

Informed consent. The procedure in which clients or subjects choose whether to participate in therapy or research after being informed of certain facts. These usually include (1) the fact that their involvement must be voluntary; (2) the nature of the therapy/research; (3) the costs and benefits of participation; and (4) the fact that they may withdraw from participation at any time. For examples of informed consent forms and suggestions on developing one's own, see Schultz (1982) and Everstine *et al.* (1980).

Libel. Written defamation of character. Possible defenses for this tort, according to Schultz (1982), include (1) that the revelation was *true;* (2) that an informed consent form was signed; (3) that the doctrine of "qualified privilege" was invoked; or (4) that there was an overarching social duty to release the information.

Malpractice. Legal liability for improper treatment. The four key elements that constitute malpractice are as follows: (1) A therapist–patient relationship existed; (2) the therapist's conduct fell below the acceptable standard of care; (3) the conduct was the proximate cause of injury; and (4) an injury actually occurred (Schultz, 1982).

National Council on Family Relations (NCFR). A national organization concerned with theory, research, practice, and public policy as they relate to the family. The national office of NCFR is located at 1910 West Country Road B, Suite 147, Saint Paul, MN 55113-5493.

Privileged communication. "A statutory declaration of a right to keep certain information, as long as it conforms to the reasonable basis of privacy and confidentiality, from legal proceedings" (Woody & Associates, 1984, p. 381). Often there is gross misunderstanding regarding the extent of privileged communication for clients of family therapists, since states vary greatly in their statutes related to privileged communication.

Slander. Oral defamation of character. Slanderous statements must be proved (1) to have been made public, and (2) to have been injurious to the reputation of the plaintiff. (See "libel" for defenses against claims of defamation of character.)

Tarasoff vs. Regents of the University of California. An important legal case that pitted the patient's right to privacy against the therapist's duty to protect members of society. In essence, the California court raised the limitations of privileged communication between a therapist and his/her client. The court noted that a psychotherapist treating a dangerous client has the duty to give threatened persons such warnings as are essential to avert foreseeable danger. For more information on this case, see Schultz (1982) and Van Hoose and Kottler (1977).

KEY ISSUES AND TEACHING TECHNIQUES

Ethical Issues

ETHICS OF AN ECOSYSTEMIC EPISTEMOLOGY

Comments on the Issue. Dell (1980) states that "patterns [of behavior] can be changed by disrupting them, but they cannot be sculpted into a planned design" (p. 329). Dell (1980, 1982) further suggests that such constructs as power and personal responsibility are epistemologically flawed. Implicit within such an ecosystemic epistemology are ethical questions related to the family therapist's and family members' responsibility for change. For example, if a therapist can disrupt, but cannot plan the outcome of change, is he/she being ethical? If the buck is passed from the individual to the system, who is personally responsible for symptomatic behavior? Who is responsible in a court of law?

Learning Activity. These ethical issues may be explored through an assigned five-page position paper. In this position paper, students respond to the following:

> Taggart (1982) writes, "Does not this emphasis on evolutionary ethics, which emerge with and within evolutionary process, destroy the possibility

of ethics, since it removes individual responsibility from the individual person?" (p. 34). Respond to Taggart's suggestion that individual responsibility may be an "epistemological error." Do you agree or disagree? If you agree, what are the ethical implications? If you disagree, respond to the possible criticism that you are employing a Newtonian, Western, linear epistemology that places a characteristic (i.e., responsibility) within the individual and not within the context of the system.

ETHICAL USE OF PARADOX

Comments on the Issue.   Paradoxical strategic interventions are considered by some to be dishonest, manipulative, disrespectful, and dangerous. When is therapeutic paradox unethical? With whom should it be employed and how? Clear, specific, comprehensive guidelines regarding the ethical use of therapeutic paradox are sadly lacking. However, certain authors (e.g., Fisher, Anderson, & Jones, 1981; Haley, 1976; O'Shea & Jessee, 1982; Raskin & Klein, 1976; Rohrbaugh, Tennen, Press, & White, 1981) have tackled this issue and provide some suggestions.

Learning Activity. The readings listed above may be assigned, and/or a debate may be set up among two or more volunteers. The title of such a debate could be "Is Paradox Ethical? Pro and Con." Our experience has been that such debates are lively and require of the moderator a variety of family therapy skills!

ETHICAL CODES

Comments on the Issue.   Family therapy trainees should be familiar with the AAMFT *Code of Ethical Principles for Family Theapists* (AAMFT, 1981a), *Procedures for Handling Complaints of Violations of the Code of Ethical Principles for Family Theapists* (AAMFT, 1981b), and *Code of Professional Ethics and Standards for Public Information and Advertising* (AAMFT, 1982a), as well as with the American Psychological Association (APA) *Standards for Providers of Psychological Services* (APA, 1977) and *Ethical Standards of Psychologists* (APA, 1979). In addition, family therapist trainees should be aware of the outcome of cases applicable to family therapy from the APA *Casebook on Ethical Standards of Psychologists* (APA, 1967).

Learning Activities. Using the AAMFT's *Procedures for Handling Complaints* (1981b), the instructor can illustrate all the possible official actions that might take place in the life of the following fictitious ethical complaint:

At your suggestion, a female client of yours wrote the AAMFT Executive Director a notarized letter stating that Dr. X, a former therapist whom she saw for divorce therapy and sex-related issues, had had sex with her "as part of therapy" on repeated occasions. This woman felt guilty and taken advantage of, and asked the Executive Director to take appropriate disciplinary action. The Executive Director referred her letter to the AAMFT Ethics Committee.

Through discussing all the possible steps in AAMFT's procedures, family therapy trainees can become sensitized to the safeguards, appeals, and possible consequences built into AAMFT's system for handling ethical violations.

The disposition of ethical issues can further be brought to life by assigning each student an AAMFT ethical principle and having him/her write down a possible violation of that principle. Then the class is broken up into groups of six. Each group "becomes" a national ethics committee and discusses and acts upon the previously conceived ethical violations. The "committee's" decisions are then presented to the entire class and discussed.

CONFIDENTIALITY AND PRIVILEGED COMMUNICATION

Comments on the Issue.   Confidentiality and privileged communication represent overlapping ethical and legal issues that can be particularly thorny for the family therapist. For a good background to these topics, students should read articles by Margolin (1982), Karpel (1980), and Gumper and Sprenkle (1981).

Learning Activity. With the readings listed above as background, illustrative situations can be read and discussed in class. Here is one example:

> You have been providing marital therapy to a couple for 3 months. During one session in which the wife is late, the husband tells you in confidence that when the wife's physical problems are stabilized he will probably divorce her. What would you do?

During the class discussion, the instructor should answer important questions (e.g., what is privileged communication and who has it?), suggest therapeutic alternatives (e.g., a presession agreement regarding secrets), and raise issues that do not emerge spontaneously from the group.

Legal Issues

FAMILY LAW

Comments on the Issue.   It is essential that family therapists have a working knowledge of family law. Since family law statutes vary from state to state, we recommend developing a relationship with a competent local attorney to serve as a consultant regarding changes in statutes and precedents. Since individual judges are typically given considerable latitude to interpret laws, knowledge about the inclinations and decisions of particular judges is frequently as important as knowledge of the laws themselves. Areas of special concern include trends in a particular state regarding custody decisions and the criteria utilized, precedents regarding the awarding of joint custody, policies and trends regarding child support, and mechanisms for changing decrees after a divorce.

Learning Activity. Actually observing divorce court proceedings can provide a student with an excellent "feel" for divorce and custody issues. In addition, local attorneys are often willing to speak to family therapy trainees about issues related to family law.

MALPRACTICE AND LEGAL LIABILITY

Comments on the Issue.   Background readings regarding a therapist's legal liability include Bernstein (1981, 1982) and Schultz (1982). Important topics related to the legal liability of the practicing family therapist include malpractice, contract law, torts, constitutional law, and criminal law. Family therapists should also be aware of how to responsibly use forms related to informed consent, therapeutic contracts, confidentiality, and releases. Ethical and responsible management of dangerous and suicidal family members is also an important area of legal liability.

Learning Activity. Therapeutic situations with legal ramifications (e.g., a difficult client who does not want to be terminated or referred) may be role-played and discussed. However, due to the important and delicate legal issues involved, it is also desirable for a lawyer with expertise in these areas to be invited into class as a guest speaker/discussant.

COURTROOM TESTIMONY

Comments on the Issue.   Several fine articles have been written to help the family therapist prepare to testify in court (e.g., Bernstein, 1979; Brodsky, 1977; Brodsky & Robey, 1973; Gardner, 1982; Meyerstein & Todd, 1980; J. Nichols, 1982).

Learning Activities. Since establishing professional credibility is essential, the therapist needs to give his/her lawyer questions about information he/she wants to come out in court. To practice this, students should be asked to bring to class a list of 5–10 questions that an attorney might ask them about their professional qualifications (they are asked to project their qualifications 5 years from now). The instructor then plays the role of the attorney.

A second simulation activity involves the instructor as prosecuting attorney putting selected students "on the witness stand" and asking them questions in an attempt to discredit them as witnesses. If a student has trouble fielding a barb, other students may try. These role plays are brief, are generally nonthreatening, and have generated a great deal of discussion. Students are prepared for the very real world of the adversarial court system by learning to grapple with how to handle such questions (adapted from Brodsky, 1977) as these:

- Is it possible that you may have some biases in this case?
- Are you testifying in a custody case and have no children yourself?
- Are you divorced? Who has custody of your children?
- How much are you being paid to say this today?
- Have you conducted follow-up studies on the consistency of your own judgments?
- Is it not true that family therapists disagree among themselves as to what brings about change?

LAWYER AND THERAPIST AS AN INTERDISCIPLINARY TEAM

Comments on the Issue. Bernstein has written about lawyer–therapist cooperation in such areas as child custody (Bernstein, 1977), the blended family (Bernstein, 1981), and child neglect (Harris & Bernstein, 1980). Bernstein asserts that the therapist must become familiar with the pragmatics of legal maneuvering. Equally important is the task of educating a lawyer about family therapy so that months of therapeutic interventions will not be undone in the courtroom. The family therapist should be aware of the advantages and practical application of such cooperation, as well as the problems in reconciling adversarial and therapeutic roles.

Learning Activity. Opportunities for lawyer–therapist cooperation (e.g., preparation for child neglect cases; see Harris & Bernstein, 1980) may be role-played and discussed. Again, a family lawyer as guest speaker/discussant also would be helpful.

Professional Issues

FAMILY THERAPY: PROFESSION OR PROFESSIONAL SPECIALTY?

Comments on the Issue. Many people believe that family therapy, with its unique history, professional associations, journals, and code of ethics, is in fact a profession, as are psychology, psychiatry, and social work. Others believe that family therapy is a legitimate specialty of each of these professions, but is not itself a profession. The question of family theapy as a profession or a professional specialty has far-reaching ramifications for family therapists in such areas as licensure, third-party payments, job security, and professional identity.

Learning Activity. Students should seek out sources regarding what constitutes a profession (e.g., Burr & Leigh, 1983), and apply their own deductive processes to the question of whether family therapy is a profession or a professional specialty. A seven-page paper is then assigned in which each student is to briefly outline the rationales for viewing family therapy as a profession and as a professional specialty. The students also present their own views on this subject.

LICENSURE AND LEGISLATIVE AWARENESS

Comments on the Issue.   The pros and cons of professional licensure (Gross, 1978; Kosinski, 1982) and the current state of family therapy licensure and certification (Sporakowski, 1982b; Sporakowski & Staniszewski, 1980) are important professional issues with which family therapy trainees should be familiar.

The licensure issue should also be understood in a larger context— that of legislative awareness. Dorken (1981), for example, provides excellent suggestions on how to affect a state legislature.

Learning Activities. One class simulation could involve the class's "becoming" a state AAMFT board faced with the task of initiating a certification or licensure bill for the next legislative session. The class should deal with whether they want a certification or a licensure bill, how to generate funds to support it, how to build a legislative network, how to choose the bill's sponsor, and how to lobby with legislators. In effect, they learn experientially the pragmatic intricacies of undertaking this important yet formidable task.

A second simulation could involve assigning each student to testify in front of a "legislative subcommittee" (the class) for 3 minutes on the merits of a family therapy certification bill they previously were assigned to read. In critiquing these legislative testimonies, important "dos" and "don'ts" should be identified and discussed.

PROFESSIONAL IDENTITY AND INSTITUTIONAL DEMANDS

Comments on the Issue.   Framo (1976) and Haley (1975) testify to the institutional roadblocks to family therapy that are often inherent in an entrenched mental health delivery system. Framo (1976) describes his own emerging identity as a family therapist in the face of such institutional pressures. It is indeed difficult to develop an identity as a family therapist because of the subtle and overt institutional pressures that discourage the practice of family therapy. For example, most of the diagnostic categories in the *Diagnostic and Statistical Manual of Mental Disorders*, third edition (DSM-III; American Psychiatric Association, 1980) place the locus of pathology within the individual rather than the system. Also, individual intake practices often support the concept of the identified patient and neglect systemic issues (Piercy, McKeon, & Laird, 1983).

Learning Activity. Family therapy trainees should read the articles listed above and then discuss and/or role-play ways to (1) maintain a professional identity as a family therapist, (2) accomodate to the mental health system, and (3) initiate change within that system (Piercy *et al.*, 1983).

JOURNALS AND PUBLISHING

Comments on the Issue.   Current (as of 7/15/86) English-language family therapy journals and newsletters, as well as their editors' names and addresses are included below (from Alan Gurman, personal communication, 1986):

- Martin G. Blinder, M.D., Editor, *Family Therapy*, 4340 Redwood Highway, San Rafael, CA 94903.
- Donald Block, M.D., Editor, *Family Systems Medicine*, Ackerman Institute for Family Therapy, 149 East 78th St., New York, NY 10021.
- Mr. Max Cornwell, Editor, *Australian and New Zealand Journal of Family Therapy*, P.O. Box 633, Lane Cove, New South Wales, Australia 2066.
- Donald Efron, Editor, *Journal of Strategic and Systemic Therapies*, Box 2484, Station A, London, Ontario, N6A 4G7, Canada.
- Craig Everett, Ph.D., Editor, *Journal of Divorce*, Sandel 106, Florida State University, Tallahassee, FL 32306.
- Charles Figley, Ph.D., Editor, *Journal of Psychotherapy and the Family*, Purdue University, 525 Russell St., West Lafayette, IN 47906.
- Alan S. Gurman, Ph.D., Editor, *Journal of Marital and Family Therapy*, Department of Psychiatry, University of Wisconsin Medical School, 600 Highland Avenue, Madison, WI, 53792.
- John Howells, M.D., Editor, *International Journal of Family Psychiatry*, Institute of Family Psychiatry, 25 Henley Road, Ipswich, England 1P1 3Tf.
- Helen Singer Kaplan, M.D., Ph.D., Editor, *Journal of Sex and Marital Therapy*, New York Hospital, Cornell University Medical Center, New York, NY 10021.
- Peter Kinney, Ed.D., Editor, *American Family Therapy Association Newsletter*, 131 North Main Street, Sharon, MA 02067.
- Dr. Bryan Lask, Editor, *Journal of Family Therapy*, Academic Press, Inc., 24-28 Oval Road, London, England NW1 7DX.
- William C. Nichols, Jr., Ed.D., Editor, *Contemporary Family Therapy: An International Journal* and *Family Therapy News*, Suite 455, 30200 Telegraph Road, Birmingham, MI 48010.

- Eileen G. Pendagast, M.A., M.Ed., Editor, *The Family*, Center for Family Learning, 10 Hanford Avenue, New Rochelle, NY 10805.
- Clifford J. Sager, M.D., Editor, *Journal of Sex and Marital Therapy*, Jewish Board of Family & Children's Services and New York Hospital–Cornell Medical Center, 65 East 76th St., New York, NY 10021.
- S. Richard Sauber, Ph.D., Editor, *American Journal of Family Therapy*, Suite 4D, 951 N.W. 13th St., Medical Arts Center, Boca Raton, FL 33432.
- Richard Simon, Ph.D., Editor, *Family Therapy Networker*, 7703, 13th Street, N.W., Washington, DC 20012.
- Carlos Sluzki, M.D., Editor, *Family Process*, Department of Psychiatry, Berkshire Medical Center, Pittsfield, MA 01201.
- Michael Sporakowski, Ph.D., Editor, *Family Relations*, 201 Wallace Hall Annex, Virginia Tech University, Blacksburg, VA 24061.

Family therapy trainees should be familiar with these journals as well as the process of getting their own names in print.

Learning Activity. Students should be assigned readings that will sharpen their writing skills (Becker, 1986; Elbow, 1981; Schultz, 1982) and demystify the publication process (Berardo, 1981; Sporakowski, 1982a). In small groups, they should be asked to discuss the tasks involved in having their own theses or dissertations published. In the class discussion that follows, the instructor should fill in any steps not mentioned by the students.

Another assignment could be the writing of a publishable 15-page paper on a relevant area of interest. This assignment may be introduced as follows:

> Each of you will choose an ethical, legal, or professional issue in family therapy of interest to you, read widely on that issue, and then write a scholarly, referenced term paper of publishable quality. To be publishable, your paper should go beyond a simple review of the current research and theory related to your issue. You should tackle your issue in some creative and imaginative way that would contribute to, rather than rehash, the literature related to your chosen topic. The following titles are only examples, but should provide a flavor for the theoretical originality or unique application of existing information that would make for a publishable paper:
>
> "Informed Consent and the Strategic Family Therapist"
>
> "Being an Advocate for Family Therapy: Guidelines for Legislative Testimony"
>
> "The Ethical Implications of an Ecosystemic Epistemology"
>
> "Institutional Demands and the Family Therapist: Some Suggestions"
>
> "DSM III and the Family Therapist: Ethical and Pragmatic Considerations"

THE MARITAL/FAMILY LIFE OF THE FAMILY THERAPIST

Comments on the Issue.   There is a growing concern regarding the emotional hazards in the field of family therapy and their possible effects on the quality of the marital and family lives of family therapists themselves. The interface of family therapists' work and family lives is worth exploring. How does their work affect their own lives and those of their families? How do their families of origin affect their choice of a profession and their day-to-day work? What happens to their work when they experience marital or family problems? While some have speculated on such questions (e.g., Charny, 1982; Piercy & Wetchler, in press; Wetchler & Piercy, 1986), there are few clear-cut answers.

Learning Activities. Students are asked to take the questionnaire developed by Wetchler and Piercy (1986) to identify work related enhancers and stressors of the marital and family lives of family therapists. Then the instructor presents and discusses the findings of Wetchler and Piercy's (1986) survey of 110 Indiana family therapists (which employed the same questionnaire). Finally, the group brainstorms ways family therapists may reduce stressors to their own marital and family lives.

The reader will find a variety of other useful procedures to help trainees explore work–family interfaces in Piercy and Wetchler (in press).

ACCREDITATION AND CONTINUING EDUCATION

Comments on the Issue.   The AAMFT procedures for accrediting family therapy programs may be found in the *Marriage and Family Therapy Manual on Accreditation* (AAMFT, 1979). Also, the rationale for accreditation is discussed in terms of accountability and professional identity by Shalett and Everett (1981). As for continuing education, practicing family therapists are expected by AAMFT to continue to develop and update their skills. However, agreement on an implementation of specific continuing education guidelines is a difficult process, as evidenced by the changes in AAMFT's guidelines in recent years. Continuing education procedures have been outlined by AAMFT (1982b); these identify specific hours necessary in certain educational categories, but generally leave issues of quality control to state AAMFT associations.

Learning Activity. The difficulty in deciding upon and implementing a continuing education program for family therapists may be experienced through a stimulation activity. The class is broken up into groups of six, and each group "becomes" a continuing education committee charged with arriving at continuing education standards, and procedures for their implementation. Forty-five minutes later, each "committee" reports its decision to the rest of the class; the strengths and deficiencies of the newly created standards and procedures are discussed. AAMFT's current continuing education procedures (AAMFT, 1982b) are presented and discussed in light of the preceding exercise.

ESTABLISHING A PRIVATE PRACTICE; PUBLIC RELATIONS

Comments on the Issue.   Family therapists considering going into private practice should be familiar with public relations procedures (Kilgore, 1979), office forms and procedures, financing, fee structures, collection procedures, and means of making contact with potential clients and referral sources (e.g., cards, brochures, speaking engagements, media, and personal contacts). An excellent source for such information is Keller and Ritt's (1982, 1983, 1984, 1985) *Innovations in Clinical Practice: A Source Book.* Four volumes (each different from the others) of this compendium of resources are available.

Learning Activities. A successful family therapist should be asked to discuss his/her own experiences in setting up a practice and developing a caseload. If possible, the therapist should share copies of business forms and discuss the technical aspects of carrying on a private practice.

Also, the ethical and pragmatic considerations of one current public relations trend—the family therapist as expert on a radio or TV talk show—should be examined. Specifically, the difference between therapy and public education should be explored, in addition to appropriate answers to difficult interview questions. Mock talk show interview could be held to illustrate ethical dilemmas and to practice appropriate responses (cf. Kilgore, 1979; Myers-Walls & Piercy, 1985).

JOB HUNTING

Comments on the Issue.   For those students interested in academic or agency positions, three broad job-hunting skills are necessary. The first is "getting sellable." Since many jobs have sources of applicants, students should use their academic careers to seek out experiences and develop skills that will allow them to stand out in the job market. This process involves the more-than-is-expected activities of running community groups, publishing articles, making speeches, attending workshops, joining professional organizations, holding offices, and reading journals and books that are *not* assigned.

Second, a "sellable" applicant must get his/her "foot in the door." Getting the attention of a prospective employer involves the development of a well-organized and compelling *curriculum vita.*

Third, the job interview—the final step in most selection processes—is a critical one (see Darley & Zanna, 1981).

Learning Activity. Students are asked to specify in small groups their rights within a job interview, the skills they want to emphasize, and the questions they want to ask during the interview (McGovern, 1976). Finally, mock job interviews are held in groups of three. Upon completion of each interview, the interviewee should be given feedback regarding his/her answers and style of presentation.

RESEARCH ISSUES

There has been virtually no research conducted on ethical, legal, or professional issues in family therapy, despite their importance. The lack of research probably stems from the relative youth of the field and the focus on initial research on the clinical utility of family therapy approaches. However, ethical, legal, and professional issues are operationalizable and researchable. Examples of possible research questions include the following:

- What dimensions of therapeutic paradox contribute to its perceived "ethicality"?
- What are the effects of a therapeutic contract on outcome in family therapy?
- What is the relationship between knowledge of ethical codes and the ethical behavior of family therapists?
- What factors correlate with credibility in the courtroom testimony of family therapists?
- What articles or books do experts identify to be key works within family therapy?
- What do family therapists perceive to be the future trends in the field?
- What are the effects of sexual relationships between clients and therapists?
- What are therapists' policies regarding seeing clients who are seeing other therapists and are dissatisfied with the therapists or the therapy? What are the therapists' policies regarding other ethical and legal issues?
- To what extent do family therapists (who may also be licensed as psychologists or psychiatrists) manipulate DSM-III codes to gain third-party payments?
- What do family therapists perceive as ethical restraints related to advertising?

Questions such as these reflect untapped yet important areas of inquiry for the family therapy researcher. In the years ahead, we expect to see much more research on such ethical, legal, and professional questions.

KEY BOOKS AND ARTICLES

American Association for Marriage and Family Therapy (AAMFT) (1982). *Code of professional ethics and standards for public information and advertising.* Upland, CA: Author.

Becker, H. S. (1986). *Writing for social scientists.* Chicago: University of Chicago Press.

In this clear, readable book, Becker shares his own experiences with writing and provides a variety of useful insights. He humorously hits the mark in discussing the foibles of beginning writers, and seems to have pinpointed the elusive work habits that contribute to good writing. Although most of Becker's examples are drawn from the sociological literature, this is an excellent source for family therapists struggling with the writing process.

Bernstein, B. E. (1979). Lawyer and therapist as an interdisciplinary team: Trial preparation. *Journal of Marital and Family Therapy, 5*(4), 93–100.

This article reviews trial preparation and illustrates examination and cross-examination, opinion testimony, and hypothetical questions. Bernstein's illustrations underline potential hazards of an adversarial court system, and his practical suggestions provide a means of averting these hazards.

Brodsky, S. L. (1977). The mental health professional on the witness stand: A survival guide. In B.D. Sales (Ed.), *Psychology in the legal process.* New York: Spectrum.

Brodsky provides useful suggestions for coping with cross-examination. He examines the "gambits" that lawyers use to discredit witnesses and provides the reader with excellent "responses that degambitize."

Brodsky, S. L., & Robey, A. (1973). On becoming an expert witness: Issues of orientation and effectiveness. *Professional Psychology, 3,* 173–176.

This article is frequently cited in the literature and, while dated, is still quite helpful in preparing the therapist for the witness stand.

Charny, I. (1982). The personal and family mental health of family therapists. In F. Kaslow (Ed.), *International book of family therapy.* New York: Brunner/Mazel.

This important chapter provides one of the first looks at the personal and family life of family therapists. Charney details many of the ways in which family therapy work may heighten the possibility of family problems. His recommendations for weathering life's storms (including the need to "live with imperfection") are particularly worth reading.

Coogler, O. J. (1978). *Structured mediation in divorce settlements.* Lexington, MA: Lexington Books.

This book is destined to be a seminal work in divorce mediation.

Dorken, H. (1981). Coming of age legislatively in 21 steps. *American Psychologist, 2,* 167–173.

Family therapists reading this article will learn alot about legislative activism from Dorken, a psychologist.

Fisher, L, Anderson, A., & Jones, J. E. (1981). Types of paradoxical interventions and contraindications for use in clinical practice. *Family Process, 20*, 25–35.

This is one of the few articles that deals with the ethicality and indications–contradindications for the use of paradox in family therapy.

Framo, J. (1968). My families, my family. *Voices, 4*(33), 18–27.

Framo provides a telling commentary of how events in his own life have spilled over into his professional work. This should be required reading for all beginning family therapists.

Framo, J. (1975). Personal reflections of a family therapist. *Journal of Marriage and Family Counseling, 1*, 15–27.

This is a moving article in which Framo traces his developemnt as a family therapist. In a very personal style, Framo deals with issues regarding professional identity and the interface between values and therapy.

Gardner, R. (1982). *Family evaluation in child custody litigation.* Cresskill, NJ: Creative Therapeutics.

An excellent guide by a therapist with considerable experience in child custody litigation. The chapter on providing testimony in court is particularly good at demystifying the courtroom process and providing specific, down-to-earth, and detailed suggestions.

Gross, S. (1978). The myth of professional licensing. *American Psychologist, 33*, 1009–1016.

Gross questions the usefulness of professional licensure by outlining the history and present state of licensure in medicine. Presented are similar shortcomings of licensure for psychology.

Gumper, L. L., & Sprenkle, D. H. (1981). Privileged communication in therapy: Special problems for the family and couples therapist. *Family Process, 20*, 11–23.

Discussed are the legal status and the ethical and legal implications of privileged communications for the family therapist.

Haley, J. (1976). *Problem solving therapy.* San Francisco: Jossey-Bass.

Chapter 8 provides a clear, compelling defense of the use of paradoxical interventions in family therapy.

Haynes, J. M. (1981). *Divorce mediation: A practical guide for therapists and counselors.* New York: Springer.

This is probably the most comprehensive and practical book on the subject; it contains many charts, worksheets, and case examples. The atuhor has been President of the Academy of Family Mediators and leads nationally recognized workshops.

Hare-Mustin, R. T. (1980). Family therapy may be dangerous for your health. *Professional Psychology, 11*, 935–938.

Hare-Mustin suggests potential risks of family therapy in such areas as the subordination of one's own goals and the loss of confidentiality and privacy. This article is an irreverent eye-opener and an excellent discussion starter.

Hines, P. M., & Hare-Mustin, R. T. (1978). Ethical concerns in family therapy. *Professional Psychology, 9,* 165–171.

The authors explore the ethical implications of such family therapy techniques as encouraging ventilation of hostile feelings, forming alliances with particular family members, and requiring reluctant members to attend sessions. Also, issues related to confidentiality are examined.

Irving, H. H. (1980). *Divorce mediation: A rational alternative to the adversary system.* New York: Universe Books.

This book presents an historical and philosophical rationale for divorce mediation as opposed to the traditional adversary method. A good place to start one's reading on divorce mediation.

Karpel, M. A. (1980). Family secrets: I. Conceptual and ethical issues in the relational context. II. Ethical and practical considerations in therapeutic management. *Family Process, 19,* 295–306.

Ethical issues regarding family secrets and confidentiality in family therapy are discussed. Means of dealing with secrets in family therapy are also presented.

Kilgore, J. (1979). The marriage and family therapist's use of media for public education. *Journal of Marital and Family Therapy, 5*(4), 87–92.

Kilgore presents some helpful suggestions for the family therapist who wishes to impart information to the public through radio, TV, and the printed word. His application of Anon's P-LI-SS-IT approach (see Chapter 5, "Key Clinical Terms" section) is particularly useful in determining what information to provide.

Lefferts, R. (1982). *Getting a grant in the 1980s.* Englewood Cliffs, NJ: Prentice-Hall.

This small book is a good first step in demystifying the process of grant proposal writing. The author provides useful guidelines for writing good proposals, clearly identifies the components of a proposal, as well as criteria for evaluating proposals. Lefferts's appendices of funding guides and resources are particularly useful.

Lemmon, J. A. (Ed.). (1984). Ethics, standards, and professional challenges (special issue). *Mediation Quarterly, 4.*

Five excellent articles discuss ethical issues in mediation. The article on neutrality in mediation is especially useful in its examination of a neutral versus proponent role for the mediator.

Margolin, G. (1982). Ethical and legal considerations in marital and family therapy. *American Psychologist, 37,* 788–802.

This article is must reading. Margolin identifies and cogently discusses such important ethical and legal issues as (1) therapist responsibility, (2) confidentiality, (3) privileged communication, (4) informed consent, (5) therapist values, and (6) training and supervision.

Meyerstein, I., & Todd, J. C. (1980). On the witness stand: The family therapist and expert testimony. *American Journal of Family Therapy, 8*(4), 43–51.

The authors discuss the application of certain family therapy skills to courtroom testimony. This article is well written and useful.

O'Shea, M, & Jessee, E. (1982). Ethical, value, and professional conflicts in systems therapy. In L. L'Abate (Ed.), *Values, ethics, legalities and the family therapist.* Rockville, MD: Aspen Systems Corporation.

This chapter identifies a variety of ethical issues in family therapy, but discusses none of them in depth.

Piercy, F., & Wetchler, J. (in press). Family–work interfaces of psychotherapists: I. A summary of the literature. II. A didactic-experiential workshop. *Journal of Psychotherapy and the Family.*

This article reviews the literature on the interfaces of therapists' work and family lives. Part II outlines a useful workshop that can easily be adapted to family therapists. The workshop helps therapists examine the effects of their present family lives and family of origin on their work, as well as the potential effects of their work on them personally and on their spouses and/or children.

Rice, D. G., & Rice, J. K. (1977). Non-sexist "marital" therapy. *Journal of Marriage and Family Counseling, 3*(1), 3–10.

The authors provide suggestions for the therapist to use in promoting egalitarian, non-sexist marriages through the restructuring of traditional marriage patterns.

Schultz, B. M. (1982). *Legal liability in psychotherapy.* San Francisco: Jossey-Bass.

This is one of the best books of its kind. Discussed are malpractice, contract law, torts, constitutional law, and criminal law, and their relevance to psychotherapy. Also discussed are the dangerous and suicidal client and legal and practical precautions the therapist should take.

Sporakowski, M. (1982). The regulation of marital and family therapy. In L. L'Abate (Ed.), *Values, ethics, legalities and the family therapist.* Rockville, MD: Aspen Systems Corporation.

This chapter discusses the state of licensure and certification (as of 1982) in family therapy. Of particular interest to the practitioner are issues such as who and what are covered in licensure/certification, academic experience and qualifications, and the licensure/certification process itself.

Shalett, J. S. (1979). Continuing education: An interprofessional endeavor. *Journal of Marital and Family Therapy, 5*(3), 101–105.

This article discusses the rationale and status (as of 1979) of continuing education in AAMFT. The value of this article is in the background it provides regarding continuing education in general in the mental health professions, since the AAMFT guidelines presented are already outdated.

Taggart, M. (1982). Linear versus systemic values: Implications for family therapy. In L. L'Abate (Ed.), *Values, ethics, legalities and the family therapist.* Rockville, MD: Aspen Systems Corporation.

This provocative chapter explores the role of values within a systemic episte-mology. The questions Taggart raises regarding responsibility are important ones for the family therapist.

Woody, R. H., & Associates. (1984) *The law and the practice of human services*. San Francisco: Jossey-Bass.

This book was written to introduce human service professionals to aspects of the law they are likely to deal with in their work. It is clearly written and up-to-date, and includes chapters on criminal law, juvenile law, family law, personal injury law, employment discrimination law, wills and contracts, rights of institutionalized patients and handicapped children, and professional responsibilities and liabilities.

Wetchler, J. L., & Piercy, F. P. (1986). The marital/family life of the family therapist: Stressors and enhancers. *American Journal of Family Therapy, 14*(2), 99–109.

This interesting study examined the number and relative strength of stressors and enhancers of marital and family life for 110 family therapists in Indiana. More enhancers were reported than stressors. The results also were examined in terms of respondent's (1) gender, (2) work setting, (3) theoretical orientation, (4) number of hours worked, (5) income, and (6) age.

REFERENCES

American Association for Marriage and Family Therapy (AAMFT). (1979). *Marriage and family therapy manual on accreditation*. Upland, CA: Author.

American Association for Marriage and Family Therapy (AAMFT). (1981a, January). New AAMFT code of ethics adopted. *AAMFT Newsletter*, pp. 1–3.

American Association for Marriage and Family Therapy (AAMFT). (1981b). *Procedures for handling complaints of violations of the code of ethical principles for family therapists*. Upland, CA: Author.

American Association for Marriage and Family Therapy (AAMFT). (1982a). *Code of professional ethics and standards for public information and advertising*. Upland, CA: Author.

American Association for Marriage and Family Therapy (AAMFT). (1982b, March). Committee recommends simplification of categories and more responsibility to divisions. *Family Therapy News*, p. 7.

American Psychiatric Association. (1980). *Diagnostic and statistical manual of mental disorders* (3rd ed.). Washington, DC: Author.

American Psychological Association (APA). (1967). *Casebook on ethical standards of psychologists*. Washington, DC: Author.

American Psychological Association (APA). (1977). *Standards for providers of psychological services*. Washington, DC: Author.

American Psychological Association (APA). (1979). *Ethical standards of psychologists*. Washington, DC: Author.

Becker, H. S. (1986). *Writing for social scientists*. Chicago: University of Chicago Press.

Berardo, F. M. (1981). The publication process: An editor's perspective. *Journal of Marriage and the Family, 43*, 771–779.

Bernstein, B. E. (1977). Lawyer and counselor as an interdisciplinary team: Preparing the father for custody. *Journal of Marriage and Family Counseling, 3*(3), 29–40.

Bernstein, B. E. (1979). Lawyer and counselor as an interdisciplinary team. *Journal of Marital and Family Therapy, 5*(4), 93–100.

Bernstein, B. E. (1981). Malpractice: Future shock of the 1980s. *Social Casework: The Journal of Contemporary Social Work, 62*, 175–181.

Bernstein, B. E. (1982). Ignorance is no excuse. In L'Abate (Ed.), *Values, ethics, legalities and the family therapist.* Rockville, MD: Aspen Systems Corporation.

Brodsky, S. L. (1977). The mental health professional on the witness stand: A survival guide. In B. D. Sales (Ed.), *Psychology in the legal process.* New York: Spectrum.

Brodsky, S. L., & Robey, A. (1973). On becoming an expert witness: Issues of orientation and effectiveness. *Professional Psychology, 3*, 173–176.

Burr, W. R., & Leigh, G. K. (1983). Famology: A new discipline. *Journal of Marriage and the Family, 45*, 467–480.

Charny, I. (1982). The personal and family mental health of family thought. In F. Kaslow (Ed.), *International book of family therapy.* New York: Brunner/Mazel.

Darley, J. M., & Zanna, M. (1981). An introduction to the hiring process in academic psychology. *Canadian Psychology, 22*, 228–238.

Dell, P. (1980). Researching the family theories of schizophrenia: An exercise in epistemological confusion. *Family Process, 19*, 321–335.

Dell, P. (1982). Beyond homeostasis: Toward a concept of coherence. *Family Process, 21*, 21–41.

Dorken, H. (1981). Coming of age legislatively in 21 steps. *American Psychologist, 2*, 167–173.

Elbow, P . (1981). *Writing with power: Techniques for mastering the writing process.* New York: Oxford University, Press.

Everstine, L., Everstine, D. S., Heymann, G. M., True, R. H., Frey, D. H., Johnson, H. G., & Seiden, R. H. (1980). Privacy and confidentiality in psychotherapy. *American Psychologist, 35*, 828–840.

Fisher, L., Anderson, A., & Jones, J. E. (1981). Types of paradoxical interventions and indications/contraindications for use in clinical practice. *Family Process, 20*, 25–35.

Framo, J. L. (1976). Chronicle of a struggle to establish a family unit within a community mental health center. In P. L. Guerin, Jr. (Ed.), *Family therapy: Theory and practice.* New York: Gardner Press.

Gardner, R. (1982). *Family evaluation in child custody litigation.* Cresskill, NJ: Creative Therapeutics.

Gross, S. (1978). The myth of professional licensing. *American Psychologist, 33*, 1009–1016.

Gumper, L. L., & Sprenkle, D. H. (1981). Privileged communication in therapy: Special problems for the family and couples therapist. *Family Process, 20*, 11–23.

Haley, J. (1975). Why mental health clinics should avoid family therapy. *Journal of Marriage and Family Counseling, 1*, 3–13.

Haley, J. (1976). *Problem solving therapy.* San Francisco: Jossey-Bass.

Harris, J. C., & Bernstein, B. E. (1980). Lawyer and social worker as a team: Preparing for trial in neglect cases. *Child Welfare, 59*, 469–477.

Karpel, M. A. (1980). Family secrets: I. Conceptual and ethical issues in the relational context. II. Ethical and practical considerations in therapeutic management. *Family Process, 19*, 295–306.

Keller, P. A., & Ritt, L. G. (Eds.). (1982, 1983, 1984, 1985). *Innovations in clinical practice: A source book.* (Vols. 1–4). Sarasota, FL: Professional Resource Exchange.

Kilgore, J. (1979). The marriage and family therapist's use of media for public education. *Journal of Marital and Family Therapy, 5*(4), 87–92.

Kosinski, F. A. (1982). Standards, accreditation, and licensure in marital and family therapy. *Personnel and Guidance Journal, 60*, 350–352.

Margolin, G. (1982). Ethical and legal considerations in marital and family therapy. *American Psychologist, 37*, 788–802.

McGovern, T. V. (1976). Assertion training for job interviewing and management/staff development. In A. J. Lange & P. Jakubowski (Eds.), *Responsible assertive behavior.* Champaign, IL: Research Press.

Meyerstein, I., & Todd, J. C. (1980). On the witness stand: The family therapist and expert testimony. *American Journal of Family Therapy, 8*(4), 43–51.

Mudd, E. (1967). *The American Association of Marriage Counselors: The first 25 years.* Dallas, TX: American Association of Marriage Couselors.

Myers-Walls, J. & Piercy, F. (1985). Mass media and prevention: Guidelines for family life professionals. *Primary Prevention, 5*(2), 124–133.

Nichols, J. (1982). The mental health professional as expert witness. In P. A. Keller & R. G. Ritt (Eds.), *Innovations in clinical practice: A source book.* Sarasota, FL: Professional Resource Exchange.

Nichols, W. (1979). Guest editor's introduction. *Journal of Marital and Family Therapy, 5*(3), 3–5.

O'Shea, M., & Jessee, E. (1982). Ethical, value, and professional conflicts in systems therapy. In L. L'Abate (Ed.), *Values, ethics, legalities and the family therapist.* Rockville, MD: Aspen Systems Corporation.

Piercy, F., McKeon, D., & Laird, R. (1983). A family assessment process for community mental health clinics. *American Mental Health Counselors Association Journal, 5*(3), 94–105.

Piercy, F. & Wetchler, J. (in press). Family–work interfaces of psychotherapy: I. A summary of the literature. II. A didactic–experiential workshop. *Journal of Psychotherapy and the Family.*

Raskin, D. E., & Klein, Z. E. (1976). Losing a symptom through keeping it: A review of paradoxical treatment techniques and rationale. *Archives of General Psychiatry, 33*, 548–555.

Rohrbaugh, M., Tennen, H., Press, S., & White, L. (1981). Compliance, defiance, and therapeutic paradox: Guidlelines for strategic use of paradoxical interventions. *American Journal of Orthopsychiatry, 51*, 454–467.

Schultz, B. M. (1982). *Legal liability in psychotherapy.* San Francisco: Jossey-Bass.

Schultz, J. (1982). *Writing from start to finish.* Upper Montclair, NJ: Boynton/Cook Publishers.

Schwitzgebel, R. L., & Schwitzgebel, R. K. (1980). *Law and psychological practice.* New York: Wiley.

Sporakowski, M. J. (1982a). From the editor. *Family Relations, 31*, 315–316.

Sporakowski, M. J. (1982b). The regulation of marital and family therapy. In L. L'Abate (Ed.), *Values, ethics, legalities and the family therapist*. Rockville, MD: Aspen Systems Corporation.

Sporakowski, M. J., & Staniszewski, W. P. (1980). The regulation of marriage and family therapy: An update. *Journal of Marital and Family Therapy, 6*, 335–348.

Shalett, J. S., & Everett, C. A. (1981). Accreditation in family therapy education: Its history and role. *American Journal of Family Therapy, 9*(4), 82–84.

Taggart, M. (1982). Linear versus systemic values: Implications for family therapy. In L. L'Abate (Ed.), *Values, ethics, legalities and the family therapist*. Rockville, MD: Aspen Systems Corporation.

Van Hoose, W. H., & Kottler, J. A. (1977). *Ethical and legal issues in counseling and psychotherapy*. San Francisco: Jossey-Bass.

Wetchler, J. L., & Piercy, F. P. (1986). The marital/family life of the family therapist: Stressors and enhancers. *American Journal of Family Therapy, 14*(2), 99–109.

Winkle, C. W., Piercy, F. P., & Hovestadt, A. (1981). A curriculum for graduate level marriage and family therapy education. *Journal of Marital and Family Therapy, 7*, 201–210.

Woody, R. H., & Associates. (1984). *The law and the practice of human services*. San Francisco: Jossey-Bass.

NAME INDEX

Colleta, S. D., 158
Comfort, Alex, 98
Commission on Accreditation for Marriage and Family Therapy Education, 301
Cone, J. D., 70
Conger, R. E., 90, 333
Connell, G. M., 299
Constantine, J. A., 78, 295, 298, 302, 309, 313, 314
Constantine, L., 57, 63
Conway, J. B., 83
Coogler, O. J., 129, 133, 150, 365
Cookerly, J. R., 323, 334, 338–339
Coppersmith, E. I., 44–45, 294, 295, 308
Cotten-Huston, A. L., 119
Coufal, J., 333
Courant, R., 284
Cox, M., 132, 151
Cox, R., 132, 151
Coyne, J. C., M.44
Crane, R. D., 327, 332, 339
Cranewell, F., 124
Crohn, H., 153
Cromwell, R. E., 332, 333, 339
Cronbach, 327
Crosbie-Burnett, M., 134
Cyrus, C. L., 131, 135, 139, 157–158

D

Dammann, C., 295, 307–308
Darley, J. M., 363
D'Augelli, A., 165
Davidson, N., 70–71, 84
Davis, C., 204
Davis, E. C., 206
de Bruijun, G., 119
Deckert, P., 159
Dekker, J., 100, 119
Dell, P., 354
Demarest, D., 203, 206
Dent, J., 179
Dent, L., 179
Denton, J. H., 206
Denton, W., 179–180, 206
Derogatis, L. R., 99, 119–120
DeShazer, S., 295
Deutsch, M., 144
Deyss, C., 165
Dezen, A. E., 331, 346
Dicks, Henry V., 4, 7, 16–17, 173
Dinnerstein, D., 218–219, 233

Dixon-Murphy, T., 290, 291
Doane, J. A., 73, 340
Doherty, W. J., 206–208
Donso, J., 207
Dorken, H., 359, 365–366
Drake, E. A., 132, 151
Druckman, J. M., 174
DSM-III, 359
Duhl, Bunny S., 51–55, 63, 64
Duhl, Fred J., 51–53, 55, 63, 64
Duvall, E. M., 174
D'Zurilla, T. J., 85

E

Edelman, R. I., 71
Edwards, R., 165
Ehrenreich, B., 233
Ehrentraut, G., 165
Eisenstein, H., 221, 233–234
Elbow, P., 361
Elkin, W., 165
Ellis, A., 94, 100
Ellison, C., 104
Ellman, B., 221
Embry, L. H., 87–88
Engel, T., 153
English, D., 233
Eno, M. M., 134
Epstein, N., 334, 339
Erickson, G. D., 254
Erickson, Milton H., 24, 29, 42, 271, 275, 284
Ericson, P. M., 176
Erikson, E. K., 136
Espenshade, T. J., 155
Evans, M., 99–100, 121, 125, 335
Everaerd, W., 100, 119
Everett, C., 133, 291–292, 301, 362
Everstine, L., 353
Eysenck, H. J., 329

F

Fairbairn, W. R. D., 4, 6, 7, 17, 18
Falicov, C. J., 298, 314
Falloon, Ian R. H., 72–73, 84
Feldman, L., 234
Fernandez, V., 88, 216, 237
Fichten, C. S., 100, 120
Figley, C. R., 180
Fine, M., 15, 18
Fisch, R., 25, 42, 44, 49, 285
Fish, L., 98, 101

SUBJECT INDEX

Absolute global dysfunction, 101
Acceptance of Marital Termination (AMT), 137
Accommodation, 33
Accreditation of family therapy programs, 290–291, 353, 362–363
Aesthetics, 280
  pragmatics versus, 262–263
Aesthetics of Change (Keeney), 263
Affect, in experiential family therapy, 52–53
Alienation, 55
Allred Interaction Analysis for Counselors, 303–304, 328
American Association for Marriage and Family Therapy (AAMFT), 187, 352–353
Commission on Accreditation for Marriage and Family Therapy Education of, 290, 291
American Association of Marriage Counselors (AAMC), 187
American Family Therapy Association (AFTA), 291–292, 353
Amplified deviation, 266
Analogical message, 31
Anorexia nervosa, key books and articles on, 43, 45
Anorgasmia, 102
Antipanic medication, 105–106
Anxiety
  existential, 54
  feedback and, 265
  performance, 95–97, 104, 105
Assessment, core battery of instruments of, 323
Association of Couples for Marriage Enrichment (ACME), 189, 191, 193–195, 197–202
  key books and articles on, 208–209
Astigmatic awareness. *See* Alienation

Attachment, in divorce therapy, 136–137
Audiotapes
  family-of-origin, 12–13
  in supervision and training, 296–297
Authority, personal, 6, 9
  key books and articles on, 21
Autobiography, family, 11–12
Autonomy of a system, 280
Awareness, 55

B

Baseline, in behavioral family therapy, 73
Behavioral exchange theory, 73
Behavioral family therapy, 69–91
  feminist critique of, key books and articles on, 234–235, 237
  key books and articles on, 81, 82
  key concepts and interventions in, 73–76
  parent skills training in, 70–71
  problem-solving/communication skills training in, 71
  research in, 72–73, 80–81
  strategic family therapy and, 75–77
  structural family therapy and, 75–77
  systemic family therapy and, 84
  teaching tools and techniques in, 75–80
  therapist in, 71–72
Behavioral marital therapy (BMT), 237
Behavioral rehearsal, 78
Binuclear family, 137
Biofeedback, in sex therapy, 123
Birth order, 9
  exercises dealing with, 13
  key books and articles on, 20
Blanton–Peale Graduate Institute, 291
Boundaries, 30–31, 49
Boundary marking, 33
Box score, 325–326

385